Seeing the Elephant

Seeing the Elephant

Understanding Globalization from Trunk to Tail

Peter Marber

WILEY

John Wiley & Sons, Inc.

Published by John Wiley & Sons, Inc., Hoboken, New Jersey.
Published simultaneously in Canada.

For general information on our other products and services or for technical support, please
contact our Customer Care Department within the United States at (800) 762-2974,
outside the United States at (317) 572-3993 or fax (317) 572-4002.

Wiley also publishes its books in a variety of electronic formats. Some content that appears
in print may not be available in electronic books. For more information about Wiley
products, visit our web site at www.wiley.com.

Library of Congress Cataloging-in-Publication Data:
Marber, Peter.
    Seeing the elephant : understanding globalization from trunk to tail / Peter Marber.
       p.   cm.
    Includes bibliographical references and index.
    ISBN 978-0-470-28385-1 (cloth)
        1. Globalization—Economic aspects.   2. Globalization—Social aspects.
    3. Globalization—Environmental aspects.   4. Quality of life.   5. Twenty-first century.
    I. Title.   II. Title: Understanding globalization from trunk to tail.
    HF1359.M363   2009
    337—dc22
                                                                    2008040633

Printed in the United States of America
10 9 8 7 6 5 4 3 2 1

In memory of Hugh Kenner, who always saw the elephant.

Contents

Acknowledgments   ix
Introduction   xiii

Chapter 1: Seeing the Elephant in the Twenty-First Century   1
Chapter 2: Trade and Finance: Money, Money Everywhere   43
Chapter 3: Energy: Twilight of the Hydrocarbons?   95
Chapter 4: Defense and Security: Preventing the Next War,
               Not Fighting the Last   137
Chapter 5: Immigration: People, People Anywhere   181
Chapter 6: Promoting Tomorrow's Health Instead of Paying
               for Yesterday's Ills   215
Chapter 7: Environment: The Hidden Cost of Everything   249
Chapter 8: Poverty: Remembering the Bottom of the Pyramid   291
Chapter 9: Driving with a New Dashboard in the
               Macro Quantum World   323

Notes   349
Index   401

Acknowledgments

Multidisciplinary studies like this book require an immense amount of support from friends and acquaintances, and this one is no exception.

First, thanks to my agents Will Lippincott and Maria Massie who encouraged me to write ambitiously, along with Debra Englander, Kelly O'Connor, and Kevin Holm, from my publisher John Wiley & Sons, who pushed and prodded the book into excellent shape amid late updates to address the unfolding global financial crisis.

My friends and colleagues at Columbia University have always been incredibly inspirational and thought provoking. Without their expertise and encouragement, many of the book's themes would never have surfaced. Lisa Anderson, Jagdish Baghwati, Dick Betts, John Coatesworth, Rob Garris (and other friends in the Global Public Policy Network), Merit Janow, Jose Antonio Ocampo, Mary Robinson, among others, have provided me with great resources, and dozens of useful comments and suggestions. I am also very grateful to Joe Stiglitz for indulging me on a wide range of inquiries. Columbia has also blessed me with dozens of student interns since 1991, and many have contributed work and ideas for this book. Amelia Erwitt, Kamil Kaluza, Debbie Landres, and Nadiya Satyamurthy helped me frame out the book's premise and related articles I've written. Special kudos go to the figurative and literal "Angels"—Priscilla Adams, Gloria Hartner, Sophy Miles, Nancy Ferrante, and Kim McGinnis, industrious women who helped counter my endless ranting with great karma. Kim, particularly, has worked with me enthusiastically to the chaotic end, and there are few pages in this book that haven't been improved by her astute observations and gifted sense of language.

I have many more intellectual debts to pay. Friends from the World Policy Institute helped me formulate the book's key argument in an article published in 2006. Ian Cuthbertson, Mira Kamdar, Karl Meyer (and his wife Shareen Blair Brysac), Ben Pauker, Steve Schlesinger, Sherle Schwenninger, John Watts, Linda Wrigley, and Michelle Wucker all have provided conversations and ideas for this book. At New America Foundation (NAF), I have to thank Ted Halstead, not only for introducing me to a fabulous community of big picture people, but his own policy thoughts have shaped much of my thinking. Other NAF related friends—Peter Bergen, Sharon Brownlee, Steve Coll, Frank Fukuyama, Jacob Hacker, Zach Karabell, Parag Khanna, Jeffrey Lewis, John Nagl , Rachel White, Dan Yergin—have also offered great insights and observations that are strewn throughout the book.

There are many concepts in these chapters that spring from dozens of conversations with writers and scholars over the years; I can't begin to name them all. However, several deserve mention including Sam Brittan, Paul Blustein, David Brooks, Steven David, Peter Feaver, Jeff Garten, Richard Goldberg, Robert William Fogel, Steve Hanke, Craig Karmin, Ed Lincoln, John Mueller, Amity Schlaes, Jim Twitchell, and Martin Wolf. A special thanks to President Bill Clinton, who graciously offered me some insights into several issues amid his hectic schedule.

My colleagues at HSBC have been incredibly encouraging. First, the organization has provided me with great opportunities to witness firsthand the megatrends I describe; indeed, the practical experience working and investing globally everyday has been some of the best education I've ever received. Specific thanks to Markus Ackermann, Rudolf Apenbrinck, Sten Ankarcrona, Nigel Brown, Chris Cheetham, Lisa Chin, Paul Dawe, Christian Deseglise, Mike Gagliardi, Steve Gibbon, Sara Grillo, Clair Hammond, Kat Harley, Arif Joshi, Erica

Maisonet, Mark McCombe, Bill McKinzie, Aimee Mihalko, Chris Milonopoulos, Rekha Ramdas, Chas Robinson, Jean Luc Roghe, Paul Seary, Denise Simon, Jeanie Sun, Nick Timberlake, George Varino, and Heiner Weber, for their varied contributions to this endeavor.

Whenever I take on a writing project like this, many voices of past teachers echo in my head. The late Hugh Kenner has always been my great intellectual inspiration, a man who could chat effortlessly and authoritatively about everything from James Joyce to computers to cartoons. It's to him I dedicate this book. Past conversations with and lessons from Milton Cummings, Pasquale DeVito, Nancy Melser, Ron Paulson, Peter Sachs, Frimi Sagan, and Larzer Ziff, among others, often filled my brain as I pored through the manuscript.

Lastly, I must thank my wife Andrea and our two daughters, who have been suffered through yet another one of my book ordeals. Andrea has been my best soundboard since college and provided me with trusty sanity checks through every step in the book.

Introduction

A nyone writing today about globalization—the complicated web of life through trade, investment, technology, ideas, and migration—needs to thank Tom Friedman and Al Gore. Whether you agree with their alarmist messages, *The World Is Flat* and *An Inconvenient Truth* helped educate and inform while elevating the debate above the whiny emotional anti-everything protests of the late 1990s.

Friedman and Gore's best sellers, along with several other books by commendable authors, discuss some of the most important facets of globalization.[1] However, like the blind men in the parable of the elephant who only feel and describe a tusk, ear, or trunk but don't comprehend the whole animal, most of these writers tend to comment on a feature or two of globalization; few attempt to describe all the phenomena and understand their holistic connections. So, while *The World Is Flat* (and Friedman's other books), vividly dramatizes international economic competition and *An Inconvenient Truth* shocks us with the perils of accelerated environmental degradation, these topics need to be considered with the many other interlocking features of a twenty-first century planet in which more than 6.7 billion people are working and consuming at an alarming rate. Only by stepping back from the fray can we begin to see the interlocking, overlapping, and colliding aspects of globalization as a whole and begin to formulate national and international policies that take account of these rapid changes and interconnections.

That's what this book is about. It is nearly impossible to talk about basic concerns like mortgages, retirement plans, and gas prices, for example, without examining global intersections in trade, finance, energy, immigration, the environment and defense. But we, as U.S. citizens, seem blind to how twenty-first century civilization is connecting more nations and peoples than ever before. Our elected officials, too, are fumbling with major policy decisions amid the world's changing power structure. Without recognizing, admitting, and understanding these connections, we can't even begin to discuss how the United States and other countries can craft and harness effective policies amid this breathtaking progress.

A Different Lens

It is somewhat understandable that we Americans can't get our heads into the chaos of globalization. For most of the twentieth century, we lived in an easy-to-understand world. The U.S. economy was the largest and most competitive but fairly insular and domestic; trade was less than 10 percent of our total economic activity. Our comparative advantages in technology—coupled with a strong dollar and cheap oil—helped propel a living standard that surpassed much of the world. After World War II, we dominated the global scene and lived large— literally. Automobiles grew longer and heavier, people grew taller and fatter, homes grew bigger, and the nation's political and economic influence grew ever grander. Because of the vast U.S. marketplace, many outward looking countries naturally wanted to do business with us and emulate our rich lifestyle—wearing designer and logo-bearing clothes, driving big flashy cars, listening to popular music, watching TV and movies, and eating too much. We were seen as leaders of the free capitalist world, a bit gauche but with our heads and hearts essentially in the right places.

There was little competition to challenge our position as the world's most powerful nation through most of the twentieth century. Europe and Japan were rebuilding; the former Soviet Union, Communist China, postcolonial Africa, and other Socialist countries in Asia and Latin America traded very little, and compared to the United States their domestic markets were tiny. The United States was, indeed, number one with no close second for decades. In foreign policy, we maintained supremacy from 1945 through the 1990s by offering select countries protection under our NATO/nuclear umbrellas against the purported Soviet threat. We built military bases abroad and planted troops and weapons in many countries. Washington maintained a simple but effective global strategy amid a simple bipolar world: Protect those who traded with us. But the post–Cold War era requires a wider, more sophisticated perspective.

The United States is still the single most important economy today, but it competes with many more countries in many more industries than just a generation ago. Global trade—hundreds of times greater today than in the 1950s—has become a mind-boggling human activity. Millions of tons of natural resources are hyperefficiently extracted, mined, and moved in and out of dozens of countries; millions of factories worldwide manufacture billions of high- and low-tech items; dense transportation networks coordinate the global distribution of resources and goods by land, air, and sea to far-flung markets previously familiar to us only from spices and old poems. And this entire system (if one could even call freewheeling, frenetic, global trade a "system") is supported by a wide range of financial players and marketplaces connecting savers, investors, manufacturers, workers, and consumers. Trillions in currencies circle the world electronically 24/7. Revved up trade has reduced poverty worldwide with hundreds of millions of people living longer and better, and with more hope than ever before.

If the world is going to continue to grow sustainably and pull the remaining poor out of deprivation, we must begin to recognize the complex interactions and interconnections that constitute the blurring new millennium—one in which countries are clearly separate yet inexorably bound in a global system at the same time.[2] And with this flurry of cross-border activity comes new risks and threats—such as terrorism, diverging demographics, resource shortages, financial imbalances, and environmental stress—that we have yet to adequately assess and safeguard against. Just consider how the tremors that started to shake the U.S. banking system in 2007 have spread through financial markets and economies worldwide.

In fact, the twenty-first century demands a very different lens for viewing the world. To survive and thrive, we will need to change the fundamental *thinking behind our thinking*. For decades, the United States and some of its close allies have used linear, compartmentalized approaches to solve problems—a "Micro Domestic" viewpoint—in which policies are fragmented and considered separately. As a result, U.S. policies have been geared to manipulate the levers of power under the belief that we could—and perhaps did—control global change. But the world is not compartmentalized as it was in the postwar period; it is far more connected than many would like to believe. To move forward, to continue to prosper, we will need a new approach: a "Macro Quantum" paradigm.

In contrast to the old ways of postwar thinking, a Macro Quantum perspective understands that power is fluid, not fixed; that future events are not 100 percent predictable; and that control, in the classic geopolitical sense, is somewhat illusory. In this shift, the United States' unilateral worldview should evolve into by one of multiple possibilities. Our absolute perspective should recognize and appreciate contextualism, simplicity should be replaced by complexity, certainty by ambiguity, and uniformity by pluralism. Such a holistic perspective emphasizes organic, free-flowing interaction and codetermination versus rigid beliefs in compartmentalized segmentation and self-determination. In this Macro Quantum world, we must learn to go with the flow of powerful forces beyond our control; indeed, attempts at control—as we witnessed in Iraq—can be counterproductive, and even exacerbate problems.

Yes, this is a dizzying concept. And the more complex life becomes, the more people want simple answers. But there are no simple answers anymore. The few highly active, independent, dominant economies of the mid-twentieth century now must negotiate an intricate, highly interconnected web of trade and investment involving billions of workers and consumers that inherently are affected by increasingly complex and intertwined security, energy, and environmental issues. We live in a time when very small individual changes in certain aspects of life can have large global consequences in what Steven Levitt might call a *Freakonomic* world.[3] While most people want black-and-white answers, the twenty-first century is a world cast in varying shades of grey.

Americans face complex threats in the world and new commercial and financial patterns involving countries with which we have little experience. Amid these changes, many U.S. government policies during this millennium have seemed almost naïve. Instead of fostering intelligent discourse and exploring new approaches, for much of this decade our government—perhaps as a knee-jerk, fearful reaction to 9/11—has been infected by an unfortunate strain of ignorance, anti-rationalism and anti-intellectualism. Critics cite the Bush administration's unabashed rejection of hard data and expert opinions on many topics—from global warming to government spending to the Iraq invasion—as evidence. Many, including me, believe that traditional policy channels involving careful analysis and debate have been hijacked in favor of bold, faith-based, gut-level decisions for most of this decade. Reasoned public discussions have increasingly given way to a noisy, partisan yell-fest among politicians and the media. While the Bush administration's policies and personalities have certainly hurt the United States in both international standing and treasure, globalization was set in motion long before the neoconservatives stormed Washington. Globalization's momentum has been building for decades; its exponential pace has made recent insular, dogmatic politics seem futile. Even the distinction between foreign and domestic policy has blurred beyond distinction.

Why can't we grapple with today's quantum complexities? Americans have always resisted policy debates, but we seem to distrust them more than ever at a time when serious discourse is needed the most. Our students have lagged in science and math for more than a generation, and most are fundamentally ignorant of basic civic concepts. The United States is a country where less than half the population votes, where only one in six citizens hold valid passports (and only one in three elected officials!), and two out of three can't name our three branches of government or one Supreme Court justice.[4] Amid our national attention deficit disorder, should it surprise us that we accept the partisan punditry and comedy of Bill O'Reilly, Lou Dobbs, Bill Maher, and Steve Colbert (as entertaining as they may be) as a substitute for meaningful policy dialogue?

This is just part of why the 2008 presidential hopefuls ignored ambiguous but pressing questions pertaining to global happenings, instead feeding us partisan proclamations on the financial crisis and Iraq, occasionally peppered with morality crumbs regarding abortion, same sex marriage, stem cell research, religion, gun control, and the death penalty. Amid the 2007–2008 economic slowdown we heard some discussion of the Colombia free trade agreement, largely in protectionist rhetoric. Few candidates spoke on our most urgent issue: the relative decline of the United States and our historic allies amid the rapid economic integration of China, India, and other non-Western countries. As the mortgage problem intensified, presidential candidates still failed to discuss how our economic troubles were international in nature: The United States' subprime crisis was actually part of a wider *global* credit meltdown. One can only hope that President Obama will dare to lead the United States—and perhaps the world—in the new global economic reality. This will necessitate dramatic policy changes including overhauling postwar multilateral institutions (the United Nations and the World Bank, among others), and/or creating new ones to coordinate cross-border affairs in a world no longer dominated by the largely white, Christian societies of the West.

Quantum World, New Players

Many of the historic advances since World War II have been pushed by the United States in concert with Europe and some other close allies that form what's known as the Group of Seven (the G7, consisting of the United States, the United Kingdom, France, Italy, Germany, Canada, and Japan). In past decades, these countries have formed the nuclei of several forums that helped codify rules, behavioral standards, and mechanisms for international collective progress and orderly conflict resolution. But today, there are signs of diverging interests and opinions among the G7 that, together with the proliferation of nonstate actors (NSAs) and the rise of powerful emerging market nations, have eroded the G7's global relevance. In many ways, the G7 countries have lost much of the economic and political clout that allowed them to control the global agenda in the last century, but an appropriate alternative has yet to fill this vacuum.

In the new millennium, many countries once pegged as "developing" nations now wield greater economic and political influence than smaller G7 members. Large nations like Russia and those from Asia (including China, India, South Korea, and Indonesia, among others), Latin America (such as Brazil and Mexico), and Africa (Egypt, Nigeria, and South Africa) have mushrooming middle classes and educated, competitive labor forces that are growing daily. Many formerly poor nations have boosted world output and are active players in financial markets. By managing their economies well, many former debtor nations have now become creditors of the United States and other G7 members that run budget deficits and highly leveraged economies. Over time, emerging countries' financial positions have solidified and their share of global trade and income has soared.

And while twentieth century crossborder activity was largely the domain of governments, today's world has a variety of civilian players—what political scientists like to call "nonstate actors"—that are assuming roles formerly reserved for sovereigns. Banks, multinational corporations (MNCs), mutual and hedge funds, journalists, nongovernmental organizations (NGOs), and even terrorist and paramilitary groups now have crossborder capabilities that were unimaginable in the years following World War II. These new players drive the Macro Quantum world by creating jobs and financing governments and investments; they provide educational, medical, and humanitarian services; they inform and shape public opinion; they influence policy decisions at the highest levels of government; and, in some cases, they wage military conflict.

In a world of countries that have been historically disconnected with limited crossborder activity, how do we now approach the chaotic stampede of economic and financial integration? With another one billion people on the planet by 2020, how can we guard against potential resource imbalances, shortages, and environmental suicide? Is it simply the market that will govern cross-border behavior? Will old governing bodies compete with new alternative blocs forming among the economic upstarts? How will we combat terrorism and weapons proliferation? How do we safeguard against financial and economic meltdowns? In short, as globalization storms forward, what new realities must we face in a world where the helm inevitably is shared with countries of which we have little knowledge, experience and—possibly—trust?

These are the questions that President Obama's administration will need to focus on, and the ones this book will attempt to investigate.

Whatever the answers, they must be rooted in sound public policies formulated in a holistic, noncompartmentalized manner. Since 1987, I've traveled to and invested in more than 50 developing countries from Latin America, the Caribbean, Africa, the Middle East, Central Europe, Russia and the former Soviet Union, and Asia. I've focused largely on government bonds and currencies, trying to figure out which countries were on successful, prosperous paths, and which weren't. This has been reinforced by nearly 20 years of research and teaching at Columbia University's School of International and Public Affairs, a community dedicated to multidisciplinary policy formulation. Professionally, I've worn three hats to analyze these trends: the first, a political scientist studying the public policies of countries in various stages of transition; the second, one of an economist trying to understand the long- and short-term economic ramifications of these policies; and the third, the hat of a pragmatic trader formulating active investment bets on which countries were doing better or worse than others.

To understand the long-term connection between sound government policy and economic success, one needs only to look at the Korean peninsula, one of the poorest places on earth just three generations ago. After war split the country in 1953, two very different policy paths were chosen. The North followed a statist-style, centralized economy, while the South focused on education and trade. Today, South Korea's per capita income is some 16 times that of North Korea's, which regularly experiences food and energy shortages. Over the last 22 years I've seen countries skillfully harmonize domestic policies toward desired future outcomes, as well as others that have fumbled miserably and fallen squarely on their faces.

The combination of Wall Street pragmatism and academic research has taught me to appreciate the kaleidoscope of globalization, in which each new element and each turn creates a unique pattern. And having bet billions of dollars over the last two decades on the outcomes of countries' policies, I (along with many investors and academic commentators) am worried that our country may be an increasingly bad bet, what market traders call a "short." Indeed, speculators betting against the U.S. dollar for much of the millennium have profited nicely. But this tide can easily reverse with fresh policy thinking. That's what we'll explore in *Seeing the Elephant*.

In my last two books, I attempted to draw attention to global trends, emphasizing the rise of emerging markets and the cultural divides that exist between these and wealthier nations. I have seen firsthand how the state has retreated from much of its dominance over human interaction in the mid-twentieth century. It's clear that the marketplace today can do certain things arguably better than governments: create productive jobs, factories, and infrastructure. But markets have weaknesses as well, as the recent credit crisis shows, and in today's hyperactive, hyper-creative financial climate they inevitably suffer from short attention spans. Against the great chaotic rise of the marketplace, government's role—particularly at the multilateral level—must be revived to focus on longer-term policies that may be unpopular and appear fruitless in the short term. And that brings us back to the United States.

The Capitalist Peace at Risk

The United States has long been a champion of the "capitalist peace," the idea that free trade and unimpeded investments can bind nations together and discourage military conflict. War, with its interruption of business and destruction of life and property, is simply too costly for all involved; that's one of the great history lessons of the twentieth century. Looking at the dramatic reductions in crossborder warfare in the last few decades, one would think that we have entered such a golden interval, but visible cracks have appeared in this otherwise strong capital peace foundation: the breakdown of international financial markets, the recent collapse of the Doha trade talks, the failure of any true global uptake of the Kyoto environmental protocol, circumvention of and stagnation in the UN Security Council, the demise of the International Court system and protectionist responses to select crossborder acquisitions not to mention consensus failure over the Iraq invasion and its consequences. In total, these problems suggest that global tensions are stewing, and that we are perhaps at a crossroad in history regarding multilateralism and future prosperity.

The quantum future is not set in stone and depends on decisions made today. The United States can ignore globalization, and continue to act as an isolated, narrow-minded bully, trying to mold every country to fit its unilateral worldview. This would be a mistake that would provoke more resentment and risk than we can imagine. Another tack to take would be to subject ourselves passively to the new global trends, understanding fully that the United States—and much of the G7—will float with the market winds that blow the sails of others and push them faster. This is preferable to recent aggressive unilateral behavior, although it leaves us little control over what is to follow the Pax Americana. In such a scenario, we'll certainly remain economically important, but our position might quietly fade as Britain's did in the twentieth century. Finally, perhaps the best way to manage the inevitable change is for the U.S. to orchestrate policies and support institutions that harmonize with the Macro Quantum world, using our waning but still potent influence to evoke better outcomes. Global relations are clearly in a state of flux but could fall into place with properly directed effort. It will not be easy, and it requires a reinvigorated spirit of international cooperation, in contrast to the United States' recent ethos of Micro Domestic control.

Globalization's promise has only been partly realized in the last decade or so, with far greater benefits potentially ahead. However, globalization is not risk-free, and historic trading, finance, and security alliances can flourish indefinitely without acknowledging the inevitable multipolarity. More than ever, the world needs broader forums for managing multidimensional cross-border relations. The one-for-all, all-for-one spirit that bred the United Nations, the World Bank, and the World Trade Organization—the bedrock of greater wealth for more people than ever before—requires renewed commitment to reflect recent history. Without reviving multilateralism the risks of instability, armed conflict, protectionism, and further financial panics, will steadily increase as they did before World War I, with potentially devastating consequences.

The optimistic path in a quantum world will require a holistic policy formulation that accurately gauges the United States' position vis-à-vis its peers. This book's first chapter takes stock of the dramatic reorientation of world power over the last century, but especially in the last two decades. It also examines the rise of new nonstate actors in today's accelerated global convergence.

The subsequent chapters focus on seven key cross-border, interlinking issues that need greater coordination:

1. Trade and finance
2. Energy
3. Security
4. Immigration
5. Health
6. The environment
7. Poverty

None of these areas can be understood in a vacuum; a multidisciplinary perspective must be employed to tame and shape a peaceful and prosperous globalization.

The last chapter focuses on the United States and the great leadership challenge—or opportunity—that now exists. There is little debate that the United States, or at least the *U.S. government*, has lost a certain amount of respect in the international community in the new millennium. It should be clear from the first eight chapters that the United States' stature has been eroded by growing economic competition, weaker relationships with old and new powers, bull-headed unilateral actions, and a general clumsiness in its approach to managing globalization. Instead of forging strong alliances with rising powers, the United States has been slow to understand a world that is rapidly recalibrating. However, this trend is not irreparable.

The United States must reestablish itself as the foremost supporter of the global system of governance that begat this quantum world. We need to reverse the vicious cycle of chaotic unilateralism that has plagued the new millennium toward the virtuous cycle of collective problem solving that makes all countries better off. To rebuild its leadership position, the United States must underscore the centricity of international protocols, rules, and institutions. President Obama needs to create a climate that encourages other countries to coordinate with the United States and restores trust in the global system and bolsters the capitalist peace.

This will require modernizing multilateral institutions like the United Nations and the World Bank, among others. The United States needs to trumpet the value of multilateralism, the philosophical foundation of our global system. This is the unifying force that can both harness the power of nonstate actors and defend against influences that can destroy such order that has been built since World War II's end.

The United States will never be able to stop the rise of emerging markets like China, India, and Russia—or any others for that matter—but it certainly can weave them into the evolving tapestry of rules and institutions that have developed in the last 60 years. The strategies I'm proposing do not necessarily ensure that the Unites States will remain on top economically but rather that our postwar multilateral system triumphs in the end; it should be the only game in town. They also serve to protect against the rise of new powers splitting the world into fierce competing spheres—exactly what happened before World War I. The more that economic, security, energy, health, immigration, and environmental rules are multilateral and all-encompassing, the more the global system retains its coherence. Whether the United States can thrive in this system rests on the policy decisions we make today. The challenge for President Obama will be to not only voice this philosophy, but to demonstrate it with better behavior. The United States must practice what it preaches.

We have an opportunity, but it's a time-based opportunity. For most of the twentieth century, the United States was globalization's shepherd, but it fell asleep sometime in the last decade while the flock has grown and strayed. The time to awaken is now. Indeed, the global financial crisis may be the perfect catalyst. Retreating would only squander our last opportunity to forge a global order that serves future U.S. interests. We should be working at this moment to shape the global system so that the institutional legacies of today's actions put the United States in the best position possible amid an increasingly crowded, more competitive landscape. The world is thirsting today for a revived system of rules and tools for collective action and, with policy shifts we'll discuss, the United States still remains the best chance at building an enduring capitalist peace.

Chapter 1

Seeing the Elephant in the Twenty-First Century

Progress is impossible without change, and those who cannot change their minds cannot change anything.

—George Bernard Shaw

There is a traditional Hindu fable in which several blind men encounter an elephant for the first time. One man feels the trunk and states the elephant resembles a snake; another touches the tail and is convinced the elephant must be like a rope. A third man grabs an ear and compares the elephant to a fan, while another pats the belly and believes it to be like a wall. The blind men start arguing, each insisting that he alone is right. A man passing by asks what the commotion is all about, and the blind men reply, "We can't agree on what the elephant is like." After hearing them all, the bystander calmly explains that each of the men is describing a piece of the animal correctly, but not one perceived the elephant in its entirety. The blind men leave feeling both vindicated and enlightened.

By titling this book *Seeing the Elephant*, I'm hoping to underscore not that conventional views on globalization—our elephant—are parochial or untrustworthy but rather to emphasize that all reasonable perspectives add value to this important dialogue. Because, when it comes to globalization, perceiving the big picture is just as essential and maybe more important than focusing on one or two areas. The title also refers to the expression "the elephant in the room," that is, an uncomfortable situation where something major is on everyone's mind, but no one says or does anything about it. Globalization is enormous and a bit frightening, so many people choose to ignore rather than confront it.

The extraordinary changes of the last century—the ways we work, eat, communicate, stay safe, and entertain ourselves—are multifaceted, yet also form a coherent whole. Today's elected officials, corporate and financial titans, media commentators, and scholars have taken a magnifying lens to various aspects of the dramatic changes of the past 20 years, providing useful snapshots of information. But we still struggle to see the how the parts are linked together.

The result of these incomplete efforts is a checklist of worries instead of a logical plan for tackling our thoroughly new challenges. When the Twin Towers topple, we fear global terrorism. Al Gore wins an Oscar for *An Inconvenient Truth*, and we fixate on global warming. An Indian customer service representative answers our toll-free call in Bangalore, and we add outsourcing to the worry list. Brazilian supermodel Gisele Bündchen demands to be paid in euros, then a weak dollar grabs the headlines. Gas rises above $4 a gallon, we proclaim an energy crisis. We discover tainted shipments of Chinese pet food, and protectionist tempers flare. We see pictures of George Clooney, Bono, or Angelina Jolie in Africa and add genocide, poverty, and AIDS to our anxieties. Lehman Brothers goes bust, and we worry if our savings accounts are safe.

This patchwork of international problems deserves more than the scattershot attention it now receives. The parts of the elephant—poverty, energy, business, environment, and security—need to be understood as a systematic whole. Americans can no longer avoid this elephant. While globalization is incredibly complex, the meteoric rise of economic powerhouses and nonstate actors demand new forums where tough questions and policy prescriptions can be discussed. But first, let's look at the path we followed to where we are today.

What's Old Is New Again

Walking through the thirteenth century, one would be surprised by how similar lifestyles were in Mesoamerica, continental Europe, Africa, and Asia. The key bio-social markers of progress—life expectancy, daily caloric intake, infant mortality rates, literacy—were fairly similar in ancient Mexico City, London, Istanbul, and Beijing. Most people farmed, went to market, lived, and died close to where they were born. Family size was roughly similar in each location (that's to say large), and no civilization looked much better off than another. Certainly no country back then could be considered rich by today's rubric. Compared to our modern existence, Hobbes was right: Life was nasty, brutish, and short.

With the advent of the Renaissance, a renewed interest in learning helped Europe break free from the Dark Ages. This led to the watershed late eighteenth-century invention of steam power in Great Britain. Adam Smith's 1776 *Wealth of Nations* provided the philosophical framework for organized capitalism, and the Industrial Revolution was born. Machine-driven capacities dwarfed animal and human labor, output soared, and costs declined. Trade accelerated as improved canals and railways and the invention of the internal combustion engine allowed more goods to move farther, faster. Great Britain's mass education system generated skilled workers capable of operating the new mechanical inventions. After millennia of struggling with scarcity, Homo sapiens had found a formula for producing abundantly while working less.

Great Britain was the first industrial economy, but its lead did not last for long. Goods, ideas, and formal education spread throughout Europe and North America in the late nineteenth and early twentieth centuries leading to the convergence of living standards (or flattening as Tom Friedman might say). By the late 1800s, poor countries around the southern European periphery—the emerging markets of their day—were growing fast, catching up to the rich industrial leaders at the European core.

Asia did not join the action until late in the nineteenth century, when the establishment of the Suez Canal, innovations in marine transport, and penetration of the continent's massive interior by railroad liberated it from the tyranny of geographic isolation. Thereafter, the West rapidly engaged Asia in exchange. China opened its ports in 1842 and Thailand in 1855, both with small tariff barriers. India followed Britain's free trade model in 1846, and Indonesia mimicked Holland in 1870. The most dramatic change, even by the standards of the recent Asian Miracle, occurred in Japan, which went from being an isolated feudal country to an open economy in the mid-1850s. Some 15 years after the arrival of Commodore Perry, Japan's foreign trade rose from 0 to 7 percent of national income, which itself grew an estimated 50 percent![1]

Outside of Japan, Asian nations' living standards continued to lag. These countries' huge populations, with education and literacy trailing the West, left them unable to switch from manual labor to machinery-based economies. From the dawn of Industrial Revolution through the late twentieth century, per capita income in India relative to Britain dropped from assumed parity to 15 percent, a fall of 85 percentage points.[2] India and China had already lost ground to the U.K., United States, and Russia that they would not start to regain until the 1990s. (See Table 1.1.)

In the late nineteenth century, after a half-century of open trade and relatively peaceful relations throughout the continent, short-sighted politicians across Europe began erecting commercial barriers. A lack of forums for cross-border economic coordination led to distrust and misperception. Trade competitiveness and protectionist policies resulted, countries started forming alliances and blocs and markets ended culminating in military conflict, commercial stagnation, and 30 years of destruction. In World War I, 28 million people were injured

Table 1.1 Historic Power Shifts, 1820–2050 (Percentage of Global Economic Output)

1820	1870	1950	2000	2050
China 33%	China 17.2%	US 27.3%	US 22.2%	China 28.1%
India 16%	India 12.2%	USSR 9.6%	China 14.6%	US 21.9%
France 5.5%	UK 9.1%	UK 6.7%	Japan 6.6%	India 17.2%
Russia 5.4%	US 8.9%	Germany 6.5%	India 5.9%	Japan 4.8%
UK 5.2%	Russia 7.6%	China 5.0%	Germany 4.1%	Brazil 4.4%

SOURCE: OECD, Goldman Sachs.

and 13 million people died, with military costs and property destruction the equivalent of trillions of dollars. The bleak intrawar years
brought further protectionist measures. As tempers flared among trading partners, a worldwide depression set in, allowing for the rise of fas-
cist and nationalist movements, and ultimately leading to World War II.
The Second World War's death toll totaled between 50 and 70 million
including fatalities from famine and disease.[3] More than $1 trillion was
spent by countries in combat and an estimated $3 trillion in property
was destroyed.[4] Not until well after World War II did trade begin to
approximate the late nineteenth-century volume.

The Postwar Period: An Uneasy Peace, an Uneven Global Economy

After the destruction, chaos, and economic stagnation of the two
world wars, a new era of stability dawned. The United States emerged
as a superpower, leading unprecedented multilateral efforts across the
realms of trade, security, and finance. In the years following World War
II, the United States engineered multilateral hallmarks, including the
Bretton Woods Agreement on monetary and financial coordination,
the United Nations, the World Bank group, the International Court
of Justice, the General Agreement on Tariffs and Trade/World Trade
Organization (GATT/WTO), the predecessor to the Organization for
Economic Cooperation and Development (OECD), and the North
Atlantic Treaty Organization (NATO). Whereas the late nineteenth-
century trade boom had been largely unregulated, these neoliberal,
free-market-oriented institutions shined as beacons of hope to counter the postwar socialist, centrally planned approaches of the Soviet
Union and much of Asia (including China), Latin America, and Africa.
By setting protocols for the orderly exchange of goods apart from the
authority of any single ruling country, they insured mutual prosperity and security. A quantum leap in living standards resulted, creating a
massive socio-economic gap between the Western camp and the rest of
the world. Between 1945 and 2000, not only did the per capita gross
domestic product (GDP) of the United States and Western European

countries grow several times faster than that of the socialist/communist world, but Westerners were living longer and were generally healthier as well.[5]

In 1974, the United States took multilateralism to the next step, creating the Library Group, an informal gathering of senior financial officials from the United States, the United Kingdom, West Germany, Japan, and France. This casual forum for the world's leading industrialized democracies was to become a steering group for global policy. The countries agreed to an annual meeting under a rotating presidency, forming the Group of 6, or G6, which later added Canada to become the G7. For the next 20 years this forum would manage economic and financial interactions but also touched on defense and security issues.

During the 1970s and 1980s, the G7 was *the* world's dominant economic and political power bloc, with several smaller trading nations slowly grafting themselves to the system including the four "Asian Tigers": Hong Kong, Singapore, Taiwan, and South Korea. These countries had adopted similar policies to Japan's "educate and export" model. It took the Japanese only 50 years to cultivate mandatory universal education (versus 150 years in the United Kingdom and 100 years in the United States), but South Korea cut this to roughly 30 years. All the Tigers focused on education. (See Figure 1.1.) By leveraging their relatively cheap but skilled workforces, they posted unprecedented double-digit growth and trade integration for nearly three decades.

For much of the postwar period, authoritarian nations like the former Soviet Union and Communist China opted for central planning and domestic protectionist policies over free trade. When the Soviet Union finally collapsed in 1991, it tolled the death knell of centrally planned economies. Then China generated dramatic momentum in the 1980s with Deng Xiaoping's vision of a "socialist market economy." With a large population and nearly 80 percent literacy, China didn't have 12-year compulsory education like the Tigers or Japan, but its sheer size allowed its economy to integrate into the global economy. By accepting more than $250 billion in private foreign direct investment from U.S. and other G7 multinational corporations, China used the 1990s to build up world-class manufacturing capabilities as the Four Tigers did in previous decades, posting similar double-digit growth rates that continue today.

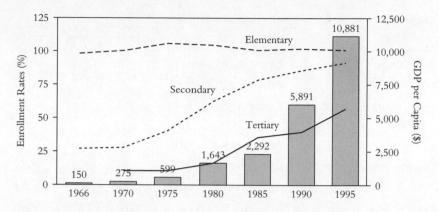

Figure 1.1   Education and Wealth: South Korean Enrollment Rates vs. Economic Growth, 1966–1995
SOURCE: IMF, World Economic Outlook 2001.

In Latin America, reform and privatization in Chile, Mexico, and Brazil, along with massive debt cancellation and restructurings through the Brady Plan, helped restore sovereign solvency and paved the way for greater global integration. Similar progress in statist South Asia— particularly India—could be witnessed. Africa, while slower than other regions, also trended toward privatization and integration programs, with South Africa emerging successfully after apartheid ended in the early 1990s.[6]

Several free trade converts, such as China and India, rapidly closed postwar living standard gaps in one of the greatest socio-economic convergences of all time. In developing countries, many indicators— education, life expectancy, daily caloric intake—began approaching G7 levels and will catch up sometime this century (see Table 1.2).

New Multipolar Power

After the Soviet Union's 1991 collapse many critics proclaimed the United States as the world's sole "hyperpower," the dominant global leader on all fronts. However, power by any definition has shifted in the twenty-first century. Consider economic power: the United States may be at the top, but other nations are nipping at its heels.

Table 1.2   Global Convergence, 1950–2050

		1950	2000	2050E
% of Global GDP	Emerging Markets	5	25	55
	Advanced Countries	95	75	45
% of Global Financial Capital	Emerging Markets	3	12	68
	Advanced Countries	97	88	32
Life Expectancy (years)	Emerging Markets	41	64	78
	Advanced Countries	65	77	83
Daily Caloric Intake	Emerging Markets	1200	2600	3000
	Advanced Countries	2200	3100	3200
Infant Mortality, (per 1000)	Emerging Markets	140	65	10
	Advanced Countries	30	8	4
Literacy Rate (per 100)	Emerging Markets	33	64	93
	Advanced Countries	95	98	99

SOURCE: Bloomberg, World Bank, UNDP, Goldman Sachs and author's estimates. GDP and stock market capitalization figures are inflation adjusted.

Japan is one of the largest world economies, dominating industries from automobiles to electronics. Much of Europe has evolved into the European Union (EU), a potent free-trade zone-*cum*-political union. The eastern European countries once left to languish under Soviet auspices have experienced rapid trade growth—many will eventually merge into the growing EU marketplace. China, after nearly 20 years of reform, now wields growing international political and economic clout and is on target to be the largest economy later this century. India, too, has shed its statist development model and emerged as a rising star. Elsewhere, Brazil, Mexico, Turkey, South Korea, and others in Asia have become major global trade participants. South Africa, Egypt, and Nigeria have become regional power brokers. With the spike in global economic activity, demand for energy has vaulted many Middle Eastern petro-states into the world's center ring along with Russia. In short, the United States and the other G7 members are no longer the locus of economic activity.

Dramatic advances in technology (particularly in telecoms and computing), the abandonment of centrally planned statist philosophies, the adoption of free market policies, and the cultivation of relatively youthful, better-fed and better-educated populations in developing countries have led to the success of many emerging states. Better human capital in developing countries—growing populations with improving living standards—is narrowing the West's lead. According to the United Nations Human Development Index (HDI), in 1960, lower and middle income countries posted HDI levels of only 20 percent and 32 percent of high income nations.[7] By 1993, these indicators grew to 34 percent and 62 percent, and in the latest spurt of globalization, by 2006, they had climbed to more than 65 percent and 85 percent, respectively. Already, the nations of what I have termed the "Emerging 7" (E7)—China, Russia, India, Indonesia, Mexico, Brazil, and South Korea—have a combined population of more than four times that of the G7 nations. By 2050, their populations will be more than five times greater, as birth rates slow in the G7. Some countries, like Germany, Italy, and Japan may even shrink in population. In the same period, the aggregate GDP of the E7 nations will be twice as large as the G7, as Table 1.3 shows.

These E7 nations are by no means the only emerging markets worth watching, but they do offer an interesting mix of risk and reward that demands serious attention for longer-term public policy formulation.[8] The prosperity that these and other formerly poor countries have gained thanks to globalization offer the United States and the G7 novel opportunities—but only if we understand the trends and engage emerging powers constructively.

The E7 and Other Rising Powers

The G7 is a chummy clique of influential and wealthy states. But with growing populations of skilled workers and consumers, many countries outside this elite club are increasingly important in the global trade system. The policies of these rising powers affect U.S. and European economies and vice versa. The E7's collective economies are already about 75 percent of the G7 on a purchasing power parity (PPP) basis,

Table 1.3   G7 vs. E7 by the Numbers

	Current Population	Est Population in 2050	Current Economy (billions, PPP)	Est Economy in 2050 (billions, PPP)
United States	295,734,134	467,480,550	$12,454	$37,666
Japan	127,417,244	124,283,183	$3,942	$8,040
Germany	82,431,390	80,395,649	$2,417	$5,440
France	60,656,178	72,957,719	$1,829	$4,870
United Kingdom	60,441,457	69,510,624	$1,926	$5,067
Italy	58,103,033	56,668,110	$1,667	$3,128
Canada	32,805,041	51,345,087	$1,061	$2,983
G7 Totals	**717,588,477**	**922,640,923**	**$25,296**	**$67,194**
China	1,306,313,812	1,744,331,739	$8,572	$48,571
India	1,080,264,388	2,164,849,996	$3,815	$27,235
Indonesia	241,973,879	497,016,784	$847	$3,923
Brazil	186,112,794	315,312,308	$1,627	$8,028
Mexico	106,202,903	189,987,001	$1,052	$7,838
South Korea	48,422,644	58,533,982	$1,056	$3,684
Russia	143,420,309	119,156,344	$1,559	$6,162
E7 Totals	**3,182,371,288**	**5,208,971,595**	**$19,140**	**$105,441**

but by 2050 they will be nearly twice as big, as Table 1.3 shows. And the E7 are more than export-reliant economies like the smaller Asian Tigers; they are large countries with growing populations, some with sizeable armies and nuclear weapons, and they should be incorporated into the world's multilateral governing bodies. Consider them country by country:

China: This 5,000-plus-year-old civilization was the world's largest economy in 1820 and should be again by 2050.[9] With enormous, skilled workforces in both low- and high-tech sectors, China has already surpassed the United States as the leading exporter to Europe, leaving its trade partners to ask, when will its artificially cheap currency become more freely traded and fairly valued? On the security front, while China has long been a nuclear superpower, it has quietly stayed out of military skirmishes for decades. Will and should this continue? With nearly $2 trillion in hard currency reserves, China is one of the world's largest buyers of U.S. government bonds, and many Chinese companies (some with state-ownership) are aggressively acquiring overseas assets. This will be *the* crucial relationship to forge in the coming decades.

India: The second largest economy in 1820, India is an amalgamation of a high-tech aristocracy that rivals Silicon Valley for its multitude of engineers and computer specialists[10]; a growing 50-million-person middle class that matches in size some G7 members; and a near-permanent underclass that constitutes 10 percent of the Earth's population. When you combine India's mix of Hindu and Muslim populations, colonial past, nuclear weapons, and the world's largest functioning, English-speaking democracy, one can see why this giant should be a greater part of our multilateral system of governance.

Brazil: South America's largest economy covers more square miles than the continental United States' 48 states and has over 160 million inhabitants. While bogged down by poorly performing and corrupt state-owned enterprises in the past, Brazil now has a diversified economy spanning agriculture to aviation and is the world's leading ethanol producer. Brazil also has taken the lead in trade discussions related to the global roadblock over agricultural subsidies. Brazil exerts strong regional influence and can have a stabilizing effect on other Latin countries, notably Venezuela, Bolivia, and Argentina, where more populist and nationalist politicians have made headway in recent years.

Russia: Ten years ago, Russia was nearly bankrupt. Yet the 150-plus million people of the former world power bounced back faster and stronger than anyone predicted. Russia holds the world's third largest foreign reserves. While a member of the G8, it is still excluded from G7 financial and trade discussions. Russia has sought greater global influence by exploiting its abundant natural resource reserves. With a revived economy, what are Russia's true intentions on the global scene? With the country's permanent status on the U.N. Security Council and improved financial footing, isn't the country worthy of increased dialogue and coordination?

Indonesia: Think about Islam and the Middle East comes to mind, yet Indonesia's 245 million people comprise a quarter of the world's Muslim population. This large nation has significant oil reserves and a skilled workforce but also ethnic tension spread across hundreds of islands in the southeast Pacific Rim. Already one of the world's 20 largest economy, Indonesia will be among the world's top seven economies by 2050. Understanding and working with this complex nation could help the G7 in future dealings with the Muslim world.[11]

Mexico: Already one of the United States' largest trading partners, Mexico has become even more interlinked since the North American Free Trade Agreement (NAFTA) was signed in 1993. With a population of nearly 110 million, Mexico is in the thick of the U.S. immigration debate.[12] We also should not take its free market and democratic status for granted. It is possible that Mexico can slip back to its socialist, statist past if ignored by the United States. Mexico should be viewed as a partner promoting greater global integration in Latin America and the Caribbean.

South Korea: Fifty years ago, South Korea was among the planet's poorest countries. Today, it is the 13th largest economy in the world. A longtime U.S. ally, South Korea sits in a geographically important corner of East Asia, though recent strains over policy toward Pyongyang have led to growing resentment of the U.S. military presence. Given its world-class corporations and its strategic location, greater inclusion of South Korea in global forums seems clearly warranted.

These seven countries represent huge segments of the world's population and a convenient standard of comparison to the G7, but by no means are they the only important emerging powers. In Africa, oil-rich Nigeria with more than 120 million people, Egypt with 70-plus million people, and wealthy South Africa are clearly important countries in a continent that is showing more promise everyday. Many central European players like Poland, Romania, Ukraine, and Turkey—with 200 million people in total—are rapidly pushing for EU integration. In Asia, several smaller countries like Singapore and Taiwan, along with larger ones like Thailand, Malaysia, and newcomer Vietnam, have vital economic and financial places in the world's economy.

The Rise of Nonstate Actors

Alongside the rise of new sovereign powers, the increasing prominence of nonstate actors (NSAs) have also complicated cross-border relations. There have always been a few civil players that were part of cross-border activity—missionaries, merchants, and explorers. Today, a remarkable variety of NSAs are active globally. Some of these players are loosely regulated and monitored by governments, but most are independent on a day-to-day basis. Understanding what they are, how they function, and how they can be influenced will be perhaps government's greatest challenge in policy making.

Multinational Corporations: Totaling over 100,000, multinational corporations (MNCs) are the economic emissaries of the modern world, seeking higher profits by scouring the globe for cheaper labor and new consumers. Today, it is common for production and supply chains of these corporate giants to cross not one but several borders. MNCs like GE and Nike have built tens of thousands of factories globally, employing millions of people. Some companies today are large and complex, and many have greater revenues, employees, and customers than some nations.[13]

Financial Institutions: The globalization of finance has accelerated briskly in the last two decades. In 1980, roughly 73 cents of every dollar that went from the first world to developing countries came from a couple of dozen commercial banks and the World Bank; there were no meaningful emerging market stock and bond markets attracting investor capital. Today, the amount of money and number of players can barely be calculated. As the current credit crisis underscores, our 24/7 system of finance now includes not only thousands of regulated intermediaries—like banks, brokerage firms, insurers, mutual funds, and pension funds—but many new ones that fly under the radar. Private hedge funds and private equity firms raise and invest money globally with little oversight in home or local markets and little allegiance to anything but profit. In addition, dozens of newly founded sovereign wealth funds (SWFs), semiautonomous investment pools, complicate this incredible web of money.

Media: While newspapers have been with us for centuries, the rise of television and the Internet as shapers of public opinion should not be underestimated. Information floods the airwaves and cyber streams of modern existence. Indeed, CNN, Fox News, Al-Jazeera, blogs, MySpace, and YouTube all have far more influence with more eyeballs watching than ever before. Some truly enlighten and some entertain, while some promote hate, fear, and insecurity.

Nongovernmental Organizations: In the past, nonprofit organizations such as the Red Cross, Oxfam, and Greenpeace seemed to only represent a limited set of humanitarian causes. Today, some NGOs have become important agents of cross-border socio-economic progress and hope. Grameen Bank, a pioneer in microlending, and the Gates Foundation, with its goal of solving global health problems, have proven to be far more effective in certain areas than multilateral organizations like the World Bank and the World Health Organization. Governments could probably learn a few lessons from these players.

Paramilitary Groups: War has traditionally been waged by governments. But one of the dual-edged swords of globalization is the rise of decentralized paramilitary groups including mercenaries, private military corporations like Blackwater and Titan, guerilla movements, warlords and subnational and cross-border terrorists like Al-Qaeda. And while all of these actors are not necessarily unjustified or wrong, they nonetheless dramatically complicate the global arena of defense and security.

All these NSAs add to the quantum web that is our world. And because their activities are so dispersed and complicated, they cannot be controlled in the classic sense. At a bare minimum, however, they need to be better understood to see how public policies can influence and harness them properly.

Working Toward the Capitalist Peace

Whether we are talking about rising emerging markets or nonstate actors, the peaceful integration of these important players rests upon the harmonization of old and new interests. While conventional wisdom draws upon the theory that democracies generally don't war with each other, there is a long "capitalist peace" tradition that includes many great historic thinkers like Charles de Montesquieu, Adam Smith, Norman Angell, and even Tom Friedman that would attribute our current Pax Americana to free trade and open markets. In 1846, British classical liberal statesman Richard Cobden described trade, which was just taking off as a result of the Industrial Revolution, "as the principle of gravitation in the universe, drawing men together, thrusting aside the antagonism of race, and creed, and language, and uniting us in the bonds of eternal peace."[14]

Open markets lessen incentives to war by changing the way societies produce wealth and increasing exchanges between states. For the better part of the sixteenth, seventeenth, and eighteenth centuries, under state-centered mercantilism, land and natural resources were the largest sources of wealth. With the advent of capitalism and the Industrial Revolution, wealth became linked to the production of goods instead. Capitalism requires property rights and free decisions by market participants to work. In the old days, seizing gold bullion may have made it yours, but now seizing a factory cannot make its assembly line workers work.

Under capitalism, war becomes a bad bet; the costs of destroying property, plant, equipment, and human capital—combined with out-of-pocket military costs—far outweigh the modest gains of territorial conquest. Moreover, capitalism and trade not only reduce incentives to fight, they also provide an alternative mechanism for countries to compete yet cooperate—and everyone goes home a winner. Countries with excess capital don't conquer those with a lot of labor; they increase immigration or outsource production overseas. Conversely, developing countries with skilled workers don't plunder their neighbors for money; they rely on global financial markets and foreign direct investment from capital-rich places, so long as they remain open, friendly, and respect the rule of law. Only in rare exceptions do trade-engaged nations now seize or nationalize foreign-owned plants, factories, or industries, because that unnerves foreign investors who will quickly cut off capital access.[15]

Rising affluence associated with capitalism, in turn, also makes war look like a bad deal. To echo Bob Dylan, when countries got something, they've got something to lose. In the postwar period, we've seen many countries grow wealthier. In 1950, only six countries in the world had

50 percent of U.S. per capita GDP; by 2006 that number was over 35 with probably a few more on a PPP basis.[16] Moreover, the number of countries with at least 25 percent of U.S. GDP per capita has grown from 20 to more than 50.[17] Much of this has to do with the abandonment of centrally planned economies for market-based philosophies and the build out of economic freedom, not necessarily the spread of U.S.-style democracy and universal suffrage.[18] In this respect, democracy probably has been overrated and capitalism underrated, as John Mueller has written.[19]

While it is true that capitalist countries tend to be democratic, economist Milton Friedman reminds us that "history suggests that capitalism is a necessary condition for political freedom,"[20] even in the absence of democracy, the inverse relationship between free markets and war holds. Empirical evidence also weighs in capitalist peace theory's favor. Like we'd expect, the world today is quite peaceful compared to a century ago. According to the *Human Security Report*, all forms of warfare—from interstate to even intrastate conflicts—have fallen precipitously in the postwar period.[21] The number of international and civil conflicts fell from more than 50 in 1990 to just over 30 in 2005 with the annual death toll from conflict falling from more than 200,000 to less than 20,000 in the same time frame.[22] Recent research from Erik Gartzke confirms that economic freedom has a high predictive value of whether a state will engage in war; in fact, his studies note that capitalism has proved to be a much stronger—actually 50 times stronger—correlate of peace than democracy.[23]

These are key lessons in the postwar period, and the United States' post–Cold War insistence on pushing democracy and human rights globally has likely made the world less safe by failing to focus on economic issues and the capitalist peace. Arguably, a wealthier world is more in humanity's best interest than a romanticized vision of homogenized self-governance. In this light, the neoconservatives' misplaced emphasis on democracy has been problematic or even counterproductive.

The Moment of Misperception

The rise of new players and the United States' failure to react begs the question, how long have the United States and the G7 misread the global tea leaves? The first sign of the G7-led world order's impending derailment came in 1997, with the G7's curiously mixed invitation to Russia to join as the eighth member. Even though its economy remained fragile, Russia—despite its dangerously large nuclear arsenal—was invited into the G7 but was barred from key discussions that coordinated global trade and interest rates, the group's *raison d'être*. The G7's refusal to aid Russia during its 1998 financial crisis underscored that country's second-class status in the fraternity. Would the United States have let Canada or the United Kingdom default on its obligations if a similar situation existed? Probably not. Instead of taking Russia into the flock and building a new ally, the G7 cast it out and made it a black sheep.

The treatment of Russia makes it seem like the G7 didn't believe its own multilateral rhetoric. High on Cold War victory euphoria, policy makers rested on their laurels. Except for a few unpopular humanitarian efforts under Bill Clinton in Mogadishu and Kosovo, foreign policy became an ad hoc extension of Cold War reflexes. As such, the G7 chose to engage Russia politically when Russia badly needed economic engagement. With oil prices hovering around $12 a barrel, no one thought Russia was terribly important. The G7 completely misunderstood the great economic convergence that was to begin in the late 1990s and what that would mean to global energy demand and Russia's future.

With oil above $30 a barrel for years—and now having peaked at $147—Russia has built a war chest of half a trillion dollars. In the first seven months of 2008 alone, Russian firms invested more than $4.2 billion in U.S. companies and assets as well as another $17.4 billion in companies outside of the U.S.[24] Even in spite of recent turmoil in its banking sector and falling commodity prices, Russia is a geopolitical force to be reckoned with. The country now regularly asserts itself in touchy cross-border debates (such as in Iraq, North Korea, and Iran) with little regard for American or G7 approval. Moscow exerts great pressure on its immediate neighbors, invading Georgia at whim, and often threatening Belarus and Ukraine. Russia's relationship with several European G7 members has grown tense given their addiction to Russian energy, complicated by disagreements on the eastward expansion of NATO with its proposed antiballistic missile defense system. Moreover, Venezuelan President Hugo Chávez and Russian President Dmitri Medvedev have declared plans to closely coordinate their actions on global oil and gas markets and foreign policy efforts. Even as late as October 2008, Russia was conspicuously absent from the G7's emergency discussions over the global credit crisis.

In addition to the misstep with Russia, the tragedy of 9/11 also exacerbated intra-G7 tensions. The attacks on New York and Washington, D.C., and the subsequent bombings in Madrid and London, created a weak, vulnerable mindset in the United States and Europe. Once bastions of security, many postwar powers looked prone in ways they could not have dreamed a decade earlier. This psyche of vulnerability has lead to unhealthy cross-border policy postures. Much of Europe seemed bewildered, tentative, paralyzed—perhaps understandable given the continent's historic monetary union, aging populations, stubborn unemployment, and sluggish economies. While Europe dealt with problems at home, the United States has turned aggressive, lashing out on the world scene. The controversial U.S.-led invasion of Iraq in 2003 marked Washington's ultimate stumble. The offensive has drained America of more than $1 trillion in direct costs (and another $10+ billion each month) and some estimate multiples of that amount in indirect costs, creating deficits financed by foreign creditors—including many emerging market central banks and sovereign wealth funds. Whether we like it or not, the United States now needs these foreign investments to close fiscal and trade gaps. The largely unilateral invasion, carried out without UN Security approval, and the subsequent occupation of Iraq have also created animosity between G7 members and alienated many rising countries. In turn, these countries quietly minded their own business, grabbing bigger slices of the world economic and financial pies. Although this began before Iraq, it has accelerated in the last few years.

The Iraqi invasion has promoted a hostile image of the United States as a paranoid unilateralist. Many outside the United States (and inside as well) view the Bush administration as dishonest. Popular Arab media portray the invasion as a ruthless oil grab, while many U.S. critics cite it similarly as a strategic oil diversification away from Saudi Arabia. The markets tell us that the United States' position is weakening, and the U.S. dollar—once a sign of the country's rock-solid strength and stability—is not nearly as valuable as it was a decade ago. Commodity markets have gyrated, stock markets imploded, housing bubbles have burst, and credit markets have frozen. Will the great trade success we have witnessed begin to reverse?

U.S. relations abroad are growing strained. In Europe, anger over Washington's policy in Iraq, Israel and Palestine, and even the handling of the credit crisis have caused strains. The United Kingdom still maintains the notion of a "special relationship," but public polls hint that this friendship is also waning. In the Americas, the rise of socialist, left-leaning governments and anti-U.S. sentiments in Bolivia, Ecuador, and Venezuela, leave the United States with fewer allies. Moreover, the U.S. congressional vote to build a 2,100-mile fence on the Mexican border certainly has not been embraced by our southern neighbor. In Asia, the United States' tenuous alliance with Pakistan in the War on Terror has not enthused India at a time when the United States would like to forge a closer relationship with the world's largest democracy. The North Korea nuclear escalation and the U.S. military's lost luster in South Korea has also rekindled Japanese rumblings over possible remilitarization, which spooks China and entangles three countries that have little historic love for each other. Are things falling apart? Can the center hold?

The New Financial Arena

Amid the global credit crisis, the United States and the G7's financial weaknesses are being exposed, to the detriment of markets worldwide. As we learned during the emerging market crises of the 1990s, everyone's policies now greatly affect one other. Yet the United Nations, the World Bank, and NATO are still dominated by white, Christian economies from North America and Western Europe that represent but a small minority of the planet. As a result of the dramatic recalibration of world power over the past two decades, U.S. and G7 global influence relative to that of other states is shrinking. Countries are sidestepping protocols and treaties, ignoring what suits them, and paying little mind to global civic responsibilities. Where are the United States and the G7 in this debate?

The G7, unfortunately, is bogged down in a struggle with its own demons. Critics question the lack of representation from the "global south," as well as the exclusion of China. In 2007, French President

Nicolas Sarkozy made a long overdue public statement recommending the expansion of the G7 to include China, India, Brazil, Mexico, and South Africa.[25] Others call for more Persian Gulf representation. If it cannot evolve, the G7 brand will be increasingly challenged in the coming years.

Not incorporating China may be the United States' biggest faux pas. China's rapidly growing economy has created a trade and investment codependency that many economists view as unhealthy. For years the United States has posted huge monthly trade deficits with China, which in turn, buys billions in U.S. Treasury bonds to help finance U.S. deficits. This unbalanced trade puts pressure on the Chinese to revalue their U.S. dollar-linked currency[26]—a discussion that would normally be within the domain of the G7; however, China is not a G7 member. China, of course, prefers a weak currency that keeps its exports flowing and its large population working. China's weak currency is beginning to irk the EU as well.

There are other important issues that strain U.S./G7 relations with China including human rights violations, intellectual and commercial piracy, and the country's murky long-term military ambitions. China's surprise ballistic missile launch in early 2007 to destroy an aging weather satellite promoted formal protests by the United States, Canada, and Australia, largely for not forewarning the world community. While the Chinese assert the test as a nonthreatening event, some U.S. critics view it as a demonstration of a significant military capability. At the same time, there are fears over Chinese companies' increased investments overseas as well as Chinese sovereign wealth funds taking strategic positions in U.S. and European corporations. All told, this is a relationship that has not been well cultivated in recent years, which is unfortunate given China's immense economic momentum and influence.

According to the International Monetary Fund, the leading 20 emerging market economies have seen their hard currency reserves swell from approximately $500 billion in 1996 to more than $3.5 trillion in mid-2008.[27] During this same period, the E7 and Russia alone saw their reserves jump from $255 billion to $2.5 trillion. Places like Hong Kong have become financial rivals for the United States for capital surpassing it in initial public offerings, while banks from China are able to borrow more cheaply than the United States' blue-blooded J.P. Morgan. Even Las Vegas has been displaced by Macau as the world's leading gambling center.

To emphasize the point, take a look at the recent fallout from the credit crisis with European and U.S. banks needing not only home country bailouts, but foreign investments totaling more than $100 billion from governments in Asia and the Middle East to bolster their capital bases from subprime losses. Imagine that: Some of the largest, mightiest U.S. and European banking groups had to borrow from countries among the world's poorest just a generation ago. Whereas the 20 most valuable financial groups in 1988 were American, Japanese, and European, by 2008, many were Chinese, Indian, Brazilian, and Russian. The world, indeed, has changed dramatically.

A major factor of this change is global capital flows. According to the International Monetary Fund, cross-border capital flows tripled in a 10-year period, reaching $6.4 trillion—roughly 15 percent of world GDP—by 2005.[28] Moreover, money flows are rapidly changing in origin, direction, and character. The remarkable growth of financial markets outside of developed economies since the bursting of the U.S. technology stock bubble in 2001 is notable for its diversity—stretching from East Asia through the Middle East and Eastern Europe to Latin America. The Mexican peso crisis of 1994, the East Asian financial crisis of 1997, and the Russian sovereign debt default in 1998 increasingly look like bumps in the road rather than the ominous end points these events seemed as they unfolded. Notably the latest credit crisis and bank failures are taking place in developed—not emerging— countries. As Figure 1.2 illustrates, a list of the world's largest economies will dramatically shift by 2050. China and the United States will move to the top two with India as the third, but look at the remaining countries. We will have some from Africa, more from the Far East, including some countries today that are barely on the United States' radar screen.

With newfound success, many emerging markets have created sovereign wealth funds outside their central banks to accelerate global financial and economic integration. SWFs are state-owned entities that manage portions of national savings. Today, many of these funds are flush with trillions of dollars due to record-high oil and natural resource prices.[29] As long as prices for energy and other commodities

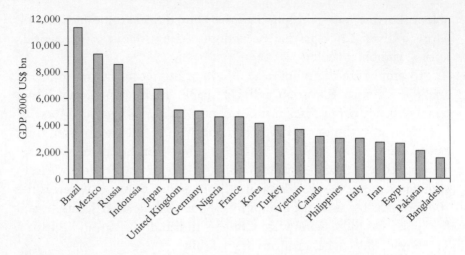

Figure 1.2 The World in 2050 (ex–China, United States, and India)
SOURCE: Goldman Sachs.

stay high, this trend will persist. And because the United States and the
G7 have less experience in dealing with these new players, the motivations of SWFs have become the subject of endless speculation. Calls
for greater transparency and disclosure by the Western media and government officials occur daily, underscoring the nervousness over these
powerful entities.

Whether or not G7 countries better integrate with emerging
markets, the newcomers are now directly investing in each other's markets. Foreign direct investment (FDI) between emerging markets has
increased significantly in recent years, reaching approximately $220
billion in 2006, double from just 10 years earlier.[30] Developing countries attracted about 36 percent of global FDI in 2006, and while it is
commonly assumed that these investment flows originate in the developed world, there has been a surge in FDI from emerging markets.[31]
According to the World Bank, FDI between developing countries
increased from about $14 billion in 1995 to $55 billion in 2006, indi-
cating intensifying commercial and financial activity that is now completely outside the G7's purview.[32]

A striking surge in intra–emerging market investment flows can
be seen between China and Africa. In large oil-exporting countries
like Angola and Nigeria, China is building railroads; in mineral-rich

countries like the Democratic Republic of Congo, Chinese companies are active in mining cobalt, copper, and bauxite. China is investing in agricultural countries like Cote d'Ivoire, building a new capital in Yamoussoukro financed by Chinese loans.[33] All across Africa generous Chinese aid packages and low-cost loans with few strings attached have made World Bank loans seem paltry and cumbersome. The World Bank and International Monetary Fund have voiced concerns that China's unrestricted lending, including a $2 billion credit line for corruption-plagued Angola, has undermined years of painstaking efforts to arrange conditional debt relief. The World Bank is also upset at lending by Chinese banks that do not follow Equator Principles, project-financing standards that emphasize certain social and environmental goals.[34] But the Chinese view all this differently. "The Western approach of imposing its values and political system on other countries is not acceptable to China," said Wang Hongyi, of the China Institute of International Studies.[35] Critics say Chinese efforts not only give their companies an edge in the competition for resources, but also that it will give China's diplomats an advantage at the United Nations and other international organizations, where African countries can constitute a powerful voting bloc.

This China cash diplomacy has also spilled into war-torn Sri Lanka where Chinese assistance has grown to nearly $1 billion, pushing it past Sri Lanka's longtime largest donor, Japan. The Chinese are building highways, developing two power plants and putting up a new port in the hometown of the Sri Lankan president. In turn, the Sri Lankan government buys weapons from China for its ongoing conflict with the Tamil Tigers,[36] allowing it to bypass Western human rights concerns.[37]

Perhaps the greatest criticism has been China's recent relationship with Sudan. Since 2003, more than 200,000 people have been killed and some 2.5 million made homeless in Sudan. During this period, China has largely ignored the atrocities in Darfur, purportedly strengthening its political, economic, and military relationship with the government of Sudan through long-term energy contracts. China is currently the largest known provider of small arms and ammunition that have been used by agents of the Sudanese government to wreak havoc in Darfur, although the Chinese government has publicly denied any wrongdoing.[38]

Moreover, Gerhardt Schroeder, the former chancellor of Germany, spoke of an impending "China-Russia combination," a relationship that would truly weaken G7 relationships with Asia. Schroeder supports the strengthening of the EU-Russia relationship, and is critical of the United States "containment policy" toward Russia, which he believes will only deepen the gap between energy policy and trade initiatives.[39] It is now only a matter of time: Russian President Dmitry Medvedev has called on Russian business to follow China's lead and invest in companies abroad in order to aggressively pursue global assets and foreign technology, as well as suggesting Russia dumps the U.S. dollar as a reserve currency.

Backlash: Where Is Globalization Taking Us?

Never in the postwar period have so many countries' economic and political policies affected the global economy and capital markets as they are today. On the surface, this development seems healthy. But trouble is brewing. In the last few years, a variety of crises—including financial meltdowns, food shortages, civil wars, terrorism, environmental stress, energy insecurities, and the formation of new security blocs—have arisen with the potential to cripple economic growth and frustrate flows of money, goods, and people. These looming worries stoke of a reversion to protectionism, capital controls, and other regressive, inward-oriented policies. Such warnings along these lines came from historians such as Niall Ferguson and Harold James, Nobel Laureate economists such as Joseph Stiglitz, and even mega-investors like George Soros, long before credit crisis began.

One sign of the looming trouble is the U.S. dollar's troubled swings. The U.S. dollar's hegemony is clearly under attack. The U.S. economy has outstripped almost all of its competitors for much of the past century and enjoyed monetary privileges due to its market power. But now, most countries whose currencies were once pegged to the dollar have made the difficult break and now float freely. Those that did not, like some countries in the Gulf region, are now in talks to do so, or have begun to use a basket of currencies rather than the dollar alone. Weak countries that pegged themselves to the U.S. dollar in recent years have suffered deeply, unable to bear the dollar's depreciation with their weak central banks and fickle fiscal policies. Currently, many of the world's central banks are holding more dollars than they really want or need—though not often out of loyalty to the United States. East Asian countries, especially, bought U.S. public sector debt in order to keep the dollar from depreciating relative to their own currencies and to maintain the levels of U.S. imports necessary to sustain their export-driven economies. If they were to dump the dollar it would surely create panics and reverberations not seen since the last Great Depression. While the flight to quality in late 2008 has stymied the decline in the dollar's value, in the long run, its value remains questionable.

Many commentators draw parallels to the pre-World War I period of economic integration that bloomed from 1880 to 1914. That globalization era—once assumed to be irreversible—was ultimately obliterated by 30 years of world war and depression. Do we face such risks today? Are we less secure in our cross-border relationships than we believe? Can the United States, once unquestionably the leader of the free world, speak for the entire planet in the twenty-first century? Should it try? And are we—citizens, businesspeople, and politicians—even aware of this historic opportunity and the diminishing time frame for action?

While most people around the world feel that the globalizing economy has been beneficial, antiglobalization sentiments are rising, and may intensify with the fallout from the credit crisis. Such concerns are strongest in the richest nations, while Africans have the most positive attitudes toward globalization. In a recent *Financial Times*/Harris Poll, citizens in Britain, France, the United States, and Spain were about three times more likely to say globalization was having a negative rather than a positive effect on their countries.[40]

These fears give rise to policies of protectionism. The largest European economies are especially prone because of their combination of weak growth, aging populations, high unemployment, and fear of job losses to lower-wage countries in Eastern Europe and Asia. This can also be seen in the resistance to EU expansion. In much of Europe, there is strong public opposition to Turkey joining the EU. In 2005, Angela Merkel and Nicolas Sarkozy, who oppose Turkish accession, came to power in Germany and France, respectively, giving elite support to widespread public sentiment.

Alongside protectionism, nationalism has also returned. In the more developed European states such as France, Austria, the Netherlands it is often expressed in anti-immigrant or ethnic- and language-oriented policies. In some new EU member states a potentially more dangerous form of nativism has emerged. In Poland, Hungary, and Romania, for example, nationalist, anti-Semitic, and anti-Western political messages have become commonplace.[41] The EU accession process stifled some of these impulses, as these countries understood the need to adhere broadly to the secular democratic values of the core EU states. But once these countries have gained EU admission, that constraint becomes less binding.

Across the Western world, political constituencies that favor tougher limits on immigration are gaining support despite evidence that increased restrictions on immigration will hamper the supply of skilled workers and raise costs. Fringe political groups have been successful in creating messages built around opposition to immigration. In many European countries, mainstream parties are finding it difficult to assemble governing majorities. As a result, they take strange bedfellows, embracing supporters who are sympathetic to the anti-immigration message of the fringe who encourage mainstream politicians to push for more restrictive immigration legislation.[42] At the same time, the European Commission forecasts that the EU needs to open the door to an extra 20 million workers, particularly highly skilled workers, over the next two decades to fill the gaps in the workforce.[43] Several European countries remain torn between the economic case for more immigration and an attachment to the traditional idea of a homogeneous nation-state.

Protectionist measures invite a spiral of retaliation. The impact on economic growth of a rise in protectionism could be severe. The Economist Intelligence Unit forecasts that even a relatively modest backlash against globalization could shave nearly a full percentage point off annual world GDP growth during the period 2011–2020.[44] Meanwhile, trade protectionist pressures are rising. In the United States, the president's Trade Promotion Authority (TPA) expired in July 2007. TPA is a procedural device that gives the White House power to negotiate trade deals and then present the final product to Congress for an up-or-down vote with no amendments. It is considered critical to the U.S. free trade agenda because trading partners are reluctant to engage in trade talks when they know that the U.S. Congress could potentially alter the terms of the completed deal afterward.[45]

Political turmoil in Europe over EU enlargement and foreign competition, pressed by aggressive hard-right factions in member states, may fracture Europe's ongoing economic and political integration and cause the continent's hard-won consensus on trade policy to unravel. Given the EU's stature as a pillar of the global trading system and its close relationship with the United States, its dissonance on trade would provide cover for other countries to adjust their own trade policies away from multilateralism.[46]

Emerging market countries also face growing opposition to globalization, especially trade liberalization. Responding to domestic constituencies, Brazil has imposed tight capital controls and high import tariffs that are particularly disruptive to U.S. business interests.[47] Brazil's perspective resonates with other South American countries, and it will increasingly become a leader in a growing bloc of harder-line developing countries that has already helped to delay the Doha Round of WTO negotiations.

As emerging market countries, Russia, India, and China among them, have grown in economic and political power they have intensified their regulatory scrutiny of cross-border FDI and merger and acquisition activity based on political and national security grounds. Regardless of the pretext, these measures are often intended to shield uncompetitive domestic industries and firms and drive global prices higher for lucrative natural resources. These pressures are causing governments to consider a variety of measures to tighten assessment of FDI flows, including introducing legislation fencing off "strategic sectors," such as defense industries and critical infrastructure, to potential foreign acquirers.[48]

Although it is deemed too important to fail, progress on concluding the WTO's global trade talks has been unfortunately slow. Launched in November 2001, Doha aimed to further liberalize global trade by cutting industrial and agricultural tariffs and by reducing farm subsidies, emphasizing benefits for developing countries. A conclusion to the talks has proved elusive, with the EU and the United States in particular being accused of failing to reduce farm support while such emerging market countries as Brazil and India have refused to open their markets to industrial goods and services. While majorities of developing countries around the world believe international trade benefits their national economies and corporations, many people, particularly in G7 countries, feel that free trade threatens jobs, lowers worker protections, and harms the environment.[49]

In place of the slow-moving global talks, trading nations are pursuing Bilateral Trade Agreements (BTAs) as more expedient alternatives. There are about 300 BTAs in force in 2007 worldwide and the number is growing, covering about half of the global trade volume. China is especially efficient in using BTAs as a strategic foreign policy tool to gain access to natural resources and develop new alliances in Africa and Latin America. The United States is also employing BTAs but on a much smaller scale given congressional protectionist sentiment and outright resistance as well as demands for additional labor, environmental, and enforcement safeguards. Ultimately, the proliferation of BTAs and the stagnation of Doha raise the prospect of weakening the multilateral system that has governed global commerce for the past six decades, possibly leading to a splintering of the global trading system into regional blocs. Another potential development is an erosion of respect for the WTO's authority to settle disputes, increasing the chances that countries will resort to tit-for-tat trade wars that could disrupt the global economy.[50]

The extended delay of the Doha Round is a sign of this new period of uncertainty. Not too long ago, Bush administration officials spoke optimistically about a free trade zone "from Alaska to Tierra del Fuego," and a world free of industrial tariffs by 2015. Today, that vision looks unlikely. It is up to Washington to consolidate what clout it has left, and be generous toward rising powers, engaging these nations in formulating new multilateral, international policies that tackle the global challenges of energy, environment, health, and security.

Converging or Diverging Interests?

The rise of emerging markets has come so quickly, and the potential for their influence is so huge, that today we need to consider them not only as economic opportunities but also as cooperators and partners in managing the global risks of the twenty-first century. However, the G7 and these new emerging powers have diverging perspectives on trade, human rights, the environment, and energy that have stymied progress in multilateral forums like the World Bank, the WTO, and the UN, where rising powers are relatively underrepresented. Can these nations continue using the global economic system, its capital markets, its stability, and laws without paying the dues owed to keep the system intact? Yet how can these players be asked to act more responsibly without adequate representation in global governance forums? This is the global chicken versus the egg conundrum.

Without insitutional reform, many of these developing countries—as well as some G7 nations—may continue to free ride and circumvent international norms, and some may even evolve into fierce, cutthroat competitors, rendering the United States less relevant globally. And, lest we forget, increased competition inevitably will strain internal G7 relations as diverging interests grow. The tense relationship with its eighth member, Russia, on everything from energy policy, nuclear proliferation, democracy, and human rights to the future of NATO potentially could undermine global stability. And the United States is tangled up in all of these webs. The real question of the moment is: Will America wake up and see the elephant?

Toward a Quantum Framework for the New Millennium

For much of this millennium, the United States has relied on familiar linear, unilateral problem-solving approaches—a "Micro Domestic" paradigm. This atavistic bias makes U.S. policy increasingly ill suited for today. President Bush's foreign policy, for example, could be a page stolen from Ronald Reagan's early 1980s playbook. His "war on terror" is akin to the "war against communism," with the "axis of evil" supplanting the "evil empire." The great reliance on increased military spending is reminiscent of Reagan, with our economy increasingly exhibiting the twin deficits that developed under that administration. Beyond defense, U.S. postures and policies on energy and fossil fuel use, agriculture, and the environment also seem woefully out of step with twenty-first century realities.

While the Micro Domestic approach may have worked well enough in a bipolar world, it demands serious reappraisal today. We live in what physicists might call a "quantum" world, one of infinite connections. As we've outlined, there are now many, not only one or two, power brokers. Additionally, the scale of global interaction that occurs today is dizzying compared to 100 years ago or even 20 years ago. The amount of information, goods, money, and people that now cross borders, and the velocity of these movements, has permanently altered the international landscape.

To prosper in this new environment, we need a new approach— what I call a "Macro Quantum" paradigm—that can better cope with more players, greater interconnectivity, and less predictability. Just as a modern medical doctor wouldn't operate on a heart without monitoring the brain and lungs; similarly, we must not operate in world without thinking of the ramifications to Beijing, London, and Brasilia, as well as to the earth itself. In simple terms, we must see the entire elephant not just individual parts.

Whereas a Micro Domestic paradigm relies on past strategies, the Macro Quantum perspective is forward thinking, understanding that new ways are needed for further progress. A Macro Quantum perspective assumes cross-border relations are unpredictable not fixed. Importantly, the Macro Quantum paradigm acknowledges that there are many ways forward, and the right choice depends on situational context as opposed to one correct approach. While some Americans may pine for the sense of moral clarity of an us-versus-them world, we must readjust our thinking to realize there are no right or wrong solutions anymore, just better or worse. And lately the latter have won out. For example, American-style democracy may work for us, but that doesn't mean imposing a constitution and a bicameral parliament on every nation will create functional government, let alone a prosperous country. The highly differentiated states of the Macro Quantum world, each with unique traditions and histories, demand custom-made solutions not one-size-fits-all.

Whereas under the Micro Domestic approach, the United States aimed to *control* countries and events, in the Macro Quantum world we endeavor to build partnerships to *influence* and help *manage* trends. During the Cold War, the United States never had to question the allegiance of its NATO allies. In addition to the looming threat of the Soviet Union, the United States used its massive economy and military might to push allies to accept its decisions. In the new millennium, this is no longer the case: The United States' attack on Iraq bothered some of its closest allies and caused significant discomfort in many European capitals. Learning to play nice with other countries will be a tough but ultimately rewarding lesson for the United States in the new millennium.

Beyond working with more countries, understanding and constructively managing relationships with nonstate actors will also be a valuable survival skill. Instead of eyeing newcomers with caution and suspicion, we must acknowledge their potentially useful roles and set clear rules that will allow these players to function in a transparent and helpful way. In the case of terrorists and paramilitaries, devising new strategies to neutralize their influence over the global rule-based system of interaction will be invaluable.

Finally, in the Macro Quantum world, policy-making must be a proactive, constant process, involving many actors, both sovereign and civilian. Whereas a Micro Domestic stance views policy issues as separate and distinct from each other, Macro Quantum strives to foster integrative policies that kill many birds with a few stones. Moreover, domestic policies must be adaptive and synchronized to global phenomena rather than unilateral. Table 1.4 compares my Micro Domestic and Macro Quantum paradigms.

With this philosophical shift, the United States and its allies can begin to examine seven large, interlinking areas that will demand serious attention in the coming years, and which will consequently be the subjects of the chapters in this book (also see Table 1.5).[51]

1. **Trade and Finance:** For decades, global trade volume has been growing twice as fast as world output and is the basis for greater cross-border interaction and wealth creation. But the recent collapse of the Doha trade talks underscores acute policy divides that exist and the rise of bilateralism. The G7 members subsidize agriculture by more than $300 billion annually, and key developing markets now retaliate with tariff protections in many manufacturing and high-tech sectors. Without breaking the multilateral logjam, the goal of poverty eradication by trade engagement—the world's most successful model—may never be achieved.

Table 1.4 Micro Domestic vs. Macro Quantum Paradigm

Micro Domestic	Macro Quantum
A present, or worse—a historic—time bias.	A forward time bias.
Assumes a larger degree of certainty and predictability in cross-border relations.	Assumes a larger degree of uncertainty, ambiguity, and unpredictability in cross-border relations.
There is only one best way, often from a domestic or small group perspective.	There are many ways forward depending on many global moving parts.
A primary emphasis on control with concentrated power among a few allies.	An emphasis on influence derived from positive behavior distributed widely among a broader range of players.
Countries are viewed cautiously, as competitors with disparate interests; little focus on nonstate actors.	Countries, working with nonstate actors, are cocreative partners with common interests.
Policy change is reactive, initiated by the hegemon.	Policy change is proactive, constant, involving many actors, sovereign and civilian.
View policy issues as separate, compartmentalized, and domestic.	View policy issues as interrelated, integrative, and global.

With more trade and capital flowing than ever before, the need for coordination is greater than ever. Whether the World Bank is currently configured to shepherd this transition is debatable. The surprising flip of E7 debtors to creditors of the G7 in the last decade muddies the World Bank's original objectives. Other global accords, such as Basel II, need to be revaluated for their usefulness in a rapidly globalizing world. Indeed, the global scope of the credit crisis underscores the need for multilateral coordination in the financial markets.

Moreover, financial imbalances due to government and trade deficits, demographic immigration patterns, and flawed energy policies, among others, need to be addressed within the context of long-term trade and investment ramifications. In the United States consumption-led policies (including excess borrowing) may need to be altered toward savings, and the entire focus on GDP expansion

Table 1.5 The Seven Policy Areas under the Micro Domestic and Macro Quantum Paradigms

Global Issue	Links	Micro Domestic	Macro Quantum
Trade & Finance	Energy, Security, Immigration, Health, Environment, Poverty	Rearward, domestic perspective; subsidies for old industries; trade-stunting policies; fossil fuel orientation; hostile to foreigners; highly leveraged, consumption-focus; little value on environment; little interest in low GDP countries; focus on domestic GDP at any cost.	Forward, external perspective; subsidies for future viable industries; trade-enhancing policies; diversified energy approach; encouraging foreign participation; less leveraged, investment-focus; greater value on environment; greater interest in low GDP countries; focus on well-being beyond traditional yardsticks.
Energy	Trade, Security, Immigration, Health, Environment, Poverty	Heavy dependence on imports for oil, reliance on coal for electricity, few public incentives for renewables.	Less reliance on imported oil; diversified approach to electricity; more public incentives for renewables, with focus on solar.
Security & Defense	Energy, Security, Immigration, Health, Environment, Poverty	Nuclear deterrence; NATO forces; containment strategies; majority underwriter of global defense; defense geared toward low probability scenarios; peace through strength; physical U.S. armed presence overseas; protecting oil access; arms sales.	Nonproliferation; wider NATO membership; flexible, rapid response strategies; smaller underwriter of global defense; defense geared toward higher probability scenarios; peace through cooperation; reduced physical U.S. armed presence overseas; greater UN peacekeeping efforts; reducing U.S. oil access commitments; limited arms sales.

(Continued)

Table 1.5 (*Continued*)

Global Issue	Links	Micro Domestic	Macro Quantum
Immigration	Trade, Security, Health, Environment, Poverty	Zero-sum perspective, protectionist orientation, lesser skilled focus, prohibitive legal framework since 9/11, viewed as a one-way street.	Opportunity to attract needed labor, stemming tide of outsourcing; higher skill focus; strategic immigration as economic tool; viewed as a two-way street.
Health	Trade, Security, Immigration, Health, Environment, Poverty	Domestic focus, emphasizes curative solutions.	International focus, emphasizes preventative policy.
Environment	Trade, Energy, Security, Immigration, Health, Environment, Poverty	No major domestic or global policies, overreliance on fossil fuels, misdirected subsidies, no global accords.	Greater global oversight of environmental standards; commitment to renewable energy; push for global accords on several stress points, especially agriculture.
Poverty	Trade, Energy, Security, Immigration, Health, Environment	Limited foreign aid channeled through multilaterals, sporadic commitments to foreign governments through the UN and World Bank.	Increased foreign aid channeled through NGOs, micro lenders, and BOP strategies with MNCs; longer term commitments with new social entrepreneurial organizations.

at any cost also requires serious refinement. Progress in the twenty-first century quantum world cannot be measured by GDP alone, and may require alternative indicators to guide policies.

2. **Energy:** With expanding economies and wealth comes greater demand for power. Few countries are energy independent, and most are addicted to fossil fuel for transport and electricity. The concerns over global warming and the waning availability of

hydrocarbons will continue to polarize rich and developing countries, exacerbating tensions with the G7, unless common environmental and energy policy solutions are found.

New demand for energy has also generated unprecedented hard currency flows to Russia and other oil exporting nations over a very short period. To guard against further concentrations and imbalances, greater cooperation toward efficient energy usage and in spurring renewable and domestic power production needs urgent encouragement. Promotion of nuclear energy, too, calls out for global coordination as it holds the potential for weapons conversion.

3. **Security:** While overall cross-border warfare has declined with greater trade integration, there remain major security threats that all countries need to consider. Nuclear proliferation is a universal issue, regardless of domestic agendas. Moreover, all military conflicts— conventional or guerilla, cross-border or domestic—threaten the global system by draining resources and damaging productive capabilities. And while weapons of mass destruction grab the headlines, a more deadly threat are simple conventional weapons. The United States' 2009 military budget of $700 billion—more than the military expenditures of the next 10 nations combined—represents resources that could be deployed elsewhere more productively.

One cost of membership in any expanded club of nations is greater responsibility for security. Broader global defense coordination should involve greater roles for other G7 members, as well as new rising powers, to deal with the more fragmented security issues the world collectively faces today. In building a greater collective capitalist peace, many new security strategies need to be reconsidered including an expanded, reconfigured NATO, greater global commitments to UN security and peacekeeping forces, greater global networks of local intelligence and law enforcement, a nuclear glidedown and bans on weapon sales, among others.

4. **Immigration:** The free flow of people has benefited the world, providing wealthier countries with fresh labor amid declining birth rates. In turn, developing countries see the gains of this labor export in the form of remittances. But immigration is a volatile issue across the globe that influences trade competitiveness and poverty and ignites protectionist sentiments. Understanding the

importance of freer movement of people could slow demographic trends in aging countries and promote freer movement of trade and help eradicate poverty over time. This would be a very different approach to immigration in wealthy economies, which have grown very protectionist in the last decade. Discouraging immigration increases the chances for outsourcing, which has also come under attack in wealthy countries. Finally, helping generate greater economic opportunity in developing countries may be seen as part of the global immigration solution, because most migrants are generally seeking better economic alternatives.

5. **Health and Drugs:** Whether HIV/AIDS, Avian flu, SARS-style outbreaks, or tainted food and medicine exports, health issues are no longer confined to one country's borders. Increased global interaction poses potential future health risks the magnitude and scale of which may be hard to comprehend. We forget that better health is a prerequisite for participating in the global economy. Seemingly simple programs in poor countries to raise daily caloric intake, alleviate childhood disease, and prevent infectious diseases like malaria, actually have great positive benefits that reverberate throughout entire societies. Health issues also will be a major concern for rich countries, as wealth gives rise to life-style-linked illnesses that cost societies billions in unnecessary, curative spending.

6. **Environment:** Setting aside the red-hot issue of global warming, there are a number of immediate concerns related to the environmental stress caused by G7 and emerging markets' economic activity. Shortages of energy, food, and water will reverberate globally if longer-term plans are not devised. One reason that the Kyoto Accord has stalled is the failure of both G7 and E7 members to acknowledge each other's environmental abuses, something an expanded working group might seriously address. But this rift cannot be addressed bilaterally, and action surely must be taken immediately if the world is to begin to turn the tide against the devastating consequences of global climate change. This clearly ties into energy usage, but the general environmental stress of greater demands across many areas outside of energy have spurred domestic and cross-border conflicts. One can only imagine the financial, security, and social ramifications of melting Arctic glaciers and ice

sheets in Greenland, events that could raise sea levels 40 or 50 feet, imperiling hundreds of millions of wealthy and poor populations that live on coasts around the world.

7. **Poverty:** More than two billion people globally still live on the margin of sustainability, something easy to forget amid globalization's broad gains. But for each new member of the middle class in China and India there are several impoverished and embattled in those countries as well as many in other parts of the developing world. Beyond the obvious moral implications, both G7 and emerging nations need to appreciate the demoralizing political frustrations that poverty creates around the world—and the security risks it foments. Moreover, the G7 needs to understand the pressures many E7 countries face internally given the massive economic gaps that have accompanied rapid industrialization and development, and rethink foreign aid and economic and financial engagement. Both the E7 and G7 need to begin to promote poverty eradication and more global economic opportunities beyond their borders. Most of the world's civil wars occur in relatively poor places and can spill across borders very easily.

America's Latest Challenge and New Global Agenda

After a disappointing start to the twenty-first century, President Obama will have a unique—and frustratingly short—window of opportunity to reassert American leadership and influence in global affairs. It will not be easy. Our leaders need to understand that what appears to be divergent interests among the G7 nations and rising powers are only superficial and that greater gains can be won for all if we are prepared to make bold and unorthodox choices with a Macro Quantum perspective.

It is today's great paradox: Countries are clearly moving closer economically, increasingly depending upon each other for commodities, trade, and capital, but they are unfortunately moving farther apart politically. In the past, forums like the G7 have helped forge multilateral working relationships—rules, behavioral codes, and mechanisms for collective progress and orderly conflict resolution. But, even if we are to ignore the signs of diverging interests and opinions among the current members, the very composition of G7 is surely less relevant today and no longer adequately represents the global system's expanded roster. The economic and demographic engines that have driven this new, unprecedented wave of globalization show no signs of slowing, and there is pressing need for multilateral, holistic coordination among old and new powers. The challenges are many, and as the world's waning but still strong hegemon, the responsibility of influencing the future rests with the United States, first and foremost. Although the United States has lost some global goodwill, it still has unmatched human and economic capital. But it is up to us to set the ball in motion. We must engage old allies, emerging markets, rising powers, and nonstate actors.

With fresh, comprehensive approaches across a broad spectrum of policy areas, the United States can reassert itself with an overarching, somewhat ironic goal: *to lead the world into an era no longer dominated by the United States.* In doing so, the country actually will be promoting its own self-interests by promoting collective interests. By shepherding new approaches and new institutions and by better understanding the interlinkages of global issues, the United States can increase chances for a bright future by winning the influence and leadership role with the global community it has seemingly lost.

Global Convergence and Sports

Standing 7-ft. 5-in., Yao Ming is one of the world's most recognizable athletes as the Houston Rockets starting center in the National Basketball Association (NBA). Ming is a poster boy for Apple, Nike, and Visa, and has received the most fan-generated ballots in several all-star games due in part to Chinese citizens voting in astonishing numbers. But more important, Ming is one among many foreign-born twenty-first century sports icons to make his name on the world scene. This is a major break from the recent past and provides a snapshot into global economic convergence and where the Macro Quantum world is heading.

Historically, professional sports have been dominated by the United States. But with increased globalization and wealth creation, upgraded overseas training has produced more competitive athletes for more sports from more countries than ever before. Professional basketball was one of the first U.S.-dominated sports to embrace the trend. In 1970, the NBA drafted its first two foreigners (neither made the league). Today, almost every team has at least one international player, and the league hosts approximately 100 overseas players (out of 450) from nearly 40 countries. With standouts like Ming, the NBA routinely scours the globe for stars such as Dirk Nowitzki from Germany, Dikembe Mutombo and DJ Mbenga from the Congo, Manu Ginobili from Argentina, and Peja Stojakovic from Serbia. Drafting talent internationally has become commonplace; now 50 percent of NBA-drafted players now come from abroad.

The globalization of sports goes beyond basketball. Take hockey, a popular international sport historically professionally dominated by Canadians and Americans. In 1970, 90 percent of NHL players were from the United States and Canada; by 2008, that number was down to 60 percent. Some of the game's best players in recent years have come from Eastern Europe, including Russians Alex Ovechkin—the world's highest paid player—Alexei Yashin, Sergei Federov, and Alexei Kovalev, and Czech star Jaromir Jagr.

In Major League Baseball (MLB), Japan has been producing talent in the last two decades including new sensation Daisuke Matsuzaka, former batting champion Ichiro Suzuki, and Yankee outfielder Hideki Matsui, while Latinos like David Ortiz and Albert Pujols comprise nearly 30 percent of MLB's players rosters.

In ladies' professional golf, South Korea fielded five of the world's top 15 ranked players in mid-2008. In fact, only 30 percent

(*Continued*)

(*Continued*)

of the top 50 ladies players today are Americans compared to more than 60 percent in 1990.

In professional tennis, only two each in of both the top 10 ranked men and women hailed from the United States in 2008, with many former Soviet Union and Central Europeans dominating.

And the former Soviets also have toppled boxing, dominated by American men for much of the twentieth century. Brothers Vitali and Wladimir Klitschko of Ukraine and Uzbek Ruslan Chagaev have been boxing champions for most of the new millennium, with many younger Russians and Kazakhs also highly ranked.

And soccer, perhaps the world's most popular sport, has also seen a similar internationalization of talent. Twenty years ago, virtually all the players in the United Kingdom's famed Premier League were born in the British Isles. But take a look at the country's Chelsea (owned by Russian billionaire Ivan Abromovich) or Arsenal team rosters today. On Arsenal, only two out of 32 players were born in England (and they are rookies who rarely play). The rest of the squad comes from Brazil, Mexico, Togo, Ivory Coast, Switzerland, France, Spain, and Germany. Similar international rosters dominate Europe's Champions League. And these leagues increasingly have a global fan base. Many team web sites use multiple languages; Manchester United's site actually has versions in Chinese, Japanese, and Korean.

The internationalization of sports talent can also be seen more broadly in the Olympics. For the past five summer games through Athens in 2004, the concentration of gold medal winning countries has shifted dramatically. In 1988, 63 percent of the gold medals won were from just five countries; by 2004 it dropped to 41 percent. Moreover, in 1988 only 31 countries won the gold, jumping to 57 by 2004. While the Cold

War's splintering of the former Soviet Union explains part of this phenomenon, only seven nations that won gold medals in 2004 were newly created countries. But the greatest—and perhaps least surprising—Olympic rise is China, the world's largest country by population and one of the fastest growing economy for nearly two decades. In 1976, China failed to win one medal—not even a bronze—at the Montreal summer games. In 2008 in Beijing, America captured 36 gold medals (110 medals over all), but was surpassed by China's 51 gold medals (100 medals over all).

This global convergence of athletic talent, like global economic convergence, will continue. Poorer countries, for decades short on funds for sports, now have the disposable income needed to invest in and develop athletes. In fact, economics has a lot to do with Olympic medal winning outcomes. In a recent study, Andrew Bernard and Meghan R. Busse examined summer Olympic medal counts for the past 40 years to see what factors determine how many medals each nation wins. Statistically, just two factors account for 95 percent of a nation's predicted medal count: the number of medals it won at a previous Olympics and the overall size of its economy, bigger being better.

Per-capita income, oddly, is irrelevant. A large, poor country will win as many medals as a small, wealthy country, assuming they have the same overall gross national product (GNP). Of still greater importance than GNP is a winning Olympic legacy. Bernard has noted, if you have done well in the past, that's going to persist. "Once you develop infrastructure and training and facilities, and once you develop athletes, they do last for a couple of Olympics," he said.★

As more countries grow wealthier with economic globalization, this will continue. With more world-class facilities and training programs globally, we can expect to see more

(*Continued*)

(*Continued*)

countries on the Olympic medal platforms over time as well as more participating and dominating professional sports in the near future. This will be no different in business, as many emerging market countries now produce talented individuals and companies to rival the United States' and Europe's former dominant positions.

---

*Alex Berenson, "We Know the Winners. Now, Let the Games Begin," the *New York Times*, September, 10, 2000.

Chapter 2

Trade and Finance

Money, Money Everywhere

Shanghai looks like the future.

—Paris Hilton on a 2007 Trip to China

As hotel heiress and tabloid star Paris Hilton proves, you don't need a Nobel Prize in economics to read the writing on the wall. After more than a century of relative decline, Shanghai is at the epicenter of China's triumphant return to the global economy, replete with glittering office towers, decadent shopping plazas, and a surprising number of Ferraris. Growing by 9 to 10 percent per annum for 20-odd years now, China's economy is one the world's hotbeds of human activity that amazes on so many levels:

- Once a country of peasant farmers, China now has 175 cities with populations greater than one million.
- Since 1990, 22 million new private businesses employing 135 million people have been created.
- China has exported more in the last three weeks than it did in all of 1978.

- The country has the world's largest foreign currency reserves—now nearly $2 trillion, up from less than $90 billion in 1997.
- Chinese citizens have opened 120+ million individual brokerage accounts in the last decade, more than the United Kingdom, France, and Germany combined.
- China has more science, engineering, and doctoral students than any other nation—it pumps 600,000 new technicians and engineers into the workforce each year.
- China will produce 70 million new workers in the next 20 years, while the European and Japanese labor forces are set to shrink over the same period.
- By year end 2007, the Chinese mainland boasts 41 billionaires, and more millionaires than Danes in Denmark.
- Beijing's new airport—the world's largest—was planned and built in only four years (ahead of schedule). The main terminal is 1.8 miles long, with a footprint that's 17 percent larger than all of London Heathrow Airport's five terminals combined.
- Between 2001 and 2005, $50 billion was spent on Chinese road and rail systems—more than was spent in the previous 50 years. Between 2006 and 2010, $200 billion is slated for new railways alone.
- There are plans to build a Shanghai skyscraper more than twice the size of the world's current tallest buildings, Malaysia's Petronas Towers, that could house 100,000 people in 300 stories.

We could go on and on about the growth and size of China, from the record amount of commodities it consumes, to the number of new Internet users going online each day, to how many millions are served daily at McDonald's and Kentucky Fried Chicken. The list of superlatives is endless, pages upon pages of sparkling footnotes documenting China's resumption of its historical place as the world's largest economy.

While China is the biggest and most dynamic emerging market (EM), it is not the only country profiting from the current wave of trade and financial integration. Over the past two decades there has been unbelievable socioeconomic progress virtually everywhere on earth; as described earlier, we are witnessing one of the great economic convergences of all time. Commerce, trade and finance have evolved quickly from small, isolated disciplines into one of the densest webs of human interaction in history, with volumes of goods, money, people and ideas whirling around the planet that can scarcely be measured.

China is the cornerstone of the BRIC countries—the acronym for Brazil, Russia, India, and China coined by Jim O'Neill and his Goldman Sachs team in a landmark 2003 paper describing the increasing importance of these economies. Their combined populations represent more than 40 percent of the world's people. Based on current trajectories, BRIC should surpass the G7's economic output between 2040 and 2050, while O'Neill's "Next 11" (N11) emerging markets are projected to eclipse the G7 sometime before 2075.[1]

The long-term, rapid growth of EMs will alter trade, labor, and consumption patterns dramatically, warranting a quantum reestimation of the United State's and the G7's future place in the global system. While Great Britain and the United States took 50-plus years to ascend to world power status, how did these countries—formerly among the earth's poorest—turn the corner so quickly? As we'll see, their youthful, educated workforces, combined with the adoption of free market reforms and new technologies have changed the planet faster than anyone could have ever predicted.

Comparative Advantage and Free Trade: Converting to the New Religion

Just one generation ago, most of humanity lived under economically segregated communist or socialist governments. Even in the early 1980s, global trade was largely the domain of the G7 and a dozen other countries. But the abandonment of statist policies in favor of free markets has unleashed unprecedented growth in places previously unconnected to the global trade and investment web. Figure 2.1 shows the magnitude of changes in trade patterns.

All around the world, thousands of state-owned enterprises have been sold, privatized or shut down, encouraging the forces of competition and changing forever the economic ecosystem. Meanwhile, the world's growing number of skilled laborers has dramatically

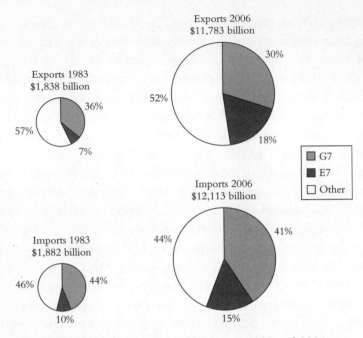

Figure 2.1   Shares of Global Imports and Exports, 1983 and 2006
SOURCE: WTO, EIU country data.

reduced the cost of most manufactured goods for consumers every-where. According to UBS, from 1990 through 2007, emerging market exports to industrial countries have soared from $45 billion per month to almost $240 billion. More impressively, the total value of emerging market exports to *other* emerging markets has grown from $30 billion per month to a remarkable $245 billion—actually surpassing exports to rich countries.[2]

This is a seminal shift. We now have massive amounts of trade that does not directly touch the G7 at all. We're not just talking about trading bananas and sandals, we're talking about everything. Old trade routes like the Silk Road that were blazed hundreds and thousands of years before the United States was born, are all being reincarnated in modern form with trucks replacing camels, and electronics, steel, machinery, and fossil fuels supplementing tea, silk, and foodstuffs.

To understand how and why labor and trade patterns have shifted recently, take a look in your closet. Where were most of your clothes made? Probably not in the United States, Western Europe, or Japan anymore. Labor is simply too expensive in these regions to produce $4 underwear or even a $40 Banana Republic shirt.

Now look at the tag inside your favorite blue jeans. For decades, companies like Levi's and Wrangler produced cheap dungarees in the United States, but as U.S. living standards rose and labor costs increased starting in the 1950s, most clothing makers shifted production overseas. An American working in a U.S. jeans factory today at $16 per hour (an average factory wage) could be very productive, sewing eight pairs each hour, the equivalent of $2 in labor per unit. In this example, a denim manufacturer operating in the United States might incur a per pair cost of $8 including the labor, then sell to a retailer like Macy's for $10 a pair—making a $2 profit per unit. In developing countries like Mexico or China, labor is less productive but also less expensive. While a worker in a developing country may only be able to sew four pairs of jeans in an hour for a $2 wage, the per unit labor cost drops to only 50 cents (compared to $2 in the United States). So by simply moving production, the jeans company can shave $1.50 off costs, making $3.50 profit per pair sewn abroad versus $2 domestically—a 75 percent increase. Or it could lower jeans prices by $1.00 (still making an extra 50 cents per pair) and sell a greater volume. Either way, the jeans company is more competitive manufacturing in a country where the productivity-to-cost ratio is higher even if absolute productivity is lower.[3] This is the essence of comparative advantage, as well as a driving force in keeping inflation curbed amid unprecedented global growth.[4] Whether we're talking about jeans, washing machines, computers, automobiles, or even data processing, seeking out cost advantages abroad has defined the Macro Quantum global economy and converted billions of emerging market citizens into global workers and consumers.

The Next Stages of Trade

How do countries evolve amid greater competition? Let's look at a basic trade model with two nations: a wealthy one like the United States and a lesser developed country like Mexico. Labor cost and productivity differentials make it more advantageous for the wealthier nation to shift work from a high-labor sector like agriculture to manufacturing and services, as the United States did for most of the twentieth century. In the first phase of the process, the United States begins to import agricultural goods from Mexico, freeing American workers to focus on manufacturing, which pays higher wages and provides greater profit. Trade develops, and both countries prosper. Eventually, as the model progresses, Mexico's profits from agriculture allow it to import manufactured goods—say blue jeans—from the United States. In phase two of trade, the Mexican economy strengthens and it is able to better utilize its lower-cost labor to produce blue jeans on its own more inexpensively than the United States (as in the previous example). U.S. labor, seeing that it can't compete in blue jeans anymore, shifts to manufacturing televisions and begins a new two-way pattern with Mexico exporting TVs and importing blue jeans. In phase three of globalization, Mexico refocuses on blue jeans for export and begins to import agriculture from a lesser developed country, say Guatemala, whose labor force can now produce agricultural products less expensively than Mexicans, who earn more sewing jeans. After time, Guatemala starts importing Mexican blue jeans and so goes the pattern. These phases move from appliances to automobiles, to aircraft, to computers, to financial services, ad infinitum.[5]

As labor productivity increases globally, strands of trade intertwine a greater number of countries, thereby weaving the capitalist peace of economic dependency and mutual profit. We forget that in the late 1800s, nearly all Americans were farmers. By 1950, half were factory workers. Today less than 2 percent of Americans work on farms and less than 25 percent are in factories. The vast majority—more than 70 percent—work in the service sector. This pattern will likely continue as countries keep innovating, improving their productivity and avoiding protectionist tendencies. As Figure 2.2 illustrates, the makeup of EM output has followed the pattern we've described. While more than 80 percent of EM exports in 1981 were in natural resources like oil and iron, today EM exports are a mix of low, medium, and high-tech manufactured goods, while resources comprise only 22 percent.

The result of this process is an extraordinary increase in global trade. And keep in mind, trade is not simply finished goods; a large

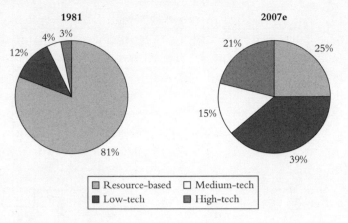

Figure 2.2   Structural Changes in Emerging Market Exports, 1981–2007
Source: World Bank; Eurostat; IMF; IEA.

share includes intermediate goods that are processed in different places and only assembled in a final country. The modern production chain of automobile manufacturing is a perfect example: The Mini Cooper, a small, fashionable, distinctly British car is actually produced and owned by the German manufacturer BMW. BMW imports engines from Brazil and other parts (brakes, glass, tires) from up to a dozen countries depending on market costs. In the end, only final assembly happens in the United Kingdom.

Barring a prolonged worldwide depression (a possibility given the current global financial crisis), the globalization of labor and manufacturing should continue for decades, and EMs are driving economic expansion. The G7 has a combined labor force of less than 500 million people, while the 15 leading emerging markets have 2.5 billion people as of 2007.[6] By 2050, the G7 labor force will be smaller than it is today. In contrast to the aging, shrinking populations of Germany, Japan, and Italy, emerging markets will add an additional 375 million skilled workers in the same period.[7]

Let us not forget what Henry Ford knew more than 100 years ago: Today's well-paid workers are tomorrow's new customers. Figure 2.3 shows just how fast EM consumption is growing. With rising disposable incomes, two or three billion emerging market workers are

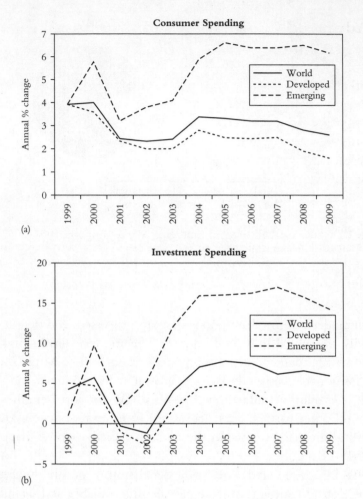

Figure 2.3   New Engines of Growth: Consumer and Investment Spending
Source: HSBC, 2008.

becoming the most desired new customers for multinationals that suffer from saturated home country markets. While the average person in
the United States currently drinks more than 360 beverages like Pepsi
or Snapple each year, in China and India this number is less than 60.
Expanding global markets present enormous opportunity in the form
of underserviced populations thirsty for basic food, clothing, medicines
and electronics we take for granted in the West.

Advanced Information and Communications Technology: The Turbo Trade Booster

Remarkable technological advances have hastened the integration of new economic players. Just as innovations in transportation reshaped the twentieth century economy, today's information technology revolution—faster computing, increased communications capacity, and denser information networks—has transformed the twenty-first century economy. Three major principles that have accelerated economic activity are especially important to keep in mind:

1. *Moore's Law* states that computer-processing speed doubles every 18 months with transistor improvements. This simple calculation has held true for decades: Just try to imagine how much faster (and cheaper!) your current computer is today than one of five years ago.
2. *Gilder's Law* postulates that communications bandwidth (like fiber-optic phone lines and satellites) grows at least three times faster than computer power. Therefore, if computer power doubles every 18 months, communications power doubles every six months.
3. *Metcalfe's Law* proposes that the usefulness, or value, of a network rises exponentially with the number of users. The more users, the more useful and valuable is the network (or market). If only two people comprise a market, it isn't particularly useful. But if two to three billion people are in your market, do the math. Consider how many people are now on the Internet today.

These somewhat arcane (and geeky!) technology laws are actually powerful gears in the Macro Quantum world. We now have immense amounts of information moving around the planet on the cheap: A $500 notebook computer can process information so quickly it makes a 1960s NASA computer seem like an abacus. Now, for example, doctors in Nigeria can watch new surgery techniques performed at a Los Angeles hospital live on the Internet and download supporting medical research instantly. If the local doctor lacks the medical tools to perform such a surgery, the necessary items can be shipped in a day. Some surgeries can even be performed remotely via computer.

Likewise, technology has enabled MNCs to become truly global. MNCs can control and monitor operations on all continents in real time and track shipments via GPS, all of which bolsters confidence in trade. Combine these three axioms with the larger number of trade participants, and our Metcalfe marketplace has expanded from about 500 million people in 1990 to almost three billion today and growing each minute. The new millennium equation: Moore's Law + Gilder's Law + Metcalfe's Law = Macro Quantum Globalization.

The More the Merrier: Unprecedented Interaction

As we've seen, new technology and the abandonment of statist economics have helped prosperity spread more quickly than the common cold. Global trade is approaching 50 percent of world GDP, and global GDP itself has risen by more than 40 percent between 2000 and 2008, according to the World Bank. Half of humanity lives in countries where the economy has been growing at 7 percent or more annually, a rate that doubles output when sustained for a decade. Figure 2.4 shows recent soaring EM growth rates. In a historic context, today's growth rate is miraculous; until the Industrial Revolution, global growth averaged less than one-fifth of 1 percent per year. At that rate, it took the world economy 500 years *to double output.* By comparison, China's economy is growing at 10-plus percent a year and will roughly double output in only seven years. Maintaining recent 5 percent growth, global output will double in about 14 years, turning our current $45 trillion global economy into more than $350 trillion by 2050. Compounded growth leads to convergence: If a country today has only 30 percent the GDP of the United States, but grows at 4.5 percent for 50 years (like Japan did after World War II) versus 2 percent for the United States, at the end of 50 years, both countries will have approximately the same GDP. In today's world, that means a country like Mexico may have only a third of France's GDP but in less than two generations their economies will be roughly the same.

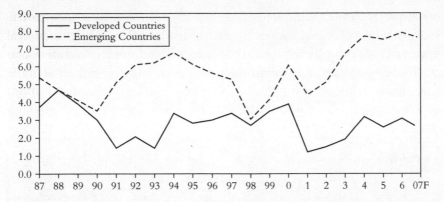

Figure 2.4 Emerging vs. Developed Nations: GDP Growth, 1987–2007 Forecast
SOURCE: IMF World Economic Outlook, April 2007.

G7 economic growth has been much slower than that of emerging markets, due to lower birth rates, saturated markets, and already-high GDPs and productivity. But the G7 has still benefited from what is happening in developing countries. Some of the biggest winners of this era are G7 consumers and the G7 companies that have expanded overseas. The success of other nations through economic liberalization is partly responsible for higher real wages and an upwardly mobile middle class in the United States. Globalization has democratized wealth by making former luxuries into everyday items. From 1960 through 2008, U.S. exports multiplied by nearly 80 times, from $30.5 billion to more than $2.4 trillion, with overall GDP jumping from $2.5 trillion to $11.6 trillion.[8] The percentage of the population in the United States living below 125 percent of the poverty line decreased from 31.1 percent in 1959 to around 16.8 percent in the most recent census data.[9] And while the U.S. middle class (roughly defined as households earning $35,000 to $75,000 a year in 2005 dollars) did shrink between 1967 and 2005, from 40.1 percent to 33.3 percent, these displaced middle Americans were not getting poorer. The share of the population earning less than $35,000 dropped 4 percent, while the number of households earning more than $75,000 has actually jumped 10.6 percent to 56.6 percent.[10]

We cannot, nor should we, wish these globalizing trends away. More people worldwide are being unshackled from scarcity, illness, illiteracy, and poverty faster than ever before, and this can continue indefinitely with strategic planning and maintenance to the Macro Quantum trade system. But doing so requires us to adopt a different worldview, one that focuses on the interplay of countless more players in the trade and investment game.

Old Money, New Money

In 1987, *Forbes* magazine launched its first world billionaires ranking. Roughly one-third of the list was American, 18.5 percent Japanese (reflecting Japan's economic zenith before its bubble burst), and 26.7 percent European.

While the United States' total share has grown to 44.3 percent of the 2008 list, the rise of emerging markets is noteworthy including the first billionaires from Cyprus, Oman, Romania, and Serbia. India accounted for an impressive 36 billionaires, outpacing Japan as home to Asia's largest number of extremely wealthy individuals. Russia weighed in third, after the United States and Germany, with 53 billionaires. South Korea contributed 10 super-wealthy (up from two in 1987); Brazil and mainland China boasted 20 billionaires apiece (with another 21 from Hong Kong and eight from Taiwan), while Turkey had 25 (no Turks made the list in 1987).

The rich list's demographic transformation reflects the amazing wealth creation that has occurred in newly industrialized and developing states over the past two decades. Not long ago, private ownership was taboo in many of the countries that now boast nearly as many Horatio Alger tales as the United States. For example, Russia's wealthiest man, Roman Abramovich, was an orphan who went on to become a state governor and eventually sold his majority stake in oil company Sibneft in 2005 for 13 billion dollars. Young Russians make up the bulk of the top 25, filling seven seats. Many have prospered in resource companies including aluminum, nickel, oil, and gas. And the average age of these seven Russian billionaires? Less than 44 years old.

Back in the late 1980s, no names would have been found from countries like China, Russia, India, or Mexico. But in 2008, only four of the top 25 in the *Forbes* list were Americans and just five were from Europe. A remarkable 16 of the 25 come from formerly poor countries. Mexican telecom magnate Carlos Slim has been wrestling for Forbes' top spot with perennial uber-rich tycoons Bill Gates and Warren Buffett (by some accounts his net worth has surpassed that of the two Americans). To put it into perspective: Slim's wealth is roughly 6.5 percent of Mexico's annual economic output. If Bill Gates had a similar share of U.S. wealth, he would be worth a remarkable $784 billion—nearly eight times his current holdings. Four Indians—Lakshmi Mittal (owner of the world's largest steelmaker), the bickering Ambani brothers (inheritors of the Reliance group, India's most valuable company), and KP Singh (real estate)—make up half the top eight slots. India now has more billionaires in the uppermost echelon of rich than any other country, save the United States. While recent stock market volatility may have reduced some billionaires into mere centamillionaires, there nonetheless has been a great proliferation of wealth.

Nonstate Actors on the World Stage

The growing importance of multinational corporations (MNCs) in spurring global trade has coincided with the rise of new financial institutions. Today, of the largest 100 economic entities in the world, roughly half are companies.[11] By encouraging the transfer of knowledge and skills and allocating capital where it is most needed, the growth of these new actors has been one of the most positive human developments in the postwar period.

Great globalizing pioneers like American Express, Caterpillar, Colgate-Palmolive, GE, HSBC, Komatsu, McDonald's, Nokia, and

Siemens, among hundreds of others were mostly founded in the G7 and other industrialized nations, but EM companies are also gaining global market share. According to a recent Boston Consulting Group (BCG) study, many new world multinationals have both the resources and ambition to upset dominant old world players. BCG's 2008 report listed 100 firms (see Table 2.1) from EMs with revenues approaching

Table 2.1   100 EM Companies to Watch

Argentina (1)	China (cont.)	India (cont.)
Tenaris*	Galanz Group Company	Reliance Group
	Gree Electric Appliances	Satyam Computer Services
Brazil (13)	Haier Company	Suzlon Energy*
Braskem	Hisense	Tata Consultancy Services (TCS)
Companhia Vale do Rio Doce (CVRD)	Huawei Technologies Company	Tata Motors
Coteminas	Johnson Electric	Tata Steel
Embraer	Lenovo Group	Tata Tea
Gerdau Steel	Li & Fung Group	Videocon Industries
JBS-Friboi*	Midea Holding Company	Videsh Sanchar Nigam (VSNL)
Marcopolo*	Nine Dragons Paper Holdings*	Wipro
Natura	PetroChina Company	Indofood Sukses Makmur
Perdigão	Shanghai Automotive Industry Corporation Group (SAIC)	
Petrobrás		**Malaysia (2)**
Sadia		Malaysia International Shipping Company (MISC)
Votorantim Group	Shanghai Baosteel Group Corporation	Petronas
WEG	Shanghai Zhenhua Port* Machinery Co. (ZPMC)	
Chile (1)	Shougang Group	**Mexico (7)**
CSAV*	Sinochem Corporation	América Móvil
China (41)	Sinomach*	Cemex
Aluminum Corporation of China (Chalco)	TCL Corporation	Femsa
		Gruma

BYD Company

Changhong Electric★

Chery Automobile★

China Aviation I

China FAW Group Corporation

China International Marine Containers Group Company (CIMC)

China Minmetals Corporation

China Mobile Communications Corporation

China National Heavy Duty Truck Corporation

China Petroleum & Chemical Corporation (Sinopec)

China Shipping Group

CNOOC

COFCO★

COSCO Group

CSIC (China Shipbuilding Industry Corporation)

Dongfeng Motor Company

Founder Group

Techtronic Industries Company

Tsingtao Brewery

VTech Holdings★

Wanxiang Group Corporation

ZTE Corporation

Egypt (1)

Orascom Telecom Holding

Hungary (1)

MOL Group★

India (20)

Bajaj Auto

Bharat Forge

Cipla

Crompton Greaves

Dr. Reddy's Laboratories

Hindalco Industries

Infosys Technologies

Larsen & Toubro

Mahindra & Mahindra

Ranbaxy Pharmaceuticals

Grupo Bimbo★

Grupo Modelo

Nemak

Poland (1)

PKN Orlen★

Russia (6)

Gazprom

Inter RAO UES★

Lukoil

MMC Norilsk Nickel Group

Rusal

Severstal

Thailand (2)

Charoen Pokphand Foods

Thai Union Frozen Products

Turkey (3)

Koç Holding

Sabanci Holding

Vestel Group

SOURCE: Boston Consulting Group.

$1 billion that are expanding aggressively overseas. These firms have many competitive advantages that will challenge many incumbent players.[12] Already 48 corporations on the global Fortune 500 are based in developing countries. With vastly improved access to capital, even more EM firms are set to take off. From 2002 to 2007, 727 EM corporations issued international bonds and 2,998 borrowed from international syndicated bank loan markets. In the same period, EM corporations issued a full one-third of all global shares cross-listed on major exchanges. Today EM economies boast more than 15,000 MNCs, many of which have achieved global recognition.[13]

This is not the first time economic batons have been passed. British companies ceded preeminence to U.S. corporations after World War II, and over the past two decades, Japan—the great twentieth century emerging market—has likewise displaced many American and European sector leaders. Indeed, General Motors, Ford, and Chrysler have all seen their historic positions erode (and now teeter on bankruptcy) with the rise of Toyota, Nissan, and Honda. Toyota now ranks as the world's largest auto producer. And yet in the blink of an eye, South Korean automakers like Hyundai have ascended from the butt of jokes to respected global manufacturers. Or consider the Indian automaker Tata Motors, which recently bought luxury brands Land Rover and Jaguar from Ford. There are many prominent EM companies in other sectors, as well: Mexico's Cemex now dominates the global cement market; steel production is controlled by CSN from Brazil and Arcelor-Mittal of India (now headquartered in Luxembourg), both of whom have acquired some of the world's largest old steel names in Europe, the United States, and elsewhere. To put things in perspective, take a look at the world's twenty most valuable companies in 1997, versus those in mid-2008 (see Table 2.2). Once dominated by large U.S. companies and a few from Europe and Japan, note that seven of the top 25 today are from BRIC countries, versus none in 1997. Japan has completely dropped off the list, and only two European firms made the cut.

Clearly many emerging market companies are on the move. Using their strong stocks as currency, they are able to make massive acquisitions not only in G7 countries but also in other developing countries where they may feel more comfortable and better understand the economic environment.[14] Many of these EM companies also are at

Table 2.2 Most Valuable Companies by Market Cap, 1997 and 2008

Top 20 Valuable Companies 1997 ($ millions)	Country	Market Cap ($millions)	Top 20 Valuable Companies 2008	Country	Market Cap ($ millions)
1. General Electric	U.S.	239,539.44	Exxon Mobil Corp.	U.S.	504,989
2. Coca-Cola Co.	U.S.	164,760.08	Petrochina CO-H	China	413,930
3. Microsoft Corp.	U.S.	152,155.50	China Mobile	China	339,026
4. Exxon Mobil Corp.	U.S.	150,337.70	General Electric	U.S.	322,714
5. BP PLC	U.K.	126,533.50	Gazprom	Russia	318,957
6. Merck & Co.	U.S.	126,526.69	Industrial and Comm. Bk.	China	293,209
7. Citigroup Inc.	U.S.	122,830.85	Microsoft Corp.	U.S	281,536
8. Intel Corp.	U.S.	115,384.50	Commercial Bank ZI	China	273,658
9. Nippon Telegraph	Japan	112,112.52	Petrobras Pref.	Brazil	257,423
10. Novartis AG-REG	Switzerland	111,110.29	Royal Dutch Shell	Netherlands	240,079
11. Bank of America	U.S.	104,751.80	AT&T Inc.	U.S.	228,211
12. IBM	U.S.	100,240.29	BHP Billiton PLC	U.K.	226,958
13. Pfizer Inc.	U.S.	96,483.88	Wal-Mart Stores	U.S.	223,625
14. Toyota Motor	Japan	95,992.80	BP PLC	U.K.	216,681
15. Procter & Gamble	U.S.	95,400.25	Procter & Gamble	U.S.	207,639
16. Roche Hldg-Genus	Sweden	91,473.66	HSBC Holdings PLC	U.K.	200,398

(*Continued*)

Table 2.2   (*Continued*)

Top 20 Valuable Companies 1997 ($ millions)	Country	Market Cap ($millions)	Top 20 Valuable Companies 2008	Country	Market Cap ($ millions)
17. Johnson & Johnson	U.S.	87,265.76	China Const. BA-H	China	199,225
18. Eli Lilly & Co.	U.S.	77,320.09	Total SA	France	198,282
19. American Intl. Group	U.S.	76,072.58	Berkshire Hathaway	U.S.	197,020
20. AT&T Inc.	U.S.	71,579.90	Chevron Corp.	U.S.	195,270

SOURCE: Bloomberg, May 2008.

an advantage when selling to the bottom of the pyramid (BOP), the four billion people who live on $10 a day or less (including two billion who live on $2 or less). This massive class of people forms the majority of the Earth's inhabitants, and yet they have been largely ignored by MNCs from the rich world due to their limited buying power. EM companies may have a better feel for how to position products for the BOP and burgeoning middle classes in other developing countries. The Tata's Nano, for example, is a four-seat automobile that will sell for as little as $2,500, less than the price of a GPS system in most European luxury cars. In poorer countries where transportation alternatives are scooters and bicycles, this car may be the new Volkswagen, or "people's car." To compete in this new Macro Quantum world, older MNCs must actively embrace and seek these BOP opportunities.

Capital Access and Waves of Money

The global financial landscape has been transformed by this historic economic integration. In 1980, the World Bank supplied more than 27 percent of cross-border capital flows into emerging markets and G7 commercial banks provided 43 percent.[15] Today, World Bank capital flows to EMs are less than 5 percent, and G7 banks supply less than 15 percent. There are so many more forms of money available today: stock and bond issuance (by companies from countries that never

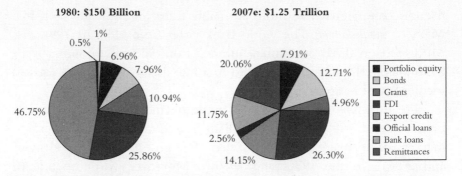

Figure 2.5 Profound Changes in Capital Flows to Emerging Markets
Source: IMF, World Bank, Bloomberg, EIU.

participated before), export finance and foreign direct investment (FDI) by MNCs that are trading more and building factories overseas at record rates, and local banks and institutions now offer liquidity (all shown in Figure 2.5). This newly diversified access has happened amazingly quickly thanks to improving EM credit ratings, local stock and bond market development, and greater savings rates in these countries that are channeling their newfound wealth into these new investments and making local financial markets broader and deeper, even if the current credit crisis slows this trend. In old Soviet-style economies, stock and bond markets didn't exist. The World Bank notes that emerging markets now absorb almost a trillion dollars in foreign flows, up from less than $150 billion in 1985.

In the last quarter century, there have been six identifiable, over-lapping significant waves of cross-border capital flows including today's stage of economic globalization. In the first wave of the early 1980s, G7 institutional investors began a process of globally diversifying capital into foreign stock markets, focusing on the G7 as well as a few Western European countries, and Australia and New Zealand. The idea was for G7 investors to improve portfolio returns while reducing overall risk through country diversification. Back then this was considered exotic; today it is seen as basic portfolio allocation.

Shortly after this wave, a second swell occurred, in which G7 multinationals globally shopped for cheap labor and lower production costs. Companies like GE and IBM, looked for skilled workers in friendly countries where more profitable factories could be built like Mexico's *maquiladoras*. The World Bank notes from 1986 to 1994 that MNC foreign direct investment jumped from $39 billion annually to $156 billion, the majority going to Asia but also to Latin America and former Soviet nations.

The third wave brought a new mode of financial investing, which began around 1989 as the Brady Plan helped dislodge the emerging market debt overhang that stifled foreign financial investment and growth in the 1970s and 1980s.[16] Moreover, with the tide of privatization and financial liberalization that swept markets in the wake of the Soviet Union's fall, local stock markets took root around the globe. In the spring of 1993, the International Finance Corporation launched its first investable equity index for emerging markets, providing G7 nations, global banks, and other investors with a bench-mark for this new asset class to help them further diversify portfolios and boost returns.

In 1994, the fourth wave broke. Mature, broadened EM stock and bond markets had arrived in the former Soviet Union countries, China, India, and other previously isolated economies. These newly capitalist countries offered financial markets that could be tapped by foreign investors for the first time in decades.

By 2000, hard currency reserves were mounting in EMs due to rapid export earnings and high savings rates. This generated a fifth wave, as successful EM countries invested in other rapidly expanding financial markets for diversification. For example, South Korean insurance companies bought vast amounts of Mexican and Russian bonds; Singaporean government investment funds bought shares of Latin American companies; and Brazilian banks invested in Asian hedge funds. This process has only accelerated since.

We are now smack in the middle of the sixth wave, perhaps the significant yet. In recent years, tremendous capital flows have been directed from emerging markets to *developed* countries, including the G7. The leading 20 EM economies have seen their hard currency reserves swell to more than $3.5 trillion by mid-2008. These developing country central banks use their coffers to regularly buy hundreds of bil-lions of U.S. Treasury bonds that help fund the Unites States' trade and government deficits. The sixth wave also includes direct investments, including billions that sovereign wealth funds have used to buy stakes in Western financial institutions amid the recent U.S. subprime mortgage meltdown. It also includes emerging market MNCs buying companies in the G7. The sheer weight of this money has helped keep interest rates low, which, in turn, fanned not only the flames of cross-border investment and consumption, but also contributed to the asset bubbles that have sprung up around the globe.

This current wave and credit crisis should be a wake-up call to the G7. There are now so many economically powerful countries, so many competitive global companies, and so many new financial players amid so many markets that a complex rethinking of financial strategies is required by all governments and companies. The G7 is clearly no longer the only game in town, but part of a highly interconnected global capital system with dozens of countries. The credit crisis underscores the interconnected nature of finance. (See Figure 2.6.)

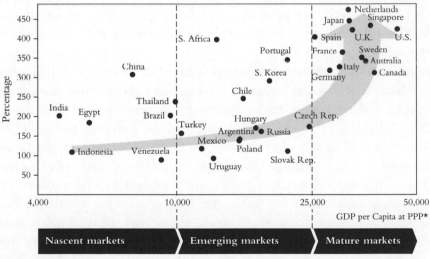

* Log scale.

Figure 2.6 Map of Global Financial Depth
SOURCE: McKinsey Global Institute Global Financial Stock Database.
NOTE: Value of Bank Deposits, Bonds, and Equity as a Percentage of GDP, 2006.

Changing Financial Hubs

In the past, most blue-chip companies would list on the New York or London stock exchanges to gain prestige and access to capital. But money is everywhere today, creating financial hubs in places such as Dubai, Singapore, and Hong Kong. As economic might shifts toward China, India, and other emerging countries, competition in financial services has never been so intense.

For example, as of May 2008, Hong Kong's stock market ranked seventh largest in the world in terms of market capitalization, with over 1,200 companies listed and a market cap of nearly $2.5 trillion. Well-positioned to capitalize on the China boom, Hong Kong is also the largest venture capital center in Asia, managing about 29 percent of the total capital pool in the region.[17] Newcomers Dubai and Abu Dhabi are also becoming hubs for investments, with their proximity to the wealthy major oil producers where vast wealth has been created. *The Economist* estimates that nearly $2 trillion in investments come from the Gulf region, most of which is currently invested abroad. In 2006, McKinsey estimated at least $200 billion petrodollars were invested in global equity markets, $100 billion in fixed-income markets, and $40 billion in hedge funds, private equity, and other alternative investments. After just a few short years of rising oil prices, this region has some of the world's deepest pockets.

Moreover, stricter rules for U.S.-listed companies also have encouraged companies to list elsewhere. According to McKinsey, in 2005 only one of the world's 24 largest initial public offerings (IPOs) was registered in the United States. In 2007, more money was raised through IPOs in Hong Kong than either New York or London. The Sarbanes-Oxley Act of 2002, which sought to clamp down on corporate malfeasance by tightening U.S. accounting standards, may scare away foreign firms eager to list their stock on U.S. exchanges. Even a well-known foreign corporation like Nestle has been unable or unwilling to meet the requirements to list on the New York Stock Exchange.[18] The United States still is the perceived leader in securitization and debt markets, but legal and regulatory stringency coupled with the growth of other financial centers means a listing on a U.S. exchange is no longer *de rigueur*. Who needs the red tape when there may be places to raise money? One only can imagine what new U.S. regulation inevitably will emanate from the global financial crisis that took down such large institutions as Bear Stearns, Lehman Brothers, AIG, Freddie Mac, and Fannie Mae.

The United States' and the G7's ability to shape capital markets (through regulatory regimes and otherwise) has been diluted as economic power spreads across the globe, and other nations now have a say in setting the rules for international finance. EM financial market capitalization grew from approximately $1 trillion in 1990 to almost $24 trillion by mid-2008 (see Figure 2.7). The battle for global capital will intensify over the next few years as competing global finance centers in Asia and the Middle East become increasingly influential. The globalization of capital is facilitating the regionalization of capital markets, cross-ownership by many EM countries in exchanges, and a diversifying investor base will raise the demand for new financial products, services, as well as regulatory frameworks.[19]

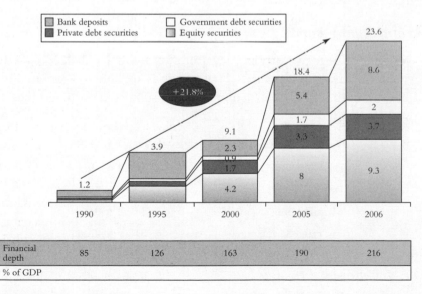

Figure 2.7   Growth in Emerging Market Financial Assets (in U.S. dollars, trillions)
SOURCE: HSBC

The New Bizarre Bazaar

Never before has there been a greater ability to access money or assets so quickly, and with the rise of EMs, highly mobile capital can exit U.S. financial markets and enter Asia and vice versa in mere seconds. It is now truly a 24/7 marketplace, and we can see global markets gyrate tick by tick on TV and the Internet. While traditional institutions like commercial banks, mutual and pension funds, as well as insurance companies, are still among the world's largest financial players, new challengers have arisen that operate with different objectives and protocols than in the past. In 1980, 73 percent of all wealthy countries flows to emerging markets were controlled through a few commercial banks and the World Bank. Very little investment flowed from EMs to the G7. Today it's a blur, with money coming in and going out from so many sources—some regulated, with others operating below the radar of financial regulators (see Table 2.3). While on the surface this seems like a positive development, the recent experience of increased market volatility, imbalances, asset bubbles, and credit freeze-ups show the dual-edged nature of the Macro Quantum world.

Private Equity Funds

The tight U.S. regulatory and legal environment has helped spur the growth of private equity funds. These entities are able to avoid much of the scrutiny to which public companies are subjected, although they are

Table 2.3   Key Investment Players, Year-End 2006

Banks	$63.5 trillion
Pension Funds	$21.6 trillion
Mutual Funds	$19.3 trillion
Insurance Companies	$18.5 trillion
Sovereign Wealth Funds	$3.1 trillion
Hedge Funds	$2.1 trillion
Private Equity Funds	$1 trillion

SOURCE: McKinsey, DB Research, Hedge Fund Intelligence, author estimates.

criticized for their lack of transparency. Private equity funds buy companies with the explicit goal of reselling them later at a profit. Private equity assets under management are now nearing $400 billion in the United States, nearly $200 billion in Europe, and $400 billion in Asia and the rest of the world. While the largest private equity firms such as Blackstone, the Carlyle Group, Texas Pacific Group, and Kohlberg Kravis Roberts & Co. (KKR), have only $1 trillion in investable equity between them, they routinely borrow enormous sums of money from banks and other financial institutions for leveraged buyouts of companies, sometimes with only 10 percent down.[20] That means that some funds control numerous companies, in effect making them large industrial and financial conglomerates, the private equivalent of Warren Buffett's publicly traded Berkshire Hathaway.

Hedge Funds

More than twice the size of private equity, hedge funds have also changed the global financial landscape. Hedge funds are private investment pools for wealthy individuals and institutional investors, trading in the public markets going both long and short.[21] Therefore, hedge funds are protected somewhat from market movements. Like private equity, they use leverage, which means that the industry's $2-plus trillion may actually control $5 to $6 trillion in assets.[22] By mid-2008, more than 390 firms worldwide manage hedge fund assets of $1 billion or more according to Hedge Fund Intelligence. Most hedge funds are still based out of the United States. International Financial Services indicates approximately two-thirds of the world's hedge fund assets are managed out of New York, but new ones are creeping up in Europe, Asia, and the Middle East.

In the past, hedge funds have been blamed for a variety of mishaps. Some hedge funds are extremely active in foreign exchange markets that directly affect governments. In 1992, one of the most famous hedge fund investors, George Soros, bet against the British pound and beat the Bank of England on what is known as "Black Wednesday" to the tune of one billion pounds Sterling. Indeed, Soros was accused by former Malaysian premier Mahathir Mohamad of undermining South East Asian economies with currency speculation.[23] Hedge funds argue that they make markets more efficient by their activities. Regardless of their intentions, which are basically to make profit wherever they can, hedge funds need to be understood by governments and market participants alike given their size, speed, and predisposition toward short-term trading, which is inherently volatile. As the recent credit crisis shows, understanding hedge funds is essential to understanding market conditions: the deleveraging of hedge funds in mid-2008 exacerbated the crisis through unprecedented asset sales worldwide.

Sovereign Wealth Funds

A sovereign wealth fund (SWF) is an investment vehicle held by governments, typically funded by the extra liquidity from current account surpluses. Often linked to nationalized assets,[24] SWFs fall into one of two categories: stabilization funds, which aim to insulate the budgetary and fiscal policies of a country from fluctuations in market prices and foreign exchange conditions; and intergenerational funds, used to anticipate depletion of natural resources, a sort of long-term "resource retirement account."[25] Governments allocate excess funds to these separate, often independent, operational entities that are run by professional portfolio managers.

However, SWFs have been met with hesitation in the rich world. They are perceived as potentially irrational economic investors acting out political agendas. According to the IMF, in 1990, sovereign funds probably held about $500 billion; the current total is estimated at $3 trillion—larger than the global hedge fund industry, but still only 2 percent of the world's $165 trillion worth of traded securities. Morgan Stanley projects that these investment funds could grow to $17.5 trillion within 10 years.[26] That's part of the concern; they are big players and becoming bigger by the day. Abu Dhabi's was the first to hit the $1 trillion mark in 2008 (see Table 2.4).

With the exception of Norway's Government Pension Fund, SWFs have traditionally published little information about their assets, liabilities and investment strategies. In the past, SWFs have followed long-term investment strategies that promoted financial stability, buying mostly government bonds. But in light of China Investment Corporation's purchase of a $3 billion stake of U.S. private equity firm Blackstone in

Table 2.4   Leading SWFs

Country	Fund	Assets under Management ($ Billions)	Inception Year	Source
United Arab Emirates	Abu Dhabi Investment Authority (ADIA)	875	1976	Oil
Singapore	Government of Singapore Investment Corporation (GIC)	330	1981	Noncommodity
Norway	Government Pension Fund Global (GPFG)	322	1990	Oil
Saudi Arabia	Various funds	300	NA	Oil
Kuwait	Kuwait Investment Authority (KIA)	250	1953	Oil
China	China Investment Company Ltd.	200	2007	Noncommodity
Hong Kong	Hong Kong Monetary Authority Investment Portfolio	140	1998	Noncommodity
Russia Stabilization	Fund of the Russian Federation (SFRF)	127	2003	Oil
China	Central Hujin Investment Corp.	100	2003	Noncommodity
Singapore	Temasek Holdings	108	1974	Noncommodity

SOURCE: Deutsche Bank.

May 2007, there is speculation that some SWFs are shifting investment strategies toward more diversified and riskier foreign assets.

These concerns are overblown. SWFs are misunderstood by many Westerners. Emerging market governments have been big buyers of U.S. and European bonds for some time, and their recent forays into other asset classes are rooted in a reasonable desire for asset diversification like most G7 institutions of comparable size. Many SWFs also have their money managed by foreign managers, largely based in the G7. Lately, some of these funds have been the white knights of the global financial system. Early in the subprime crisis, SWFs infused more than $100 billion into U.S. and European banks, helping to keep them solvent and operating (even though many of these led to losses). However these benign investments are being eyed with suspicion, largely due to the origins of the investors: Kuwait, the United Arab Emirates, Russia, China, Brunei, and Saudi Arabia.[27] SWFs are not likely to be a huge threat, but a push toward greater transparency is in order. In May 2008, the IMF and 25 sovereign wealth funds established a working group to draft the first-ever best-practice guidelines. Since these countries are new to global markets, it is important to integrate them properly—as other countries have been—to strengthen the global financial system.

The fact that pension funds, insurers, and SWFs often invest in hedge funds and private equity (as well the underlying assets of hedge funds and private equity funds), and that global banks often lend to these institutions and make markets in underlying investments, means that trouble in any one corner of the financial system can wreak havoc for the whole system.

Anatomy of a Macro Quantum Crisis

To understand today's interconnected quantum world, simply take a look at the recent U.S. credit crisis and its links to globalization. This financial meltdown happened not in a developing country with weak controls, but in the United States, the world's financial leader. By examining the tangled web of global economics, capital markets, labor, immigration, energy, and regulatory regimes that contributed to (and resulted from) the U.S. subprime mortgage bubble and broader credit meltdown, we see just how interdependent the world has become.

In the early 1990s, a nearly balanced federal budget under the Clinton administration pushed down global interest rates making U.S. mortgages more affordable than they had been in the late 1980s.

Interest rates dropped from a high of more than 11 percent in mid-1989 to 7.25 percent in 1995 and continued to dip for the remainder of the decade, according to HSH Associates.[28] Because financing was cheaper, U.S. real estate sales and prices soared. Residential mortgage volume jumped from $2.95 trillion at year-end 1992 to $5.1 trillion by 2000. The housing boom resulted in a need for construction workers. Lured by high wages, many Mexicans and Central Americans (some legal, some undocumented) immigrated to fill these open jobs.[29] In turn, billions of dollars worth of capital remittances were sent back to families in Latin America, sparking domestic booms in these countries. A similar economic expansion in the Middle East and Europe led to parallel immigration and remittance patterns with laborers from India, Bangladesh, Pakistan, Turkey, and the Philippines.

This real estate boom also ushered a great U.S. import binge from China. Americans began to fill their houses with everything that could be bought from the local Home Depot or Wal-Mart and jammed into a plus-sized SUV. The seeds of our widening trade deficit, weaker dollar, and the rises in commodities prices were planted. As the real estate boom continued, banks targeted less qualified or subprime borrowers for mortgages. With the rise of interest-only and adjustable-rate mortgages, as well as personal mortgage insurance, many "NINJA" borrowers (No Income, No Job, No Assets) were able to buy houses with little or no money down—the resulting combination of a debt-prone culture, some predatory lending practices, as well as some outright fraud in mortgage applications.

With surging U.S. real estate and a sizzling economy, the U.S. trade deficit jumped from $111 billion to $370 billion from 1995 to 2000 sending dollars abroad and building wealth overseas in places like China. The 2000 bursting of the Silicon Valley bubble and resulting crash in tech stocks, only further whet appetites for U.S. real estate because property values held up better than the NASDAQ. So Americans continued to build, buy, and renovate houses, (not to mention speculate on pre-built properties) as well as piling into their mammoth SUVs, consuming more gasoline, and buying more and more imported goodies.

In the wake of the 9/11 terrorist attacks, the U.S. Federal Reserve Bank kept the U.S. economy afloat with huge interest rate cuts, pushing mortgage rates—particularly adjustables—historically low. By 2002, "teaser" mortgages were offered at less than 3 percent for the first two years, with 15-year mortgages averaging 5 percent or less—half of what they were in 1992. Coupled with Wall Street innovations for slicing and dicing pools of mortgages, low interest rates created untold liquidity that continued to fuel the surge in home ownership and construction. Residential mortgages ballooned from $5.6 trillion at year-end 2001 to $8.8 trillion by the end of 2005.

The Bush administration's "global war on terror" required massive defense spending, financed with U.S. government bonds, often purchased by foreign central banks. Oil, which had been $19 a barrel in 1992, had risen to $28 before the Iraqi invasion. By 2003, the U.S. and world economies started to hum again, the U.S. housing market continued to grow, and Wall Street peddled record volumes of mortgages to global investors from banks everywhere from Boston to Beijing. But this growth was based on rocky foundations: By 2005, the U.S. trade deficit spiked to an unprecedented $726 billion and oil had climbed to $50 a barrel.

Speaking of Beijing, in the early millenium China's export economy began to reap the benefits of the long global expansion. China ravenously imported industrial metals and fossil fuels needed for its red-hot economy. Newly wealthy Chinese began consuming more as well as speculating on their own real estate and local stocks. Beyond China, stock market and real estate bubbles were developing in the United Kingdom and Spain as well as in emerging markets like Russia, Kazakhstan, and Vietnam, to name a few. According to Bloomberg, from 2002 to 2006, emerging stock markets on average rose more than 400 percent.

The real estate and other asset bubbles were exacerbated by the 1988 Basel Accord (Basel I), a banking framework established by the G7 plus a few other small European countries.[30] Basel I aimed to standardize capital requirements across banks. In June 2004, the refined Basel II Accords were released. Under both frameworks, the more risky loans a bank assumes, the more capital it needs to hold. The new Basel II emphasized public security ratings (such as Moody's, Fitch, and S&P) to determine risk. As a result, balance sheets were built on the decisions of these credit rating agencies that bore little liability for their actions. This was a break from the past when banks cultivated in-house credit departments to review exposures, and developed deep relationships with borrowers. As a result, the large commercial banks lost their historic connections to borrowers, and risk management became a game of statistical odds.[31]

To minimize Basel capital requirements, structured finance gurus utilized a loophole called a Special Investment Vehicle (SIV). By putting a small amount of money into SIVs, banks could actually bet on a lot more assets off balance sheet with no Basel capital needed. SIVs would fund themselves with short-term debt and reinvest that borrowing in longer term slightly higher yielding investments, such as AAA-rated pools of mortgages, credit cards, student loans, car loans, and commercial paper. Everyone believed the underlying assets were among the most liquid bonds available, with years of purported data and high credit ratings in tow. The trouble was that some SIVs invested in assets that were nominally rated as AAA but may not have been even close to AAA in risk. There was a dearth of NINJA defaults data amid a slowdown and rising interest rates.

Because the SIVs were buying some longer term bonds but funding their investments through short-term debt, SIVs continuously needed to reissue short-term debt. It is estimated that some $400 billion in SIV debt had been issued before the crisis. By August 2007, due to worries over subprime defaults, SIV borrowing rates rose more than 1 percent—making many SIV structures suddenly unprofitable. The gig was up. SIV managers scrambled to sell their mortgage-backed and other securities to deleverage and unwind the trades, but the markets dried up. Many banks sponsoring SIVs were forced to assume SIV debt on their balance sheets to avoid reputation damage. Stuffed with assets they thought they'd never have to take on their balance sheets, banks suddenly stopped normal commercial lending because they now had to allot capital for the SIV bailouts under Basel rules.[32] The credit markets froze and housing and the economy slowed, creating worldwide panic for months. Some financial institutions like Bear Stearns and AIG needed to be rescued, while others like Lehman Brothers failed, creating panics in the interbank credit market. In recent months, U.S. Treasury had to orchestrate major bailouts of Freddie Mac and Fannie Mae, as well as provide a $700 billion bailout for U.S. banks which included taking stakes in the nations biggest banking players to shore up the financial system.

But systemic banking problems were not ring-fenced in the United States. Banking systems all over the world were hit but the resulting credit crisis in which banks ceased lending or trading with each other due to bankruptcy fears. While Basel II was designed by the G7 and a few of its fellow rich-world cronies, it was adopted by more than 100 countries. This explains why U.S. subprime problems reverberated globally, appearing in the most unlikely of places. Walter Molano of Columbia University notes that Basel inadvertently "was a conduit to expand the U.S. credit crunch to pandemic proportions by allowing the few investment banks that controlled the credit rating agencies to determine the use of the world's savings pool."[33] Moreover, both European and EM central banks were also put in the unimaginable position of making liquidity available to their local markets and to support their banks in the wake of this credit freeze. Never before has the world witnessed such an internationalized banking crisis.

Beyond the financial contagion, the financial crisis had important economic reverberations. With bank lending curtailed and no SIVs to soak up mortgages, the U.S. housing market predictably slowed, and the fallout quickly spread to Europe, Latin America and other regions. Molano found that of 15 Latin American economies, for example, 12 showed better than a 90 percent correlation between U.S. housing starts and remittances. The results included pressure on their current account balances, dampened domestic consumption, slower GDP growth, and weaker exchange rates as transfers decline. The troubled U.S. housing sector would also cool home construction activity in Europe and the Middle East, affecting emerging market countries in North Africa, as well as India, Pakistan, and the Philippines, which relied heavy on remittances. As mentioned earlier, the global growth fueled a dramatic increase in cross-border labor remittances: From 1995 to 2007, the UN's International Fund for Agricultural Development notes they grew from $101 billion per annum to approximately $318 billion.[34] It also had pumped up stock markets globally. With the havoc created in the United States and elsewhere, many emerging stock markets (pumped up by growth from record

U.S. imports and global growth) peaked in October 2007 and then dropped 50 percent by October 2008. House prices in places like Mexico City and Shanghai (not to mention London and Madrid) also crashed.

The U.S. dollar jerked around like a rag doll through all of this. At one point in this millennium, it only took 80 cents to buy one euro; by early 2008 it took nearly $1.60, only to fall back to $1.35 by October 2008. With a devaluing dollar, all commodity prices, which are quoted in dollars, also reached record levels and rollercoastered violently. Europe, for example, was willing to pay more in dollars because commodities actually cost less in euros with the devaluation. And then speculators added fuel to the fire contributing to price spikes in metal, energy, corn, wheat, and rice.

Wildly fluctuating commodity markets, along with rising global wealth and growing caloric intake, shifting grains, soy, and corn from human to livestock consumption, and U.S. grain shifting from food to ethanol production also resulted in massive global food shortages in mid-2008. Skyrocketing grain prices incited riots in more than a dozen countries from Haiti to Cameroon to the Philippines, with deadly violence in many cities. These food shortages also underscore the problem of wealthy nations' agricultural subsidies that distort world supply and demand and have stalled completion of the WTO's Doha round.

This global credit crisis should be a wake-up call. In addition to trillions of dollars of paper wealth lost in stock, bond, and real estate values, banks everywhere still are taking sizable hits, requiring trillions of dollars from governments to solidify the global economy and financial system. In addition to the unprecedented structural and institutional stress, millions of individuals are losing homes and livelihoods with this collapse, many are going hungry, and some even dying (including farmers who committed suicide).[35] As a result, data collection, market intelligence, better regulation, personal responsibility and cross-border coordination need to be rethought to avoid the losses and suffering that we have witnessed. Policy makers everywhere can no longer avoid what is happening in far away places; they need to rethink domestic policies considering their global links.

The Future of the Greenback

The subprime and global credit crises also raise concerns over the U.S. dollar, the world's dominant currency for more than six decades. Currency exchange rates form the basis of comparative advantage and free trade, and the dollar's recent downward plunge raises serious questions about the United States and the global economy's future along with new systemic financial risks.

During the nineteenth and early twentieth centuries, the gold standard helped anchor exchange rates between countries. Up until World War I, the United Kingdom was one of the world's strongest economies, holding 40 percent of all overseas investment. The British pound was equal to roughly $5. However, by accumulating a huge amount of war debt, the United Kingdom was forced to devalue several times between the wars to approximately $2.80 against the U.S. dollar. With the breakdown of Bretton Woods in 1971, the pound has free floated and has fluctuated between $1 and $2. This is what happens when a financial power incurs massive overseas debt.

We have seen similar patterns with economic catch-ups in the late twentieth century. The Japanese yen lost much of its value during and after World War II, and was fixed at ¥360 against the U.S. dollar by Bretton Woods. By 1971, the yen had become undervalued. Japanese goods were incredibly cheap, and imports from abroad were costing the Japanese too much.[36] The Japanese current account balance rose from the deficits of the early 1960s to a surplus in 1971. The belief that the yen was undervalued motivated the United States and Europe to push the yen to ¥308 per $1. In 1971, the fixed rate system was scrapped, and the major nations of the world allowed their currencies to float.

In the 1970s, Japan grew concerned that a strong yen would hurt export growth. The government intervened heavily in foreign-exchange marketing (buying or selling dollars), even after the 1973 decision to allow the yen to float. Trade surpluses helped strengthen the yen to the mid ¥200s against the dollar by 1980. This continued in the 1980s, and in 1985, key nations signed the Plaza Accord to acknowledge that the yen was undervalued. This agreement, coupled with shifting market supply and demand, led to a rapid rise in the value of the yen. By 1995, the yen strengthened to less than ¥80 against the dollar, temporarily making Japan's economy nearly the size of that of the United States. In the wake of the late 1980s and early 1990s Japanese asset bubble, the Bank of Japan kept interest rates extremely low (even less than 1 percent) to keep the yen weak. It has since settled in around ¥100 to the dollar, reflecting the massive economic leveling Japan made against the United States in the last few decades.

Floating currencies tend to more honestly reflect currency value, but some stability is sacrificed in the process. In the 1990s, many developing countries, struggling with hyperinflation and monetary instability, pegged their currencies to the U.S. dollar in an attempt to gain better monetary control. While this policy helped stabilize economies, over time the strengthening U.S. dollar meant that many countries— including Mexico, South Korea, Brazil, and Russia, among others— saw their trade competiveness erode. Large foreign debt loads forced countries to raise interest rates to attract capital, which ultimately depressed their local economies. The dam burst with Mexico in late 1994, Thailand in 1997, followed by South Korea and Russia in 1998, Brazil in 1999, with Argentina being the last major de-peg in late 2001.

In the wake of these currency de-peggings and free floats, most developing countries have reversed their trade deficits and have recorded record growth, trade surpluses, and hard currency reserves. Oil exporting nations—including several from the Gulf—have also amassed trillions since oil prices have risen. In short, much of the world is now awash in U.S. dollars which, along with the structural problems in the American banking system raising uncertainties over the dollar's value.

Even with these currency free-floats and phenomenal trade successes, the World Bank suggests that many EM currencies may still be theoretically undervalued. Over time, many should gain against the dollar, just as the dollar gained against the British pound and the Japanese yen against the dollar as trade and investment integration accelerated. Note that from the mid-1990s through 2007, fast integrators like Mexico and South Korea have seen their currencies move from roughly 30 percent to 80 percent of theoretical value.[37] Russia, rebounding from its meltdown with higher oil prices, saw its currency climb from 25 percent to 62 percent between 2000 and 2007, but several Asian currencies still lag. India and China, which still do not allow full-currency conversions, have currencies valued at less than half what economists think they should be worth. Given the dramatic U.S. trade deficit with China, Beijing's currency policy has become a sore issue with U.S. government officials with routine public calls for a revaluation policy. Will the Chinese eventually allow the value gap to narrow by either market forces or government intervention? Only time will tell, but the situation is more complex than it appears.

China's weak currency has created a precarious codependency with the United States. With nearly $2 trillion in currency reserves in mid-2008, a potent export machine, capital controls, and a lack of foreign debt, China can maintain its dollar peg whereas most emerging economies in the late 1990s could not. In fact, now the Chinese are financing the United States' debt. Japan is the second biggest buyer, but Japan has been a major U.S. economic and financial ally for decades, and people worry that China may be different. There are some Washington, D.C., hawks who believe that the Chinese are more than a new economic rival. They argue that China is accumulating dollars for geopolitical leverage. Between its undervalued currency and the U.S. deficits, the Chinese admittedly have some control of the dollar's value. Xia Bin, a government official, once publicly called such influence China's "bargaining chip."[38]

How would China use its leverage over the dollar for political ends? Imagine a scenario in which China disagrees with U.S. policy, say over Taiwan's independence, and decides it wants to shape U.S. behavior. Instead of taking military action, China could opt to sell U.S. bonds, causing a spike in interest rates. This would send a body blow to the already-bruised U.S. housing market, throwing the United States into a deep recession. The crisis in confidence ripples to the foreign exchange and commodities markets and the dollar plunges and commodities prices soar—it's what Chinese state media have called a financial "nuclear option."[39]

A couple of generations ago, the United States and Britain had a similar financial umbilical cord. During the Suez Crisis in 1956, experts speculate that President Eisenhower threatened to dump British pound reserves to prompt the United Kingdom to retreat. As international relation theorists like to remind us, when a foreign nation gains economic influence over another, sovereignty is at risk and ultimately exploitable.

Today, the risks are not the same for a number of reasons. China's wealth is hinged to the dollar's value and the U.S. economy—the largest market for its exports. A U.S. recession would upset the profitable trade pattern with China. Dumping even a couple hundred billion U.S. Treasury bonds would signal a loss in confidence and trigger dollar weakness in foreign exchange markets. So as China dumps its unsold reserves lose value. That's why many optimistic economists and Wall Streeters argue it's actually in China's best interest to keep the dollar moderately strong. Destabilizing the dollar would ultimately derail China's trajectory by hurting its largest export client, and the country still has more than 650 million very poor people who've not yet benefited from globalization. Some have called this situation "mutual assured economic destruction," and believe that while China and the United States go eyeball to eyeball financially, neither one is likely to blink. More likely, China will diversify its reserves into other currencies and buy key assets in the United States and other Western nations like ports and energy-related firms that can help China's growth. Western nations, as well as EMs, will see growing Chinese ownership and economic influence will be more evenly spread throughout the globe.

While the mutual assured economic destruction argument may hold true, keep in mind that circumstances could change. Remember, many countries have accumulated large U.S. dollar reserves. Some act less rationally and more politically. If just a single country began dumping dollars, the worry is that others might follow. Barry Eichengreen noted that in 1968 France converted dollars into gold under the old Bretton Woods fixed-convertibility arrangement. This, in turn, plunged Lyndon Johnson's administration into a mini-financial crisis during the Vietnam War.[40] Moreover, Asian, Middle Eastern, and other private investors whose holdings of U.S. assets—including not only bonds but stocks and real estate—are predicated on dollar stability could divest in response to a sharp dollar decline unless U.S. interest rates rose significantly to compensate for the greater risk, which itself would negatively impact the U.S. economy.

The durability of the current tacit agreement ultimately depends on many nations continuing to finance U.S. external debt largely because the consequences of not doing so would hurt their own economies as much as that of the United States. In other words, the continuing funding of U.S. deficits is dependent on the confidence of foreign countries—many new to the global financial system—of the mutual benefits. Dumping dollars may not be so far-fetched with the global economy and balance of financial interests in major flux. To prevent a financial meltdown will require careful multilateral communication, coordination, and relationship building as soon as possible. In this respect, the October 2008 meeting of G7 heads to discuss joint efforts to combat the crisis was encouraging, although concrete action will be needed in addition to supportive rhetoric.

Amid this turmoil the United States still can exert some control over this trajectory. Currency values and exchange rates are tied to a mix of government and private sector practices and choices. The U.S. current account deficit, rooted in a stubborn trade gap (partially due to rising energy prices but also to heavy Asian and European imports, excessive defense costs tied to Iraq, and Middle Eastern oil imports, as well as interest payments on debt to foreigners) has ballooned in the last decade to roughly 5 to 6 percent of GDP. The United States is tied into a codependency with many countries that fund its borrowing in order that their export-driven economies have the benefit of competitive exchange rates to sell their goods to Americans. Although some analysts have characterized this relationship as an unspoken, unofficial "Bretton Woods II," it is unstable. The United States requires many countries (especially China and Japan) to continue purchasing U.S. Treasury bonds, but these countries' capacity, need, and willingness may not last forever. If foreign investors—or even just China—stop buying dollars, this will not only spell trouble for the United States but also for the stability of the growing, entangled Macro Quantum economy. To diffuse this risk, the United States needs to reduce its own governmental budget deficit and promote wider international agreement for currency and other economic adjustments that can help to rebalance trade flows.

The United States helped pioneer the liberal economic order in the postwar period and has been the global markets' shepherd ever since. No other nation has yet to emerge as a leader. But this position is based on confidence, and global confidence in the United States may be eroding. The dollar's slide between 2000 and 2008, coupled with the subprime and credit meltdowns, has left the United States economically vulnerable. This situation must be addressed through responsible public policies. The United States' dependency on foreign capital requires greater fiscal prudence from the government, which has amounted massive deficits under the Bush administration. The most obvious area of retrenchment is in defense spending. Our short but useful experience in the twenty-first century underscores the need for balanced trade and investment flows. Some suggest a new framework to limit exchange rate fluctuations from their theoretical equilibrium values through close cooperation between policy makers in both older industrial and emerging markets—something that has been the role of the G7 but now requires much broader participation. We also need closer coordination of fiscal and monetary policy by large exporters (China, Japan, Gulf countries, and some in Europe) that might be encouraged to stimulate domestic demand and imports. The U.S. government could also encourage domestic savings plans, discourage rampant consumption, and enact policies to slow energy imports.

Of course, this won't be easy. It will only work with radical changes in U.S. domestic attitude and policies and a renewed emphasis on negotiation and collective coordination rather than unilateral control. Perhaps the current global financial stress will serve as a catalyst for such cross-border efforts. As the world's largest creditor, the United States can easily bring the right parties to the table. This should be supported by prudent domestic policies that could alleviate some market pressures. In any event, the global system—as well as the dollar's value and America's role as a financial leader—is visibly at stake.

Recoiling from the Capitalist Peace?

Only by promoting a capitalist peace can the United States and the G7 reconcile the well-being of established and up-and-coming players before imbalances and competition create frictions that harm the overall system. But public attitudes have turned more pessimistic: The proportion of Americans who think their country should be active in the world is down to 42 percent, the lowest it has been since the early 1990s.[41] According to a Pew Research Center poll, the share of Americans who believe that trade is good for their country has plunged from 78 percent in 2002 to 59 percent in 2006, the lowest proportion among the 47 countries included in the survey. Yet in 2007, the global economy entered its fifth year of greater than 4 percent annual growth, maintaining the longest period of such strong expansion since the early 1970s. Despite financial market woes, world growth pushed forward, and trade grew at 9 percent according to the World Bank. The benefits of free trade tend to be dispersed widely, while the costs of it—such as bankruptcies and job losses—tend to be concentrated and highly visible. But as Hayek noted, prosperous countries make better trade partners than impoverished ones, so trading states should maintain a "selfish" interest in the freedom and prosperity of other nations.[42]

While economic liberalization can bear negative consequences such as the spectacular imbalances and volatility of the credit crisis, protectionism is far more damning. Protectionist sentiment has left thousands impoverished needlessly and destroyed economic opportunities for G7 and emerging states alike. In 2007, for the first time in a quarter century, the World Bank's *World Development Report* put agriculture and the productivity of small farmers at the top of its global agenda to reduce poverty. Yet the continued refusal by the United States, the EU, and Japan to reduce agricultural subsidies has led the Doha round of trade talks to stall and denied rural poor in developing nations access to developed nations' markets. As Nobel Prize Laureate Joseph Stiglitz noted, the attack on U.S.-style globalization is "driven by Luddites and protectionists."[43] Despite the immense vitriol of antiglobalization forces, increased global competition has raised the living standards of the average American. Instead of attacking globalization, we should work to create a healthy economic environment that mitigates the risks of an interdependent economic system.

The biggest threat to U.S. prosperity is not China, India, or even terrorism. It is not the rise of sovereign wealth funds and hedge funds nor increased capital flows from abroad. The greatest threat to U.S. prosperity *is not properly integrating new economic actors in an increasingly complex world*. Policy makers worldwide have struggled to understand the confluence of financial, commodity trade, and labor markets and have not adequately monitored unprecedented capital flows to prevent speculative and disruptive market volatility, which

stokes nationalist fears. The United States has reacted to rising economies as threats to domestic jobs and security, instituting protectionist
measures (including blocking several U.S. acquisitions by foreigners[44])
that hurt everyone financially and create public opinion backlashes in
the rest of the world instead of using trade and openness as a platform
for cooperation.

The United States and its old cohorts are growing comparatively less powerful, less coordinated, and less influential each day.
The multilateral institutions that the world has relied upon historically to help shape economic interaction, especially the G7 and World
Bank, are increasingly irrelevant in this dynamic new power landscape.
Through institutional reform, the United States can co-opt emerging economies and nonstate actors into a mutually beneficial system
predicated on free trade and economic coordination. Without it, problems such as high commodity prices, food shortages, property bubbles,
financial panics and other imbalances may lead to problems such as
protectionism or worse, the military conflict we witnessed in the early
twentieth century.

Institutional Reform:
Another Quantum Way Forward

To safeguard against doomsday scenarios, rising powers should be
integrated into the global order through holistic, rule-based institutions.
This has been done successfully in the past; indeed, the G7 arose in a
situation similar to today. This group helped forge the rules, behavioral
codes, and mechanisms for the collective progress and orderly conflict
resolution of the past three decades. Before the creation of the G7,
financial affairs were managed through the Bretton Woods agreement,
which set fixed exchange rates. [45]

As Japan and Western Europe recovered from World War II, the
global economy changed drastically. The return to convertibility of
Western European currencies at the end of 1958 and of the Japanese
yen in 1964 facilitated the vast expansion of international financial
transactions and deepened monetary interdependence. A new pluralistic
distribution of economic power led to increasing dissatisfaction with

the privileged role of the U.S. dollar as the international currency. Additionally, the emergence of large private banking groups allowed for huge international transfers of capital for investment purposes as well as for hedging and speculating against exchange rate fluctuations. By 1970, the United States was no longer the sole economic superpower. The United States consistently ran a current account deficit and held less than 16 percent of international reserves. By 1973, the weakening dollar led to the demise of Bretton Woods. The United States could no longer afford to be banker to the world. A global recession took hold as currencies were floated.

G7 Evolution

In 1975, the G7 emerged out of the rubble of Bretton Woods as an informal forum to manage the international monetary regime. The G7 members were the major economic players of the era. The rise of new economies and private actors has thrown the utility of the G7/G8 order into question. The countries of the G7 are still an essential part of the global economy: Together, they represent 14 percent of the world population and nearly two-thirds of the world's GDP, but the group no longer adequately represents the global system's expanded roster. At the fall 2007 G7 financial ministers' meeting, China's growing current account surplus and the need for the Renmindi (RMB) exchange rate to rise dominated the debate.[46] *But China is not a member of the G7.*

As we've seen, China is fast becoming a key linchpin of the global economic system along with a few other countries. Its reserves fuel U.S. spending, and this unhealthy relationship has held down interest rates the world over. A decade or two ago, speedy monetary growth in emerging economies was of little concern to the central banks of the developed world. If the Central Bank of Turkey pumped out cash, it would simply cause hyperinflation there. But today these economies play a larger role in the world economy and cross-border financial flows are much bigger. The liquidity pumped out by central banks is flowing into global financial markets.

The United States and the G7 should work on reforming the institutional framework so that more countries can benefit from economic openness and become vested in the global system. While the United States still carries the most economic and political clout, it needs to give rising powers incentives to buy in to the system and create a strong oversight system to ensure private actors are behaving.

The existing international organizations—the World Bank, WTO, and G7—are based on the precepts of free trade and capitalist peace, but they risk becoming structurally ossified as they fail to make room for nonstate actors and accord emerging nations a role proportional to their growing economic might. Institutional reforms must address the global trade and current account imbalances without significantly slowing growth. The new framework must also find a way to successfully conclude the Doha Round of trade negotiations. Finally, the framework must strengthen the international financial system and reduce volatility to avoid further financial crises.

Outside of the economic sphere, properly functioning institutions can also mitigate negative side effects of openness. While increased economic interdependence has resulted in reduced cross-border warfare and poverty, and the improvement of living standards, liberalization is by no means a panacea. Economic openness and growth have complicated environmental, health, and security challenges. With increased commerce comes the increased movement of people and greater possibilities for the spread of terrorism and contagious diseases. Greater prosperity also leads to heightened demand for commodities and energy, creating new environmental stresses. A successful economic framework must address all these issues.

The holistic platform of the G7 model makes the organization uniquely equipped to handle the reverberations of economic liberalization and is worth replicating. The original scope of the G7 was macroeconomic management, international trade, and relations with developing countries. From this initial foundation the summit agenda has broadened to include everything from environmental standards to health. The central problem with the G7 is not design but membership. Currently, the G7 focuses on issues over which it has little to no direct control.[47] For example, the G7 finance ministers have called on oil-producing countries to expand production to restrain the upward rise in crude oil prices and on non–G7 Asian nations to adopt more flexible currency regimes.

The apparent solution would be to expand the G7 membership or increase the role of an already existing G20 (or most likely with some roster changes). Established in 1999, the G20 comprises the G8, the European Union, Australia, and several important emerging economies, including China, India, Brazil, South Korea, Argentina, Indonesia, Mexico, Saudi Arabia, South Africa, and Turkey. While a larger organization of states with diverse interests will likely lack the flexibility and cohesiveness of the G7, it is an obvious natural evolution. For the key monetary agreements traditionally in the G7's domain, a smaller subgroup could meet regularly to coordinate policy and occasionally meet in plenary. Under this scheme, in addition to large countries and blocs with important currencies like the United States, the European Union, the United Kingdom, Russia, and China, some regional clusters could also be included from Mercosur, the Gulf Cooperation Council, and ASEAN. By abolishing the G7 and acknowledging the G20, we would engender a new era of multilateralism.

WTO and Trade Progress

As the private sector and EMs play a greater role in the global economy, the role of the state and intergovernmental organizations must reflect this change. *Laissez-faire* economies have always required strong institutional and regulatory support. The market alone cannot force consumers to pay $20 for a DVD when they can easily purchase a pirated copy for a tenth of the price. Nor can it persuade a government to stop doling out subsidies to inefficient or romanticized industries or strengthen regulations of financial markets. There will still be a need for a more formal rule-setting and judicial body to make sure terms of trade are universally applied.

As the successor to the postwar General Agreements on Tariffs and Trade (GATT) formed in 1947, the WTO has played this role since 1994. GATT rounds began at the end of World War II and were aimed at reducing tariffs and boosting trade based on the Most Favored Nation (MFN) clause, under which the lowest tariff applicable to one member must be extended to all members.

Today the WTO aims to help all countries obtain MFN status so that no single country will be at a trading advantage over others. WTO rules also become part of a country's domestic legal system and apply to companies operating internationally. If a country is a WTO member, its local laws are not supposed to contradict WTO rules and regulations, which govern nearly 97 percent of all world trade. While this organization has achieved immense success in the postwar period (tariffs have been reduced by nearly 90 percent), the latest round of WTO talks, started in Doha, Qatar, in 2001, has stalled, and with it we have witnessed increased bilateral agreements outside the WTO framework. The proliferation of some 300 bilateral free trade agreements has become a web of conflicts whereby different conditions pertain to different countries creating a variety of cross-border inconsistencies and resentments that, in total, vitiate the concept of MFN.

One logjam in Doha has been an age-old debate over agriculture subsidies by wealthy nations (virtually all of which are guilty) and the retaliatory postures taken by developing countries on opening their countries to manufactured goods and restricting foreign ownership. On the tail of the round's kickoff, the Bush administration supported a farm bill in 2002 that actually provided *more* subsidies for U.S. farm products, setting the stage for a battle. The same year, French President Jacques Chirac persuaded German Prime Minister Gerhard Schröder to postpone for another decade serious attempts to reduce agricultural subsidies in the European Union. And even as late as 2007, the U.S. Congress approved the 2007 Farm Bill, which expanded subsidies to nonstaple foods as well.[48]

The G7's $300 billion plus dollars of yearly subsidies stifles perhaps $1 trillion of trade globally. For decades (up until the recent commodity shocks), artificially depressed global prices have damaged agriculture in developing nations that can't profitably compete with subsidized agribusinesses in the G7, thereby cutting many counties off from the first entry point in global trade. This harm to agricultural producers abroad hinders many G7 efforts, resulting in retributive subsidies, tariffs, and barriers in manufacturing and foreign ownership. The well-publicized food shortages and riots in 2008 underscored the urgency of promoting freer agriculture with far more nations producing than today.

In the United States the estimated damage of maintaining farm subsidies for agricultural producers over the last 20 years is more than $1.7 trillion.[49] While small U.S. farmers are part of the national lore, farmers are actually quite wealthy and have a powerful lobby in D.C. The median wealth of farm households is more than five times that of the overall average U.S. household. Farmers' average annual incomes have exceeded the overall average household income by 5 to 17 percent every year since 1996.[50] Removing barriers to agricultural imports will provide cheaper food for consumers by injecting competition and dynamism into agricultural markets. The resources currently devoted to these subsidies could be better shifted into a variety of transportation and energy technologies—not farming. And given the rising demand for food tied to increasing incomes abroad, swift resolution is needed. As WTO Chief Pascal Lamy said in the wake of May 2008 food riots, "Although the WTO cannot provide anything immediate to help solve the current crisis, it can, through the Doha Round negotiations, provide medium to long-term solutions" to increase world output to stabilize commodity markets.[51]

Another key WTO issue for wealthier countries is phasing out foreign ownership limits in private and publicly traded companies, particularly in service areas that provide a comparative advantage for older advanced economies such as banking and finance. The issue was hotly debated by U.S. and Russian negotiators during WTO accession talks in 2006. India has pledged more openness by 2009; meanwhile, China has begun to make headway. Until this year, foreign banks could participate only from the sidelines in China's growing consumer banking industry, having been barred from offering loans or banking services directly to Chinese citizens. Currently, foreign securities companies can only own up to 33 percent of a joint venture. Foreign investors can only own up to a 25 percent stake in Chinese banks. Smaller and less integrated economies, such as Vietnam and Libya, are currently preparing strategies for opening their banking sectors to foreign capital and competition.

The G7 and emerging nations must foster faster integration through mergers and acquisitions between countries. In the last few years we've witnessed protectionist tendencies justified for purported national security reasons. Given that countries with vested economic interests in one another are far less likely to attack each other, cross-border transactions should provide the basis for greater relationship building because of practical common interests. It goes to the heart of capitalist peace theory.

Both rich and developing nations must recognize that global trade is a two-way street. It must also address such key issues as protecting intellectual property rights. The first step in reinvigorating the WTO, therefore, is for both the United States and European Union to commit to a multiyear glide-down plan phasing protectionist policies out completely in exchange for a similar timed reduction and relaxation of developing country barriers in manufacturing and services.

World Bank Reform

With the stated goals of reducing poverty and providing global financial stability, the World Bank and its subsidiary organizations have been reinventing themselves for decades, from technocrats in the 1950s to developmental lenders in 1960s through the 1980s to crisis managers in the 1990s. However, the organization needs a new mission for the new millennium. With the shift to market-based systems and the new access to capital, net transfers (disbursements minus repayments minus interest payments) to developing countries from the World Bank and the International Bank for Reconstruction and Development (IBRD) have been negative every year since 1991.[52] Sixty-three percent of World Bank loans are received by Middle Income Countries (MICs), but during the past 12 years, MICs have outpaced the growth of rich countries and repaid an annual average of $3.8 billion more than they have taken out in new loans. [53] More stable and better managed than previous decades, coupled with reliance on local and global capital markets, many of these MICs are now able to finance themselves outside the World Bank system.

With its traditional role as a regular lender fading in the new millennium, the World Bank group needs to reposition itself. First, it needs to address its skewed voting structure to create broader ownership stakes from developing countries. Like many postwar institutions, the World Bank is dominated by the G7 (with roughly 45 percent of the quota and votes) and many small European nations have large stakes as well. The BRIC countries, in contrast, have less than 10 percent of the voting power; Brazil and India have a little more than 1 percent, China less than 4 percent, and Russia about 2.6 percent (the same as Belgium!). There have been various plans to restructure this with the idea of vesting several nations—China, Mexico, and Korea have been mentioned (all of which used to be borrowers from the World Bank)— with greater stakes in the institution. It should come as no surprise that China and Russia routinely make developmental loans outside the World Bank system as influence building exercises, often with few noneconomic strings attached. World Bank loans come with a variety of social and environmental conditions. While World Bank stipulations are sound advice, for a debtor nation it may simply seem like a hassle compared to China's no-strings-attached offer of funds.

The World Bank must embrace China, Russia, and the other nations tempted to circumvent its rules to prevent these sideline deals and to save the organization itself. With few members borrowing from the World Bank and the IMF income has been reduced, forcing restructuring and cutbacks within the organization. Current managing director Dominique Strauss-Kahn recently announced a 15 percent reduction in staff and an overhaul of its noncore activities. Yet, it seems that more than ever the global financial system needs more resources to monitor capital flows and coordinate complex activities not fewer. As one Wall Street analyst notes, "Retrenching now is tantamount to downsizing a fire department when there is a low incidence of fire."[54] Indeed, the global credit crisis has created many vulnerable countries—both emerging and industrialized—that have petitioned the World Bank for support.

While a May 2008 modification shifted 2.7 percent of the vote away from advanced (largely European) economies in favor of developing countries, there needs to be a more aggressive shift. One suggestion is to rebalance the voting based on percentage GDP adjusted for PPP over a 10-year period, allowing BRICs, for example, to move toward a 45 percent stake (in line with their percentage of world output), along with the N11 and other Asian and Gulf countries to have greater voting rights. In turn, greater voting rights will also require greater financial commitments from these countries. U.S. and European influence would be dramatically reduced, and the ownership and the operations of the World Bank system would be democratized dramatically with considerably more vested parties than today.

Without a doubt the IMF and World Bank will be needed for emergency lending like during the Asian and Latin American financial crises of the 1990s, and should be reincarnated as defenders of global financial stability, with expanded roles in information and risk monitoring. As we have seen, with increased financial openness and liquidity comes the need for oversight. In addition to being a lender to countries without capital access, the World Bank could become a global authority that could track aggregate flows to protect against imbalances and speculative attacks.

Finally, on the financial front, the IMF and World Bank should take this opportunity to evolve into more dynamic financial players than in the past. As of February 2008, the IMF had dwindled down its balance sheet to roughly $5 billion in outstanding credits versus $50 billion in 2004. Stephen Jen of Morgan Stanley proposed selling the IMF's 100 million ounces of gold reserves, worth more than $90 billion at current prices (see Figure 2.8).[55] With the proceeds, the IMF could start a supranational endowment for longer term investing. In additional to generating new income (which gold sitting in a vault does not), the

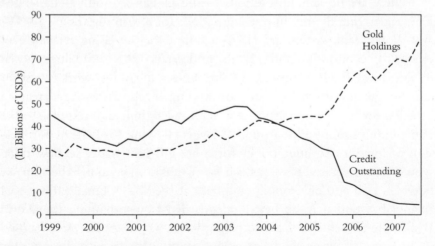

Figure 2.8   The IMF's Gold Holdings and Credit Outstanding
Source: IMF.

IMF could redirect this capital to areas proven beneficial and necessary in the World Bank Group's mission to eradicate poverty, including:

1. Microlending, either directly or to existing successful operators.
2. Bottom of the pyramid business that seeks to cultivate commercial and entrepreneurial spiriting engage very low income world citizens.
3. Renewable energy sources, that will have lower impact on the environment hopefully reducing climate change and environmental degradation.
4. Sustainable agriculture, an imperative with rising wealth and population growth.
5. Strengthening local financial institutions and local markets.

The suggestion is controversial, because making the IMF a big player in financial markets would give it more influence over the world economy. There are also questions about how it would be managed on behalf of its members, something that may be resolved if the voting structure and membership evolves as mentioned above. In total, a recapitalized, repurposed World Bank system, with broader ownership and voting structure, should be an extremely useful institution in the Macro Quantum world.

There are no simple solutions to the global economy's challenges. The underlying themes in our suggestions for reforming the G7, WTO, and World Bank system are (1) to account for the rising relevance of emerging economies and (2) to understand the difficulties posed by an increasingly complex world. These measures work together for the greater capitalist peace on several levels. First, they create a broader forum for discussion by acknowledging and respecting the contributions of a wider group of players allowing for better coordination of foreign exchange policy for more efficient trade. Second, trade would be accelerated if we abolish farm subsidies, breaking the impasse between rich and developing countries at the WTO. Finally, the global financial system may be better safeguarded by overhauling the World Bank's membership and modernizing its tactics while keeping focused on its original goals, which are as important in the twenty-first century as they were in 1944. Of course, this will take immense courage on

the part of the United States as well as longtime European allies, both
in recalibrating domestic policies with a new worldview and making
significant shifts in its multilateral postures. However, this window
of opportunity to salvage such forums is closing as Macro Quantum
activities and players are quickly making them less relevant and jeopardizing the capitalist peace.

Why Do Markets Spike and Collapse in the Macro Quantum World?

When oil and food prices hit record levels in 2008, many people wondered what was driving the rise in commodity prices.
If, for example, oil jumps from $50 a barrel to $100, does that
mean global demand has doubled? No, the relationship is more
complex: If demand rises 10 percent, we may very well see
prices rise of a multiple amount.

Many markets are flexible, whereby supply can easily be
tweaked to meet modest demand changes. Commodities and
certain other assets like real estate, however, aren't very flexible.
It takes time to grow crops, refine oil, or construct buildings,
leaving these assets especially prone to speculation which can
also push markets up or down.

Most oil is sold before it is even produced, leaving very little wiggle room in the market if supply or demand should suddenly change. As we'll discuss in Chapter 3, structural demand
has been steadily increasing in many emerging markets (as well
as in SUV driving America).[20] In recent years, a shortage of
global oil refineries (some starting with Hurricane Katrina) has
also stifled supply. Moreover, Iraq isn't pumping as much since
the invasion, and labor problems in Nigeria and other countries also have intermittently cut global oil output.

In the case of food and agriculture markets, the effects of
excess demand and new investors have been compounded by
the increasing amount of grain and soy used for livestock feed

(Continued)

(*Continued*)

and Ethanol production. So while supply of some grains has been historically high, prices spiked recently because global demand for grains—not only just for human consumption but also for animals and alternative energy—grew faster. Moreover, in oil and agriculture markets, financial speculators have driven up demand for commodities (although they can quickly change their market views).

Adding another layer of complexity, commodity prices are tied to foreign exchange markets. Most world commodity contracts are denominated in U.S. dollars. So the value of goods like oil, gold, and grains, fluctuate with the dollar's value. Consider, for example, what would happen if the dollar depreciates against the euro. Say $1 was originally worth €1. If a barrel of oil cost $100, it would have also cost €100. Then, the dollar weakened so that $1 is now worth only €.8. After the depreciation, oil would only cost €80. Since the underlying value of the oil hasn't changed, its dollar price may get pushed closer to $125 (the new equivalent of €100). That means only dollar-based buyers see a spike in oil prices, while euro prices remain more constant, and oil sellers aren't hurt as much by the dollar's fall.

The relatively inflexible supply of commodities and the effects of foreign exchange and speculative investing drove oil and food prices to new heights by mid-2008. As quickly as prices rose, however, they fell, proving that commodity markets are just as prone to collapsing as they are to spiking. The recent market gyrations are warning signs of the new potential stresses in our Macro Quantum world, with many complex variables now affecting markets and lifestyles.

Chapter 3

Energy

Twilight of the Hydrocarbons?

Hydrocarbon Man shows little inclination to give up his cars, his suburban home, and what he takes to be not only the conveniences but the essentials of his way of life....The people of the developing world give no inclination that they want to deny themselves the benefits of [a fossil fuel] powered economy, whatever the environmental questions. And any notion of scaling back the world consumption of [fossil fuel] will be influenced by the extraordinary population growth ahead.

—DANIEL YERGIN[1]

O ne of the few aspects of globalization that economists, politicians, scientists, and ordinary people agree on is that it boosts energy demand. As world living standards rise, so does the need for power. Over the last century, this increase has been met almost exclusively by fossil-based sources—oil, gas, coal, and related products. But it can't continue forever. Uncertain supplies and unprecedented demand have made our hydrocarbon economy extremely pricey, even before considering its nasty side effects: Fossil fuel dependence concentrates wealth in a few geopolitical hotspots and produces greenhouse emissions, both of which jeopardize the capitalist peace.

Our contemporary lifestyle is predicated on relatively cheap and reliable power. Compare an old episode of *Little House on the Prairie*

95

with *Desperate Housewives* to understand this quick historic evolution. The cost and form of energy available determines almost everything an individual or an entire country can accomplish, including where we live and work, how we travel, what we eat, how we entertain ourselves and even how we sleep.

It's tough to imagine a world without hydrocarbons, but our dependence is a recent condition. During the early Industrial Revolution, lamplight was fueled by whale oil and chopped wood provided heat. But in 1856 the Polish chemist Ignacy Lukasiewicz developed an easier way of refining kerosene from petroleum. His discovery brought an end to the whaling industry, and ushered in the brighter (literally!) modern era. Following major oil discoveries in 1859 and the late nineteenth century refinements in coal-burning power plants, Daniel Yergin's "Hydrocarbon Man" was born.

Very few countries are self-sufficient in power, putting energy at the heart of Macro Quantum cross-border discussions. It is symbiotically bound with trade, influencing and being influenced by international capital flows, as well as inflation and exchange rates. Energy affects security not only because it is necessary for economic growth, but also because one form—nuclear—can be converted to horrific weaponry. And of course, it poses huge environmental impacts. Our current power paradigm has failed to deal with the challenges of these interlinkages, requiring a major rethinking of energy's uses, sources, and costs.

Ever-Increasing Demand

Worldwide energy consumption has increased 20-fold during the twentieth century. Today, the aggregate energy used around the world equals the physical work of 306 billion human beings. It is as if every man, woman, and child on the planet each had a crew of 46 people working for them. In the high-tech United States every person has 238 such hypothetical workers.[2]

Rising levels of productivity and consumption create a snowball of energy usage. Americans today consume 30 times what they did in 1929, and they live in houses five times larger than a century ago.[3] These huge houses are filled with heating, air conditioning, microwave ovens, and dozens of electronic gadgets and appliances that *The Little House on the Prairie*'s Laura Ingalls couldn't have dreamt of. Moreover, we have more than 800 million cars globally shuttling us from homes to work to shopping centers; and then there are the factories that produce this lifestyle. A look at the recent past shows the quickening pace of energy use. Between 1970 and 2004 total world energy consumption more than doubled from 204 quadrillion Btu to 447 quadrillion Btu—an annual growth of 2 percent, occurring predominantly in the G7.[4] With the rise of emerging markets, the U.S. Energy Information Administration (EIA) estimates an increase of 57 percent of total world demand from 2004 to 2030 (see Figure 3.1).[5]

Growing prosperity means we can expect one to two billion formerly poor people to soon adopt energy-intensive U.S. lifestyle patterns. While traditionally wealthy countries should see a 24 percent increase in energy usage by 2030, emerging market energy use may

Table 3.1 Energy Consumption, 2006

Country	MTOE	Percent of World Usage
United States	1,721	21.8%
China	1,147	14.5%
Russia	518	6.5%
Japan	386	4.9%
India	277	3.5%
Germany	248	3.1%
Canada	245	3.1%
France	195	2.5%
United Kingdom	171	2.2%
Brazil	160	2.0%
World Total	**7,912**	**100.0%**

SOURCE: U.S. Energy Administration, International Energy Annual, 2007.

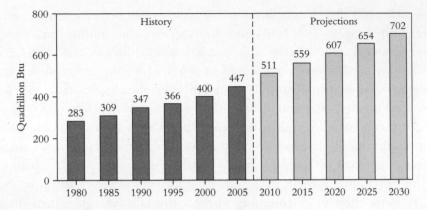

Figure 3.1   World Energy Consumption, 1980–2030
SOURCE: Energy Information Administration.

double in that time. Overall, energy demand by developing countries should surpass that of industrialized countries by 2010 and be a third larger by 2030, as these developing countries continue to industrialize and urbanize.[6] China alone is creating huge demand: After only two decades of rapid expansion, China is now the second largest energy consumer in the world, on its way to surpassing the United States. China's energy consumption has been growing at an average 11 percent since 2002, and the current low per-capita energy use—*only one-seventh of that of the United States*—suggests that this growth will be sustained for the next several years.[7] By the end of 2007, China had 159 million total motor vehicles including 60 million cars, a 10.2 percent increase over 2006, according to the Chinese government's statistics.[8] Experts forecast continuing annual car sale increases of about 10 percent in the Chinese market for decades to come, as ownership grows from just 44 per 1,000 citizens toward levels found in wealthy nations—between 300 and 600 per 1,000 for European countries and more than a whopping 750 in the United States.[9] Considering trends in both the industrialized world and in emerging countries (shown in Figure 3.2), there is a desperate need for global cooperation to face the challenges of ever-increasing energy demand.

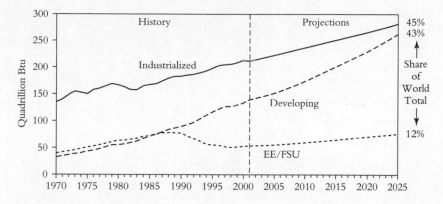

Figure 3.2 World Energy Consumption, Industrialized and Developing
Countries: 1970–2025
SOURCE: Energy Information Administration.

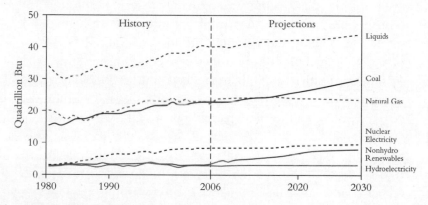

Figure 3.3 World Energy Consumption by Fuel, 1980 to 2030
(quadrillion Btu)
SOURCE: BP Statistical Review of World Energy 2007.

China: From the Bucket to the Drum

Laundering was one of the earliest domestic activities of
human society. The evolution from traditional clothes washing
on riverbeds, to the scrubboard in 1797, to modern washing
machines today, is a great metaphor for human development
and industrialization. Without running water, gas or electricity,

(*Continued*)

(Continued)

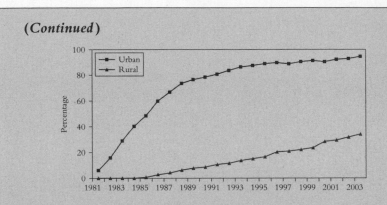

Figure 3.4   Penetration of Clothes Washers in China
SOURCE: China Statistical Yearbook 2003.

even simple hand-laundry required staggering amounts of human time and labor. A typical preindustrial wash involved scrubbing, boiling, and rinsing. One load required 400 gallons of water—weighing 400 pounds—moved from pump or well or faucet to stove and tub in buckets and wash boilers. The innovation and spread of mechanical clothes washers in the last century put an end to these painful but necessary processes.

By 1940, already 60 percent of the 25,000,000 electrically wired homes in the United States had a washing machine.[*] It has taken China another 40 years to come to this point. China is currently the largest market for washing machines in the world. Annual imports of clothes washers rose from 1.28 million in 1981 to 19.4 million in 2003. About 95 percent of urban Chinese families and more than 40 percent of rural families have one.[†]

Currently washing machines require 1,600 kilowatt hours (kWh) of electricity per urban household in China. As China continues to modernize, it aims to switch from the simpler but

---

[*]Answers.com. "Washing Machine," www.answers.com/topic/washing-machine.

[†]Jiang Lin and Maithili Iyer, "Cold or Hot Wash: Technological Choices, Cultural Change, and Their Impact on Clothes-Washing Energy Use in China," *Energy Policy*, Volume 35 (2007): 3046–3052.

less energy consuming cold-water impeller machines to hot-water drum machines. If a third of all machines are of the latter type, electricity usage will increase by 25 percent—the equivalent of 12 large base-load power plants at 300 MW each.*

We can extrapolate how these household lifestyle changes like acquiring washing machines drive energy demands. As the next one billion consumers begin a modern lifestyle with household appliances, one can only imagine the spike in energy demand globally throughout the twenty-first century. Public policy that could curb this demand: the introduction of metering devices to change the washing behavior of households (once they know how much energy a single wash consumes, they won't turn it on unless it's completely filled) or the introduction of energy saving washing machines. Curbing wasteful behavior early in a country's life cycle and developing an energy-efficient culture is often cited by experts as the best check on long-term energy usage.

---

*Ibid.

The Geography and Math of Global Energy

How does the world quench this growing thirst for energy? Table 3.2 underscores our great fossil fuel reliance. Roughly 80 percent of energy comes from oil, coal, or natural gas. Earth-friendly renewable sources like solar, geothermal, and wind while growing, contribute only one half of 1 percent of global energy production.

Petroleum

Oil is the largest single energy source today, about two-thirds of it is used for transportation. The world economy doesn't move much without oil: cars, trucks, boats, and planes need oil, and there is no easy alternative in sight. As Table 3.3 shows, many countries produce the stuff, but only a few use less than they produce, and even fewer are making

Table 3.2   Sources of Global Energy

Energy Source	Percent of Total
Oil	35.0%
Coal	25.3%
Natural Gas	20.7%
Combustible Waste	10.0%
Nuclear	6.3%
Hydro	2.2%
Other*	0.5%

*Includes geothermal, solar, wind.
SOURCE: International Energy Agency, *Key World Energy Statistics 2007*.

Table 3.3   Leading Oil Producers

Country	MTOE	World Total	Total Production as % of Reserves
Saudi Arabia	507	12.9%	1.4%
Russia	477	12.1%	4.7%
United States	310	7.9%	10.7%
Iran	216	5.5%	1.1%
China	184	7%	8.3%
Mexico	183	4.6%	10.8%
Venezuela	151	3.8%	0.6%
Kuwait	139	3.5%	1.4%
U.A.E.	134	3.4%	1.0%
World Total	**3,936**	**100.0%**	**2.2%**

SOURCE: International Energy Agency, *Key World Energy Statistics 2007*.

new finds. The data on production as a percent of proven reserves suggest that the United States, China, Mexico, and others are depleting their reserves at a very rapid rate. Until 1948, the United States had very large crude oil reserves and was a net oil exporter. Since 1980, the U.S. consumption to production ratio has outstripped new supply, driving down reserves by 65 billion barrels to approximately 21 billion.

U.S. reserves are equivalent to less than 10 percent of Saudi Arabia's purported 264 billion barrel reserve. Unless new oil is found in the United States, or consumption radically changes, it is speculated U.S. domestic oil production will only last another 10 to 20 years. China, too, after decades of being self-sufficient in oil, has begun the transition to importer, giving the world a major impetus to worry about how much oil there is to go around.

There are differing views on oil supply. Some catastrophists suggest worldwide oil production peaked in 2000 and that as oil reserves dwindle, there will be worldwide food shortages and other crises.[10] U.S. lifestyles will be the most vulnerable: People living in suburbs 30-plus miles from their jobs and driving gas-guzzling SUVs, large cars, and trucks need cheap oil. As gasoline becomes more expensive, people will start to move closer to their jobs, resulting in a collapse of the suburban housing market and recession—effects that we are seeing today. On the other hand, technologists argue that known oil reserves may have peaked, but human innovation and adaptation will evolve. Like whale oil 150 years ago, as petroleum becomes more expensive, alternatives will become more competitive and—if intelligent plans are formalized quickly—imbalances may subside over time.

Whether you're optimistic or pessimistic, we have probably reached the end of the era of "cheap" oil. Current supply and demand are in such tight balance that there is steady upward pressure on world oil prices: A barrel cost $12 in 1998 but rose to $147 in mid-2008 only to fall below $50 by year-end. Current projects for expanding oil capacity over the next few years (including everything from deeper drilling, extracting oil from sand and shale, other high-tech methods, and new refineries) are encouraging, but they'll be hard-pressed to keep up with demand. Add to that the market distorting demand created by financial speculators and investors. Increased oil imports will continue to create trade deficits and financial imbalances and spew more pollution and greenhouse gases. But oil is not the only fossil fuel we have to worry about.

Coal

Because we don't fill our cars with it on a weekly basis, most of us are less familiar with coal's massive contribution to the global energy system. In the United States., coal-fired power plants supply us with roughly two-thirds of all our electricity. Measured in metric tons of oil equivalent (MTOE) terms, the world's coal reserves are greater than those of oil or gas. And geographically, coal is distributed very differently than oil. China and the United States are the world's leaders by a wide margin, with China producing nearly twice the output of the United States, and the United States producing three times what the third place country—Australia—does. Nor are we in grave danger of coal running out in the short term. Looking forward, the United States, Russia, India, and China have more than 100 years of coal reserves at current production rates. (See Table 3.4.)

There has been steady growth in coal consumption since the late 1960s in tandem with rising GDP, as Figure 3.4 shows. Since 2001, coal has been the fastest-growing hydrocarbon while oil was actually the slowest growing. According to the U.S. Department of Energy, this trend is set to continue, with coal accounting for 28 percent of world energy and 45 percent of world electricity in 2030.[11]

Because China and the United States are major oil importers but have abundant coal, logically they could offset oil imports with coal.

Table 3.4 Leading Coal Producers

Country	MTOE	% of World	Total Prod. as % of Proven Reserves
China	1,317	38.1%	1.0%
U.S.	676	19.5%	0.3%
Australia	233	6.7%	0.3%
India	202	5.8%	0.2%
Russia	168	4.9%	0.1%
South Africa	138	4.0%	0.3%
Indonesia	104	3.0%	1.9%
Poland	86	2.5%	0.6%
Kazakhstan	43	1.2%	0.1%
World Total	3,459	100.0%	0.3%

SOURCE: International Energy Agency, *Key World Energy Statistics 2007.*

But coal is not a long-term answer to the crisis. It is expensive to extract and the physical process of transporting and prepping coal for energy itself uses immense energy, creating greenhouse gases and other waste products. While there are many politicians and coal lobbyists trying to promote "clean" coal—using high-tech processes that reduce CO_2. While "clean coal" may be cleaner, it isn't particularly green compared to renewable energies and it won't cut down oil imports by much. Unfortunately, the growth of emerging markets is only contributing to more coal being mined and burned. Every 10 days, another coal-fired power plant opens somewhere in China that is big enough to power a city the size of Dallas. India is right behind China in increasing coal-fired power plants to support its growing population, which is expected to outstrip China's by 2030.[12]

Burning coal is a leading emitter of man-made particulate matter (PM). What you think of as soot, dust, or grime is particulate matter, and more than 159 million Americans—over half the nation's population—live in areas with high levels of PM.[13] This is not just a problem in the United States; anyone who has traveled to China and India can attest to the bad air quality in many of their cities. Moreover, PM is a primary contributor to lung cancer and other respiratory illnesses. Consider asthma, just one illness linked to poor air quality. An estimated 30 percent of childhood asthma is due to environmental exposures, costing the nation $2 billion per year.[14] Asthma keeps kids out of school (14 million lost school days each year in the United States), and employees home from work (12 million lost workdays every year).[15] These hidden costs of coal need to be considered when discussing future energy options.

Natural Gas

Like coal, natural gas is used mostly for electricity and is still relatively abundant worldwide: current natural gas reserves are estimated to last between 50 and 100 years. And proven reserves are increasing as new discoveries are being made. But as Table 3.5 shows, Russia has a massive hold on gas and has suggested creating a cartel to manage the gas marketplace. This has major consequences for energy deficient countries in Europe that depend on Russian gas for electricity.

Table 3.5   Leading Natural Gas Producers

Country	MTOE	% of World Total	Prod as % of Proven Reserves	Total Reserves
Russia	627	22.0%	1.1%	57,000
United States	501	17.6%	8.6%	5,826
Canada	181	6.4%	10.0%	1,810
Iran	94	3.3%	15.1%	623
Norway	88	3.1%	1.7%	5,176
Algeria	85	3.0%	4.3%	1,977
United Kingdom	80	2.8%	3.5%	2,286
Netherlands	74	2.6%	0.3%	24,667
Indonesia	69	2.4%	2.7%	2,556
Turkmenistan	64	2.3%	0.8%	8,000
World	**2,845**	**100.0%**	**1.6%**	**1,777,813**

SOURCE: International Energy Agency, *Key World Energy Statistics 2007*.

Table 3.5 also shows that the United States has sizeable natural gas deposits. But as it has done with oil, the United States is depleting its reserves quickly and may have little left by 2025. Canada may run out even sooner.

One major difficulty in the use of natural gas is transportation and storage. Natural gas pipelines are economical, but they are impractical across oceans, subject to attacks, and can lead to squabbles when they cross international borders. Consider the series of bombings in Veracruz, Mexico, in September 2007 by a Marxist Guerilla group that resulted in 60 percent of the country's steel industry shutting down.[16] Ships and trucks are also a transport option, but these are more expensive. All-in-all, limited domestic supplies, security issues, and Russia's politicking in doling out its gas means natural gas is probably not a viable long-term option for the United States or many other G7 members.

Nuclear

The only major non-fossil fuel is nuclear energy, which comes with unique risks attached. The United States is the largest absolute producer of nuclear power, but it constitutes only 12 percent of U.S. total energy production, while nuclear energy contributes 87 percent and 69 percent in France and Japan respectively, as Table 3.6 shows.

Virtually all nuclear energy is used to produce electricity, and unlike fossil fuels, it does not contribute materially to global warming. Until recently, the costs of using nuclear energy compared to coal and gas to produce electricity were high, but with fossil fuel prices creeping up, they are now more reasonable. Currently there are 435 atomic reactors generating electricity in 31 countries across the globe, as well as nearly 30 more under construction and another 222 under consideration. India may build 20 or so new reactors, while China wants to construct more than 60 facilities to supply a projected 50 gigawatts of power.[17]

While the United States has not built new commercial nuclear reactors since the 1970s, they are under serious consideration again. The conservative Heritage Foundation, for example, claims that the 104 U.S. nuclear plants prevent nearly 700 million metric tons of CO_2 emissions per annum, comparable to taking 96 percent of cars off the roads.[18] The challenge of nuclear waste is often overstated. With newer reprocessing technologies, approximately 97 percent of spent fuel is reprocessed,

Table 3.6 Leading Nuclear Producers

Country	MTOE	% of World Total
United States	211	29.3%
France	118	16.3%
Japan	79	11.0%
Germany	42	5.9%
Russia	39	5.4%
Korea	38	5.3%
Canada	24	3.3%
Ukraine	23	3.2%
United Kingdom	21	3.0%
Sweden	19	2.6%
World Total	720	100.0%

SOURCE: International Energy Agency, *Key World Energy Statistics 2007*.

and only 3 percent is waste. It's also highly efficient: one kilogram of enriched fuel produces the same amount of electricity as 160 tons of coal with only 30 grams of waste—less than one ounce.[19]

On the other hand, nuclear power can potentially lead to dangerous radiation-releasing accidents, radioactive waste, and air pollution. A March 2007 report by the Oxford Research Group notes that while nuclear plants may not generate CO_2 emissions while they operate, the necessary steps to produce energy, including the mining of uranium and waste storage, does spew substantial CO_2 pollution.[20]

Nuclear energy also generates political and security issues. The conversion process from energy to weapons technology isn't very complicated, so spreading nuclear energy is tantamount to spreading nuclear weapons. However, it is difficult to deny underpowered countries access to nuclear technology. Consider Iran, whose nuclear program was ironically launched with the help of the United States as part of the Atoms for Peace program in the 1950s.[21] The development of a civilian nuclear power program is allowed under the terms of the nuclear Nonproliferation Treaty (NPT), and the Iranian government's desire to build a civilian nuclear energy program is reasonable, considering that its current oil reserves are only estimated to last through the next 74 to 89 years.[22] But it only takes one year for an average civilian nuclear power plant to produce enough plutonium for a small nuclear bomb and we know that Iran continues its enrichment processes.[23] In the end, it is the enriched uranium and plutonium that makes building the bomb so difficult. Once raw materials are in place via nuclear power facilities, it is only a question of a couple of years (or even months) before warheads can be produced.[24] So the real question is: Can we encourage peaceful nuclear energy in view of fossil fuels' contribution to global warming while at the same time minimizing the inherent dangers of weapons proliferation? Or better yet, aren't there alternatives to nuclear power that should be encouraged?

Energy Balances and the Capitalist Peace

Energy dependent countries find their foreign policies increasingly linked to energy. The United States is the world's largest consumer, using 50 percent more energy than the next country, China. The big policy question for all countries that consume more than they produce (and these are mostly G7) is how to plug their energy deficit.

Japan, the United States, and Germany are the biggest importers of energy, but they are also the world's largest economies. EMs and smaller economies are popping up on the list quickly. Particularly worrisome are India and China, which are both experiencing growing energy deficits. China gets about 60 percent of its oil from the Gulf Region. But it is striving to diversify its sources of supply and has recently made shopping trips to Central Asia, West Africa, and the Americas and, in some cases, has been reported to offer military equipment for petroleum. China has oil deals with Iran and Sudan, muddying foreign policy efforts—including sanctions—to deal with their regimes.

It is also interesting to look at countries most dependent on energy imports as measured by the deficit as a percent of total use. What jumps out from Table 3.7 is that these countries are all among the world's poorest. Given that energy imports are not only less reliable but also more expensive than indigenous sources, there are few opportunities for these countries to modernize and improve living standards. Yet what is also striking about the countries in the table is

Table 3.7 Largest Energy Deficits

Country	Deficit as % of Country Total Use
Sierra Leone	100.0%
Somalia	100.0%
Wake Island	100.0%
British Virgin Islands	100.0%
Benin	100.0%
Togo	97.0%
Israel	95.4%
Morocco	95.0%
Jordan	94.5%
Cambodia	92.5%

SOURCE: U.S. Energy Administration, 2007.

their above-average exposure to sunlight. Why must a country like Sierra Leone or Somalia, with almost year-round uninterrupted sunshine rely on expensive foreign oil and gas when it potentially could get the energy (almost) for free from the sky? In any event, when discussing global poverty, access to energy is inextricably bound to a country's socioeconomic trajectory. All of these dependencies complicate the quest for capitalist peace.

The Realities of Supply

The connection between global demand, soaring energy prices, and recent geopolitical events provide insights into the challenges that lie ahead. As domestic production in major industrialized and industrializing economies can no longer keep pace with increasing consumption, most of the world has become increasingly dependent on fossil fuel imports from a handful of countries.

During the first oil crisis in the 1970s, U.S. imports had already risen to 37 percent of total consumption. At the end of 2006, this number stood at 65 percent—more than 12 million barrels every single day—and should top 13.5 billion by 2010.[25] The U.S. Department of Energy estimates that by the year 2020 expected U.S. oil imports will amount to two-thirds of our entire consumption.[26] And by 2025, the National Commission on Energy expects U.S. daily demand for oil to increase more than 40 percent to nearly 30 million barrels a day. At $80 a barrel, 13.5 million barrels is roughly $400 billion in imports a year—nearly 75 percent of the United States' current trade deficit. Some speculate that the United States may have invaded Iraq to keep the flow of oil open and keep prices down. If this was the case, it has been a painfully failed strategy; once the mid-2003 war began, oil has rose from $35 a barrel (double its price during the Asian financial crises in the late 1990s) to record levels in 2008. This reliance is not just a U.S. problem. According to the International Energy Agency (IEA), other wealthy countries are projected to import two-thirds of their oil needs by 2030 compared to 56 percent today.[27]

And the cost of oil does not include the huge portion of U.S. defense spending, which is a byproduct of the United States' oil dependence. U.S. troops are tasked with protecting pipelines and refineries from terrorist and insurgent attacks. The U.S. Department of Defense has been supporting Angola and Nigeria with arms and military training to help them protect themselves against assaults on their energy production sites; for the same reasons, the U.S. military is currently stationed in Colombia, Saudi Arabia, and the Republic of Georgia. The U.S. Navy is patrolling the tanker routes of the Persian Gulf, the Strait of Hormuz, the South China Sea, the Strait of Malacca, and other places.[28] And there is the war in Iraq, which has cost the United States more than $1 trillion in its first five years, currently $10–$20 billion per month and potentially another $1 trillion in postwar medical and disability costs.[29] These massive security measures are not excessive, however, as long as we are dependent on fossil fuels for our energy. A single attack on the sulfur-cleaning towers near Ras Tanura in northeastern Saudi Arabia, for example, could take six to seven million barrels of oil off the marketplace for two years, sending oil prices to unseen records.[30]

As dire as the energy supply situation seems in the United States, other countries may be even worse off. With a threefold increase in its energy demand, China has turned from energy self-sufficiency to being the third largest net importer of crude—behind the Unites States and Japan—in only 20 years.[31] As the gap between domestic energy production and consumption rapidly increases in China and other emerging countries, these nations rightly fear that their dreams of first-world living standards may be thwarted by energy shortages or prohibitive costs.

The stress that the United States, Europe, and Japan places on the energy markets combined with growing pressure from China, India, and other rising countries will also have devastating economic and political repercussions around the world. Think about potential shortages in electricity, for example. What happens to the world of steel, building materials, clothing, electronics, and office outsourcing if Chinese and Indian companies are short electricity and cannot fully operate? Even if we have enough power, what are the inflation implications? Already in recent years, we have seen food price spikes linked to the rising price of the energy needed to support modern agriculture.

Energy and the Global Financial System

Energy is the single greatest force shaping international capital flows, inflation, exchange rates, and wealth distribution. Indeed, oil is the largest internationally traded good, both in volume and value terms.[32] During the past century, several countries have transitioned from being among the poorest to being among the wealthiest by finding oil and gas underground. A study by McKinsey suggests that if oil stays above $50 a barrel for the next five years, oil exporters could add more than $1 billion each day to the world's capital markets—or more than $1.8 trillion in total.[33] However, if oil even hovers around $50 to $60 a barrel, we may see a tilt in the world's scales of economic power. Let's take a closer look at some of these fuel-rich regions listed in Table 3.8.

The Middle East

The Middle East exemplifies how the new economic and political power of petro-states is a two-edged sword for the international economy. Until a generation or so ago, the sheikhdoms of the Middle East existed in a small world circumscribed by desert. They were remote places with lifestyles that had scarcely changed over a millennium. Then oil riches abruptly thrust these states into the center of the world's economy and political stage.

Table 3.8 Largest Energy Surpluses

Country	(MTOE) Absolute Surplus	Country Surplus % of Use
Russia	561.577	75%
Saudi Arabia	469.429	285%
Norway	213.140	412%
Algeria	156.137	444%
Iran	143.946	80%
Australia	143.277	106%
Nigeria	136.280	516%
UAE	131.716	231%
Venezuela	126.947	164%
Kuwait	123.322	429%

SOURCE: U.S. Energy Administration, International Energy Annual, 2007.

Smaller states like Kuwait, the United Arab Emirates (including Abu Dhabi and Dubai), and Qatar have made great efforts in recent years to convert their vast oil and natural gas wealth into financial wealth and modernize. They are investing heavily in their energy infrastructure to insure future capacity to deal with growing global demand. Most are also undertaking massive construction and public works projects.[34]

Three states—Saudi Arabia, Iran, and Iraq—take up most of the land surrounding the Persian Gulf, and hold the vast majority of the region's oil reserves. While we often hear about glitzy Dubai, or Kuwait's model parliament, it should be noted that these places are tiny and hold comparatively small reserves. Of the big players, only Saudi Arabia is friendly toward the United States, although this relationship may strain under high global oil prices. In 2008, for example, there was a U.S. Senate move to block four major arms sales worth $1.4 billion to the kingdom unless it boosted production by one million barrels of oil a day to alleviate market pressures.[35] While the Saudis have been extremely accommodating, increasing output at times of world market stress, despite facing opposition from other OPEC countries, even they have physical daily production limits. It may take Iraq, still tormented by civil war, years before its oil industry can modernize infrastructure and begin pumping more daily. And beyond troubled relations with the United States, Iran—another country with vast reserves—has not been investing properly in greater extraction capabilities and may, surprisingly, be running short of oil. Indeed, daily production has fallen an estimated 10 percent to 12 percent due to short-sighted government investment policies.[36] In short, the big three producers' ability to deal with surging future demand is far from comforting.

A Desert of Black Gold

Record flows of petrodollars have enabled governments in the Gulf region to spend billions on infrastructure projects and development, creating construction sites that rival China's. In addition to investing excess cash via their sovereign wealth funds, Gulf governments are fueling their own domestic economies with expensive and imaginative prestige projects—the modern equivalents

(Continued)

(*Continued*)

of the pyramids, the Forbidden City, and the Taj Mahal—making them among the world's fastest growing economies.

Before oil money started flooding into Abu Dhabi, the city had just 46,000 inhabitants, four doctors, and five schools.*

People earned their livings camel herding, growing figs and dates, fishing, and pearl diving. Most people lived in huts made of palm fronds, with only wealthy families being able to afford mud huts. Only 50 years after British explorers discovered what would turn out to be the world's fifth largest oil reserve, Abu Dhabi is perhaps the earth's richest state. Its population has grown to 420,000, and each citizen is theoretically worth nearly $20 million. Abu Dhabi's GDP per capita reached $63,000 in 2006, the third highest after Luxembourg and Norway, and it is expected to grow by 10 percent per annum for the foreseeable future. With more than $1 trillion in reserves, the emirate is developing itself in flamboyant fashion. As Khaldon Khalifa al Mubarak, a 31-year old, U.S.-educated developer, remarks, "How many places in the world can you say: 'I'm going to establish an airline,' and boom, two years later you have 21 planes and 37 destinations? How many places in the world can you say, 'I need 15,000 hotel rooms,' and boom, you have 100 new hotels in the works? How many places can you say, 'I want world-class hospitals, universities, and museums,' and boom, the Sorbonne, Cleveland Clinic, Guggenheim, and Louvre are on the way?" Plans call for $200 billion to be spent here over the next 10 years to dazzle the eyes. Abu Dhabi now features the $3 billion Emirates Palace hotel, with its $1,000-a-night rooms, a multibillion-dollar plan to outdo the Guggenheim in Bilbao, Spain, and a Ferrari Theme park with a racetrack, four polo fields, and a Formula One racing team.

---

*Barney Gimbel, "The Richest City in the World," *Fortune Magazine*, March 12, 2007, http://money.cnn.com/magazines/fortune/fortune_archive/2007/03/19/8402357/index.htm.

Dubai may have generated the biggest splash so far in the Gulf. With a skyline like Manhattan, yacht harbors, man-made islands in exotic formations like the Palm Isle, the future tallest building in the world (the Burj Dubai, planned to rise over 2,625 feet), and the world's largest expansion bridge, Dubai has become the place where Saudis shop, Brits tan, and Russians party. Other Middle Eastern countries, such as Saudi Arabia, Qatar, and Bahrain, used oil money to establish themselves as international finance centers, dealing with infrastructure finance, wealth management, and insurance.* With some luck and proper planning, many of these Middle Eastern petro-states may escape the feast-famine "commodities trap" that unfortunately has plagued many oil exporters in the past.

---

*"A Bouquet of Desert Flowers," *The Economist*, September 13, 2007.

Russia

After teetering financially on the brink of collapse in the late 1990s, energy has transformed Russia into one of the world's major power brokers. Only a decade after its historic default, the world's number two oil exporter has amassed the third-largest gold and hard currency reserves worth about $600 billion in mid-2008.[37] By the time Vladimir Putin ended his second term as president, soaring oil prices helped Russia's federal budget balloon tenfold since 1999. This resulted in a 6 percent budget surplus with GDP growth of 7 percent and a drop in poverty from 30 percent in 1990 to 10 percent in 2006. This comes as no surprise considering oil and gas represents around 20 percent of Russia's GDP, generates more than 64 percent of its export revenues, and attracts 30 percent of all foreign direct investment.[38]

Internationally, concerns remain that Russia may be using its energy clout to peddle influence. All of Russia's gas is managed by one of the world's most valuable state-controlled companies, Gazprom. At present, Europe relies on Russia for over a quarter of its energy needs, with Germany importing some 40 percent of its gas from Gazprom. Several states from Eastern Europe are even more dependent on Russia for electricity. And these trends are projected to intensify significantly during the coming decades. Some analysts expect that by 2020, Europe will depend on Russia for close to 70 percent of its gas supply.[39]

Putin has made it clear that he sees his nation's vast energy resources as a political tool to recover some of his country's international influence that was lost after the Soviet Union's dissolution. The key to his strategy is Gazprom and the immense leverage it can exert on its Western European electricity clientele. Russian pipeline routes encircle the EU from the north and south. As we witnessed in the winter of 2006, Russia can turn its gas spigot off anytime it wants to "influence" its neighbors. When Russia stopped supplying gas to the Ukraine in the beginning of 2006, it prompted immediate gas shortages in European countries because Ukrainian pipelines transport 80 percent of all gas from Russia to Europe.[40] In countries as far west as France, gas supplies dropped 30 percent to 40 percent.[41] Fearful of spending the winter without light, heat, and cooking appliances, the Ukrainian government soon reached a deal with Russia to end the supply disruption with a fourfold increase in price.[42] Russia similarly employed its influence with Georgia, Belarus, Azerbaijan, Armenia, and Lithuania. Further pipeline developments, currently under construction, are even more alarming. In the future, they will allow Russia to turn off gas supplies to Ukraine, Poland, and Belarus without affecting "more important" European customers.[43]

Reinforcing the importance of energy in Russia's global master plan, upon his retirement as the country's president in May 2008, Putin was named the new chairman of Gazprom as well as the country's prime minister, putting an immense amount of Russian power (literally!) in his hands. In the same spirit, the Kremlin has flatly ruled out ratifying the EU's energy-charter treaty, which would require it to open up its gas pipelines to other countries and other suppliers. Just two days after the negotiations, Putin enshrined into law Gazprom's monopoly position as the sole exporter of gas. Even more unnerving to the Europeans is the prospect of an equivalent to the OPEC oil-exporters' cartel, which Putin has recently advanced with several gas players such as Qatar.

Africa

In Africa, oil-exporting countries Nigeria, Sudan, and Chad have massively profited from high oil prices, in some cases freeing these countries from G7 influence. Sudan's capital, Khartoum, is booming, with new skyscrapers and luxury hotels on the rise, offsetting sanctions aimed at pressuring the country to halt attacks against minorities in Darfur. Likewise, Chad has used its oil money to buy weapons rather than to develop its economy.

Nigeria is the continent's key energy country, with the largest proven reserves in Africa.[44] Unfortunately, Nigeria has suffered domestic unrest that has hurt its energy output. Frequent insurgencies and labor strikes clipped production by 475,000 to 675,000 barrels a day in 2007, almost 25 percent from peak daily output.[45] Government corruption, while lessening, has also hampered full development of this sector. James Ibori, the former governor of Delta state, one of the key oil-producing regions, has been charged with 129 counts of money laundering and other financial crimes. Ibori was also linked financially to Nigerian President Umaru Yar'Adua.[46]

When China turned to the African continent as a source of oil, the United States and its allies found out that tying trade with Africa to human rights and democracy measures would no longer work. Chinese government firms have invested billions of dollars in foreign exchange, no strings attached, and have used Chinese engineering and construction resources on infrastructure for developing oil, gas, mineral, and other natural resources in dozens of African countries, including Algeria, Angola, Gabon, Nigeria, Sudan, and Zimbabwe.[47] During the 1990s, Sino-African trade grew by 700 percent, and by 2006 reached $32.17 billion.[48] This makes China Africa's third most important trading partner, behind the United States and France, and ahead of Britain.

Latin America

In Latin America, Mexico and Brazil continue to be friendly and steady world suppliers, although without further new finds, Mexican oil reserves may run out in a couple of decades, and Hurricane Katrina damaged much of its infrastructure in 2005. Brazil may prove to be the region's bright spot; a recently discovered deep-water exploration area off its coast could contain as much as 33 billion barrels of oil, making it the world's third-largest known oil reserve.[49] While this may take years to fully develop, it adds further to Brazil's acceleration to a world power.

Outside these two reliable countries, Latin America's energy map is littered with political problem spots, starting with the largest oil producer, Venezuela. Without oil, Hugo Chavez's bravado would be nothing but bluster. But with an eightfold increase in oil prices since the late 1990s, the Venezuelan president has used this oil wealth to dispense patronage around South America, offering below-market crude to win friends and inflammatory rhetoric to anyone who will listen. Driven by his anti-Americanism and anticapitalism rhetoric, Chavez has made it a centerpiece of his policies to consolidate the continent's energy network including a 2005 deal to build a 5,000-mile intracontinental pipeline connecting Brazil and Argentina.[50] His recent legal battles with Exxon Mobil, prompted by his 2007 decision to nationalize Venezuela's oil fields, led to a new low in U.S.-Venezuelan relations. The court order allowing Exxon Mobil to freeze up to $12 billion of PDVSA (the Venezuelan national oil company) assets overseas, prompted Chavez to threaten cutting energy supplies to the United States.[51]

In spite of having the region's second largest natural gas reserves after Venezuela, Bolivia is among Latin America's poorest nations. The landlocked country has also been marked by political instability, with recent presidents barely able to stay in office for a year. One of them, Gonzalo "Goni" Sánchez de Lozad, was forced to resign in 2003 after protests against plans to export Bolivian gas turned violent. In 2007, a decree stated that foreign companies—including both Spanish and Brazilian companies, which had already invested almost $4 billion since Bolivia opened up its energy sector in the late 1990s—must hand majority control over to state-owned Yacimientos Petrolíferos Fiscales Bolivianos (YPFB). Firms had 180 days to renegotiate energy contracts with the Bolivian state, which experts say will likely lead to price increases.[52]

Similar consolidations have occurred in Ecuador, the second largest source of U.S. oil imports in the region. In May 2006, the government took over the operations of the U.S. oil giant Occidental Petroleum,[53] and President Rafael Correra has since been renegotiating foreign oil contracts with the aim to more than quadruple the share of crude volume received by the state.[54]

Concentration and Instability

Given that most energy exporters are state-owned entities, the fate of the global economy rests in the hands of a small group of national governments. Whether energy profits go into sovereign wealth funds or government budgets, what results is a potentially unfriendly, murky mix of politics and business that makes markets nervous. In the past, production difficulties in Venezuela and Mexico, concerns over Iran and Iraq, and violence in Nigeria have contributed to a political risk premium on oil prices that has been estimated at $25 to $50 a barrel.[55] The concentration of two-thirds of the world's known oil reserves in the Gulf States magnifies potential political risks of the region. Instability in the Middle East has caused major oil price hikes and contributed to every U.S. and global recession of the last 35 years. Indeed, oil prices' latest five-year upward trend has already significantly lowered U.S. consumer savings rates, added to U.S. inflation, worsened the U.S. trade deficit, undermined the dollar, and shaved GDP growth.

The insecurity of the world's energy supply also raises concerns about longer term economic development and poverty reduction. In past centuries, geography, access to water and trade routes, and climate might have determined the economic well-being of a country. Today, the availability of energy is equally important. As China began to modernize and grow its economy, energy consumption tripled between 1980 and 2001. During this period, the share of people living in extreme poverty (on $1 a day or less) dropped from 53 to 8 percent.[56] China and other emerging countries managed to reduce their poverty rates through the application of mechanical processes dependent on electricity. It follows that the lack of electricity exacerbates poverty by precluding most industrial activities and the jobs they create. It is no coincidence that the majority of people who currently lack electricity live on less than $2 per day.[57] Even today more than a quarter of the world—1.6 billion people—have no access to electricity, while two-fifths still rely mainly on traditional biomass for their basic energy needs.[58] Of these, more than 80 percent live in South Asia and Sub-Saharan Africa. With nearly one billion people, Africa, the poorest continent, accounts for over a sixth of the world's population, but generates only 4 percent of global electricity.[59] As Africa has recently experienced healthy economic growth, the significance of a reliable energy supply has come to the forefront. In late 2007 and early 2008, South Africa, which is generally seen as the strongest of the African economies, witnessed what it meant to run out of power. Because of insufficient energy supplies, it had to suspend the production in its biggest gold and platinum mines and is now fearing that power cuts could similarly hit the country when it hosts the soccer World Cup in 2010.[60]

Although the number of people without electricity will drop in the coming decades, a projected 1.4 billion people will still be without electricity in 2030.[61] To extend electricity supplies to the energy poor could spread the capitalist peace, but it will require domestic as well as international efforts.

We must also consider our current trajectory's environmental risks: As coal, oil, and gas are burned, carbon dioxide is emitted and contributes to global warming. With mean temperature increases of 1.4°F over the past century, sea levels are up by nearly 20 centimeters (7.8 inches), and the Arctic has decreased by 7 to 15 percent, depending on the season.[62] The number of category four and five hurricanes has almost doubled in the last 30 years. Hurricane Katrina, floods in Europe, and the recent forest fires in California are further glimpses of what may come—not to mention greater rates of cancer, asthma, and other disease—if we maintain our current energy usage patterns.

While rich nations are currently still the main polluters, with 23 percent of all greenhouse gases being emitted by the United States alone, the IEA estimates that between 2004 and 2030, developing countries will account for over three-quarters of the increase in global CO_2 emissions. This increase is faster than their share in energy demand, because their incremental energy use is more carbon-intensive than that of older industrialized economies. Developing countries typically use more coal and less gas. For instance, China is projected to surpass the United States as the world's biggest CO_2 emitter by 2010.[63] While many noted economists have attempted to circumscribe the potential costs of environmental degradation, the bottom line is that fossil energy usage is a root cause that needs to considered amid planned global expansion.

Moreover, oil access can provoke conventional military conflict, and nuclear energy's potential as a weapon is another plausible and frightening possibility. Other risks abound as well such as creeping geopolitical influence being amassed quietly in the form of capital reserves and financial dependency. Historians have suggested that much of World War II aggression was petroleum-linked, including Germany's 1941 attack of the Soviet Union to grab the Caspian Sea oilfields, and the Japanese attack on the United States was partially the result of the United States' oil embargo of Japan. The first Gulf War in the 1990s was driven by G7 concerns that oil from Kuwait (and the rest of the Gulf region) could end up in the hands of an unfriendly Iraq. Many critics believe the second Iraqi invasion began in 2003 was motivated by a U.S. plan to free Iraq's oil from antagonistic interests. It is likely that new demand will increase cross-border hostilities, shortages, imbalances, price volatility, and military undertakings.

Nuclear power is seen as a possible panacea to energy challenges; it is cheap, efficient, and theoretically emits little CO_2. Yet, as new nuclear power plants mushroom around the globe, especially in countries with lower safety standards, potential dangers are simmering. The reactor accidents at Harrisburg in 1979 and Chernobyl in 1986 should remind us of the massive costs when nuclear power goes awry. Moreover, nuclear waste storage creates long-term risks that need to be managed. And, most important, as discussed earlier, the easy convertibility of nuclear energy to weaponry also poses a challenge. Both North Korea and Iran claimed to be developing nuclear power for civilian purposes. However, as it turns out, at least the former had different ambitions with its program. And consider the need to protect energy facilities against terrorist attacks.

According to estimates, the world would need to triple the current stock of nuclear power plants if we wanted to achieve a real impact on CO_2 emissions and better energy independence.[64] A 2008 study by the IEA suggests the world would need to invest \$45 *trillion* to build 1,400 nuclear power plants to meet Intergovernmental Panel on Climate Change goals.[65] But this would also triple the risk of nuclear proliferation and Chernobyl-type accidents. Before resorting to this unbelievably expensive strategy, aren't there other safer mechanisms to achieve reliable energy supplies and better environmental protection?

The Big Shift: From Hydrocarbons to Renewables

Not everyone agrees on which Macro Quantum energy-induced crisis is worse—creating financial and energy dependencies, empowering questionable national leaders, or choking the environment. Who cares? Whatever theory you choose, whatever ideological perspective you represent, the common solution is to liberate ourselves from our fossil fuel addiction with a new energy paradigm, one that would tackle several global challenges at once. It would reduce the importing countries' dependency on relatively few sources; it would seek to be environmentally friendly; and it would promote a diversified portfolio of energy sources to reduce the chance of price volatility and shortages, and help as many of the world's poor as possible—all in a comprehensive plan to promote rising living standards and the capitalist peace.

Renewable energy sources should be the centerpiece of a new global energy policy. Today, renewables form a very small part of U.S. energy consumption (see Figure 3.5). Being the largest power user, and one of the least energy efficient among wealthy countries, U.S. leadership in this area would go a long way toward restoring The United States' global reputation. Few countries could argue with policies that developed greater levels of self-sufficiency and renewable sources.

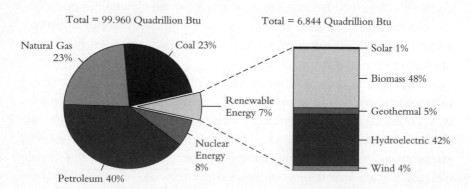

Figure 3.5   The Role of Renewable Energy Consumption in the U.S. Energy Supply (2006)
SOURCE: EIA, Renewable Energy Consumption.

The concept of using public policy to change lifestyle patterns for the greater good is not new. On the contrary, this is arguably one of government's central roles. Take a look at the U.S. interstate highway system. When President Dwight D. Eisenhower signed the Federal Aid Highway Act on June 29, 1956, he drastically altered the lifestyle patterns and economic destiny not only of U.S. citizens, but also of all of today's 6.7 billion people worldwide. With personal transportation came the freedom to live and work where one chooses. No longer constrained to the remote farm or crowded urban center where he worked, your average American had the choice to live in an idyllic suburban town amid amenities once reserved only for the extremely wealthy: swimming pools, tree-lined streets, climate control, as well as all sorts of gizmos and gadgets that made life a little easier. With the advent of the highway system, a family vacation to the Grand Canyon or Disneyland was just a short drive away; and delicacies like Maine lobster or Georgia peaches could be shipped freshly and quickly via truck to your local supermarket. Indeed, driving a convertible down an open road is a potent image of freedom, choice, leisure—parts of the American lifestyle that remain immensely alluring today not just here but around the world. But given the problems surrounding fossil fuel dependency, isn't it time to have an American—now global—shift in thinking? This does not mean giving up pools or Disneyland or Maine lobster, but simply making our choices in a way that ensures the world's children have the same abundance and freedom we have enjoyed.

Contrary to popular belief, in the long run, renewable energy sources might be cheaper than traditional sources. The watershed 2006 study by Sir Nicholas Stern, the head of the United Kingdom's Government Economics Service, compared the costs of preventing climate change to the likely economic consequences of a warming planet if we keep our present energy usage patterns. The Stern report concludes that the status quo is likely to lead to a loss of 5 to 10 percent of global economic growth. In contrast, an investment in alternative energies and environmentally friendly technologies to offset these changes would lower GDP growth by only 1 percent.[66] While the Stern report has raised methodological questions,[67] it is hardly alone in its conclusion that poor energy policy hurts our economy.

Moreover, a cleaner, greener energy may actually boost our economy. A study by the California Public Interest Research Group found that renewable energy generates four times the number of jobs per megawatt as does natural gas. Similarly, renewables create 40 percent more jobs per dollar of investment than coal plants.[68] The two energy sources have very different economic equations. While fossil fuel costs are mainly driven by the extraction of oil, gas, and coal, the costs of alternative energies mainly depend on capital investment and skilled labor, *something we have an abundance of in the United States*. The economic potential of alternative energies is further illustrated by a study by the University of Tennessee that discovered that if the production of alternative energy comprised 25 percent (up from its current 7 percent today) of all U.S. energy, $700 billion of economic activity would be generated and five million new jobs created, all while reducing carbon emissions by one million tons.[69]

Several countries are already benefiting from sustainable technologies and could share their experiences. Brazil, for example, began its ethanol-based fuel program in the mid-1970s. In 2003, the Brazilian ethanol program provided nearly 700,000 jobs, and oil imports were cut by $50 billion during the period from 1975 to 2002. Today, Brazil gets almost 40 percent of its automobile fuels from sugar cane-based ethanol. Due to improved technologies, Brazil has managed to offer hydrous ethanol at a lower price per gallon (before tax) than gasoline. The United States could abolish trade barriers—implemented to protect U.S. sugar growers—that currently prevent Brazilian ethanol from entering the U.S. market. A technology sharing agreement signed by President Bush and Brazil's President Lula da Silva in March 2007 is a promising step in this direction.[70]

Similar developments are occurring with other renewables. Hydropower has been spearheaded by a developing country: China. Hubei, China, is home to the Three Gorges Dam, which—upon completion in 2009—will be the largest hydroelectric project in the world.[71] While dams are sometimes criticized for their ecological impacts, improvements in free-standing turbines and other hydroelectric technologies are making offshore tidal power into a viable option. In one of the first deals of its kind, Pacific Gas & Electric, a U.S. utility, agreed to buy electricity from a wave farm being built off the coast of California and due to open in 2012.[72]

When it comes to wind power, Denmark is prominent in the manufacturing and use of wind turbines. Currently, Denmark generates more than 20 percent of its electricity with wind turbines, the highest percentage of any country and is fifth in the world in total wind power generation.[73] It also manufactures more than 30 percent of wind turbines sold globally, contributing mightily to its GDP. These and other technologies, such as solar power, biomass, tidal power, and geothermal power are areas with huge potential. With sufficient research and development (R&D), technology sharing, and trade, these sources might become the power generators of the future. Using projections from the Department of Energy, the group estimated that 4.5 percent of CO_2 emissions could be offset with wind power by 2020, a fraction of the potential in the United States given vast wind "reserves" with the United States' coastlines and gusty prairies.[74]

The U.S. federal budget for energy is just a paltry $3-odd billion. Comparing this to the $111 billion the United States paid for energy imports from OPEC countries alone[75] or to the current regular military budget of more than $500 billion,[76] this sum demonstrates a clear lack of government commitment. In 2006, the government spent $6 billion alone on the development of a fighter plane![77]

In the past three years, U.S. private investments into renewable energy technologies have doubled, and accumulated investment over the past 10 years amounted to $180 billion.[78] But this is peanuts in the big picture. With the right government incentives to support R&D, think what could be mobilized. By directing and harnessing the United States' greatest strength—nonstate actors like scientists, corporations, venture capital, and Wall Street—an enormous economic boom could help the United States become a new technological leader in so many renewable energy areas.

Waste Not, Want Not

While alternative energy sources require time and money to develop, the quickest, cheapest, and least contested means to reduce our dependency on fossil fuels is to just use less energy. It is amazing what a difference can be made by simply becoming more energy efficient. McKinsey studies cite economically viable ways of cutting power

demand growth from a forecasted 2.2 percent annually to a mere 1 percent. These would also bring the United States halfway to the emissions
cap of 450 to 550 parts per million, which has been set by the Kyoto
Protocol to control global warming.[79] However, market forces alone
won't suffice.

While energy efficiency does not contribute a positive addition
to our power supply, it lowers our use of other fuels—and is sometimes referred to as the "fifth fuel," after oil, gas, coal, and nuclear. Why
hasn't government been promoting this fifth fuel? A new national
energy strategy should aim to reduce fossil fuel usage, which is largely
a matter of legislation within our current technological capabilities.
While improving, the United States is extremely inefficient relative to
other countries in Europe or Japan, so seeking out greater efficiency
shouldn't be hard. And it has been done before: Consider that in the
four years between 1979 and 1983, following the last spike in gas
prices, the United States weaned itself off of 3.3 million barrels a day,
a drop of nearly 20 percent. Not until 1997 did the United States get
back to the same level of oil consumption it had in 1979.[80] And when
oil prices peaked in 2008, oil consumption in the United States fell by
800,000 barrels a day, the biggest decrease since 1982.

Taking up the largest share of end-use energy consumption at 25
percent, the U.S. residential sector is ripe for energy savings. The technologies are ready and available: By installing high-insulation building
shells, compact fluorescent lighting, and high-efficiency water heating,
the sector's energy per annum growth rate would shrink by more than
half from 2.4 percent to only 1 percent.[81] Oddly enough, the main
obstacle to the introduction of these technologies has not been the
price of those investments—in fact, these technologies would save the
average consumer a lot of money over the years—but ignorance about
these opportunities and the costs associated with everyday energy use.

The U.S. government could help by implementing limits on
standby power-saving technologies, as California successfully did with
refrigerators (see Figure 3.6). Electrical devices that are plugged in 24
hours a day use between two and 20 watts of "standby," or "vampire,"
power—even when the device is fully charged or off. Standby power
accounts for 10 percent of U.S. residential electricity consumption or
more than $6 billion annually. Manufacturers could easily build power

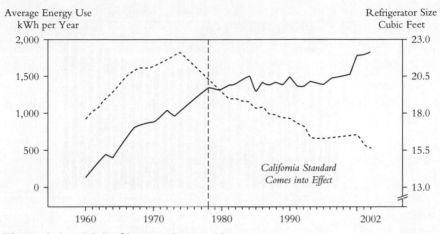

Figure 3.6 U.S. Refrigerator Energy Use
SOURCE: David Goldstein, Natural Resources Defense Council.

supplies for electronic devices that draw as little as 0.25 watts for little additional cost. Also, utility companies could aid in the efficiency
quest by billing with better breakdowns that allow the consumers to
see the actual cost of individual appliances. People are more likely to
save energy (and money) when they know what's being consumed.[82]

In the transportation sector, increasing fuel economy standards globally would help curb oil usage and cut down on emissions.
Raising average fuel standards by approximately one mile per gallon
saves nearly one million barrels of oil imports every day. In this respect,
the recent congressional approval to boost U.S. corporate average fuel
economy (CAFE) from roughly 25 miles per gallon today to 35 miles
per gallon in 2020—the first meaningful increase in the CAFE standards since 1984—will make a difference. The Union of Concerned
Scientists estimates the higher standard will eliminate greenhouse gas
emissions equivalent to taking 28 million of today's cars and trucks off
the road and save consumers at least $30 billion per year (if gasoline at
the pump stays above $3.25 per gallon).[83] You wonder why the United
States waited 24 years for such new legislation. If we pushed toward
fuel standards that have been adopted in other countries, it is very easy
to see how four to five million barrels of oil imports could be reduced
from our current 12 to 13 million barrels. Moreover, by mandating the
55-mile-per-hour speed limit, an additional two million barrels a day
could be saved (see Figure 3.7).

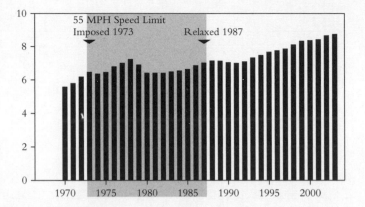

Figure 3.7   U.S. Gasoline Use (Million Barrel's Per Day)
SOURCE: Energy Information Administration.

Industry has less room for improvement than the residential sector, which represents 5 percent of United States' energy usage. In the industrialized world, industrial energy efficiency has been pursued vigorously since the oil crises in the 1970s and is reflected by the lower levels of energy intensity in most countries that are members of the Organization of Economic Cooperation and Development (OECD). As GDP in these countries grows their use of energy becomes more efficient. In fact, since 1970 the costs for producing every dollar of national income have shrunk by 49 percent in the United States.[84] Yet there are still technologies available to save energy in the industrial sector, and the government could support industry in its energy savings efforts by undertaking demonstration projects and energy audits.

Although energy intensity in emerging market countries is slowly decreasing, those countries still have a long way to go before achieving the standards of the industrialized world (see Figure 3.8). Considering the stakes for the entire world if energy demand goes out of control, wealthy countries have a real interest in helping their less developed neighbors to increase their energy efficiency. Technology and knowledge sharing, a reduction of tariff barriers for energy-effective technologies, and high domestic taxes for inefficient technologies coming out of the developing world can produce the right incentives to accelerate a less energy consuming pattern in the developing world. You might find it surprising

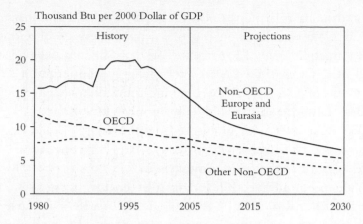

Thousand Btu per 2000 Dollar of GDP

Figure 3.8   Energy Intensity by Region, 1980–2030
SOURCE: Energy Information Administration.

that countries still subsidize energy (especially fossil fuel), but they do. McKinsey estimates that average fuel efficiency in countries with fuel subsidies are half of what they are in countries without subsidies. Cut them out, and the world theoretically can save three million barrels of oil a day.[85]

The Really Bright Idea: Here Comes the Sun

The greatest potential for redefining energy use in the United States— and eventually throughout the world—comes from solar energy. The eternal pipe dream of hippies, granola-crunchers, and lately a growing bet for venture capitalists and progressive politicians, sunlight should be thought of as an abundant global resource that could potentially help many poor countries that are wholly dependent on foreign sources for energy needs. Given the United States' impressive technology/ venture capital machine, one could see solar technology spur the next big wave of U.S. economic growth and wealth creation, similar to the way the computing and communications boom has in the recent past.

The amount of energy that 40 minutes of sunlight on Earth produces is more than the world's annual total energy consumption. Even better, the United States, given its large, temperate land mass, has huge sunlight "reserves." In parts of Nevada, Arizona, New Mexico, and California alone there are 250,000 square miles of desert land suitable for constructing solar power plants.[86] A patch of land like that receives more than 4,500 quadrillion Btu of solar radiation a year. Converting a small fraction—say 2.5 percent—of that sunlight into electricity would match the United States' total energy consumption in 2006. Two-thirds of U.S. electricity and one-third of total energy (which includes transportation) could conceivably come from solar power by 2050. Moreover, with proper scaling, this energy could be sold to consumers at rates equivalent to today's rates for conventional power sources, about five cents per kilowatt hour.[87]

With recent advances, including solar energy storage systems, the United States may already be technologically capable. Of course, a plan to build this greener, safer, less energy-dependent U.S. economy is neither cheap nor easy. U.S. public policy would need to change dramatically. Currently, Japan spends six times more to promote solar technology than the United States even though the U.S. economy is more than three times the size of Japan's. To usher the United States from hydrocarbons to a renewable future, experts suggest huge tracts of land—perhaps 30,000 square miles—would have to be covered with photovoltaic (PV) panels and solar transmission equipment. Although this area may sound enormous, the land required for each gigawatt hour of solar energy produced is *less* than that needed for a coal-powered plant when factoring in land for mining.[88] Studies by the U.S. Department of Energy's National Renewable Energy Laboratory show that more than enough land in the Southwest is available without touching environmentally sensitive areas, population centers, or difficult terrain.[89] In addition to PV farms to capture solar energy, a direct-current (DC) transmission backbone would also have to be erected to send that energy efficiently across the nation.

Skeptics say solar has issues. The efficiency of photovoltaic cells (currently the world record set by a University of Delaware-led consortium is 42.8 percent) falls just shy of the 50 percent efficiency goal set by the Defense Advanced Research Projects Agency (DARPA) to make solar cost effective.[90] While production costs have dropped and efficiency levels have risen significantly in recent years, more progress is needed for solar energy to become the backbone of the U.S. energy supply. But this is not impossible. Why is this not a stated national goal, today's equivalent of sending a man to the moon? Imagine a new Silicon Valley for energy—a "Solar Valley." An entrepreneurial technology cluster that works together, along with venture capital and Wall Street money, to bring a new industry to life led by the equivalent of Bill Gates or Henry Ford could bring about a whole new way to live and work. If the computer and other telecommunication advances have revolutionized life in the last two decades, isn't there even greater potential in a new energy paradigm?

Why not also create a "Wind Valley," an "Alternative Fuel Valley," and a "Hydrogen Valley"? The major car companies including Ford, General Motors, Toyota, and BMW all see hybrids and hydrogen fuels as the auto technology of the future.[91] If hydrogen technology is fully developed, the United States alone could save 28 percent of all the energy we consume today.[92] The picture becomes clear: If biomass, geothermal, hydrogen, tidal, and wind sources were also developed, renewable energy theoretically could provide all of the nation's electricity and 90 percent of its energy by 2100.[93]

Like Eisenhower's national highway legislation, a master energy plan to build a renewable energy economy won't happen without government support. Depending on the final plan, most energy experts estimate the U.S. government would have to invest $500 billion to $1 trillion over the next 10 years to complete this kind of paradigm shift. Couple that with a comparable investment from private funds and industry, and a major revolution could be under way. According to his election web site, President Obama planned to earmark an extra $50 billion for alternative energy research and development—chump change compared to the costs of the Iraq War or routine defense spending. And unlike the war, the payoff for the U.S. economy and the world would be enormous. For example, solar plants consume little or no fuel (like wind farms and some other renewables), saving billions of dollars year after year. The Southwest solar infrastructure described previously—just one of many viable plans floating around—would displace hundreds of large coal-fired and natural gas power plants. Such a long-term plan could effectively eliminate all imported oil in roughly a generation, fundamentally cutting U.S. trade deficits and easing political tensions globally. Because solar technologies and other renewables are almost pollution-free, the plan would also reduce greenhouse gas emissions from power plants by 1.7 billion tons a year, far in excess of recommended cuts under the Kyoto Protocol. With some shifts in automobile design, such as plug-in electric hybrid engines, another two billion tons from gasoline vehicles would be displaced by plug-in hybrids refueled by the new solar power grid. In 2050, U.S. carbon dioxide emissions would be roughly two-thirds less than 2005 levels, putting a major brake on global warming.[94]

The price tag for the overhaul of the nation's energy infrastructure could be met through a carbon tax. A carbon tax of half a cent per kilowatt hour—about 10 percent more than today—will be required to induce electric companies to adopt solar capture and storage systems to replace coal and gas power plants. This might start as a sliding scale increasing over time to give producers and consumers time to adapt. It may also be added to gasoline prices—say 50 cents a gallon—which isn't much compared to places like Europe where taxes are routinely $2 to $4 a gallon. One of the most interesting developments during oil's rise from $25 per barrel to $147 was how the United States—and the global economy—have adjusted relatively well compared to the oil shocks of the 1970s and 1980s. Establishing a multiyear phase in of one or several carbon taxes would provide a decent amount time for the U.S. energy community to digest this cost, causing no worse of a shock than the recent oil price spike. Although $500 billion is substantial, it is also less than a third of the $1.7 trillion in subsidies U.S. agriculture has received in the last 35 years. Imagine if government had forward bias versus a Micro Domestic perspective when farm subsidies began in the early 1970s—the same time as the first oil crisis. Most important, these subsidies will kick-start the United States' freedom from policy and budget issues driven by international energy conflicts, perhaps allowing new perspectives to emerge in managing many global relationships and insuring the capitalist peace in the Macro Quantum world.

To Lead or Lag

Energy remains the greatest link to most twenty-first century cross-border issues we've been discussing. Potential shortages and resulting imbalances, along with climate change, can easily thwart the capitalist peace in the more crowded, wealthier world of the future. The task now is to face the facts, harmonize public policy with private sector innovation, and shape consumer patterns in progressive ways. While the United States' global position may be slowly weakening, there is no reason why poor energy choices should be part of that equation. On the contrary, the United States may be able to reassert its legitimacy and voice in global affairs with a bold new plan. Dozens of energy-starved countries may be the beneficiaries of U.S. innovation, as well as dozens of countries saved from unforeseen environmental havoc. A new energy paradigm set by the government could allow U.S. industry and labor to revitalize itself with renewable energy technologies on the brink of phenomenal growth. Financially, we can reduce trade deficits while easing pressure on the dollar and keeping interest rates down. We just may be at the cusp of the next great technological revolution like those spurred by railroads, electricity, and the computer. It is an historic opportunity too important to take lightly.

Car Talk

Since the mid-nineteenth century invention of fossil fuel-powered combustion engines, the automobile has become a fixture of modernity, not just as a personal form of transportation but also as a symbol of status and individual style. Why, given all the oil crises, hasn't some new type of engine surfaced? Why do cars, and even airplanes, only run on oil? Imagine if the automobile ran on, say, salt water. While we can't readily convert salt water to energy, the point is, with some creative thinking, we may not need to throw in the towel on automobiles.

Cars offer unparalleled flexibility in transportation: the ability to move one to eight people (and their stuff) at once to and from very specific land-based locations. Trains can't do it, planes can't do it, boats can't do it. And while those single-person-moving Segways look cool, they're not much better than an old bicycle. These days, tree huggers regard cars as yester-tech;

(Continued)

(Continued)

symbols of excess, contributors of noise, pollution, traffic, and greenhouse gases. But they're missing something.

An efficient interstate road system has great advantages to an economy, as the United States' postwar history showed. With cheap oil, cars, and trucks, the interstate roadways helped crystallize the American dream: The road system created access to our vast country, putting houses, picket fences, and garages within reach of all who could afford a mortgage and car payment. Keep in mind, many developing nations, too, are on the path to their own similar dreams of urbanization and suburbanization.

But cars are not carbon efficient. A car that averages 20 miles per gallon with two passengers, for example, gets 40 people miles per gallon (PMPG). By comparison, filled passenger jets average something like 65 to 100 PMPG, while trains—as Europeans like to remind us—can approach some 300 to 400 PMPG if fully loaded. But trains are rarely fully loaded and neither are planes. And the big problem is *neither are cars*. Imagine if a minivan or SUV averages 17 miles per gallon but always carried five people. That would dramatically improve PMPG to the same levels as aircraft. Public policy should encourage carpooling such as by creating high-occupancy vehicle (HOV) lanes to boost average carloads. Moreover, legislation reducing U.S. highway speeds back to 55 could dramatically reduce oil imports and carbon emissions. (It has been shown that most cars are at their peak fuel efficiency at this speed.)

Furthermore, imagine using existing technologies—not experimental stuff—such as turbo diesel engines and hybrids to boost combustion engine mileage to 30 to 35 miles per gallon, that combined with policies to encourage large carloads, would help even more so. Or we can simply use smaller cars, something most countries around the world have done for decades. While the United States has been buying larger SUVs, sedans, pickups, and minivans (happily supplied by U.S., European, and Japanese auto manufacturers), the rest of the world drives smaller cars with better fuel economy. In Japan and Europe, average miles per gallon is 50 percent higher than in the United States. With $4 a gallon gas, electric-hybrid and fully electric-powered cars like Toyota's Prius and the new Chevy Volt may beat 80 miles per gallon. Even larger SUV hybrids like Ford's Escape show very respectable miles per gallon ratings in the high 20s, about 10 miles better than the oil-burning version. All the major car companies have been aggressive in offering more hybrids and E85 ethanol mix cars in the last few years, and hydrogen may be coming sooner than we think.

Electric-only cars are also gaining speed. For those of you who think that these are nothing more tricked-out golf carts, guess again. Upstart Tesla Motors, founded by PayPal entrepreneur Elon Musk, has launched a sexy two-passenger electric sports car than can accelerate faster than a Corvette and travel about 165 miles per charge. A recharge takes 3½ hours for about $7 worth of electricity, or roughly 4.2 cents a gallon. With $3 a gallon gas, a normal car would need to get 65 MPG to match Tesla's cost. With plans to develop a four-passenger model, Tesla should be hailed as a model for what can be done in a short period of time with the right entrepreneurial spirit. At $100,000, Tesla is very exclusive, but at $13,000, the Indian-made electric REVA is a bargain. The REVA uses nine units of electricity for a single full charge that gives up to 50 miles in city driving conditions, or about 3 cents per mile—roughly a third the cost of gasoline.

Policies need to be crafted to support the development and sales of electric vehicles, particularly in places where single drivers are common. For example, a United States census report found that from 2000 to 2005, the percentage of people driving alone to work increased slightly to 77 percent.* In Europe and Japan, electric car use is promoted by a variety of government tax benefits including being exempt from parking fees, congestion taxes, and sales and road tax. The Israeli government

---

*"Live Far Away? Most Likely You Drive Alone," WTOP Radio, June 14, 2007, www.wtop.com/?sid=1166861&nid=25.

(*Continued*)

(*Continued*)

has taken this to an even more ambitious level: They aim to install the world's first electric car network by 2011, which may eventually consist of 500,000 charging points and up to 200 battery-exchange stations. The initiative was aimed at addressing the country's dependence on foreign oil from unfriendly regimes and the negative health and environmental effects of gas-burning vehicles.* One can see how this, coupled with a plan for more renewable forms of electricity, could foster a very different driving situation in the United States.

Automobiles don't necessarily have to be seen as villains in the energy-economy-environment yell-fest. A push for new technologies, incentives, and fresh government policies to support better driving habits could dramatically cut down on greenhouse emissions while providing the mobility and freedom dreamt of by billions.

---

*"Israel's Electric Car Will Cut Oil Needs," *Middle East Times*, January 24, 2008, www.metimes.com/Technology/2008/01/24/israels_electric_car_will_cut_oil_needs/7949/.

Chapter 4

Defense and Security

Preventing the Next War, Not Fighting the Last

That commerce and industry of a people no longer depend upon the expansion of its political frontiers; that a nation's political and economic frontiers do not now necessarily coincide; that military power is socially and economically futile, and can have no relation to the prosperity of the people exercising it; that it is impossible for one nation to seize by force the wealth or trade of another—to enrich itself by subjugating, or imposing its will by force on another; that in short, war, even when victorious, can no longer achieve those aims for which people strive.

—NORMAN ANGELL[1]

Poor Norman Angell. In 1913, he published *The Grand Illusion*, outlining one of the first modern capitalist peace theories. History, in the words of the Nobel Peace Prize winner, had evolved beyond war between states for territorial aggrandizement; land grabs in an age of industrialization and trade made little sense.

Alas, timing is everything. About one year after *The Grand Illusion* was published, World War I began—one of the bloodiest territorial conflicts to ever take place. But was Angell completely wrong in his prediction of a new era, one in which cross-border war would be less prevalent? Nearly a century later, is it practical to attack and occupy a country to control its wealth? Today, what would a conqueror do, for example, with tiny but rich Singapore? Chain every factory worker to their electronics assembly lines so that they could fill orders for Apple and Sony?

Tom Friedman certainly agrees with Angell. His "Dell Theory of Conflict Prevention" posits that "no two countries that are both part of a major global supply chain" for multinational companies like Dell Computer fight wars against each other.[2] While tongue-in-cheek, Friedman notes how nations in today's globalized economy bear huge financial costs attacking other nations with which they have strong economic ties.

Countries still compete with one another and have different national interests; however, the changes in cross-border economic competition have also altered the ideas of security and power. From about 1500 to 1900, nations that possessed valuable land and key natural resources also held power. A country could increase power by seizing weaker nations and exploiting their physical resources. But then the terms of global competition shifted from territory to trade. By the period following World War II, a nation's power was not tied to the resources it conquered but to its productive workforce and state-of-the-art factories. For example, Germany and Japan— which both lost so much in WWII—grew stronger globally through cultivating skilled labor and competitive products, not remilitarizing.

Economic power has continued to grow in importance relative to military power. Today, natural resources remain incredibly useful and armed forces have their place, but true Macro Quantum power is measured in factories and workforces that produce goods, offices and studios that cultivate creative brainpower and services, and money for mobile investment. The historic evolution from violent competition of nation-states to a world where complex financial and trade interconnections have nearly eliminated classic cross-border warfare (see Figure 4.1) is the defining feature of our era.

But if cross-border trade encourages peace, you may wonder why the two world wars occurred after this evolution began—and if a world war could happen today. Trade alone is not enough to discourage war. Complex interdependence (interdependence in economics, security, energy, and other policy areas), cemented by international institutions,

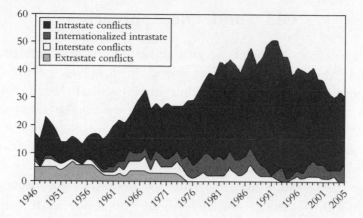

Figure 4.1 Number of State-Based Armed Conflicts by Type, 1946–2005
SOURCE: UCDP/PRIO.

is also necessary. Without these binding elements, trade can stop abruptly. Historian Niall Ferguson showed that just before WWI, trade flows actually began to ebb and protectionist policies were rampant. With no forum to dispel growing anxieties, Europe began an unhealthy arms race.[3] Increased militarization bred suspicion, insecurity, and hostility around the world, leading to the formation of alliances and blocs. With no United Nations or multilateral forums to diffuse the cycle of fear, it is easy to see how war erupted then, and how, if we don't play our cards right, it might again in the future.

WWI showed us that economic webs need to be strengthened by rules-based international forums that can diffuse suspicions and hostilities before they spin out of control. While we live in a relatively tranquil era by historical standards, we shouldn't get too comfy. There are still many looming threats—some old and some new—that can destabilize the world. That is why stagnation at the World Trade Organization and Kyoto and reforms at the UN and World Bank demand serious attention. Unfortunately, generals and their armies are notorious for their tendency to "fight the last war" —to use past successful strategies and tactics to achieve victory in the present. But today, fighting the last war may be a losing proposition: A twentieth century Micro Domestic security posture cannot completely address twenty-first century Macro Quantum risks.

Old World, Old Approaches

The security environment we face today has a vastly different look and feel than that of the postwar period. In many ways, we are better off than during the Cold War. While some egghead theorists bemoan the loss of "certainty" and "predictability" of the bipolar world, no one should wax nostalgically for the days when two nations with the power to destroy our planet pursued antagonistic and shortsighted security agendas. But there are new things to worry about.

For the first time since the Peace of Westphalia, the major source of cross-border security challenges is not other sovereign states, but "virtual states" or "nonstates" like al-Qaeda. These entities function in ways similar to landed sovereigns: They have intelligence offices and trained armies, and some even provide civil services.[4] But, as their name implies, these nonstates are borderless, their citizenries constantly shift, and you will never find them on a map. Now the United States and its allies must retool their postwar strategies in order to deal with these new nonstate threats.

For most of the twentieth century, two major schools of geopolitical thinking dominated the international scene: Liberalism and Realism. Angell represents Liberal thinking, which holds that economic interaction dominates international relations and that it is in all countries' best interests to cooperate. While most Liberal theories are fairly sophisticated, Angell showed us the danger of overreliance on an extremely simplified version of the theory. On the other hand, Realists put little faith in cooperation, maintaining that the most important, if not only, way to protect national interests is through military might. However, Realism also has its limitations, particularly its overreliance on deterrence through retaliation—that is, the schoolyard logic of "you don't hit others if you'll be hit back harder." Unfortunately, deterrence depends on knowing who and where your enemy is. With virtual states, we don't typically have this luxury. Not to mention, "peace through strength" can lead to just the opposite. Arms races, militarization, and out-of-control defense spending are hardly a recipe for harmonious living. Today, the traditional risk of country-to-country warfare, in which deterrence worked well, has largely been replaced by three areas of concern: (1) the proliferation of weapons of mass destruction (WMDs) and conventional arms, (2) pervasive civil wars, and (3) terrorism.

Because the threats we face are varied and complex, we cannot rely on any single strategy—be it deterrence or trade—to prevent conflict. Contemporary security threats require accordingly sophisticated, cooperative, multilateral solutions. Borrowing from both Liberal and Realist thinking, both increased trade and a limited strategic variety of deterrence could form parts of a much broader strategy mix that aims to reduce vulnerabilities that foment violence and war.

Weapons, Weapons Everywhere

In the Macro Quantum world, imports and exports move across borders with greater ease than ever before. Unfortunately, this includes a dizzying array of weapons, from handguns to nuclear warheads. New patterns in legal and illegal traffic of WMDs, conventional weapons, and small arms are redefining security risks and the geopolitical landscape.

Weapons of Mass Destruction

Although the Soviet Union has disbanded and many nuclear weapons have been disarmed, the threat from WMDs is still very real. While terrorists more frequently rely on low-tech weaponry, WMDs (whether nuclear or biological) pack the biggest punch. Today's atomic missiles have maximum yields of millions of casualties. The global nuclear inventory includes an estimated 30,000 warheads and enough enriched uranium and plutonium to produce 240,000 more.[5] Even with late twentieth century arms reductions, there are still more than enough atomic bombs to kill every person and much of life on Earth.[6] Moreover, a limited regional nuclear war could disrupt the global climate for at least a decade and kill more people than in all of World War II.[7]

WMDs undermine traditional theories of geopolitics by enabling weaker countries, as well as terrorists and rebel groups, to damage larger, more economically and militarily powerful nations. According to studies by the American Geophysical Union, new nuclear states like Pakistan, India, or North Korea may have the ability to release 50 or more Hiroshima-sized weapons each.[8] And with each additional country that joins the nuclear club, the potential horror scenarios multiply.

More likely than nuclear escalation between nations, fissile materials could fall into the hands of terrorists. Prior to 9/11, chances seemed remote that terrorists would indiscriminately target large numbers of civilians, but today this is a distinct possibility. Hundreds of weapons are currently stored under conditions that make them vulnerable to theft or illegal sales.[9] Potential suppliers of such material include Russia, where the collapse of the Soviet Union has left thousands of nuclear weapons in poorly maintained locations; Pakistan, which has worrisome links between its security services and al-Qaeda; and North Korea, which reputedly has already sold missiles to Egypt, Syria, Libya, Iran, Pakistan, and Yemen.[10] But other countries, including Ukraine and Ghana, maintain Soviet-supplied research reactors with enough enriched uranium for one or more nukes.[11]

While nuclear weapons—including "dirty bombs" (conventional explosives combined with radiological material)—are difficult to obtain and require significant expertise to detonate, biological and chemical WMDs are easier to access and can also cause mass casualties. The anthrax panic directly after 9/11 underscored this threat: On a clear night 100 kilograms of anthrax spores dispersed over an area of 65 square miles could cause up to three million deaths.[12] Alternatively, biological and chemical agents could be spread if someone were to crash into repositories of poisonous and radioactive materials. There are 850,000 such sites in the United States alone.[13] (See Table 4.1.)

Conventional Weapons

Technology advances have also increased the ability to inflict cross-border damage with conventional weaponry. The number of countries seeking to develop ballistic missiles that could potentially threaten the United States and NATO members has risen substantially since the Cold War's end.[14] For example, Iran's recently developed Shahab-3 missile can travel more than 1,300 miles, putting Israel and parts of southeastern Europe in target range.[15] India, Pakistan, and North Korea have developed similar

Table 4.1 Comparative WMD Effects

Using Missile Warheads	Area Covered (square km)	Deaths Assuming 300–1,000 people per square km
Chemical: 300 kg of Sarin nerve gas with a density of 70 mg per cubic meter	0.22	60–200
Biological: 30 kg of Anthrax spores with a density of 0.1 mg per cubic meter	10	30,000–100,000
Nuclear: 12.5 kt device achieving 5 lbs per cube in overpressure	10	23,000–80,000
Nuclear: 1.0 megaton hydrogen bomb	190	570,000–1,900,000

SOURCE: Abraham Wagner, Center for Advanced Studies on Terrorism (CAST).

medium-range ballistic missiles with capabilities of up to 1,900 miles.[16] China has possessed a sizeable stock of nuclear weapons and long-range missiles for years.[17] Its new intercontinental DF-31 missile can reach the U.S. West Coast, while its longer range sibling, the DF-31A, could hit most of the 48 states.[18] Requiring less launch-preparation time, China's new missiles have better odds of surviving preemptive strikes.[19] Also worrisome was China's first successful antisatellite test in January 2007. The United States and former Soviet Union, previously the only countries with these weapons, halted tests in the late 1980s because of the danger they posed to orbiting satellites, which are essential for both military operations as well as civilian communications.[20] In addition to raising the spectre of "space wars" (and a potential arms race, see Box 2), China's public display raised questions about its commitment to a peaceful global coexistence.[21]

While China's behavior is unsettling, the United States has not acted much better; it remains the top conventional arms merchant.[22] Linking arms sales to foreign policy goals has been a standard U.S. business practice for much of the postwar period. For example, the Bush administration announced in early 2008 a 10-year pledge to transfer some $20 billion in arms to U.S. Arab Gulf allies, especially Saudi Arabia, in what some consider a strategic move to counterbalance Iran.[23] Unfortunately, military technologies are highly vulnerable to theft, espionage, reverse engineering, and illegal exports. To prevent these scenarios, U.S. weapons sales are subject to regulation and licensing procedures, but these are hardly airtight. According to the Government Accountability Office (GAO), the bulk of arms transfers fall under the State Department, but unfortunately the State Department lacks the staff needed to effectively process arms export cases.[24]

Small Arms

In the age of nuclear and biological WMDs, smart bombs with tactical warheads and multibillion-dollar fighter jet fleets, the weapons responsible for the most deaths are also the most mundane. The vast majority of global conflicts continue to be fought with unglamorous, low-tech conventional weapons: rifles, machine guns, grenades, land mines, explosives, light rockets, and even machetes.

Because these weapons are easy to buy, easy to use, and require little maintenance, they are prolific. The world is now home to more than 650 million small arms and light weapons, enough to arm one in every 10 people.[25] In war-torn Mogadishu, there are one million assault rifles for two million inhabitants,[26] while in Iraq, there are estimated to be enough guns to arm every man, woman, and child.[27] In Sudan, Uganda, Sierra Leone, and Sri Lanka, the availability of weapons exceeds that of soldiers. In these conflict-ridden countries, recruitment of child soldiers (often through kidnapping) has become commonplace.

More than 59 percent of small arms are privately owned, 38 percent are in the hands of government forces, and less than 3 percent are held by police forces.[28] In Asia, 80 percent of small weapons are in the hands of civilians fighting in conflicts.[29] And while small arms may not grab headlines, they are certainly deadly: The International Network on Small Arms notes that on average 500,000 people are killed each year by armed violence—roughly one victim a minute.[30]

Unfortunately, the open Macro Quantum marketplace has exacerbated the small arms problem.[31] Although accurate data trade is sparse due to the significant black market, research and anecdotal evidence compiled by the Small Arms Survey of the Graduate Institute of International Studies in Geneva values the total trade at approximately

$4 billion per year.[32] While most arms production is state-sanctioned, the industry is rife with smuggling and reselling. Illicit trade is tough to track given it is orchestrated through a complex web of "conflict entrepreneurs": weapons manufacturers, gunrunners, merchant middlemen, and end users.[33] This unsavory group generally transfers funds that are untraceable through certain nations with lax banking regulations.[34]

Moreover, the small arms market perpetuates the crippling economic and social effects of war. Former UN Secretary General Kofi Annan explains that small arms "exacerbate conflict, spark refugee flows, undermine the rule of law, and spawn a culture of violence and impunity."[35] Conflicts fed by small arms divert investment and energy from normal productivity, disrupt education and health care, and destroy critical physical infrastructure like roads, sanitation, and water and electricity supply. Agriculture and food production suffers as people flee their homes and fields because of war or fear of land mines. Small arms violence can result in major dislocations of people, thereby drastically changing immigration, health, and poverty patterns.

The G7 and many emerging powers like China and Russia continue to pursue shortsighted and potentially dangerous policies, exporting unprecedented levels of small arms. As you can see in Figure 4.2, the United States is by far the world's largest supplier. Many of the recipients of U.S. arm shipments are important allies in the global war on terror. Yet these arms shipments help to create the political, economic, and military instability that breed terrorism. In an era without major power conflict, the world's $45 trillion economy would survive perfectly well without small arms exports, possibly through a global ban. It would be a small cost to help promote stability. A ban, combined with more financial aid earmarked for weapons collection programs including buybacks, amnesty periods, exchange for vouchers for food and goods, scholarships, infrastructure projects, and public health services, could help lessen the impact of small arms. In recent years, there have been successful programs in places as diverse as Iraq, Kazakhstan, Namibia, Brazil, and even in U.S. cities, with statistical evidence of reduced homicides and violence.[36]

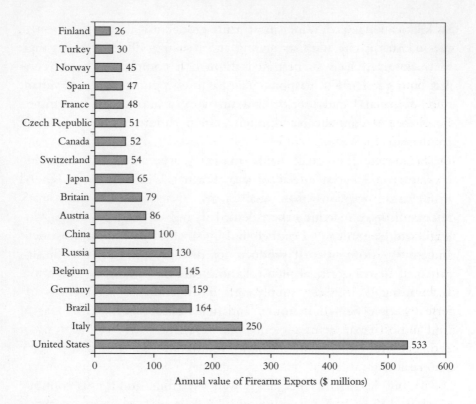

Figure 4.2   Largest Exporters of Small Arms (Annual value of firearms exports in millions of U.S. dollars)
SOURCE: *The New York Times.*

Ongoing Civil Wars

While interstate conflict is rare in the post Cold War world, civil war has remained persistent—30-plus countries are embroiled in battle within their borders at this very moment. The vast majority of these countries once served as arenas for U.S.-Soviet tensions but now hold little strategic interest to world powers. As a result, civil conflicts such as those that have occurred (or are still occurring) in Bosnia, Somalia, Israel/Palestine, Congo, and Sudan have been left to fester.

Without superpower interference, ethnic and internal conflicts repressed in the bipolar world have reemerged. Look at the Balkan Peninsula, where the acrimonious breakup of communist Yugoslavia has led to a long-term presence of international peacekeepers. Similarly, wars in Africa have mushroomed. Take Somalia, for example. Because of its strategic location along Persian Gulf oil routes, during the Cold War both the United States and the Soviet Union vied for influence there. Somalia was heavily dependent on U.S. military aid, but when the United States pulled out in 1994, the country predictably suffered from political instability and food shortages and is now the poster child for "failed states."[37] Its recent pirate troubles only highlight this failure. This unfortunate club has a long roster that continues to expand.

Beyond the destruction, poverty, and violence that befalls the citizens of these anarchic nations, failed states also pose threats to their neighbors. These states become ideal havens for terrorists, warlords, drug barons, and criminals. Readily available weapons, coupled with a lack of law and oversight, allow these nefarious activities to flourish, destabilizing entire regions. Pre-9/11 Afghanistan illustrates this perfectly. The Russian army's withdrawal in 1989 left the country in the hands of the Taliban government. Afghanistan became a haven for terrorists, who established their training camps in the Hindu Kush and found refuge in its craggy, remote mountains. This environment allowed Osama bin Laden the leisure to plan and coordinate the deadliest assault on U.S. soil to date.

Moreover, foreign policy analysts have largely ignored poverty as a security issue, but eight out of 10 of the world's poorest countries are suffering, or have recently suffered, from large-scale violent conflict, most with GDP per capita under $1,000.[38] In Darfur, Sudan, water shortages and other environmental stresses caused by overpopulation helped foment ethnic and tribal differences into full-blown civil war. Indeed, in failed states, a vicious cycle of conflict and poverty develops: War destroys all other sectors of the economy, forcing people to peddle arms or engage as mercenaries to survive.[39]

Inequity of wealth also spurs conflict. The concentration of wealth in the hands of a small clique allows that group to rival the government for influence—if it does not already control the government as well. By doling out favors, medicine, and weapons, these elites actually exacerbate factionalism and make internal revolts more likely.[40] In short, Macro Quantum defense strategists cannot afford to ignore poverty issues and their links to civil wars.

Terrorism

Terrorists have been with us for some time; From the Bolsheviks to the IRA, from the Symbionese Liberation Army to the Shining Path, al-Qaeda has a long list of predecessors. But terrorism today is different from what it was in the past. Groups are more widespread and better armed, while their targets are more vulnerable. Technological developments have changed the face of terrorism, as Philip Bobbitt notes:

> For five centuries it has taken a state to destroy another state. Only a state could raise the revenues, muster the armies and organize the logistics required to threaten the survival of another state. Soon this will no longer be true, owing to advances in computer technology, communications and weapons of mass destruction. We are entering a period in which a small number of people, operating without overt state sponsorship but using the enormous power of modern computers, biogenetic pathogens, air transport and even small nuclear weapons, will be able to exploit the tremendous vulnerabilities of contemporary open societies.[41]

Today, a single terrorist attack can have global repercussions. The speed with which people travel long distances has made containing viruses—the stuff of a modern bioterrorist attack—much more difficult. Just recall the fearsome threat of the global SARS pandemic, and how quickly it leapt from Guangzhou to Toronto. Moreover, terrorists today have much broader aims than in the past. Before, the IRA had specific grievances with Britain; and separatist movements in Latin America or Asia also were largely domestic in nature. On the other hand, Islamic fundamentalist terrorism has struck numerous countries, seemingly aiming for the millenarian destruction of the entire capitalist peace architecture we are seeking to build. Fundamentalists do not advocate overthrowing the government—ostensibly they want to overturn the world order. Additionally, these modern terrorists operate as virtual states, readily moving their base of operations across borders. The combination of increased mobility and generalized targets makes terrorism more potent than ever. As Figure 4.3 shows, general terrorism has been on the rise, even though there have been few major headline-grabbing incidents like 9/11.

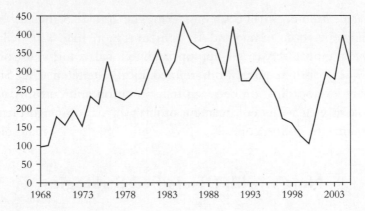

Figure 4.3 Number of International Terrorist Incidents, 1968–2005
SOURCE: MIPT Terrorism Knowledge Base.

Because people and goods are so mobile today, transportation is a logical primary terrorist target. While increased security measures have been implemented on trains and airplanes, port security should also become an essential part of defensive planning. In the United States, port security is handled jointly by the Coast Guard and U.S. Customs and Border Protection. Major ports such as Los Angeles and New York process such a high volume of goods that it is difficult to screen everything that passes through customs. While almost 95 percent of consumer goods enter the United States through a port, only 5 to 8 percent of all maritime cargo undergoes physical inspection.[42] This is one reason why allowing foreign port management companies to handle U.S. ports is so contentious. A study undertaken by the New York Port Authority recently highlighted potential risks in 361 U.S. seaports, provided specific recommendations including appointing a National Port and Cargo Security director who reports to the Secretary of Homeland Security, enacting federal legislation promoting high-tech cargo screening techniques, and establishing response and recovery plans tailored for each U.S. port.[43] While the Marine Transportation Security Act (MTSA) of 2002 legislated for some of these recommendations, the MTSA lacks a mechanism to finance these projects.[44] The U.S. Coast Guard estimates the costs of implementing the MTSA would equal $7.3 billion in the first 10 years—averaging less than a billion dollars a year (an extremely small cost considering the 2009 U.S. military budget including operations in Iraq and Afghanistan is more than $700 billion).

For a global threat, an appropriately global solution is needed. Today's terrorism requires both refined local intelligence tactics and cross-border coordination between transportation and customs administrations as well as law enforcement officials. It is a job far too large for one country to police alone.

New World, Diversified Strategies

The United States is still clearly the world's largest security power, but it appears to be immobilized like Gulliver by the Lilliputians: many small Macro Quantum variables now pin the superpower down physically, psychically, and financially. Figure 4.4 gives us one clue to just how out of balance current defense policy really is. Each year at the federal level the United States spends (much, much) more on defense than education, health, and Social Security combined. It is dubious whether our hardware-intensive, land and air combat-focused defense forces are really the answer to today's security threats; not to mention

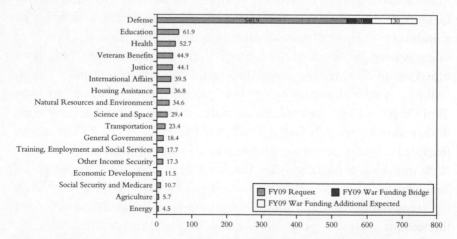

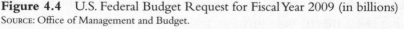

Figure 4.4 U.S. Federal Budget Request for Fiscal Year 2009 (in billions)
SOURCE: Office of Management and Budget.
NOTE: Ft'90 defense spending in this chart includes the $540.9 billions, "base" budget reques, the $70 billions placeholder figure, which is predicated on FY'08 funding levels, for expected additional war funding in FY'09.

the costs of waging this kind of war in the Macro Quantum world have become astronomically high. The United States must adopt a new paradigm of security thinking to avoid the risk of going bankrupt like the Roman Empire, the British Empire, and the former Soviet Union. Moreover, public support for such global intervention has weakened in recent years: a recent survey from the Pew Research Center notes that the percentage of Americans who believe the United States should "mind its own business internationally" has jumped from 30 percent in 2002 to 42 percent in 2005.[45]

Reforming the U.S. Military at Home and Abroad

The United States' traditional military posture is not well suited for today's threats. For nearly 60 years, the United States and its NATO allies have been preparing for land-based attacks in Europe and deterring nuclear war with a mutual assured destruction (MAD) policy. The more recent and politically popular air-based defense strategy, that is, use of aircraft and bombs to inflict maximum damage while keeping U.S. casualties low, has proven to be a politician's pipe dream. And then there is the question of who is bankrolling these efforts. The 2009 U.S. defense budget is almost as much as the rest of the world's spending combined, and it is more than eight times larger than the second biggest military spender, China. Taken together with its NATO allies, the United States is responsible for about two-thirds of the world's military outlays.[46] Although the United States has accounted for the lion's share of military expenditures since World War II, in recent years it has also been the country with the largest increases in its defense budget, as Figure 4.5 shows. Both financially and reputation-wise, the U.S. military can no longer afford to be the sole capitalist peace insurance company of the world.

Responding to the U.S. military buildup, many countries are increasing defense spending even though the world is relatively peaceful. (See Figure 4.6.) Indeed, currently China's defense budget is growing faster than its GDP, and soon Beijing's military capabilities will be on par with other Western nations. While China's overall economy grew by an average of 9.2 percent from 1996 to 2006, its annual

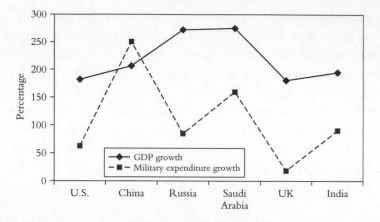

Figure 4.5   Increase in Military Spending and Increase in GDP, 1996–2007
Source: SIPRI 2008 Factbook, CIA World Factbook 1997, 2008.

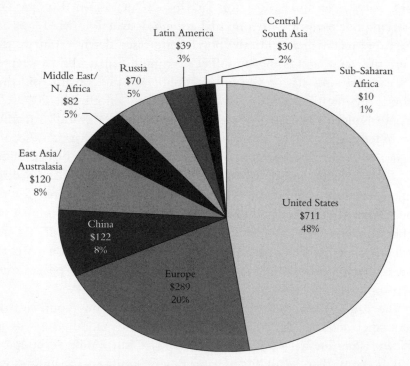

Figure 4.6   2008 U.S. Military Spending vs. the World (in Billions US$ and Percent of World Total)–$1.473 Trillion.
Source: Center for Arms Control and Non-Proliferation.

defense budget shows an average growth of 11.8 percent,[47] and more than 15 percent in the last five years.[48] India provides a similar picture. With more than 1.3 million active personnel, it has the world's third largest military. Its annual defense budget grew by 40 percent to $24 billion from 2002 to 2006.[49] Russia, too, is repositioning itself more and more again as a big military power with expenditures quadrupling in only six years to some $31 billion in 2007. Analysts estimate that this could easily increase by an additional 30 percent in coming years, particularly if the country involves itself in more skirmishes such as its 2008 intrusion into Georgia. In addition, Russia has focused on investing in new technologies rather than the maintenance of its old equipment. In 2007, the Russian government approved a $240 billion rearmament program through the year 2015. Indeed, this the growing global militarization feels eerily like the arms race of Angell's time.

In 2009, the aggregate U.S. military budget stands at more than $700 billion—more than the GDPs of 100 countries. And this number does not even include military-related items that are outside the Defense Department budget such as nuclear weapons research, maintenance and production (approximately $9.3 billion included in the Department of Energy budget), and Veterans Affairs (approximately $33.2 billion).[50] Adjusting the budget for nuclear requirements and inflation, recent budgets have exceeded the average amount spent by the Pentagon during the Cold War. And today's military troops are one third smaller than they were just over a decade ago![51]

Today, the global U.S. defense complex is one of the world's largest global operators. According to the Pentagon, the U.S. military had 1,840,062 personnel in 2005. The military was supported by an additional 473,306 Defense Department civil service employees and 203,328 local hires. In total, that makes 255,065 U.S. military personnel deployed worldwide. Furthermore, the U.S. military owns 737 bases in 63 foreign nations (including seven new countries after 9/11). The complex owns 845,441 different buildings and installations, 32,327 barracks, hangars, hospitals, and other buildings, in addition to leasing another 16,527. The size of these holdings was recorded in the inventory as covering 687,347 acres overseas and 29,819,492 acres worldwide, easily making the Pentagon one of the world's largest landlords.[52]

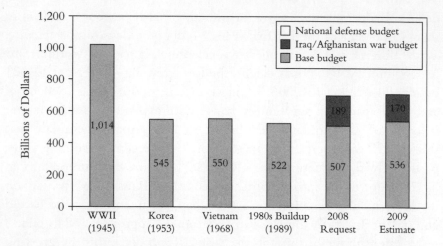

Figure 4.7   U.S. Defense Spending Historically (in Constant 2008 Dollars)
SOURCE: Office of Management and Budget.
NOTE: National Defense (function 050) historical outlays are from OMB FY2009 "Historical Tables"
Tables 3.2, adjusted for inflation using OMB GDB deflator Table 10.1 Base budget figures are for
National Define (function 050) and include Department of Enegry nuclear weapon activies and
DOD-related spending by other agencies. Iraq/Afhanisum war budget figures are from CBO, "Analysis
of the Gowth in Funding for Operation in Iraq and Afghanism," February 11, 2008.

These huge military outlays and their long-term impacts on the
U.S. economy are only beginning to be understood by the American
public. The Afghan and Iraqi invasions have become some of the
most mind-boggling financial engagements undertaken by the U.S.
government, military or otherwise. In order to conceal the real costs
of these conflicts, much of the related expenditures are categorized as
"supplementary spending," which falls outside the federal budget. (See
Figure 4.7.) According to the Stockholm International Peace Research
Institute (SIPRI), the cost of the Iraq war (including past expenditures
and estimated future outlays until 2016) to the United States will
surpass $2.3 trillion.[53] Nobel Laureate economist Joseph Stiglitz
describes Iraq as the "three trillion dollar war."

The New Cost of War: Iraq and the $3+ Trillion Mistake?
Five years after the United States invaded Iraq, Nobel Laureate
and former World Bank chief economist Joseph Stiglitz
co-authored *The Three Trillion Dollar War: The True Cost of the*

Iraq Conflict with Harvard professor Laura Bilmes. In contrast
to original estimates of the war's cost and the relatively modest
$61 billion direct expense of the first Gulf War, the two schol-
ars report that the aggregate cost of the conflict will eventually be between $3 trillion and $5 trillion—*and this is the low
end of their projection.* Alarmingly, this figure only reflects direct
costs to the United States; it does not take into account the
enormous devastation that the U.S. military has wrought upon
Iraq's infrastructure or its people. Nearly 100,000 civilians have
been killed in Iraq alone, with five million displaced by the
violence, and thousands of refugees have fled to neighboring
Syria, Jordan, and elsewhere.[*]

Officially, the United States spends $16 billion every
month while in Iraq and Afghanistan, but this figure includes
only direct expenses.[†] One of the biggest costs will be future
health-care and disability costs for veterans. The authors note
that in previous wars the ratio of wounded to dead was two-
to-one or three-to-one; however, new medical technologies
have allowed many who might otherwise have died to survive
extremely serious injuries. In the past, wounded-to-fatality
ratios were 4 or 5-to-1; In Iraq, the wounded-to-fatality rate
is approximately 15-to-1. The new reality is that the United
States has extensive long-term care costs for many thousands of
disabled veterans for the rest of their lives.

After factoring in the cost of weapons and operations,
health care, interest on debt used to fund the invasion, and
future borrowing, the authors believe Iraq and Afghanistan will
actually cost Americans $5 to $7 trillion.

---

[*]"Documented Civilian Deaths," Iraq Body Count, www.iraqbodycount
.org/database/ (last accessed June 3, 2008).
[†]Joseph Stiglitz, "The Three Trillion Dollar War," *Times of London,* Feb
23, 2008, www.timesonline.co.uk/tol/comment/columnists/guest_
contributors/article3419840.ece.

(*Continued*)

(*Continued*)

In a world of resource choices, the Bush administration made an irreversible public policy choice: Every $1 trillion spent equals eight million forgone housing units, university scholarships for 43 million students, the salaries for 15 million U.S. public school teachers, and some minimum health care for the United States' 40-plus million uninsured. $1 trillion could have covered the costs of building a U.S. solar energy backbone we discussed earlier.

What about broader costs outside the United States to the Macro Quantum world? Stiglitz estimates that for industrialized countries, the premium to oil prices—which have more than tripled—attributable to the war is also in the trillions. And remember, higher oil costs have hurt the U.S. economy and created spikes in other commodity products leading to food shortages in dozens of countries. Observers like Jeff Sachs and others estimate that funds expended in one year of Iraq fighting—approximately $200 billion—could go a long way toward eradicating global health problems like AIDS, measles, tuberculosis, and malaria. One can barely calculate these opportunity costs to the capitalist peace with so much human capital squandered and so much trade suppressed.

While some U.S. hawks refute the book's charges by pointing out that Stiglitz and Bilmes didn't factor costs saved in preventing potential future attacks and maintaining access to oil, shouldn't the costs of such access and prevention have been scrutinized more closely in the months building up to the invasion? As we'll see, there are many other cheaper, potentially more effective strategies in preventing terrorism (if indeed we prevented any), as well as the diversified energy alternatives to Gulf oil.

Affirming a quantum worldview on the Iraq miscalculation, Stiglitz believes that to hold off recession in the wake of 9/11, the invasion plans ballooned the U.S. government's deficit, and the U.S. Federal Reserve flooded the economy with liquidity (and low interest rates), which will lead not only to massive future debts, but also to the dollar's potential devaluation, further trade deficits, and have contributed in part to the housing bubble, subprime mortgage crisis, and the spike in commodity prices.

More important, the experience in Iraq underscores the weaknesses of applying an old-world approach to a new-world problem: Traditional warfare cannot diffuse terrorism. To remedy this situation, hopefully the Obama administration will begin a long overdue overhaul of the U.S. defense system with greater emphasis on "soft" power—increased intelligence, diplomacy, and preparedness—and less on hardware and a "peace through strength" philosophy.

In addition to the massive financial burden, the U.S. military will be unable to keep current soldier deployments—more than 250,000 troops in 100-plus countries—for much longer. With this intensity, many analysts, including former President Clinton, are questioning whether the United States military is stretched in ways that could undermine its future capabilities should new threats arise.[54] With over 500,000 National Guard personnel having served in Iraq and Afghanistan (some on second and third tours), the United States is vulnerable both internationally and domestically. It is estimated that 40 percent of Mississippi's and 35 percent of Louisiana's National Guardsmen were in Iraq during Hurricane Katrina.[55] As four-star Army Vice-Chief of Staff Richard A. Cody said, "The current demand for our forces in Iraq and Afghanistan exceeds the sustainable supply and limits our ability to provide ready forces for other contingencies."[56] With military recruitment becoming increasingly difficult, the problem is likely to get worse.

A declassified army plan from 2002 suggests that the U.S. government expected to have only 5,000 soldiers in a peaceful and well-run Iraq by 2008.[57] Instead it has 132,000 troops trapped in the middle of a sectarian civil war with no end in sight. Indeed, the U.S. troops in Iraq and Afghanistan have become so stressed that prescribing them antidepressants and sleeping pills has become commonplace.[58] Combined with the United States' military commitments on the Korean peninsula, in the Horn of Africa, and in other parts of the Middle East even the world's strongest armed forces may soon reach their limit.[59]

The U.S. military could easily cut back without jeopardizing U.S. security. The military could limit purchases of new expensive equipment. The U.S. military leads by such a great margin in terms of military equipment that it should not matter much whether it acquires 1,000 new F-35 Joint Fight Strikers at a total cost of $230 billion—the most expensive fighter planes ever. Moreover, with its nuclear superiority still intact, the U.S. Navy's $36 billion Aircraft Carrier Replacement Program may not be adding to U.S. security.[60] A reassessment of the U.S. defense budget should aim to reduce aggregate spending to no more than 3 percent to 4 percent of GDP (which is the post Cold War peace time standard set by the Clinton administration), versus the 5 percent to 6 percent range under the Bush administration. The reduction of $200 to $300 billion each year—along with the partial redeployment of such spending toward intelligence, diplomacy, and other civil preparedness efforts—might go a long way toward improving the United States' defense posture and reducing large-scale risks.

Reforming U.S. Intelligence and Diplomacy

The balance between U.S. "soft" intelligence and "hard" military has been lopsided. Overall U.S. intelligence spending is estimated at $66.5 billion, or less than 10 percent of the Department of Defense's annual spending.[61] Just as preventative medicine is cheaper and easier than corrective medicine, well-employed intelligence could prevent the need for large military outlays.

Moreover, the paltry funds the intelligence community does receive, it often squanders. The 9/11 Commission notes the U.S. Intelligence Community (IC) exhibits "inefficiencies in budgetary planning, the lack of adequate numbers of linguists, a lack of human resources, and an unwillingness to share information among agencies."[62] With 16 different intelligence agencies in the United States, some under military authority, others are under civilian control, interagency communication is essential.[63]

The 9/11 Commission wrote, "the Intelligence Community did have general indications of a possible terrorist attack against the United

States or U.S. interests overseas in the spring and summer of 2001 and promulgated strategic warnings,"[64] also stating that intelligence agencies knew prior to 9/11 about a possible employment of civilian airlines to crash into major buildings and had detailed information on some of the terrorists involved in the attacks. The report concluded by highlighting the general lack of preparedness of the Intelligence Community to deal with the challenges of global terrorism.[65]

After 9/11, U.S. military doctrine shifted to allow for preemptive military strikes in countries that represented a threat to the United States (even if that threat wasn't immediate).[66] To prevent the need for preemptive action, we should boost our abilities to accurately detect and prevent such threats. Instead, the dysfunctions of the U.S. intelligence system were showcased by its inability to deal with Saddam Hussein's Ba'ath regime. Instead of admitting to its difficulties in acquiring accurate information, the National Intelligence Estimate (NIE) of September 2002 simply claimed the existence of WMDs in Iraq, even exaggerating the extent of Iraq's programs.[67] On the basis of scarce information and shoddy analysis, the United States initiated a war without UN Security Council approval, which has so far claimed the lives of more than 4,000 U.S. soldiers and possibly many more in the future, cost American taxpayers trillions, and made the United States widely unpopular around the world.[68]

The IC's recent handling of Iran also raises doubts about its capabilities. Being "highly confident" that the Iranian government was working on WMDs, the United States threatened an invasion to destroy the country's nuclear facilities, only to find out in November 2007— again with "high confidence"—that Iran had halted its nuclear program in 2003.[69] Although in light of 2008 documents presented to the International Atomic Energy Agency (IAEA), it is possible the program had restarted,[70] with the situation in Iran murky at best, it underscores the limitations of our recent U.S. intelligence posture and how it added fodder to hawkish politicians.

Many of the U.S. Intelligence Community's challenges are organizational. Until 9/11, there was not an overarching authority to coordinate the activities of these agencies. Recognizing this deficiency, the Bush administration created the position of Director of National Intelligence as the head of the IC.[71] However, further centralization, better intelligence sharing mechanisms between agencies, improved coordination between law enforcement and intelligence gathering, as well as the elimination of functional overlaps, are still the orders of the day.

An expanded intelligence budget should include funding for greater cooperative measures between local police forces around the world, as well as with regulators to track financial flows. Roles for multinational organizations such as the International Criminal Police Organization (Interpol) should be expanded. While Interpol has one of the largest membership rosters of any organization, its budget is a paltry $59 million, something that could and should be increased tenfold.[72] Diffusing terrorism is often done at a very localized level, such as tracking money and keeping tabs on potential suspects. Recent coordinated counterterrorist efforts in Asia, which included the United States, Germany and Australia working with local forces in Indonesia and Philippines, have dealt terrorist networks in Southeast Asia significant setbacks with wide scale arrests and the killing of key terrorists.[73]

There is still a lot more that could be done in terms of national security concerns regarding the spread and misuse of sensitive intelligence. The IC is in dire need of Arabic, Farsi, and Chinese speakers. With few native speakers who fulfill the strict U.S. security requirements, an obvious measure could be to lower clearance requirements in certain intelligence areas. Given that most intelligence work is done from open source materials today, lowering clearance standards should not exacerbate security threats. How could the translation of Arabic newspapers, e-mails, or TV into English by non-Americans be more dangerous than not having any translations at all?

A Civil Defense Corps—essentially a version of the National Guard that focuses less on military security training and more on intelligence and diplomatic needs—could be one new strand of defense. With this the United States could cultivate much-needed specialists to combat Macro Quantum threats—linguists, political analysts, legal experts, computer programmers, and other service-sector functions that could help improve intelligence gathering and analysis, diplomacy, and civil preparedness. In doing so, the entire notion of defense could be refined to encompass more civil involvement—something advocated by many policy makers, including Secretary of State Condoleezza Rice.[74] Much the way the Israeli Defense Army mobilizes the entire population based on their specific talents, this Civil Defense Corps structure could also tap into the broader private sector by setting up cooperative ventures with local law enforcement groups to encourage two-way flows of information.

Some programs along these lines are already in place: NYPD Shield is a New York City effort that coordinates intelligence and threat information, training for private sector security personnel, physical security planning for special events, infrastructure protection guidelines, critical response roles for both the police and the private sector, as well as counterterrorism efforts. NYPD Shield has over 2,500 local members as well as 660 members outside of the metropolitan area, representing more than 1,500 companies and organizations from 22 sectors, including law enforcement, finance, health care, telecommunications, media, education, and transportation. Private-public coordination results in improved intelligence. In addition to enlisting thousands of other specialized individuals domestically, organizations like NYPD Shield can tap into international networks, creating a dynamic intelligence web. Most important, these efforts foster greater preparedness and provide greater abilities to bounce back quickly from potential terrorists attacks, key to preventing future attacks.[75]

As for diplomacy, the United States' image in the world has suffered massively in recent years. Jean-David Levitte, the former French ambassador to the United States, recounts a telling conversation between newly elected French President Sarkozy and former Secretary of State Rice in which she asked, "What can I do for you?" Sarkozy said bluntly, "Improve your image in the world. It's difficult when the country that is the most powerful, the most successful—that is, of necessity, the leader of our side—is one of the most unpopular countries in the world. It presents overwhelming problems for you and overwhelming problems for your allies. So do everything you can to improve the way you're perceived—that's what you can do for me."[76]

In a time when the United States truly needs the good faith of the international community, the government continues to downplay the importance of public diplomacy. The slip started before 9/11; in 1999, the State Department abolished the U.S. Information Agency (USIA), its primary public diplomacy agency.[77] The trend has continued with U.S. standoffishness to the major global multilateral initiatives of the past few years: the refusal to sign the Kyoto Protocol, the

Chemical Weapons Ban, and the Anti-Ballistic Missile Treaty; the failure to join the International Criminal Court; the weak efforts to act on the UN's Millennium Development Goals; the unilateral response to 9/11, despite unprecedented support and aid offers from international governments and publics alike; and the unpopular campaign in Iraq have brought the United States' image abroad to a historical low. A reversal of political unilateralism as well as renewed emphasis on public diplomacy would certainly be a shift in the right direction.

Yet U.S. diplomatic efforts remain extremely under-resourced. The State Department's 2009 budget, including all funds for UN dues and peacekeeping missions, totals less than $11.5 billion—just about a sixth of the Intelligence Community's estimated funding, and less than 2 percent of the Department of Defense's baseline budget (not including Iraq and Afghanistan spending).[78] Understaffed embassies hamper diplomatic efforts. According to the American Foreign Service Association, "not only does the FY08 budget leave State unable to create any of the 254 new Foreign Service positions that the President requested this year, but it cannot fund all existing operations at current levels."[79] The State Department, like the Intelligence Community, has a massive shortage of Arab speakers. The Foreign Service has just 468 students of Arabic, which is up from 173 in 2002, but still woefully inadequate from a country with 300 million people.[80]

The Bush administration certainly put little effort toward improving the United States' image via media campaigns, cultural, educational, and diplomatic exchanges and financial assistance. For example, President Bush did not make his first trip to Israel and the Palestinian territories until his final year in office. During this trip, he affirmed that his Middle East envoy was only a part-time post[81] and eschewed talks with Iran, stating that negotiating with terrorists and radicals only brings "the false comfort of appeasement."[82] As policy makers are apt to point out, speaking to the enemy is actually a routine part of diplomacy—not appeasement. Not to mention, Bush has continued six-party talks with North Korea while dismissing discussions with Iran often based on poor intelligence, leading one to wonder if Bush has any coherent scheme for U.S. diplomatic efforts. Secretary of State Rice affirmed this Iran strategy saying, "Diplomacy is not a synonym for talking" (although Rice has yet to demonstrate an alternate version of diplomacy).[83] In a similar vein, in 2006, Condoleezza Rice was asked why she wasn't talking with Syria. She replied, "The Syrians know what they need to do."[84] Let's hope that the Obama administration bucks this trend and reinvigorates diplomacy and intelligence—not military might—as our first line of defense.

Toward a New Security Framework

New Macro Quantum realities require progressive, diversified approaches, but this does not mean abandoning all our theories of international relations. Fresh interpretations of collective security and complex interdependence could prove useful in the twenty-first century. Collective security, first championed by President Woodrow Wilson after WWI, holds that the threat of a few (or many) states acting in concert can provide more effective deterrence against potential aggressors. While its first embodiment, the League of Nations, folded—partly because the United States never joined—the philosophy of collective security is alive and well in the North Atlantic Treaty Organization (NATO). Under collective security, a community of nations commits to act in unison to defend global security and prosperity. This community relies on collective retaliation as a deterrent. But as we mentioned, retaliation today has its limits: It is not effective against virtual states and nonstate actors. This is where complex interdependence kicks in. Complex interdependence is a theory of international relations that holds economic and other peaceful forms of interlinkages increase the probability of cooperation among states. If states are deeply interdependent in other ways, military force is less likely to be used. One way our collective security community could become more densely woven is through increased intelligence gathering, low-intensity peacekeeping, conflict resolution, and police action against those that would attempt to defy the system.

Collective security would also lessen the financial burden on the United States. As noted, the United States alone spends more on defense than all other countries combined. At the same time, other countries, including China, India, and Russia, now wield economic and military (including nuclear) capabilities that allow them to meaningfully contribute to global security.[85]

Giving rising Asian powers a larger role in the collective security system may gain the United States some new friends and prevent rival blocs from forming. New contenders to NATO have already surfaced: India and China signed an agreement on defense cooperation in May 2006 during the visit of former Indian Defense Minister Pranab Mukherjee to China. In December 2007, India and China began a landmark joint military exercise, the first of its kind between the two largest armies in the world.[86] And even earlier, in 2001, China, Russia, Kazakhstan, Kyrgyzstan, Tajikistan, and Uzbekistan founded the Shanghai Cooperation Organization (SCO). The SCO was designed to serve as a counterbalance to NATO and the United States. In fact, the United States was denied observer status in the SCO in 2005. Furthermore, the SCO has already proven that, if united, it can influence its will on the United States. In response to SCO pressure in the midst of the Afghan and Iraqi wars in 2005, the United States set up a timetable for withdrawing its troops from SCO member states and considered leaving Uzbekistan's K-2 air base.[87] The anti-Western stance of the SCO is worrying. Together, SCO full and observer members comprise 25 percent of the entire Earth's land surface and two of the most important economies in the world. A new collective approach will require the reshaping of the UN Security Council and NATO and an attempt to bring the SCO back into the fold.

The UN in the New World "Disorder"

No other organization in the world embodies as many dreams and delivers as many frustrations as the United Nations. For most of its history, the UN's General Assembly has often served as public theater for empty rhetoric, while the Security Council has been a closed-off power brokers' club. The whole UN security system hinges on the concerns of its founders 60 years ago—states waging aggressive war against each other—instead of preparing for the wider range of human security threats and challenges of the new millennium. The UN may be broken, but it's certainly worth fixing. As we learned when the League of Nations fell apart in the 1930s, leaving no multilateral forum to diffuse tensions in the prelude to World War II, lacking an effective global collective security institution could be the death knell of the capitalist peace. Although there has been talk of scrapping the UN and starting over, a new entity's mission would likely echo the UN's noble goals to "save succeeding generations from the scourge of war," to "promote social progress and better standards of life in larger freedom," and to "unite our strength to maintain international peace and security," without much advantage over the current body. Truth be told, without the UN, we would simply have to reinvent something like it all over again.

Instead, we should focus on reforming the organization we already have. Even in the twenty-first century—a time in which millions of nonstate actors engage in decentralized, cross-border activity 24/7—life is still organized around sovereign nations, especially in the realm of security. Although today's threats emanate largely from nonstate actors, functional states hold a monopoly on the solutions to these problems (that is, the intelligence community, military forces, and diplomatic corps). A revitalized UN could better coordinate sovereign states' responses in order to uphold stability and the rule of law.

The political nature of the UN, however, is also a source of its headaches. Deep disagreements among its founding members and between other contending forces have handicapped the organization. The Bush administration has maintained a passive-aggressive attitude toward the UN, keeping its budget impossibly small (regularly paying its relatively trivial annual dues months, in some cases years, late), and disregarding UN policies and procedures if it disagrees. The American "my way or the highway" perspective isn't appreciated by many, including close G7 allies, particularly after the invasion of Iraq. European countries often call for a stronger UN role in security matters, possibly because they have disproportionately large roles at the UN; some claim they use it as a pulpit for asserting their regional interests and overinflating the continent's influence in global affairs. China basically has what it wants out of the UN—a permanent seat and veto power in the Security Council, yet it pays little in dues and often abstains from public opinions. Small nations that would otherwise have no public voice in global affairs use the UN as a loudspeaker. Finally, the restrictive control over the Security Council exercised by the United States, Russia, and the nations of Western Europe has created considerable distrust and resentment among rising economic powers that want greater say and control in the organization.

The UN needs a fundamental structural reorganization if it is to accomplish its original mission of promoting international cooperation and maintaining peace and security, and the United States is probably the only country that can galvanize such an effort. However, it remains to be seen whether the United States will bring forward the reforms that the United Nations needs to avoid the fate that beset the League of Nations.

A reformed UN must become an integral, effective cornerstone of global civil society that combats the disruptive, lethal forces that threaten our collective capitalist peace. Pragmatically, this can happen by (1) encouraging more balanced participation beyond the dominant World War II power bloc, measures that would include a larger, more equitably shared budget and expanded permanent Security Council membership, and (2) strengthening capabilities in the spheres of peacekeeping, intelligence coordination, and nonproliferation.

More Balanced Participation: Budget Reform

For an organization that has so much theoretical prestige, it is not reflected in funding. The UN, excluding peacekeeping efforts and a few humanitarian programs such as the UN Development Program, the World Food Program, and the UN Children's Fund, operates on roughly $2 billion per year.[88] Three countries—the United States, Germany, and Japan—routinely account for half of this budget. The first step in rejuvenating the UN is simply to put more money behind it. With a more egalitarian formula for financial contributions, the UN could broaden the number of true stakeholders. Currently, a member state's capacity to pay is determined by the country's population size and gross national income, adjusted to subsidize poorer member countries. Yet the current structure has allowed several powerful nations to free ride the system. China, a permanent Security Council member, paid only $53 million in 2007, while Russia (another permanent member of the Security Council) and India routinely pay less than $20 million each, both surpassed by the contribution of tiny Switzerland. (See Table 4.2.)

One proposal is to gradually increase total funding for the UN. To weaken the grasp of a few countries over the organization, perhaps a

Table 4.2 UN Budget Assessment and Payments
(in US$ millions)

Country	2007 Assessment
U.S.	493
Japan	333
Germany	172
U.K.	133
France	126
Italy	102
Canada	60
Spain	59
China	53
Mexico	45
South Korea	43
Netherlands	37
Australia	36
Switzerland	24
Brazil	18

SOURCE: United Nations: 2007 Status of Contributions to the
Regular Budget, International Tribunals, Peacekeeping
Operations and Capital Master Plan.

new funding formula should be introduced based 50 percent on population and 50 percent on economic output (on a PPP basis). Assume a larger UN budget set at $10 billion—a dramatic increase from its current $2 billion level, but still fairly low. Under this new arrangement the United States (with 4.3 percent of the world's population) would pay approximately $228 million in population dues plus $1.066 billion in economic dues (to account for its 21.8 percent share of world output). That makes for a total payment of less than $1.3 billion, more than double today's contributions but less than 11 percent of the total UN bill versus nearly 22 percent today. This is but a small part of the United States' aggregate defense/intelligence/diplomatic spending that is currently nearing $800 billion.

China, on the other hand, would see a dramatic increase. It currently pays less than 4 cents per Chinese citizen or just 2.6 percent of the UN current budget. Under the new system, China would actually become the largest UN financier, paying more than $1.5 billion each year. While this seems high, keep in mind China now holds almost $2 trillion in hard currency reserves. No longer a poor country, China needs to be more vested in the UN system. India, too, would be required to pay considerably more as would Brazil. In contrast, several European members would actually pay less than they currently do. And small countries with very small populations and economies would not be overly penalized under this new formula.

How can we get these countries to agree to a larger budget and a new financial formula? The United States must take the lead on this front, readily offering to pay its share of the extra funds and setting a new higher standard while broadening the financial base of the UN with new players. For newcomers like India and Brazil, such increases will need the incentive of increased power, influence, and prestige. The amount of money we are discussing—$10 billion in total—is but a rounding error in the budgets of the top 20 countries that will be footing 90 percent of the bill. President Obama can take a strong multilateral stand by advancing greater financial support for the UN, paying the proposed increase on time, and setting a new stage for more reinvigorated UN participation. And with renewed interest in the UN, we would likely see the budget and scope of activities grow significantly in the near future. But these developing countries will need greater roles in the UN in exchange for such increases.

More Balanced Participation: Security Council Reform

At the heart of the UN debate over representation and financial commitments is the Security Council, a body that still reflects the global power structure of 1945. At that time, 11 countries were named to the council, with a privileged five victors of World War II—the United States, the United Kingdom, France, Russia, and China (known as the P5)—granted permanent membership with veto rights. Since 1966, this has grown to 10 elected members, but the council remains undemocratic, with a two-class system (permanent and temporary).

The veto power of the P5 allows each to turn down a resolution even if the other 14 members approve it, which often leads to UN gridlock. Skeptics question whether Security Council reform is feasible so long as certain members have an individual veto. One highly charged suggestion is to end veto rights (perhaps over a specified time frame), while also expanding the P5 to nine members (the P9). These moves alone could dramatically reinvigorate the UN on many levels. A new 19-member council would remain small enough to be efficient yet broad enough to reflect a wider range of views than it currently does. As a substitute for the current veto enjoyed by the P5, a three-quarters majority rule could be implemented to guarantee that the council's decisions reflect, at all times, a worldwide consensus. This means that the council's decisions would have to be supported by at least 15 members.

While the P5 would initially object to this realignment, there are legitimate reasons to move in this direction. First, the current veto right puts too much power in the hands of one country. Second, if there is a concern that requires a veto, a sponsor would need to gain the support of an additional four members to block a council vote. With a revised permanent status, one can see how the addition of other world powers would be far less controversial than if new permanent members had veto rights. With no changes to the permanent status of council members in 60 years, it is long overdue.

While there are many worthy countries, there is a wide consensus that political and economic powerhouses such as Japan, India, Brazil, and Germany have the size and stature deserving of membership. As the second and third largest economies in the world, Japan and Germany's candidacies should not be hugely contentious, although China may have issues with Japan. The historically contentious relationship between the two has not yet cooled: Chinese Premier Wen Jiabao told Japan that it must face up to its World War II aggression before aspiring to a bigger global role, stating, "Only a country that respects history, takes responsibility for history, and wins over the trust of peoples in Asia and the world at large can take greater responsibilities in the international community."[89] Indeed, when China, along with Russia and the United States rejected the last major effort for Security Council reform in May 2005, the strained Sino-Japanese relationship was cited as one of the key reasons.[90] However, several U.S. diplomats, including Condoleezza Rice, have promoted their inclusion.[91]

Nor should Brazil be a controversial addition. It is the largest Latin American country in population and economic power in addition to having the 11th largest defense budget and the 18th largest standing army in the world. The country is no stranger to the Security Council, having been elected to it 18 times, the most of any elected country. Brazil has contributed troops to several UN peacekeeping missions (Angola, the former Belgian Congo, Cyprus, Mozambique, and East Timor, among others), putting it among the 15 largest financial contributors to the UN budget, and it would be bumped up to sixth under the proposed new formula. Most of the Security Council would probably approve Brazil's permanent membership, although the Chinese have shown no public support. The only vocal opponents to a Brazil membership are two Latin American countries—Mexico and Argentina—which argue that Brazil is not Spanish speaking and therefore is not representative of the Latin world. Yet Brazil stands strong as an important player in the twenty-first century.

India should also be added to the permanent members of the Security Council, although its candidacy poses far more complexities than Brazil's. It is simply too big to ignore on the global scene. As the world's second largest country in terms of population (on its way to being the first), the largest democracy, a huge economy (perhaps the third largest on a PPP basis), and a nuclear power with the world's third largest standing army, India's scale speaks volumes for inclusion. It is among the largest contributors of troops to UN peacekeeping commitments, and it actually was one of the founding members of the Security Council back in 1945. However, potential opposition from countries such as Pakistan and China needs to be addressed first.[92] Oddly, the United States is now the only P5 member opposed to India's candidacy. While President Bush made some conciliatory overtures to India, including the civilian nuclear power sharing program signed in 2006, his administration's opposition to India's permanent UN Security Council seat is due to its Pakistan-centric South Asia policy, where Pakistan remains Washington's key ally in its war on terror. The United States does not want to upset Islamabad, which clearly opposes India's entry to the council. Yet India's large Muslim population—more than 160 million—might be appreciated by other Muslim countries worldwide and may ultimately help the United States and the G7 in the long run with the fight against global terror, easing tensions between the Western and Islamic world.

Keep in mind that an additional 10 countries would make up the council, and that permanent status without a veto right would no longer be nearly as prestigious or valuable as it is today. Therefore, calls for a Muslim or African country to broaden permanent representation may be less vocal. Indeed, by adding Japan, India, and Brazil and removing the veto right over time, the Security Council's complexion changes dramatically, breaking up the West's traditional stronghold.

While the combination of an expansion of the P5 to P9 with the phase-out of the veto right would make sense on many fronts, critics would argue that few of the P5 would sanction such moves. But look at the reality of the situation. For the United States, giving up the veto would be largely symbolic and should not affect it practically. To form a bloc, the United States would need only four others on the entire Security Council with four old allies—the United Kingdom, France, Germany, and Japan—already permanent members. If finding four others is a major undertaking, perhaps a message is being sent that should be heeded. The Europeans should not object strongly, given that the EU will already have three permanent members of the five nations needed for a veto. Finally, Russia and China, too, should be motivated to accept this reform since the United States alone (nor any individual country) could no longer block broader consensus. This is extremely controversial, but in many ways the downside risk of such expansion and veto change seems considerably less than what the world assumes with an impotent, ignored UN.

A revised membership that includes four new permanent members—Japan, Germany, India, and Brazil—an evolution of veto rights at the Security Council and a larger budget could potentially restore vigor, democracy, and legitimacy to the UN. The proposed new dues formula would allow for more equitable underwriting of UN activities. These reforms taken together could reduce global tensions and resentments, underscore the evolution of world power, and set the stage for a more empowered UN role in Macro Quantum management.

UN Peacekeeping

The UN peacekeeping tradition is now more than 50 years old since first raised in response to the Suez Crisis of 1956, and there have been more than 60 UN peacekeeping operations. The concept has enduring, pragmatic appeal: deploy lightly armed military personnel from member countries under UN command to war-torn areas that need a neutral party to cultivate conditions for sustainable peace. UN peacekeepers—including soldiers and military officers, civilian police officers, and personnel from many countries—deliver undeniably valuable services in postconflict situations and assist excombatants in implementing official peace accords. Such assistance comes in many forms, including confidence-building measures like power-sharing arrangements, electoral support, strengthening the rule of law, and providing some stability for renewed economic and social development.

While in theory peacekeeping is an excellent strategy to maintain the capitalist peace, one common criticism is that the UN's ad hoc, bureaucratic style often results in deployment delays when global crises occur. For example, during the Rwandan genocide, the UN was unable to garner international support for aid to the country, and 800,000 people were slaughtered. One suggestion to remedy these delays would be the creation of a rapid reaction force: a standing group that receives troops and support from Security Council members and is ready for quick deployment. This should be a permanent feature of the UN, expanding the capabilities of the organization in concert with the new realities of twenty-first century civil wars.

Currently the peacekeeping process calls on existing troops from member nations' armies to join designated missions; however, multi-country peacekeepers are typically poorly coordinated. Frequently, each country's troops live on separate bases and operate independently. In recent years, the UN has tried to overcome coordination problems by hand-picking specific battalions that already have peace-keeping experience.[93] By contrast, a dedicated full-time command structure, similar to NATO, with centralized training and communication in a common language, would allow a more effective response. Moreover, some have suggested interesting, flexible methods for allowing wealthier countries to contribute more in capital and weapons than in soldiers, with countries with larger militaries to be compensated for supplying more troops, something that may be useful if peacekeeping efforts become more commonplace.[94]

Peacekeeping should also be extended to other nonmilitary conflict situations such as natural disasters and pandemics like the Asian tsunami of late 2004 or Hurricane Katrina in 2005. A standing rapid reaction force would require increased permanent funding for a command structure, training, equipment, and deployment. As discussed earlier, the general dues structure would be increased dramatically to fund this command and training structure, with individual peacekeeping missions still kept outside the general budget.

NATO Reform

In the aftermath of WWII, the Soviet threat was very real: Its armed forces outmanned the rest of Europe significantly, and in 1949 the USSR tested its first nuclear weapon. Stalin armed both the North Koreans and Mao's Communists in China. In response, the NATO treaty was written to bind the United States, Canada, and Europe together in the case of a Soviet attack. NATO's charter states that if any of the member nations is attacked, all will respond to the attack together.

As the Cold War ended and the Soviet Union collapsed, some called for an end to NATO, claiming the *raison d'être* of the alliance has evaporated. As part of post-Cold War restructuring, NATO's military structure was cut back and new forces such as the Headquarters Allied Command Europe Rapid Reaction Corps were established. Former Eastern bloc countries including the Czech Republic, Hungary, Poland, Bulgaria, Estonia, Latvia, Lithuania, Romania, Slovakia, and Slovenia have subsequently joined the organization. In the post-Cold War era, NATO has intervened in humanitarian crises in former Yugoslavia, sent troops to Afghanistan, and (since 9/11) has increased antiterrorist cooperation.

It probably isn't said enough, but NATO is a phenomenally successful organization, perhaps the greatest traditional military force the world has seen. As such, it would seem logical for NATO to embrace new missions, as demanded by new twenty-first century threats, in addition to its traditional focus on territorial defense. These new aims include crisis management (the ability to intervene effectively in smaller-scale conflicts) and countering weapons of mass destruction.

Capitalizing on its great success, NATO could be extremely useful helping the UN strengthen the peacekeeping force by building a similar command structure and model. This is preferable to NATO expansion, because the UN is a truly global force, while NATO remains a regional group that has yet to shed its anti-USSR (and by extension, anti-Russian) image. A 2004 Russian parliament resolution warned that Russia would revoke a promise to limit troop numbers in several key strategic regions if NATO continued its eastward expansion.[95] Russian President Dmitry Medvedev echoed this sentiment in 2008, adding: "Atlantism has exhausted itself. Now we must talk about the integrity of the entire Euro-Atlantic space—from Vancouver to Vladivostok."[96] It has been suggested EU expansion is a more appropriate forum to incorporate these states. Since the EU emphasizes economic interlinkages, as opposed to security, it would be less likely to evoke a hostile Russian response.

Moreover, NATO must reassess its long-term nuclear plan. Nuclear weapons have formed part of NATO's collective defense policy since its inception, but its policies have grown contentious. While NATO has only three nuclear weapon states officially recognized by the nuclear Non-Proliferation Treaty (NPT), several others—including Belgium, Germany, Italy, the Netherlands, and Turkey—all host nuclear weapons on their territory as part of a sharing arrangement.

Every NATO member is a party to the NPT, which went into force in 1970, aiming to rid the world of all nuclear weapons. Under the NPT, states that did not possess nuclear weapons as of 1967 agreed not to obtain them, and states that did hold them agreed to reduce these weapons over time. NATO's weapons-sharing arrangement seemingly violates the principles of the NPT. Indeed, the necessity of maintaining weapons in Europe is debated by the host countries themselves, such as when former German Chancellor Gerhard Schröder called for removal of U.S. nukes in Germany in 2005.[97]

After the Cold War, NATO reduced its nuclear forces and no longer targets any single country with its weapons.[98] Still, NATO defense ministers uphold the centrality of nuclear weapons to the organization's purpose. In a communiqué responding to Belgium and German calls for the withdrawal of nuclear weapons from their states' territories in April 2005, NATO ministers responded, "the fundamental political purpose of NATO's nuclear forces: to preserve peace and prevent coercion."[99]

In a heralded 2007 editorial, distinguished statesmen George P. Schultz, William J. Perry, Henry Kissinger, and Sam Nunn argued for accelerated disarmament, writing: "In today's war waged on world order by terrorists, nuclear weapons are the ultimate means of mass devastation. And nonstate terrorist groups with nuclear weapons are conceptually outside the bounds of a deterrent strategy and present difficult new security challenges."[100] Similar ideas have been floated by U.K. Prime Minister Gordon Brown and Defense Secretary Des Browne who offered to host a conference for technical experts from all five recognized nuclear states to develop technologies for disarmament.[101] The Schultz group proposed a renewed commitment to the principles of the NPT, that is, continuing to reduce the nuclear forces in all states that possess them. They also suggest ratifying the Comprehensive Test Ban Treaty and initiating a multilateral effort to control the uranium enrichment process, which guarantees uranium for nuclear power reactors without allowing individual countries to carry out their own enrichment.

The move toward eliminating nuclear weapons should be applauded, but the feasibility of a multilateral enrichment process is limited at best. A centralized enrichment process may lessen chances than any given country will produce nuclear material to use as weaponry, but deciding who gets the enrichment contracts has provoked much political bickering. As discussed earlier, it is difficult to argue against developing nuclear power in energy-deficient countries. But there are many other clean, viable alternatives to nuclear power. We could bypass the squabbling over multilateral enrichment by simply encouraging renewable power sources instead of the development of nuclear facilities.

More important, NATO should be spearheading the global shift away from nuclear-based defense. That said, it was unfortunate to see five former NATO bigwigs—including General John Shalikashvili, the former chairman of the U.S. Joint Chiefs of Staff and NATO's ex-supreme commander in Europe; General Klaus Naumann of Germany; General Henk van den Breemen, a former Dutch Chief of Staff; Admiral Jacques Lanxade; and Lord Peter Inge of the United Kingdom—float a hawkish 2008 manifesto for NATO that underscored nuclear first-strike capability, yet another plan to fight the last war.[102]

At least the Shalikashvili group had enough insight to call for reform of NATO's inequitable funding arrangements and troop burdens.[103] Given that the United States disproportionately foots the bills and contributes troops, it accordingly has a more resounding voice setting the NATO agenda. The security challenges of the future demand equitable, effective, and coordinated action by nations with common interests. NATO has made impressive strides toward adapting itself to the demands of a changed and changing world, but its members should recognize that neither the alliance nor their own military establishments are perfectly suited to these demands. Fielding the requisite military capabilities will not come cheaply, nor will further institutional changes within NATO be without cost. But it is well worth the effort, given the myriad security challenges we now face.

Given the new emphases, a common call is for NATO's member states to be structured for more rapid deployment, similar to the recommendation for UN peacekeeping forces. Achieving a more expeditionary posture entails expanding and modernizing NATO's transportation fleets (principally military airlift, but also sealift), acquiring more mobile logistics assets, upgrading infrastructure in selected countries, and modernizing the forces themselves so that lighter, more mobile units can be more effective in a wide range of missions. This will entail, among other things, exploiting recent advances in surveillance, information processing, communications, and precision weapons so that the military assets of adversaries can be rapidly located, identified, and destroyed with minimal collateral damage. NATO must also develop a greater ability to deter and defeat chemical, biological, and nuclear weapons. Many military analysts and specialists, like the Rand Corporation, believe these "softer" plans will be far more important than new expensive hardware and weaponry for NATO's more modern posture.[104]

The Way Forward

Today's security risks cannot be controlled by endless military spending, overstretched engagements, and unilateral postures. U.S. politicians have seemingly forgotten the craft of balancing commitments and resources responsibly, while accurately detecting and gauging risk in the twenty-first century. The refinements of our global security architecture will require far greater multinational cooperation than we have ever seen before, but in the end, this would strengthen and reinforce the capitalist peace.

U.S.-led efforts should refocus security policy on prevention—not fire-fighting. After all, it is easier (and cheaper) to detect smoke than save a burning house. The primary tools of our Macro Quantum defense paradigm will be multilateral bodies and the diplomatic and intelligence communities, synchronizing to diffuse the tensions of interstate competition, monitor terrorist activity and prevent the spread of arms. In situations where violent conflict breaks out, NATO forces and UN peacekeepers will be prepared to act decisively and rapidly. The United States will continue to maintain a traditional military, but this army should be small, nimble, high-tech, and staffed by highly skilled personnel, as opposed to the cumbersome, hardware-intensive beast we have now.

The United States and G7 should no longer try to unilaterally control threats through the use of force; that's merely attacking the symptoms of the world's ills versus cooperatively curing the root causes. We must begin to explore new approaches to diffusing old threats. Weaning the world off fossil fuels and promoting energy efficiency may be a far simpler solution to solving problems in the Middle East and reduce the necessity for military intervention there. A concerted effort on the energy front would also help ease global warming and the concomitant security and social threats. Likewise, a multipronged approach to poverty could help reduce civil wars, terrorism, and nuclear proliferation. Modest global reforms such as bans on small arms production and more restrictive weapons exports could help curb global militarization and stem the worrying rise in intrastate conflict.

The proposals suggested here aim to leverage our mutual interdependence and encourage an equitable distribution of defense responsibilities in order to create a true collective security community. They seek to consider security from trunk to tail, not part by part. Twenty-first century realities put the world at risk of repeating Norman Angell's era. Without such modernizations and commitments, we may suffer worse consequences than what we witnessed in the twentieth century.

Electromagnetic Warfare and the Return of Star Wars?

Since its inception in 1958, the National Aeronautics and Space Administration (NASA) has brought the United States moments of great national pride (such as the first manned moon landing in 1969), as well as some moments of shame (such as in 2007, when diaper-clad astronaut Lisa Marie Nowak was arrested for attempted kidnapping). Yet overall, NASA's image today is largely innocuous—a bunch of physics geeks gathering moon rocks in outer space.

How soon we forget that NASA was founded in part to conduct military research in space. During the Cold War, militarization of space—once the stuff of science fiction—became an imminent threat as the Americans and Soviets raced to design and launch satellites and complex antimissile defense systems. After the fall of the USSR, military space research slowed dramatically, but did not disappear entirely: In 1996, Commander-in-Chief of U.S. Space Command (now part of the U.S. Strategic Command) Joseph W. Ashy was quoted as saying: "We're going to fight from space and we're going to fight into space. That's why the U.S. has development programs in directed energy and hit-to-kill mechanisms. We will engage terrestrial targets someday—ships, airplanes, land targets—from space."*

*Karl Grossman, "master of space," *Progressive Magazine*, January 2000, www.thirdworldtraveler.com/Pentagon_military/MasterofSpace.html.

Indeed, it appears that the space arms race may back on, although it is less clear whom we are racing. In December 2002, George W. Bush signed the National Security Presidential Directive, which essentially resumed the missile shield research that had been discontinued a decade earlier. China seems keen to develop its own space technologies, and in 2007, it carried out its first successful antisatellite test. Japan, India, and several European countries also continue space research that has potential military applications.

Beyond missiles and missile defense, space militarization includes the continued development of reconnaissance satellites and satellite navigation systems (not just for use in Range Rovers, GPS is an extremely useful military tool). Space also provides the venue for nuclear tests: High altitude nuclear explosions, reaching heights over 50 km, have been used largely for research purposes.

These explosions are actually how the United States got the idea for electromagnetic weapons, another military innovation that eerily resembles something from *Battlestar Galactica*. In 1962, the United States first exploded a nuclear bomb 20 miles up in the atmosphere. The gamma rays resulting from the explosion triggered an electromagnetic pulse that disrupted radio stations more than 700 miles away.* The pulse lasted for only a fraction of a second, but it showed that electromagnetic pulses were not only possible but also potentially useful.

Today, a device known as a virtual cathode oscillator (vircator, for short) can mimic the effects of a nuclear explosion, generating high-powered microwaves (HPMs) to similar effect. Electromagnetic weapons, sometimes called e-bombs, can be used to destroy electronic systems, as well as temporarily

---

*"Come Fry with Me," *The Economist,* Jan 30, 2003, www.economist.com/science/displaystory.cfm?story_id=E1_TVVJRPD.

(*Continued*)

(*Continued*)

incapacitate people. Although the weapons are still experimental, the U.S. Navy reportedly used electromagnetic pulse warheads during the opening hours of the first Gulf War to disrupt and destroy Iraqi electronics systems.★ Fears that terrorists will use a rudimentary form of the e-bomb, or that Iran or China will develop their own version of the technology, are rumored throughout the security community.† In some ways, this echoes the naval arms race of 1906 with the British *Dreadnought* ship.

The forward-looking time bias of the Macro Quantum paradigm requires us to anticipate new threats and incorporate new technologies—whether they come from the sky or pulse through the air. As it stands, the U.S. military budget is heavily skewed toward fighter jets and naval carriers—the technologies of yesterday. To avoid becoming a modern-day Maginot Line, the military hardware budget should shift to favor these tech-intensive applications.

★"High-power microwave (HPM) / E-Bomb," Global Security, www.globalsecurity.org/military/systems/munitions/hpm.htm, (last assessed June 9, 2008).

†"Electromagnetic Pulse Risks and Terrorism," United States Action, http://unitedstatesaction.com/emp-terror.htm (last accessed June 9, 2008).

Chapter 5

Immigration

People, People Anywhere

Immigration is the sincerest form of flattery.

S ince our ancestors left the African savannahs two million years
ago, migration and travel have been an inherent part of our
human experience. We're hardwired for movement; it's a
Darwinian instinct, a curious inclination, an encoded skill to wonder
and to wander in search of new opportunities and possibilities. From the
hunters and gatherers' trek from Africa to Eurasia and then across
the Bering Straits to the Americas, to explorers' voyages and conquests
during the Age of Exploration and colonization; from the slave trade of
the eighteenth and nineteenth centuries, to Europeans' pilgrimages to
new worlds, migration has long generated the issues and emotions we
face in the Macro Quantum twenty-first century: excitement, fear, joy,
tension, and even violence between newcomers and local populations.

Throughout history, human movement has frequently been
the result of population pressures: famine, climate change, political

instability, and powerful economic forces. While these continue to drive migration in the new millennium (see Figure 5.1), unprecedented demographic shifts and the economic success of developing countries have added unique twists to the ways—and whys—people move. First, aging populations in the G7 are creating a dearth of able-bodied workers and an overabundance of elderly. Second, while successful economies have always attracted immigrants, the source countries that once provided these immigrants are now becoming destinations. Both of these trends support the case for the creation of a coherent policy that views immigration as an opportunity rather than public nuisance.

This is easier said than done. Cross-border migration is a topic rife with contradictions and misconceptions. The far-reaching socioeconomic and cultural ripples it provokes in both sending and receiving countries invite passionate opinions from all involved. Even though roughly 10 percent of G7 populations are immigrants, some still view immigration as a zero-sum game. In the United States, this group is small—only an estimated 20 to 25 percent of voters who are

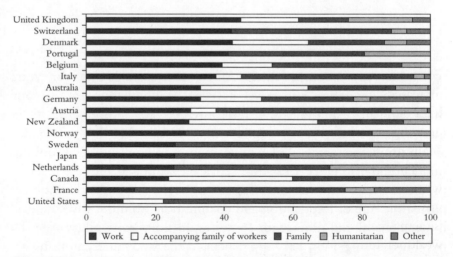

Figure 5.1   International Migration by Category, 2005
SOURCE: OECD International Migration Outlook 2007.
NOTE: For Information on the compilation of the standardised statistics, see www.oecd.org/els/migration/imo2007. startLink http://dx.dci.org/10.1787/015262881585.

mostly male, white, and lacking college degrees—but they have had a disproportionate voice in the media and in Washington. Yet these immigration naysayers are wrong to think migration is bad for the economy.[1] Like in trade, all countries that participate stand to benefit. Unfortunately, without an accurate understanding of the demographic imperatives driving migration and its actual cross-border effects, this vocal minority has drowned out proper public discourse, perpetuated stereotypes, and created a culture of discrimination. Immigrants are depicted as stealing jobs, and scientists' and scholars' research is viewed as a threat to national security.

Despite these misgivings, migration is a central link in today's worldwide web of persons, goods, customs, practices and ideas—an essential element of the elephant we're describing. We must accept the free movement of people along with the free movement of goods and capital; it is a necessary feature of the Macro Quantum world. Immigration policy needs to be viewed as a government tool to cultivate a workforce that will complement global labor force trends. This requires a revamping of both our attitudes and approaches toward this age-old (albeit increasingly complicated) phenomenon.

The Ticking Age Bomb

For virtually all of recorded time, populations everywhere have increased, and age structures were bottom-heavy (that is, more young than old). By contrast, today the populations of some countries are still growing rapidly, but many are stagnant, and some are even shrinking. Many are aging, while others remain young.

This era of divergence started with the Industrial Revolution, when some nations leapfrogged ahead of others economically. In many ways, the story of modern wealth creation and rising living standards is actually a story of changing demography. As countries become wealthier, fertility rates begin to decline. As Table 5.1 shows, the richest countries typically have the smallest families, and vice versa.

This transition was likely caused by changes in the social and economic logic of large families brought about by industrialization as well

Table 5.1   Rising Wealth, Shrinking Families

Smallest Families			Largest Families		
Country	GDP/ Capita	Household Size	Country	GDP/ Capita	Household Size
Luxembourg	80,500	2.9	Congo	300	6
Norway	53,000	2.3	Burundi	400	5.8
U.S.	45,800	2.7	Guinea-Bissau	500	5.3
Switzerland	41,100	2.5	Niger	700	5.9
Iceland	38,800	2.3	Sierra Leone	700	5.7
Demark	37,400	2.3	Malawi	800	5.9
Sweden	36,500	2.2	Mozambique	800	5.6
Belgium	35,300	2.4	Rwanda	900	5.8
Germany	34,200	2.3	Tanzania	1,300	5.4
Japan	33,600	3	Sudan	2,200	6

SOURCE: U.S. Census Bureau, CIA World Factbook 2007.

as changes in the roles of women, who were now viewed as potential workers in addition to (or even instead of) being mothers and wives.[2] Urbanization and industrialization favors smaller families; instead of being another pair of hands to work the farm, a city child is another consumer of space, time, and resources. And, because an industrial economy provides more opportunities for women to join the workforce and support themselves, it leaves them less time to rear children. In turn, this declining birthrate leads to higher wealth per capita, making more resources available to cultivate individuals—human capital—through education. Better educated workers result in higher productivity per capita and fuel the process of trade and economic development that we discussed in Chapter Two (wherein farmers become factory workers, factory workers become white-collar workers, and so on).

Across generations, these demographic trends were amplified. If a couple has only one child, and that child marries another single child, and they have only one child, the population quickly shrinks. Two sets of grandparents (four people) produce two children, who go on to have only one child: The population goes from four to two to one in only two generations. On the other hand, if a couple has three children, and

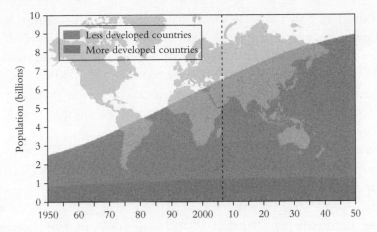

Figure 5.2 Predicted Population Growth, Developed vs. Less
Developed Countries
Source: IMF.

each of those children has three, the population grows exponentially.
And as Figure 5.2 shows, populations in the developing world are
predicted to follow the latter pattern.

What are the global implications as populations stagnate in rich
countries but continue to grow in poor ones? First, the developing world has a chance to catch up to the G7 in terms of aggregate
GDP. Think of the size of an economy with the simple equation:
Population × Per Capita Output = GDP. The more people, and the more
each individual can produce, the larger the economy. We've already
seen that wealthy countries with smaller populations can invest more in
human capital to increase per capita output, which results in a modest
GDP gain. But if a developing country with a massive population,
such as India, is able to capture even a very small increase in efficiency
(per capita output), it is multiplied by a population of 1.1 billion, and
appears as a very big gain. This is why so many of the largest emerging
markets—including Brazil, China, and India, among others—are also
some of the larger economies in the world.

Another aspect of this demographic transition is that the United
States and the G7 are aging. The lower fertility rate and longer

life expectancy in the rich world has left developing countries with younger populations than their rich world counterparts. By 2025, one in five Europeans will be more than 65 years old,[3] and more than a third of Japan's population will be over 65, winning it the title of oldest in the developed world.[4] In extreme cases, such as in Italy, Germany, and Japan, death rates now exceed birth rates; these countries are actually *depopulating*, as Figure 5.3 shows for Japan.

With fewer and older people, the G7 labor force is shrinking fast. Analysts estimate that to offset these worker declines would require a net migration of about 500,000 people per year for Japan, 150,000 for Germany, and 100,000 for Italy.[5] It is clear that aging, industrialized nations need to reconsider their immigration policies. These countries, currently the biggest players in the global economy, will experience stagnant (or negative) economic growth and a sharp decline in wealth if nothing is done. McKinsey believes by 2027 household financial wealth in the world's major economies will be roughly $31 trillion less than if historical population trends had continued.[6]

And what's more, aging populations stress pension and health care systems, as income-earners must support a growing number of retirees. In

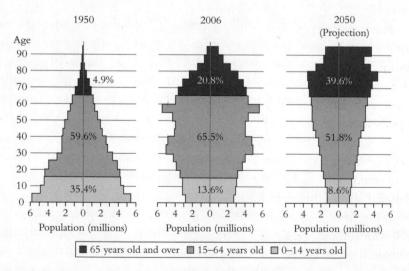

Figure 5.3 Japanese Population Transition
SOURCE: Statistics Bureau MIC.

the United States, the ratio of workers to retired people—the "dependency ratio"—was 4.5:1 in 1941.[7] By 1970, this had dropped to 3:1, then is estimated to fall to 2.7:1 by 2009, and it is expected to hit 1.6:1 by 2050 unless policies change. In Germany the current ratio of 2.3:1 is expected to fall to 1.3:1 by 2030.[8] In Japan, a steeper falloff occurred: In 1990, the country had 5.8 workers per retiree, but this dropped to 3.9:1 in 2000 and is heading to 2.1:1 by 2025.

Since 2002, the United States has experienced reduced private savings and a growing fiscal (government) deficit along with a growing current account deficit, reflecting increased borrowing from abroad. U.S. imports of goods and services continue to outstrip U.S. exports by a wide margin, leaving U.S. households and firms to borrow the difference on international capital markets. Meanwhile the U.S. federal fiscal deficit, augmented by ambitious military adventures abroad, registered at 3 percent of 2007 GDP. Because private households aren't saving, and the government isn't saving, the question becomes, who is going to cover the costs of retirement for an increasing number of Americans? The 2007 Social Security Trustees Report already raised the concern that this U.S. benefits program will face massive annual deficits in as little as a decade if no reforms are made.[9]

Fortunately the recent metamorphosis of the developing world from a net borrower to a net lender has eased the industrial aging boom. The excess savings of EMs have been held in foreign currency reserves, often invested in U.S. treasuries. But this bailout cannot last forever. In the future, cross-border savings flows may not fill such deficits for two reasons: First, the world's current supersavers represent only a small piece of the global financial pie. In China for example, financial assets have been growing extraordinarily rapidly (14.5 percent compounded annual rate over the past decade), but its share of global financial assets is still only 4 percent.[10] Second, many emerging markets are aging, too. Between 2006 and 2030, the number of older people in less developed countries is projected to increase by 140 percent as compared to an increase of 51 percent in more developed countries.[11] China is expected to have 265 million 65-year-olds by 2020, partially the result of the one-child policy, implemented in 1979.[12] Russia's working-age population is expected to shrink 34 percent by 2050, and the country's population is already decreasing by 700,000 people per year.[13] These nations will have to use their surpluses to deal with their own pension issues; they will not be able to support U.S. overspending forever.

Immigration could partially offset the problem of decreasing populations and provide an injection of fresh economic activity. It can also help meet the demand for health care providers, assisted-living facility workers, and other professions uniquely required by G7 aging populations. With no changes in the current restrictive immigration policy, the G7 will soon face unsavory pension reform decisions, including delaying formal retirement ages or reducing transfer payments, given increased life expectancies.

New Wealth, New Destination Countries

The prosperity of formerly poor countries is altering immigration patterns. Greater political stability, exploding economic opportunity, and the promise of social mobility for citizens abroad is encouraging the return of national diasporas. In fact, many people who left their countries seeking brighter economic prospects a generation ago are going home. Moreover, the children of those immigrants, who were born in the United States and elsewhere, are making the decision to immigrate to their parents' homelands. Take India as an example. Today there are at least 20 million Indians scattered throughout the world, most of whom migrated to the United States, the United Kingdom, and the United Arab Emirates.[14] Within the past decade, though, a new destination has appeared atop the list: India. Nonresident Indians, known as NRIs, have turned into "returned nonresident Indians" or RNRIs.[15] In the technological hub of Bangalore alone, it is estimated that between 30,000 and 40,000 RNRIs have come home within the past 10 years, reflecting a radical change in migration patterns.[16]

When droves of Indians packed their bags in the 1960s and 1970s, it was a combination of low pay, a lack of technological jobs, and a frustrating, socialist economy that convinced them to go. Highly skilled NRIs from India, usually the graduates of elite technical universities, tended to have a common destination, especially in the 1990s: Silicon Valley. Indians arguably became the most sought after group of employees in the Valley, and many became millionaires there. And while it is speculated that there are more successful entrepreneurs of Indian origin in Silicon Valley than in any city in India, this is changing.[17] The expertise and work experience gained by NRIs abroad can now be used back home. Since the 1990s, foreign direct investment (FDI) has taken off in India, partially the result of a more open and deregulated economy. Technology development now happens in India while technology consumption happens in the United States.[18] At the same time foreign companies are expanding into India, Indian companies have been going global, expanding abroad, giving a double boost to the national economy. The country's companies have moved beyond the phase of simply replicating U.S. pharmaceuticals and European automobiles. Instead, they are now becoming some of the world's leading innovators in areas such as biopharmaceuticals and automotive engineering. The result is what some have described as a "silent scientific repatriation" in India.[19]

This returnee trend is popping up in other countries as well. As FDI and outsourcing drive economic growth, some expatriates are being sent back by their employers to set up outsourcing operations throughout Asia, Latin America, Africa, and the Middle East.[20] Many returned expats have found that the best way to move up is to move back.[21] The returnees enjoy prestige in their homelands, often gaining some of the best-paid, most desired jobs. They are sought by companies on both sides of the globe to connect U.S. and G7 customers and workforces, often bridging cultural divides to accelerate economic integration.

In addition to returnees, emerging markets now deal with an influx of other diverse immigrants. Like in trade, a steady flow of "South-to-South" migration that never touches the rich world has developed. Although the United States continues to be the number one destination country for immigrants, its lead is shrinking. In 2005, among the 20 countries with the highest numbers (and percentages) of immigrants living within their borders were Ukraine, Saudi Arabia, India, Pakistan, the United Arab Emirates, Israel, Kazakhstan, Cote d'Ivoire, and Jordan.[22] (See Table 5.2) For example, Algeria hosts immigrants

Table 5.2   2000-2005 Net Migration, Largest Inflows and Outflows in Thousands

Outflow			Inflow		
Rank	Country		Rank	Country	
1	Mexico	400	1	U.S.	1160
2	China	390	2	Afghanistan	428
3	Pakistan	362	3	Spain	405
4	India	280	4	Germany	220
5	Iran	276	5	UAE	192
6	Indonesia	200	6	UK	137
7	Phillippines	180	7	Italy	120
8	Kazakstan	120	8	Australia	100
9	Sudan	104	9	Sierra Leone	88
10	Egypt	90	10	France	60

SOURCE: UN Data.

representing more than 44 nationalities, and Turkey has more than 600,000 immigrants in transit.[23] Countries like China and India are now among both the largest sources and destinations for immigrants.

Today, countries of destination are as diverse as countries of origin.[24] As the line between source and destination countries blurs, immigration becomes admittedly more complex, but mutually beneficial cooperation at the multinational level becomes more feasible.

Trends and Implications for the United States and the G7

Some old patterns persist. In developed countries, permanent immigration for family or work-related reasons continues to increase. In the United States, 70 percent of immigrants moved to join family members, while in Western Europe, the bulk of the immigrant population was seeking better employment opportunities.[25] Differing from the past, the number of global asylum seekers has been steadily declining.[26] This group has traditionally been one of the larger immigrant categories, reflecting people displaced by political turbulence in their home countries. Today, these refugees are disproportionately represented in the immigrant populations in Africa and Asia but shrinking elsewhere.

With growing economic opportunity overseas, the supply of qualified immigrants available to the United States and G7 will naturally decline. But because Americans and Europeans today are better educated, older, and less fertile than ever before, the need for both skilled and unskilled workers will only continue to grow. Facing a tighter labor market and low national savings, the United States (as well as Europe and Japan) must now strategize to strike a harmonious balance between what it produces domestically, what it imports, who it engages as immigrants, and what it provides its retirees.

As free trade continues, it is almost guaranteed that certain labor-intensive industries will move abroad. Eighteenth-century economist David Ricardo would have called this process of increasing specialization and trade "capturing comparative advantage," but today we refer to it by the politically unpalatable name of "outsourcing." Unpopular as it may be, it makes sense for the G7 to let some industries go, concentrating instead on businesses that require greater technological capability and less labor.

Outsourcing does eliminate some lower paying jobs, as critics point out, but by redistributing resources to the most efficient economic sectors, it can result in the creation of even more better paying ones, expanding the economic pie for everyone. This is what the Bureau of Labor Statistics (BLS) calls "net job creation." The BLS found that starting around 1990, coinciding with the advent of outsourcing, labor productivity climbed rapidly for an unprecedented 15-plus years. At the same time, more than 23 million jobs were created in excess of those lost in the United States. In the future, even as labor intensive manufacturing continues to move away, total U.S. employment is expected to increase by 10 percent from 150.6 million in 2006 to 166.2 million in 2016. The net increase of 15.6 million jobs will come almost exclusively from services—like healthcare, education, and hospitality—which cannot be outsourced nor done by machines. This should allay some irrational fears of job loss: While a call center can be moved to Calcutta, your hairdresser, dentist, and kindergarten teacher certainly cannot.[27]

Even with outsourcing, wealthy nations will still have to compensate for their aging populations by bringing in new workers. A shrinking working age population will push up wages for these new high-skill service sectors; skilled domestic workers will vie for these positions, thereby leaving a gap in low-skill jobs. A greater number of elderly means physically intensive jobs will go unfilled. What's more, the United States and other countries with aging populations might need to raise retirement ages to keep worker-retiree ratios in better balance or cut back on long-term benefits. Americans are living longer than ever before, but the retirement age (currently 62) hasn't changed since 1983. The average American born in 1983 could expect to live to 74.7; today life expectancy at birth is 78.1 years. As of April 2008, the average retired worker received $1,083 in monthly benefits.[28] If the United States doesn't scale back benefits or raise the retirement age, these extra 41 months gained in life expectancy will require additional benefits of more than $44,000 per person. Multiply this by the expanding retirement age population, and the retirement system will be sorely stressed. Faced with three unpopular options—outsourcing, increasing immigrant flows, or cutting back government benefits—strategic immigration may now appear to be the lesser of three perceived evils (although a combination of the three is probably more economically optimal).

Keep in mind that the majority of immigrants don't compete with most native-born workers. Instead they complement the U.S. marketplace, shifting the demand curve outward and resulting in a more productive economy for everyone. Immigrants tend to move into either highly skilled or unskilled jobs and very few in between. Countries with guest worker programs usually attract unskilled immigrants in housekeeping/restaurant sectors, seasonal farming, and domestic services such as childcare. In the United States, the traditional native candidates for low-skill jobs—high school dropouts—are disappearing quickly. In the early 1960s, half of adult Americans had not finished high school; today, high school dropouts from less than 7 percent of the adult population.[29] And these laborers actually help raise American wages. The National Academy of Sciences estimated that native-born incomes increased $10 billion annually due to immigration,[30] because immigrants take low paying jobs, creating a need for more higher paid supervisors and managers.

In other cases, greater demand for services by aging populations, particularly in the medical field, cannot be met by employing the native population alone. As a result, the number of doctors and nurses immigrating to these countries is increasing. Today, a similar siuation is developing in the United States where fewer Americans are graduating with technical degrees in engineering and the sciences. Between 1980 and 2000, the percentage of foreign-born scientists and engineers with Ph.D. degrees employed in the United States increased from 24 percent to 37 percent; 45 percent of physicists were foreign-born, while for engineers, the figure is over 50 percent.[31] Between 1990 and 2004, more than one third of Nobel Prizes in the United States were awarded to foreign-born scientists.[32] Indeed, our technological lead is at risk when we limit our intake of high skilled immigrants.

Although immigrants do consume government benefits and services, they tend to add more than they subtract. Data shows that many come to the United States during their prime working years, at an average age of 28, and exhibit lower rates of unemployment than do native-born Americans.[33] Immigrants generally take jobs Americans either don't want to do or can't do—or they create their own jobs. Consider, for example, the proliferation of immigrant-owned lawn care businesses, restaurants, and nail salons in recent years. One estimate suggests that immigrants'—both legal and illegal—contributions to the U.S. economy come to $700 billion a year.[34] Immigrants, after all, have to make rent, buy food and cars, and pay taxes just like any American.

As we've seen, a freer flow of people can clearly benefit the rich world, providing wealthier countries with fresh labor amid declining birth rates, but it also helps the populations of developing countries contributing those workers. Migration is a "labor export." Sending countries often benefit from financial remittances from abroad, which, according to the World Bank, totaled more than $300 billion in 2007 (see Figure 5.4). Moreover, this globalization of labor—as is the case with goods, services, and capital—helps to correct local imbalances, as excess capacity can be absorbed by overseas demand. As laborers relocate abroad, countries with an abundance of workers witness a decline in domestic unemployment creating a global win–win proposition.

While a handful of bank-to-bank transfer services exist for handling transfers between, for example, the United States and Mexico, these options are few and far between for smaller communities abroad. Western Union and its subsidiaries is the most commonly used financial service for such transactions. Western Union's rise and near monopoly control in many countries has been subject to mixed reactions. On one hand, a

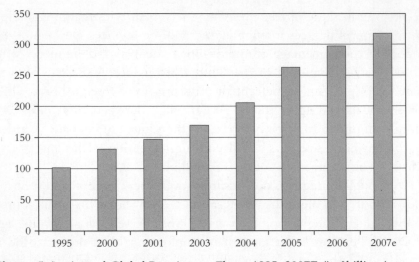

Figure 5.4   Annual Global Remittance Flows, 1995–2007E (in $billions)
The true size of remittances, including unrecorded flows through formal and informal channels, is
believed to be larger.
SOURCE: The World Bank.

150-year track record and brand recognition (especially when the local
population does not trust domestic banks) guarantees safe funds transfer
across borders. On the other, however, Western Union is still a business
and there are fees attached to the money transfers. So while citizens living in small communities underserved by banks are more than pleased
to have such an accessible way to receive funds from family members
working abroad, those sending the money are slapped with hefty fees.
For example, to send $100 in a same-day transfer from the United States
to Mexico, the sender might have to pay up to 15 percent of the amount
sent![35] Many immigrant spokespeople in the United States have added
the reduction of money transfer fees to their list of concerns alongside
better immigration legislation. The company is responding by partnering
with the communities and the Mexican government.[36]

Immigration: Interlinkages and Challenges

With so many new Macro Quantum cross-border flows, maintaining the
desired regulated but liberal immigration flow will require an overhaul

of both local and multilateral policies based upon realistic demographic and economic trends. Most countries, including the United States, have failed to see how immigration fits into the big picture. Discussions surrounding strategic immigration policy and the flow of illegal immigrants must be elevated above the nationalistic, knee-jerk banter that has dominated discourse to date.

Immigration and Poverty

Regardless of skill level, immigrants are usually moving to find better opportunities than those available in their native countries. Often, family members are left at home and depend upon the money sent back to them in the form of remittances. This is mutually beneficial to both developed and developing countries. In recipient nations, remittances are not only the best way of accruing foreign currencies but also stimulate economic activity, including trade, investment, and consumption.

As Figure 5.5 notes, some countries are highly dependent on such funds. In extreme cases, such capital flows comprise almost half of a country's GDP. Immigration is helping to mitigate poverty and

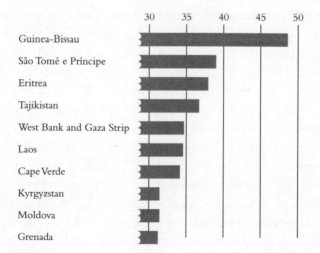

Figure 5.5 Remittances to Developing Countries, 2006 (US$ Billion)
SOURCE: International Fund for Agricultural Development.

engage poor countries that might not otherwise be linked to the global economy.

Involuntary Migration

While most of the immigration we've discussed has been voluntary in nature, there are dark chapters of forced migration in globalization's history, such as the brutal 200-year period when more than seven million sub-Saharan Africans were captured and sold as slaves in the New World. But forced migration is not ancient history: Last year an estimated 800,000 people were forcibly transported across national borders.[37] Human trafficking, frequently referred to as "modern day slavery," is the second largest criminal industry in the world and can take many forms.[38]

Human trafficking generally involves a form of involuntary servitude. This can include bonded labor, forced prostitution, child labor/child soldiers/child sex tourism, and even the extraction of bodily organs for sale. Human traffickers usually prey on people in dire economic straits with false promises of a better future. Women are offered jobs in hotels; young boys are kidnapped to work in sweatshops; girls in countries known for gender inequality are told they will receive education. The most common form of transnational human trafficking involves prostitution, and it even affects international sports. UEFA, the European arm of the soccer organization FIFA, has focused attention on cases related to underregulated qualifications for agents and recruiters. Each year, hundreds of young children are "recruited" from Africa and South America to allegedly play for European soccer clubs. Upon arrival, however, most realize the ploy. If they are fortunate enough to make it to an actual tryout, many who are cut are simply left on the streets. In cases where phony recruiters are involved, children are often forced into the sex industry.[39] Human trafficking also has ramifications for health, accounting for a disproportionate number of new HIV/AIDS victims. For example, in Nepal, 38 percent of rescued victims had been infected with the virus.[40]

The international community is currently trying to address the issue with the recent founding of the UN Global Initiative to Fight Human Trafficking, but so far, results have been mixed at best. The issue of involuntary migration is intertwined with that of illegal immigration, so it is unlikely that it will be brought under control until the international community can successfully devise broader immigration policies. Additionally, global and domestic awareness of the issue (or a lack thereof) also dampens efforts to combat the problem.

Immigration, Trade, and the Dreaded "O" Word: Outsourcing

In the Macro Quantum era, trade trends have reshaped human migration, often with unforeseen effects. The North American Free Trade Agreement (NAFTA) is a good example. Since the late-1993 free trade agreement came into effect, Mexico's foreign direct investment (FDI) has expanded by a remarkable 14-fold, nonoil exports quadrupled, and farm exports to Canada and the United States have risen threefold.[41] Yet NAFTA also altered the structure of Mexican agriculture, changing it drastically. While approximately 80 percent of Mexico's farmers worked on farms of fewer than 12 acres pre-NAFTA, these small farmers were squeezed out as large Mexican farming conglomerates that could capture the lower costs of economies of scale through capital investment and mechanization moved in.

NAFTA increased the U.S. farm labor supply from Mexico.[42] As U.S. agricultural exports increased to its NAFTA neighbors, logically there was increased demand in the United States for low-skilled agricultural laborers and migrant workers. Mexican farm workers, many unemployed due to the intrusion of highly mechanized conglomerates as noted, crossed the border to help meet this demand. Simultaneously, as we discussed in Chapter 2, the United States began to experience a huge construction boom in the mid-1990s. A need for construction workers—and the fact that the average wage difference between California and northern Mexican states is 13 to 1—gave Mexicans an incentive to move north.

This situation was exacerbated partially by the United States' failure to pass comprehensive agricultural subsidy reform. In earlier discussions, we mentioned how bilateral (or in this case, trilateral) trade agreements are not true substitutes for overarching trade organizations like the WTO. Consider what happened recently in the market for corn: Mexico's import tariff on corn ended on January 1, 2008, but the U.S. government did not stop subsidies to U.S. corn growers. So even while Mexico exports more corn today than it did before NAFTA, the switch to megafarms wiped out an estimated one million Mexican jobs in corn production.[43] This created potential migrants, many of whom would be illegal. The combination of bilateral free trade agreements and a failure to reform agricultural subsidies in the United States has contributed greatly to what some Americans perceive as undesirable low-skill immigration.

The age-old tug-of-war over whether immigrants steal jobs is being trumped by a newer debate over outsourcing. If businesses can't find cost-effective labor in their home countries, they'll go elsewhere. The net results: Nationalistic politicians and unions accuse countries like Mexico, China, and India of stealing G7 jobs as multinational companies relocate to lower cost regions to fill white-collar jobs in everything from data processing to software coding and even industrial design. This has been a hot issue in the United States where several states and unions are considering ways to prohibit or restrict offshoring. There have been U.S. government spending bills that specify in many contracts that private companies cannot farm out work outside the United States.[44]

While a backlash over lost jobs is understandable, not seeing the relationship between offshoring and immigration—and resorting to protectionism—would be counterproductive. Many people believe that the U.S. economy simply loses money spent for services abroad. But offshoring is a story of mutual gain.[45] The quantum leaps since the mid-1990s in telecommunications and computing have allowed multinational corporations to arbitrage labor costs globally. It's too compelling not to: Software developers who earn $65 an hour in the United States get $6.50 in India; data entry clerks earning $20 an hour in Cincinnati make $2 in Calcutta. Because service sector offshoring is so labor-intensive (and doesn't require the huge capital investment of setting up overseas factories as in the automotive sector) these differences translate into unbelievably quick profits. It is, from an economic perspective, a business practice that makes sense.

Surprisingly, G7 nations that outsource actually benefit *more* than the emerging market labor country. This newfound ability to capture cross-border labor efficiencies actually creates enormous value for the world economy, and studies have shown a disproportionate benefit for the nations and companies that outsource. A 2004 study found, for example, that the United States earned 78 percent of the new economic value created by its corporate offshoring versus the 22 percent that goes to the lower wage countries where these services are relocated.[46] For U.S. businesses in India, an estimated $1.46 in new economic value is created for every $1 a U.S. firm spends offshore. Both countries win. Counting the advantages such new business brings Indian workers, firms, and governments, McKinsey estimates that India gains a net benefit of at least 33 cents from every dollar the United States sends offshore. The United States, meanwhile, earns a benefit of at least $1.13 for every dollar spent.[47]

Offshoring creates value and profit for U.S. companies and frees up resources (both people and capital) for activities with more value added. Firms that outsource pass cost savings on to consumers through lower prices and to investors through higher profits. Companies also get new sales from Indian firms that boost imports from the United States. Meanwhile, the U.S. economy redeploys workers who lose their jobs from offshoring in ways that expand growth as well. Going forward, as the populations of the G7 age and more people retire, maintaining high living standards will require some combination of increased technology innovation, heightened productivity, and new labor—meaning more immigration and offshoring. While neither is politically popular, it is likely offshoring can be embraced faster, because immigration legislation seems to be deadlocked in Congress.

Different groups of people are hit disproportionately by the phenomenon: Labor-intensive manufacturing and certain white-collar jobs are moving, and workers in these sectors will have to adapt. But rarely has a shift in the labor market, similar to the one in farming and heavy manufacturing in the twentieth century, created mass unemployment. It is simply part of the bigger picture of modern progress. Job losses in some sectors are part of a never-ending economic restructuring with which G7 countries—particularly the U.S.—are well acquainted (remember our discussion in Chapter 2). Technological change, economic recessions, consumer demand fluctuations, business restructuring, and public policy decisions can result in labor shifts. Over the next decade the United States may lose roughly two million service jobs thanks to offshoring.[48] But, with an economy that employs more than 150 million people, this is small potatoes. Since the mid-1990s, the United States has created roughly 35 million new jobs in areas like education, health, and technology services. Displaced American workers find new jobs quickly—almost all within six months.[49]

Is there a way to ease the pain of offshoring? Can and should government intervene? Yes, but only in strategic and reasonable ways. Skill training programs and health insurance portability programs like COBRA are good examples.[50] But more important, wealthy countries need to adapt psychologically and not let short-term disruptions to people's lives outweigh the larger consequences of resisting this global reality. If U.S. and European companies can't move jobs abroad, they will face great risks from global competition, not just from other wealthy countries but increasingly from world-class emerging market competitors. Failure to accept twenty-first century realities and not adapt and innovate will ultimately weaken the economy and throw more people out of work. The openness of the U.S. economy, particularly its labor market, is among its greatest strengths, but the risk today is that poor immigration policy decisions will make the country less flexible and less competitive in the future.

Trade and the Expat Scene

Living abroad was once a pursuit reserved for adventurous trust fund babies, diplomats, misfits, scallywags, and do-gooders. But over the last 20 years, from Bangkok to Buenos Aires, the complexion of expat communities has radically changed. While the same clique of eccentrics and English teachers remains, a large number not only of retirees, but of managers, professionals, and skilled engineers and scientists have been added to the mix.

In the 1990s, manufacturers seeking to capture low-cost labor advantages in newly industrializing nations were faced with a dearth of local management talent. In some of these countries, the education infrastructure simply did not produce the skills needed; in others, the indigenous business culture made it difficult to instill corporate norms in local staff. In China, for example, the Cultural Revolution brought all higher education to a halt in the late 1960s and early 1970s. The generation in their teens and twenties at this time (which would be prime age for middle management positions by the 1990s) likely did not have a college degree, let alone an MBA (which was still largely an American degree, although it was catching on in Europe).[51]

Assigning home country employees to work abroad was viewed as a way to bring reliable people with top-notch management skills, specialized knowledge, and a grasp of the corporate culture to these outposts. To lure Westerners to these rough-and-tumble locales, U.S. and European expats were promised "mobility premiums" and "hardship pay."[52] These lavish packages not only multiplied base pay, but also added hefty allowances for travel, schooling, and day-to-day luxuries, like cooks, maids, and drivers.

Today, this is beginning to change. The ranks of business expats continue to expand. According to GMAC Global Relocation Services, 69 percent of multinational companies sent more people abroad in 2006 than in 2005.[53] But these are often voluntary—not forced—assignments.[54] According to the Employee Relocation Council (ERC), companies still make use of international assignments for training and development, for cultural transfers, and to groom their executive leadership. But many of these assignments are now of shorter duration—meant for exposure, not to plug talent gaps.[55] The fact is, many emerging markets have the local talent—willing to work without a plump benefits package—to staff not only manufacturing companies, but also sophisticated service sector enterprises and financial organizations as well.[56]

Local managers can probably bring knowledge of regional practices and markets to the table as well as a firm footing in business best practices. The stiff competition for jobs abroad does not mean the flow of expats will slow to a halt; as Dubai, Moscow, and Beijing become more desirable places to live, Americans and Europeans no longer require extra perks to relocate there. These postings, instead of being seen as hardships are now viewed as valuable opportunities to live in a world-class city, learn about an important market, and advance careers. Emerging markets are becoming ever more central to MNC business strategies, so moving managers between countries is viewed as a valuable tool for instilling a balanced global perspective. In the

Macro Quantum world, the United States is not the only land of opportunity anymore.

Immigration and Security

The 9/11 attacks and subsequent 2005 London subway bombings have made immigrants appear as the number one terrorist enemy of the Western world. There has been legislation to match this paranoia such as the U.S. Patriot Act requiring photographs and fingerprints of all foreigners entering the United States. Immigration law is now being used as an anti-terrorism tool. Considering that the bureau formerly in charge of immigration policy, Immigration and Naturalization Services, was folded under the Department of Homeland Security umbrella in 2003 and considering the extended wait times for visas, it appears that security—not labor markets—is the chief determinant of U.S. immigration policy post 9/11. But whether these moves actually increased security remains to be seen.

While a bit overblown, there has been a feeling that the biggest impact of post-9/11 legislation has been on the academic community including delaying or denying visas for students and professors from particular countries. According to an administrator at the Massachusetts Institute of Technology, "there is growing anecdotal evidence that while our international student population is, by and large, very happy at school, they are ambivalent about being in the United States . . . [they] report a distinct feeling of unease about the political and cultural climate in the U.S."[57] The students who have traditionally come to the United States to study have been the best and brightest of their home countries. They are clearly intelligent and not oblivious to their environment. The combination of U.S. government legislation and xenophobia seems to be sending a sad but clear message: Go home.

From the moment an international student arrives, his every movement is tracked by the U.S. government through the Student Exchange Visitor Information System (SEVIS), a database that came about as part of the Patriot Act. The program is so comprehensive that it monitors the number of credit hours taken by a student, the student's major, and other details about their whereabouts. But SEVIS is not only often inaccurate but also chronically out of date.[58] In fact, the errors that result in students being detained at airports or other points of entry of the United States are just as, if not more, likely to be the fault of the system as the fault of the student. The burden of proof ends up falling on the student, with the Customs and Border Protection authorities automatically assuming guilty until proven innocent.

This trend is disconcerting given the importance of foreign students to the U.S. economy. International students contribute on average $14.5 billion to the United States annually.[59] (See Figure 5.6.) Education is an export of sorts. And today's international students are often tomorrow's U.S. researchers and scientists. Nowadays, not only is it tough to study scientific fields in the United States, but it is even more difficult to stay after graduation. In some fields of science, including computer science, mathematics, physical sciences, and engineering, more overseas students are being awarded Ph.D. degrees than Americans. This is not a bad thing: The challenge for the United States is to harness the

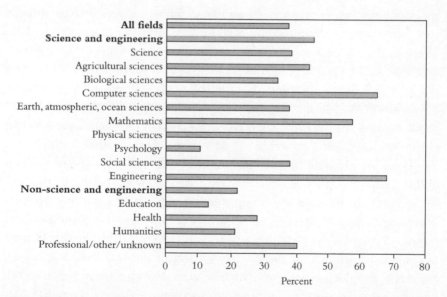

Figure 5.6 Non–U.S. Citizens' Share of Degrees Awarded by Category, 2006
SOURCE: National Science Foundation Division of Science Resources Statistics, Survey of Earned Doctorates.
NOTE: Non–U.S. Citizens include individuals holding permanent or temporary U.S. visas. Percentages are based on respondents who reported citizenship status in each field. Denominators for these percentages are not presented in this report.

capital that it has trained to keep its sciences on the cutting edge by retaining foreign-born talent.

The more stringent system for student visas post-9/11 discourages foreign students from studying life sciences in the United States in light of bioterrorism threats. Students planning to study biochemistry, genetics, molecular biology, cell biology, recombinant DNA technology, or virology—all topics covered in introductory biology classes—are often subject to visa delays or denials.[60]

While the United States is now making life more difficult for foreign students and graduates, their non-U.S. employment options are increasing. This may lead to a reverse brain drain that could severely handicap the United States (or any other developed country pursuing similarly restrictive policies). Between 2001 and 2002, U.S. visas for immigrants working in the fields of science and technology dropped by 55 percent, largely as a result of strict post-9/11 policies not because immigrants don't want to come to the United States.[61]

The United States is still an attractive place to live. The number of applicants for visas continues to climb. In 2008, more than 6.4 million applications were submitted for 50,000 visas available through the U.S. Diversity Visa Lottery (a visa that does not require a university degree or special skills),[62] up from 5.5 million applications submitted in 2007. And as Figure 5.7 shows, the United States still vastly exceeds other nations as a destination for immigrants. But as one expert put it, "Recent government policies are sending talented U.S.-based researchers overseas and clamping down on the arrival of new researchers to the country . . . the Bush administration's policies are shooting this country's economy in the brain."[63] Other countries have been actively courting talented researchers and students via funding and easier visa regulations. Foreign governments and companies are providing strong incentives to return and offering opportunities that previously were only available in the United States. We forget that in the Macro Quantum world talented scientists, engineers, and doctors are highly mobile, with skills that are in real demand, providing them a much wider range of employment than in the past.[64]

Consider how anti-immigrant anxiety has affected skilled workers in the United States on H-1B visas. H-1Bs allow employers to hire skilled foreign workers in specific professions. These visas last for three years and can be renewed for another three, and can eventually lead to green

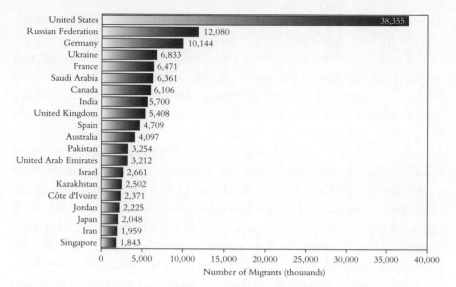

United States | 38,355
Russian Federation | 12,080
Germany | 10,144
Ukraine | 6,833
France | 6,471
Saudi Arabia | 6,361
Canada | 6,106
India | 5,700
United Kingdom | 5,408
Spain | 4,709
Australia | 4,097
Pakistan | 3,254
United Arab Emirates | 3,212
Israel | 2,661
Kazakhstan | 2,502
Côte d'Ivoire | 2,371
Jordan | 2,225
Japan | 2,048
Iran | 1,959
Singapore | 1,843

Number of Migrants (thousands)

Figure 5.7 Countries with the Largest International Migrant Stock, 2005
SOURCE: UN Department of Economic and Social Affairs.

card—but this requires a separate application process.[65] Even in the 2008 U.S. economic downturn, there simply aren't enough of these visas.[66] H-1Bs are limited by Congress, and for the last five years this number has been set at 65,000. Congress temporarily raised the H-1B cap to 195,000 during the Silicon Valley boom, but that expansion expired in 2004. In 2007, the cap was reached the very first day visa applications could be filed.[67] As Microsoft Chairman Bill Gates testified before a House committee in 2008, "the fact is that the terrible shortfall in the visa supply for highly skilled scientists and engineers stems from visa policies that have not been updated in more than 15 years. We live in a different economy now, and it makes no sense to tell well-trained, highly skilled individuals—many of whom are educated at our top universities—that they are not welcome here. I see the negative effects of these policies every day at Microsoft."[68] And the United States is not alone: Global competition for the best minds in the world is affecting other countries as well. Virtually every industrialized country is confronted with a significant labor shortage, particularly in the knowledge sectors.[69]

In addition to terrorism, there is a long-standing stereotype that immigrants are more inclined to commit crimes than the native population. When it comes to legal immigrants, however, this stereotype appears to be misguided. In the United States, research during the last two decades has concluded that immigrants commit proportionately no more crimes than native-born citizens.[70] Immigrant crime rates also tend to be overstated, because all immigration violations are considered federal offenses.[71] Crime rate statistics for illegal immigrants appear somewhat ambivalent. In the United States for example, crime rates are actually lower in cities with the most immigrants, and even as illegal immigration has increased over the past two decades, violent crime continues to fall.[72] Yet another study suggested illegal immigrants are often tied to organized crime and commit a disproportionately high rate of sex offenses.[73] This suggests that immigration policies for legal immigrants are working well to screen out shady characters. However, it also means that illegal immigration needs to be addressed better.

While the United States needs to reform its visa policies to attract the labor it needs legally, it also needs to redouble border and port security. Illegal immigrants make it much more difficult to track the flow of people meaning the United States cannot sort the bad apples from the good. Instead of swimming against market forces, the United States needs to acknowledge its labor shortage and address it through legal immigration. If farm jobs are filled legally in the United States, there will not be incentives for illegal flows. One potential policy to consider would be amnesty for the estimated 12 million illegal immigrants already in the country. Even President Bush recognized this, suggesting a Z Visa that grants amnesty to illegal immigrants willing to pay a fine.[74] In essence, these people receive a slap on the wrist, in the form of a fee, which some critics believe is not enough punishment to fit the crime. But face it: These immigrants are already here and are likely to stay whether or not they are granted legal status. By legitimizing their presence, not only could we be safer by knowing who is here, we will also be able to better monitor our population and collect taxes.

Immigration and Health

As mentioned earlier, one of the most pronounced changes in immigration is its unintended affects on global health care. While we'll explore the risks of cross-border pandemics in the next chapter, immigration linked to demographic trends and globalization are reshaping the nature of medicine in both industrialized and developing countries.

With increased health spending, medical workers are becoming globally mobile. Doctors and nurses from nearly every emerging market—Africa, Southeast Asia, Eastern Europe, Central and Latin America—are being recruited to work in countries with aging populations. For example, in 2005, one third of practicing doctors in the United Kingdom were from overseas.[75] The reasons for the health sector migration, according to the WHO, vary. On one hand, troubles in home countries encourage highly skilled workers to leave and take care of Europe's aging populations. A lack of promotion prospects, poor management, unmanageable workloads, inadequate living conditions, and high levels of violence and crime are some of the reasons a health care professional chooses to leave. These motivations are compounded by the opportunities available in other countries. Immigrating doctors and nurses can find better remuneration, upgrade their qualifications, work in a safer environment, and provide a better environment for their own families.[76]

While the immigration of health care professionals benefits the countries to which they move (as well as their own livelihoods), their emigration is often detrimental to the regions they leave behind. With 11 percent of the world's population and 24 percent of the global burden of disease, Africa is home to only 3 percent of the world's health workers.[77] According to the WHO, approximately 25 percent of doctors and 5 percent of the nurses trained in Africa are working in wealthy OECD countries. This has startling implications for those African countries losing health care workers. As health care professionals head to other countries, South Africa surfaces as the only country in the sub-Saharan region that will meet WHO guidelines for the number of health care professional per sector of the population.[78]

As the global economy accelerates, health care, too, is being pulled quickly into a market-based system. While doctors and nurses can move across borders these days to satisfy cross-border demand, so can patients. Medical tourism—where patients go abroad for better or cheaper treatments and surgeries—is becoming common. But increasingly, older Americans are simply moving for good. New innovative medical technologies and treatments allow aging Americans to live healthier and more productive lives, but at a cost: U.S. Federal Reserve Chairman Ben Bernanke recently noted, "per capita health care spending in the United States has increased at a faster rate than per capita income for a number of decades," with Americans now spending more on health care than for housing or food. Government estimates show that by 2020, health spending will exceed 22 percent of the nation's gross domestic output, largely as Americans age. [79] Indeed, growing old in the United States is becoming more expensive. Average monthly costs living in a U.S. nursing home is now more than $5,000, according to MetLife.[80] For many, this sum of money puts an assisted living facility out of reach. As a result, many American retirees have found a solution: go global, with a growing number moving south of the border to various destinations in Latin America.

In Mexico, for example, a patient can receive a studio apartment, three meals a day, laundry and cleaning service, and 24-hour care from English-speaking staff for only $1,300 a month—a quarter of what an average nursing home costs in some parts of the United States.[81] While many U.S. insurance companies and government providers such as Veterans Affairs, Medicare, and Medicaid will not cover foreign medical bills, some overseas governments will even cover foreigners living in their country. For example, the Mexican Social Security Institute (IMSS) allows foreigners to benefit from their services. An American with diabetes living in Mexico, who needs regular amounts of insulin and other medications, can pay $140 a year and have all of his medical bills covered.[82] Interestingly, the U.S. Embassy in Mexico has no reports of Americans filing complaints against Mexican nursing homes.[83] Furthermore, as the industry expands, the Mexican government has begun projects with U.S. university hospitals and health care companies to begin standardizing the care available for Americans living in retirement homes.

It's not only the price of the services that make living in places like Mexico or Panama comfortable for Americans. Many U.S. retirees live alongside other expats in enclaves such as Lake Chapala, an American-style retirement community about 50 minutes from Guadalajara and 600 miles from Texas (voted second best climate worldwide by National Geographic!). The communities here are being designed with cushy resort amenities such as restaurants, satellite television, and news-papers, libraries, social clubs and even movie theaters— all in English. There are dozens of restaurants, and the community has more than 50 English-speaking social organizations.[84]

In contrast to the United States' restrictive visa regulations, which have only become stiffer since 9/11, foreign governments have adopted legislation to facilitate this kind of immigration.[85] These foreign government incentives are not philanthropic gestures toward ex-pats, but rather shrewd commercial acumen; they are luring a potent form of foreign direct investment. U.S. (and European) retirees—like multinational corporations—are good for local business.[86] They create demand for services (such as construction of medical facilities and homes and ongoing medical treatment) and for day-to-day house-hold items. According to a survey of U.S. retirees living in Mexico and Panama, retirees spend considerable amounts of money in their newly adopted homes and on local spending—often more than $250,000 in the first 18 months of such a move.[87]

This is happening elsewhere in the world, where foreign govern-ments have been making the most of the fact that American retirees are good for their countries. American baby boomer retirees who can no longer afford to live in Florida or Arizona on a pension have figured out they can enjoy a higher standard of living elsewhere.

Toward an Immigration Policy

To address immigration challenges earnestly, the United States must accept global labor competition and integration. The United States, like other wealthy countries, is undergoing a massive demographic shift. Its citizens are better educated and less fertile than ever before, yet the need for low or unskilled workers only continues to grow and there are plenty of countries willing to supply the talent. Moreover, the flow of workers is not within U.S. policymakers' powers to stop; as long as there are jobs, workers will come, whether or not the law condones migration. However, with some foresight—and acknowledgment of the useful tool immigration can be—a combination of looser restric-tions on educational visas, amnesty for workers who are already in the

United States illegally, and guest worker measures may help achieve the balance of skilled and unskilled workers the country so direly needs to fix the ailing immigration system.

The United States is not the only country facing immigration challenges: There are more people migrating to Asia, Latin America, and Europe than ever before. As a result, one can argue that international organizations, destination countries, and origin countries all need to work together to create a comprehensive, functioning pro-immigration environment. The line between destination and source country is beginning to blur, as previous net sending countries are becoming net destinations. Still, sending countries have understandably different interests from destination countries. Destination countries are concerned about attracting the right kind of labor, protecting domestic jobs, and integrating immigrants. Source countries are focused on losing skilled workers, dependence on remittances, and the role that diaspora communities play in domestic politics. These interests would be best coordinated through a multilateral forum versus the haphazard approach of the past.

Today, the UN High Committee on Refugees (UNHCR) and the International Organization for Migration (IOM) are the two major intergovernmental bodies that work with immigration policy. The UNHCR focuses of refugees—a decreasing percentage of immigrants. The IOM, founded in 1951 to deal with displaced WWII refugees, tackles the whole spectrum of immigration policy and has 121 members. Ninety-five percent of the IOM's funding comes through voluntary contributions for projects, leaving the organization sparse funds to do more than advise on policy; it doesn't have the teeth to enforce immigration policies. To create a more effective multilateral forum, the IOM could be folded into the UN system, therefore gaining access to a wider membership and steadier funding. In addition to keeping better tabs on migration trends, this newly reincarnated UN IOM could be charged with developing a global registry of immigration and coordinating efforts between Interpol and individual countries to identify international criminals and terrorists who are trying to cross borders illegally. It could additionally work on measures to rapidly identify medical outbreaks like avian flu. More important, the UN IOM should create international guidelines and develop best practices in immigration policy for host countries to ensure that quality standards for the working conditions of migrant populations are met. It could also work to garner better financial support for refugees who are forced to immigrate during times of civil wars and natural disasters.

Facing the ticking demographic time bomb, efforts to block immigration may mean a slow, yet certain, economic strangulation. The United States and other rich nations will continually need professors, doctors and nurses, apple pickers and nannies; the countries risk depopulation and economic stagnation if they do not learn to better embrace immigrant communities. Places like the United States that are primarily destination countries need to focus on creating *realistic* policies and immigration reform. Not addressing illegal immigration or simply building a wall between countries (like the unfortunate one being built between the United States and Mexico) does not insure that immigrants are going to disappear. Destination countries should view the potential of this labor as added productivity, a tool to be used in the economy by government like monetary or fiscal policy with important links to Social Security and other retirement systems. Hopefully, such a mind-set would help lessen the xenophobic stigma attached to immigrants. After all, in the United States, virtually every citizen descended from an immigrant within the last three to four generations. The United States has always been a magnet for the world's best and brightest, but there is competition in the Macro Quantum world. In the next generation it is likely that some emerging market economies will become choice destination countries for immigrants. Mexico already receives large numbers of immigrants from Central America. Don't be surprised to find that Americans may even begin to leave for better opportunities abroad in the not-so-distant future.

Finally, there is great need for origin countries to control exit out of their own borders. Historically, the United States has served as an employment outlet for Mexican labor. This reliance was risky, because the outlet valve could be abruptly curtailed by more effective border control. While a freer flow of people across borders needs to be cultivated, there should be a structured, organized system, not a hodgepodge of country-specific policies. Moreover, origin countries should no longer free ride by relying upon wealthier destination countries to do all of the policing. After all, the line between origin and destination is increasingly blurred. Many of the states sending extra workers abroad are also playing host to inflows of workers from elsewhere. Because their interests are no longer so distinct, sending and receiving countries, working through a multilateral UN IOM, could coordinate domestic policies to maintain, and hopefully accelerate, the capitalist peace in the twenty-first century.

Good Fences Make Good Neighbors?

Ninety-six miles of wall through the heart of Berlin became an emblem of the Cold War struggle between good and evil, between freedom and oppression, between democracy and communism. Today, a wall intended to cover the 2,000-mile border between the United States and Mexico is currently under construction. It will cost an estimated $49 billion to build and maintain for 25 years.* Is there some sort of ideological message that the U.S. government is trying to send with building the fence? Is Mexico our enemy?

There are millions of illegal immigrants who enter into the United States by crossing the U.S.-Mexico border each year. The U.S. government traditionally places a lot of the blame on the Mexican government for not keeping its citizens within its own borders. Nonetheless, this is only one side of a very complicated problem.

When President Bush met with newly elected Mexican President Felipe Calderon in 2007, Bush repeatedly expressed the necessity for Mexico to do something to stem the tide of illegal immigration. Calderon made a commitment to do so, but under one condition: that President Bush better control the illegal arms entering Mexico from the United States. Ninety-five percent of illegal weapons in Mexico come

---

*Study: Price for border fence up to $49 billion Study says fence cost could reach $49 billion," *San Francisco Chronicle*, Jan 8, 2007, www.sfgate .com/cgi-bin/article.cgi?f=/c/a/2007/01/08/BAG6RNEJJG1.DTL.

from America.* Today, drug cartels are often better armed than the police and the military. In 2007, more than 2,500 Mexican citizens were killed in the cross fire with these smuggled weapons.

A second argument used to bolster support for the border fence centers upon national security in the wake of 9/11. In discussions about the fence, for example, Republican Congressman Duncan Hunter, a member of the House Armed Services Committee, said, "If you look at the list of people who have crossed that piece of the border in the last several years, there are a ton of people that come from terrorist nations and from states that back terrorism."† But Mexico isn't one of them. The construction of the border fence is an example of Micro Domestic policy made by the U.S. government that is causing unfettered resentment from our southern neighbor, and rightfully so. It has become wrapped in a mixture of ideological terms that run the gamut from illegal immigration to the global war on terrorism. This focus on the flow from south to north, however, is misplaced. If the U.S. really wanted to get political support from Mexico to patrol its border, it would enact tougher gun laws (much to the chagrin of the National Rifle Association and arms producers!) and enforce them better.

The fence has likely exacerbated crime and had a large human cost as well. because the fence surrounds strategic U.S. cities, immigrants are forced to cross in rural and inhospitable stretches of desert instead. This has increased the cost—as well as the profits—or human smugglers, but it has also resulted in

---

*Hector Tobar, "Weapons Flowing from U.S. into Mexico Leave their Mark," *The Boston Globe,* January 15, 2006, www.boston.com/news/world/latinamerica/articles/2006/01/15/weapons_flowing_from_us_into_mexico_leave_their_mark/.

† Duncan Hunter as quoted in "Battle Over U.S.-Mexico Border Fence Heats Up," *Fox News,* March 15, 2004, www.foxnews.com/story/0,2933,114090,00.html.

(*Continued*)

(*Continued*)

a larger number of deaths: Between 1996 and 2000, border crossing deaths increased fourfold.[*]

Furthermore, the United States desperately needs the immigrants from Mexico and other countries to maintain a dynamic economy. Strangely, there may be more unintended *Freakonomic* consequences of such fence building. Did anyone ever think that to build the fence we'd employ illegal, undocumented immigrants? We've already mentioned that Hispanic construction workers in the United States have drastically increased over the past 15 years. According to the Bureau of Labor and Statistics, foreign-born workers comprise 20 percent of the U.S. construction workforce.[†] If 20 percent is the official number, then one can estimate that the actual percentage of undocumented workers in construction is much higher. So even if the myriad of lawsuits and legislative debate about the fence are completed, the very people that anti-immigration Americans hope to keep out of the United States with the fence may ironically be a large part of its construction.

---

[*]Migration and Migrant Integration in the Atlantic Region Conference Report, Atlantic Conference 2007, March 22-24, 2007, Seville, Spain, 19.
[†]Amina Khan, "Could Illegal Immigrants Build the U.S.-Mexican Border Fence?" *Los Angeles Times*, June 3, 2008, http://opinion.latimes.com/opinionla/2008/06/could-illegal-i.html.

Chapter 6

Promoting Tomorrow's Health instead of Paying for Yesterday's Ills

So many people spend their health gaining wealth, and then have to spend their wealth to regain their health.

—A. J. REB MATERI

A mid today's globalization, goods are moving, people are moving, and their diseases are going with them—as microbes tucked delicately into the corners of their suitcases, as transmuted superbugs gone airborne and recycled in airplane ventilation systems, as the threat of anthrax sachets sent via mail, or even as the lead fumes of the Chinese-made toys wrapped for the holiday season. While these cross-border epidemics and bioterrorist threats have dominated the headlines lately, the Macro Quantum concept of health must extend far beyond germs, terrorists, and tainted goods. Health is a vital component of a nation's comparative advantage, and failing to treat it as such significantly handicaps the domestic labor force and impedes businesses from functioning.

Consider that the most probable killer today is mundane chronic illness—largely preventable ailments linked to smoking, inactivity, and obesity, such as heart disease, stroke, cancer, and type II diabetes. As globalization and prosperity have spread, so have sedentary, overconsumptive habits and the maladies that accompany them. Globally, chronic diseases are expected to increase 17 percent between 2005 and 2015.[1] While some of this increase is the inevitable product of aging populations, many of these afflictions could be nipped in the bud through cheap and easy preventative behaviors: regular health checks, exercise, proper nutrition, and avoiding cigarettes.

By ignoring easy preventative fixes, not only must we later spend multiples of the cost of prevention on remediation, but we're actually depleting the most valuable resource—human capital. Reliance on remediation results in shortened life spans and less productive people. Chronic conditions cause major limitations in activity for more than one of every 10 Americans, or more than 25 million people, according to the Centers for Disease Control and Prevention (CDC).[2] In addition to individual suffering, businesses saddled with huge health and pension costs also are penalized—especially in the United States where employers, not the government, foot most of the bills for employee healthcare. (See Table 6.1.)

To ensure a level global playing field for U.S. companies, we must radically shift how we think about health and health care. Remember our earlier discussion about GDP as a product of population and per capita output. Chronic illness affects both variables: population (better health makes for longer life spans and lower infant mortality) and per capita output (not only is a healthy worker much more effective than an unhealthy one, but a company unburdened by high costs of overspending on employee health care and sick days is also more efficient). (See Figure 6.1.) As President Theodore Roosevelt once said, "No nation can be strong if it is comprised of citizens who are impoverished and sick." It is only by combining good policies with lifestyle changes that health can be converted from a drag on the U.S. economy into its biggest asset: healthy, productive people.

Table 6.1 Life Expectancy by Country (Average for the 2005–2010 Period)

Rank	Country/Territory	Overall Life Expectancy At Birth (Years)	Male	Female
	World Average	67.2	65	69.5
1	Japan	82.6	79	86.1
2	Hong Kong SAR (PRC)	82.2	79.4	85.1
3	Iceland	81.8	80.2	83.3
10	France	80.7	77.1	84.1
11	Canada	80.7	78.3	82.9
12	Italy	80.5	77.5	83.5
22	United Kingdom	79.4	77.2	81.6
23	Germany	79.4	76.5	82.1
38	United States	78.2	75.6	80.8
48	Mexico	76.2	73.7	78.6
82	China	73	71.3	74.8
110	Indonesia	70.7	68.7	72.7
194	Mozambique	42.1	41.7	42.4
195	Swaziland	39.6	39.8	39.4

Source: UN 2006.

Americans are in worse shape than most believe. It should come as no surprise that as the world's richest country the United States leads the way in terms of lifestyle diseases. Chronic illnesses account for roughly 70 percent of health costs and deaths in the United States,[3] well above the 60 percent global average.[4] The nation has witnessed a quadrupling in the rate of childhood obesity and a doubling in the asthma rate over the past 30 years.[5] But what may come as a surprise is that the United States spends more than any other country on health care—a whopping $2.3 trillion in 2007, or $7,600 per person—yet the country still ranked only 38 out of 195 in terms of life expectancy.[6]

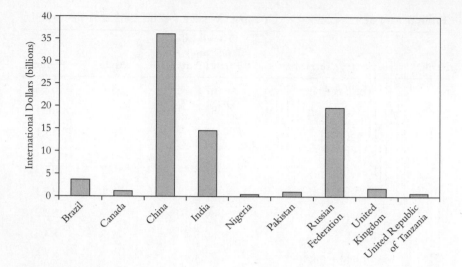

Figure 6.1   Increase in Value of Labor if Global Chronic Illness Is Reduced by 2 Percent Annually until 2015
SOURCE: WHO.

While most industrialized countries provide their citizens with at least a basic standard of care—often called "socialized medicine"—most Americans and their employers are largely responsible for their own health care costs. Yet the U.S. government's annual outlays of $600 billion tops what most foreign universal systems spend on socialized medicine.[7] One study comparing Australia, Canada, New Zealand, the United Kingdom, and the United States found that the United States performed poorest in 16 out of 30 measures of care, and "stands out for income-based disparities in patient experiences—particularly for more negative primary care experiences for adults with below-average incomes."[8] This underscores our major quandary: We're spending more on health care than any other country, yet by many measures, we aren't getting the care we need. Indeed, as the ultimate expression of the U.S. system's dysfunction, we have seen a growing number of dissatisfied Americans go abroad for health care. (See Figure 6.2.)

While lifestyle choices are ultimately the responsibility of individuals, the public sector is culpable for failing to spread awareness on health issues, allowing health care costs to rise beyond the reach of many

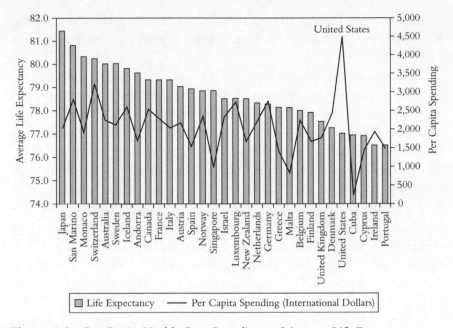

Figure 6.2   Per Capita Health Care Spending and Average Life Expectancy
SOURCE: UC Atlas, University of California Santa Clara. http://ucatlas.ucsc.edu/health/spend/cost_
longlife75.gif.

Americans, and incentivizing curative—as opposed to preventative—
medicine. National health care systems everywhere vary in the degree
of central control, regulation, and cost sharing they impose, as well as in
the role of private insurance, but the U.S. health care system is uniquely
convoluted and bloated by any standard.[9] Its complex incentive structure leads to overconsumption of medical services for some and being
priced out of the system for others, as well as misunderstandings
between doctors, insurance companies, and patients. And as far as preventative care goes, consider that for fiscal year 2009 the U.S. Centers
for Disease Control (CDC) requested $932 million for "health promo-
tion," including chronic disease prevention as well as genomic and birth
defect research—a decrease of $30 million from the previous year.[10]
This is only about two-thirds the amount requested for health-related
terrorism spending ($1.419 million) and half the amount requested
for infectious diseases ($1.870 million).[11] Addressing the United States'
skewed pricing structure and the poor delivery system could reduce

U.S. companies' burden, freeing them from the huge disadvantage they have compared to companies from countries with socialized systems of medicine.

Of course, poor service delivery and chronic illness are not the only health challenges amid globalization that merit attention. The epidemics and bioterrorist worries mentioned earlier have been international issues for as long as people have been crossing borders: The bubonic plague was carried by rats on merchant ships; European settlers in North America used rudimentary germ warfare in the form of smallpox blankets; and the Spanish flu made its way as far as the Arctic and remote Pacific islands. Despite the millennia of exposure we've had to these challenges, the infrastructure designed to tackle these cross-border contagions and hoax panaceas remains poor. From the Chinese government's secretive handling of 2003 SARS outbreak,[12] to the American man infected with a deadly strain of tuberculosis who took two transatlantic flights in 2007,[13] it is clear that better coordination is needed to prevent and prepare for low-probability, high-impact pandemics. Moreover, greater multilateral coordination is needed to create uniform safety and product trade standards combating counterfeit drugs, tainted food, and unsafe products.

Managing epidemics, bioterrorism, and counterfeit drugs should form an integral part of a Macro Quantum global health plan. But a truly comprehensive scheme must also consider the less headline-grabbing side of health—the health care incentive structure, cost of care, chronic illness management, and preventative care measures. In the Macro Quantum world, health is a competitive asset that needs to be harnessed through sound public policy. The public sector must take a more active role in defending health and combating chronic illness. As Jeanne Lambrew of the Center for American Progress writes, "disease prevention is more like homeland security than health insurance: everyone needs it, no one notices if it works, and it depends on persistent, strong leadership and systems."[14] Having a health system unable to cope with the modern challenges is a recipe for disaster, especially in a world where the G7 has aging, ailing populations.

The Bottom Line

Companies have a vested interest in healthy workers. One study shows productivity losses associated with workers with chronic disease are as much as 400 percent more than the cost of treating chronic disease.* Globally, chronic-disease-related deaths accounted for approximately 56 percent of all deaths in the working-age population, as well as about 40 percent of total lost time in 2005. Moreover, unhealthy workers force employers to manage the costs associated with disability, unplanned absences, reduced workplace effectiveness, increased accidents, and negative impacts on work quality or customer service. In the long run, many economists believe that workers actually "pay" for health care through lower wages. But in the short run, it is likely that employers are saddled with these costs. And in the United States, where according to a New America Foundation report, manufacturers spend more than twice as much for health benefits than their foreign trading partners,† this can hurt business.(See Table 6.2.)

Because of the dominant practices in pensions and retirement health benefits, U.S. companies are forced to have a vested interest in the health of their retirees as well as their employees. And these costs can be massive as life spans continue to lengthen. Indeed, some experts believe large U.S. automakers' struggle to deal with underfunded pensions—not comparative disadvantage in manufacturing—is what is strangling the industry.

---

*"Working Towards Wellness: The Business Rationale," World Economic Forum 2008.

†New America Foundation, "New Report Shows Impact of Employer Health Care Costs on Global Competition and U.S. Jobs," news release, May 7, 2008, www.newamerica.net/pressroom/2008/new_report_shows_impact_employer_health_care_costs_global_competition_and_u_s_jobs.

(Continued)

(*Continued*)

Table 6.2   Lost Productive Years of Life Due to Cardiovascular Disease

	2000 Years Lost	Rate Per 100,000	2030 Years Lost	Rate Per 100,000
Brazil	1,060,840	2,121	1,741,620	1,957
South Africa	302,265	2,753	391,980	2,667
Russia	3,314,014	5,684	3,208,265	5,887
China	6,666,990	1,595	10,460,030	1,863
India	9,221,165	3,572	17,937,070	3,707
United States	1,631,825	1,267	1,972,215	1,661

SOURCE: "A Race Against Time: The Challenge of Cardiovascular Disease in Developing Economies," Center for Global Health and Economic Development, 2004.

How do retirees' health care costs cuckold U.S. business? If you ever took a basic accounting class, you will be familiar with the discipline's fundamental principle: What a company owns (assets) must be equal to what it owes (liabilities) plus what has been invested in it (equity). But if accounting were always so straightforward, companies wouldn't need to hire a staff of specially trained experts to prepare their books. Pensions are a clear-cut example of how complicated accounting rules can obscure a company's real financial outlook. Before the 2006 U.S. Pension Protection Act was enacted, companies were able to exploit accounting rules to keep future health care and retirement benefits off the balance sheet, making the companies look more desirable. Companies made generous commitments on this front in exchange for lower salaries for unionized workers, but these companies failed to hold enough assets to fund these future commitments.

The 2006 reform required companies that underfund their pension plans to pay additional premiums and required that companies measure the obligations of their pension plans more accurately—using a principle that comes close to "mark-to-market,"[*] that is, valuing assets at their current market values, allowing for a bit of "smoothing" to keep prices fairly constant. Previously, assets used to fund pensions were recorded at historical book value. But as interest rates fell, so did the value of these assets, while the value of the liabilities continued to grow as more and more employees retired. In 2005, one expert calculated that growth in pension liabilities outpaced assets by 50 percent between 2000 and 2005.[†] With the reform, all of a sudden, companies that had vastly underfunded their pensions found themselves in hot water. Consider General Motors' predicament even before the credit crisis toppled the stock market.

The United Auto Workers union and GM made deals that were heavy on benefits, relatively light on wages. Commitments for pensions and "other postemployment benefits" (OPEB) didn't count as obligations on its balance sheet. But then GM had to start pouring cash into its pension funds as workers retired or were let go and paying out these benefits became a reality.[‡] In 2006, GM still had an unfunded liability of $85 billion solely for health care of employees and retirees— almost eight times the market value of the whole company.[§] Some joke that GM is no longer a car company, but a pension fund that makes cars to pay its debts. If it goes bankrupt, these liabilities are probably the reason.

---

[*]Office of the Press Secretary, "Fact Sheet: The Pension Protection Act of 2006: Ensuring Greater Retirement Security for American Workers," news release, August 17, 2006.

[†]Scott Burns, "Your Pension May Be Worse Off than You Think," MSN Money, moneycentral.msn.com/content/RetirementandWills/P109918.asp.

[‡]Allan Sloan, "General Motors Getting Eaten Alive by a Free Lunch," *The Washington Post*, April 19, 2005; page E03.

[§]Eduardo Porter, "Japanese Cars, American Retirees," the *New York Times*, May 19, 2006, www.nytimes.com/2006/05/19/automobiles/19auto.html.

(Continued)

> (*Continued*)
>
> According to company estimates, health care costs add about $1,500 to the cost of each GM vehicle, $1,400 per vehicle for Chrysler, and $1,100 for Ford.* Consider that Japanese car companies are still competitive despite coming from a country with high wages. In Japan, the government—not the company—is largely responsible for retiree health care costs. Pension reform and a greater public role in health care need to be defined if the beleaguered fate of the domestic auto industry is not to beset other U.S. industries.
>
> ────────
> *Eduardo Porter, "Japanese Cars, American Retirees," the *New York Times*, May 19, 2006, www.nytimes.com/2006/05/19/automobiles/19auto.html.

Unhealthy Lifestyles

In contrast to the frenetic interchange of goods and services witnessed each day, certain segments of the population aren't moving nearly enough. This sedentary lifestyle comes with a price tag: nagging ailments and shortened life spans. While breakthroughs in the health industry have continued to add years to life expectancy, our greater capacity to consume has created a culture of overconsumption.

In the United States approximately 25 million children are technically obese—a whopping one-third of American children and teens.[15] Obesity then puts our country's workers on a downward spiral for the rest of their lives, leaving them more susceptible to diseases later in life that include type II diabetes, high cholesterol, heart disease, hepatitis, liver failure, and sleep apnea.[16] And child obesity is but only the latest manifestation of poor lifestyle choices.

Between obesity rates; cigarette, drug, and narcotics usage; and the increasing amount of time Americans spend in cars and at desks, is it such a surprise that, according to UN estimates, the average life expectancy in Cuba is greater than the average life expectancy here in the United

States?[17] While Americans tout their medical care as the best in the world, capable of treating nearly any disease that arises, statistics show that the United States lags in many ways. While we do have some of the best specialist physicians in the world, adopting bad habits and relying on surgeries and specialized care later on is not wise. Better small decisions made daily can free the country from huge medical bills down the road.

Of course, government policy cannot make choices for individuals, but it can help to educate people and skew incentive structures through taxes. Consider what happened to the tobacco industry in the late twentieth century. Today we know that cigarette smoking can cause lung cancer, heart disease, emphysema, bronchitis, chronic airway obstruction, atherosclerosis, and peripheral vascular disease, just to name a few. Many of these diseases are not totally curable, and others, such as peripheral vascular disease, require extreme forms of treatment such as amputation of limbs. But when cigarettes were first introduced in the United States in the early nineteenth century, these health complications were largely unknown. Although early-1900s progressives campaigned against the habit for hygiene and moral reasons, during World War I, army surgeons praised cigarettes for helping the wounded relax and easing their pain.[18] But by the 1950s, scientists were aware of cigarettes' carcinogenic properties.

Since the 1960s, government policy toward tobacco has helped to wean more and more Americans off these "cancer sticks." Although today cigarette smoking remains the leading preventable cause of disease and death (in 2006, an estimated 20.8 percent—45.3 million—of U.S. adults were cigarette smokers[19]), as Figure 6.3 shows, this marks a significant decrease. Success is largely due to a multi-pronged government policy: limiting advertising, warning potential consumers and children of health side effects, and raising prices. Since 1969, it has been prohibited to advertise cigarettes on TV and radio, and since 1999 billboards have also been off-limits. Since 2002, 43 states and the District of Columbia have increased cigarette taxes, increasing the average state cigarette tax from 43.4 cents to $1.11 a pack. The current federal tax is 39 cents per pack.[20] The slew of lawsuits brought against tobacco companies have stipulated increased spending for anti-tobacco campaigns. The decrease in smoking over the last 40 years shows us that similar

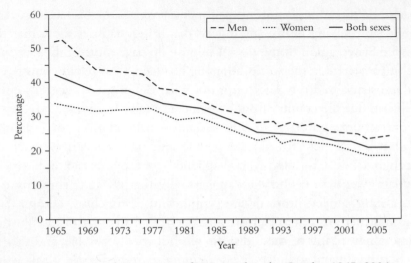

Figure 6.3   Estimated Percentage of U.S. Smokers by Gender, 1965–2006
SOURCE: CDC.

policies—taxes, limits on advertisements, and awareness campaigns—
may work when applied to other lifestyle choices.

While it appears the United States is winning the battle against
smoking, U.S. tobacco companies continue to export the addiction to
emerging markets. In 2007, more than a fifth of cigarettes produced
in the United States were destined for overseas.[21] Tobacco use is a risk
factor for six of the eight leading causes of deaths in the world, and
80 percent of tobacco-related deaths will occur within a few decades
according to the World Health Organization (WHO).[22] But research
shows that increasing tobacco taxes by 10 percent decreases tobacco
consumption by 4 percent in high-income countries and by 8 percent in lower income countries.[23] That means the strategies that have
worked in the United States could be even more effective in markets
where incomes are more limited. Alternatively, more stringent regulation of trade in tobacco and of growing illegal cigarette smuggling
could also help to slow the increase in smokers and smoking-related
health problems.

Both domestically and globally, food and diet is the next arena
that requires our attention. The Department of Agriculture reports that
in 2005, total U.S. animal protein intake (red meat, poultry, and fish)

amounted to 200 pounds per person, 22 pounds above the level in 1970.[24] Even though Americans have been gradually switching to less fatty meats, they lose the benefit by consuming more calories and less nutritious foods. Indeed, the increase in caloric intake in the United States is linked to consuming more processed foods. Back in the early 1970s during the Nixon administration, the United States faced a problem that resurfaced in 2007 and 2008: rising food prices. In 1973, food prices hit an annual inflation level of 8 percent. President Nixon devised a domestic food policy to help ease the impact on American wallets. Nixon held down the prices of processed foods while allowing the prices of raw farm produce to rise.[25] Hence, processed foods became drastically less expensive for the average American consumer than unprocessed foods. In order to support the processing and help his approval ratings, the Nixon administration began to heavily subsidize corn, a legacy still with us today. As one researcher discovered, 13 types of processed corn are found in a typical McDonald's meal. Additionally, corn and its by-products, such as high fructose corn syrup, make up about 25 percent of all of the edible items available on our supermarket shelves.[26] High fructose corn syrup permeates nearly every possible type of processed food. It's harder for your body to digest and results in the consumption of higher than normal levels of fructose. Higher levels of fructose, in turn, lead to increased levels of type II diabetes and surging rates of obesity.[27]

The dependence on corn feed and increased intake of processed foods, calories, and protein also spill over into the environmental realm: The average American diet produces an extra ton and a half of carbon dioxide-equivalent annually (in the form of actual carbon dioxide as well as methane and other greenhouse gases) compared to a strictly vegetarian diet. By cutting down on just a few eggs or hamburgers each week, greenhouse gas emissions would be drastically reduced.[28] In 2002, energy used for food production accounted for 17 percent of all fossil fuel use in the United States.[29]

In 2007, another period of food price inflation kicked off, and as prices soared, questions about the way we produce and consume food became crucial to matters of security, trade, poverty, and environment, not to mention health. Demand for food has been on the rise—both in terms of the demand for human consumption and for ethanol production. Extra calories are a good thing for people formerly afflicted by hunger, but in the United States, extra consumption is truly excess consumption. Not only is it bad for the average American's waistline, it is contributing to instability around the globe. Policies that worked for smoking can help again today. A combination of nutrition awareness (such as posting nutrition information at restaurants and elementary education programs) and consumption taxes on high fructose corn syrup could help to get Americans back into shape. We must extend prevention activities outside of traditional settings into schools, workplaces, and sites like supermarkets and pharmacies,[30] and craft policies that make nutritious foods and healthy portion sizes an appealing (and perhaps cheaper) option.

Health Care Providers and Insurance

Beyond lifestyle choices, there are a number of systemic variables that encourage poor health. The U.S. health care system is characterized by an insurance infrastructure that creates perverse incentives by emphasizing curative instead of preventative medicine and by too much demand relative to supply. These attributes are substantially interlinked, whereby health care providers, by training, focus on treating versus preventing disease. Insurers have little incentive to invest in preventive practices today that will only benefit other insurers tomorrow.[31]

Under the traditional U.S. health care scheme, doctors are paid according to how much care they provide. The more drugs they prescribe and the more surgeries they perform, the higher their paychecks. Insured patients pay only a small fraction of the cost of treatment and so have little reason to question their physician's diagnosis. Many believe this has resulted in chronic overtreatment of patients. An estimated 30,000 Americans are killed each year by unnecessary procedures and overtreatment—that's the equivalent of a 747 airliner crashing and killing everyone aboard once a week.[32] An additional 90,000 to 400,000 patients are estimated to be harmed or killed by the incorrect use of a drug (resulting from either incorrect prescription, dosage, or multiple prescriptions).[33] Some critics estimate that Americans spend between $500 billion and $700 billion dollars annually on care that does little if anything to improve our health; that is roughly 5 percent of GDP.[34] Exacerbating the overtreatment crisis, Americans' medical histories are kept largely in hard copy format. Electronic medical records (EMRs) are used by less than a quarter of primary care physicians,[35] despite the fact that centralized EMRs could help emergency care facilities and other physicians better treat patients and not prescribe unneeded or potentially harmful treatments, thereby saving billions of dollars (not to mention potentially saving lives).

Beyond the perverse incentive structure for doctors, patients, and insurers, a shortage of doctors and nurses (see box 2) pushes up prices of care in the United States, which also makes patients less willing to seek out early treatment. The average cost per day in a U.S. hospital is four times the average in the rest of the developed world.[36] This results in major imbalances: While 16 percent of our economy is dedicated to health services, we still live in a country where 47 million people lack any health insurance and millions more have inadequate coverage. The U.S. Census Bureau reports that 15.6 percent of Americans have no insurance, meaning all health costs are out-of-pocket.[37] Uninsured patients will often use emergency rooms for nonemergency care, because emergency rooms are mandated to accept patients regardless of ability to pay for services, overcrowding these critical facilities. Worse yet, uninsured Americans may wait until a condition has deteriorated to the point where emergency care is actually required.

Even for insured Americans, the picture is not much rosier. Because health insurance in the United States is considered largely a responsibility of employers, some employers looking to cut costs and reduce overconsumption are switching to "consumer driven health care," that is, health savings accounts (HSAs) and high-deductible health plans (HDHPs). HDHPs and HSAs are paired to help avoid the moral hazard of health care overconsumption associated with the traditional U.S. insurance scheme. But consumer driven health plans actually tend to reinforce the curative bias. An HDHP is an inexpensive health insurance plan that usually won't pay for the first several thousand dollars of health care expenses but will generally cover you after that. Because HDHPs are less expensive than traditional health plans, the savings can be deposited in an untaxed HSA to save for future health care costs. But what we find is that when patients are responsible for paying for routine care—even when small amounts of money are involved—they do not seek care at all. Forgoing basic annual physicals can allow medical conditions to go unnoticed and untreated until they become much bigger problems. For example, one study showed that even a $10 copay (the amount a patient is responsible for covering) caused a significant reduction in the use of mammograms, despite the fact that paying for a mammogram now is immeasurably cheaper than treating cancer down the road.[38] Another study found that targeted prevention used to control hypertension among seniors could save Medicare $890 billion over 25 years.[39]

Consider by contrast the socialized medical system of the United Kingdom, where the National Health Service (NHS) provides most medical services, although private services are available. Routine care is largely the responsibility of general practitioners, who are typically private doctors that contract with the NHS; they are paid by the NHS according to work they do and their performance. Patients pay a fixed fee for each drug prescribed regardless of the amount of drug pre-scribed or the cost to the pharmacy; the cost of drugs is charged to the NHS. General practitioners can refer their patients for more spe-cialized treatment. While the U.K. system has its detractors who claim the system discourages hospital purchase of specialized equipment and increases wait times for critical care, overall satisfaction rates are high. Because routine and preventative care is largely free of cost, the United Kingdom also avoids some of the problems of cost-conscious citizens failing to seek preventative care.

In the United States, a transition to a U.K.-style socialized medi-cine system is not only contentious but unlikely. Yet redefining the public sector's contribution to health care is necessary to fix what ails American health care. The public sector could increase immunization and screening programs and introduce more convenient care clinics that grant access to nurse practitioners and other medical professionals for quick advice and other prevention measures.

Medical Tourism

The cost of treatment is getting so out of hand that Americans are realizing that they can go abroad, even to developing countries, to get treatment for less money. Indeed, there has been a growing response by the approximately 85 million uninsured or underinsured Americans to the rising costs of care here in the United States.[40] They're going on vacation.

For about $10,000, an American citizen can fly round-trip to India, receive a heart valve replacement procedure at a hospital with U.S. board-certified doctors, and enjoy an organized vacation package.[41] While $10,000 is still a sizable amount of money, it is roughly 5 percent of the cost for the same procedure in the United States. In 2006, 150,000 U.S. citizens traveled abroad to destinations such as Argentina, Mexico, Costa Rica, Thailand, Singapore, and India for everything from LASIK eye repair to neurosurgery. Thailand boasts an official number of 600,000 medical tourists per year from all over the world.[42]

Medical outsourcing can, however, be misconstrued. Here in the United States, outsourcing as it is portrayed in the media has become synonymous with American job loss and attacks on U.S. industry. But if the average American cannot afford something as basic as health care in his or her own country, then there might be something wrong with the system. The fact that the medical tourism industry as a whole, which was valued to be worth $20 billion in 2006 (and is expected to double in value by 2010) indicates the global system is working better than the national one.[43] Americans, Canadians, Brits, and other nationalities are realizing the value of tapping into the resources available for medical care abroad.

American universities are also getting involved. Medical schools and teaching hospitals affiliated with them appear to be head-to-head in a new race to franchise themselves globally. What might have originally started as school partnerships has morphed into something completely different. For example, in Bangalore, health care facilities fall under recognizable (and well-reputed) brands such as Johns Hopkins, Tufts, and Harvard Universities. It appears, however, that the universities are not necessarily going into emerging market countries to partner with hospitals strictly to make money. As the costs of surgeries are so much lower than in developed countries, this seems to have some validity for the time being. Instead, they, like the hundreds of thousands of medical tourists each year, have recognized a growing trend, namely, "that health care is moving toward an international platform, where it will be of the same high quality no matter which region of the world one is in. In this new high stakes global playing field, brands like Harvard don't want to be left behind."[44]

International Health Infrastructure

In addition to reforming our national health system, we must also safeguard against the Macro Quantum cross-border health risks that come with increased international exchange. Like other multilateral efforts, coordinating and managing such risks will require institutional reform. In 1942, the Office of Malaria Control in War Areas, a division of the U.S. Public Health Service, realized that it needed to try to combat not only malaria but also other diseases, such as typhus, that were being found in the southeastern United States and in tropical regions outside of the country where U.S. troops were fighting.[45] It only took a few years for the nascent organization to realize that more people and resources were needed to protect the American population from such diseases. International health became part of the national agenda for the first time in U.S. history, and in 1946, the Center for Disease Control (CDC—now the Centers for Disease Control and Prevention) was born. Americans were not the only ones who realized that a new kind of effort was needed to control illnesses and promote health. During the same time period, the foundation for the birth of the World Health Organization was being laid. On April 7, 1948, the World Health Organization (WHO) constitution came into force.[46] While a tally sheet of successes and failures might cloud the reputation of the WHO, today we are realizing the same problem as the diplomats of the postwar era: The current infrastructure in place to address matters of global health is insufficient.

Although the WHO has been with us for more than 60 years, it did not truly begin to wield influence until 20 years after its establishment. Health entered onto the international stage as a global issue in the mid-1970s. It was around this time when the WHO, at the height of its influence, began the ambitious program, "Health for All by the Year 2000." The program originally focused on the principles of equity, community participation, and intersectoral collaboration. It was decided at the World Health Assembly in 1977 that the main goal of the WHO and of governments the world over should be "the attainment by all the citizens of the world by the year 2000 of a level of health that will enable them to lead a socially and economically productive life."[47]

Despite the establishment of a global vision for health, the WHO's effectiveness has been steadily declining since the 1970s. A combination of a flawed funding structure, political divides, and competition with private foundations has crippled the organization, leaving many to wonder if it is worth preserving.[48] On one hand, we should be thankful that the WHO cemented health as a global issue. On the other, it may be time to turn to new international networks focusing on addressing the issue in different ways. Several nongovernmental (NGOs) have proven more effective in part due to better funding and more focused agendas. For example, compare the resources and scope of the Bill and Melinda Gates Foundation with those of the WHO; the Gates Foundation has nearly double the WHO's annual budget ($3.05 billion as opposed to $1.66 billion) for a much more limited agenda.

The Gates Foundation is not alone. The international community has enacted a series of piecemeal solutions addressing the traditional problems of health, including UN legislation; the Gleneagles G8 commitments in 2005; the establishment of the global fund to fight AIDS, TB, and Malaria in 2006/2007; the first Advance Market Commitment for new vaccines in 2007; and the World Economic Forum's global plan to stop tuberculosis in 2006. On a limited budget, the WHO has a broad mission. Its efforts range from tobacco education to immunization finance. The WHO would have more success if it refocused attention to monitoring efforts; this would make it a powerful force in handling cross-border pandemics.

Pandemics are low-probability, high-risk events. Consider something as simple as the flu: You can find the advertisements on the subways of New York City in Spanish and in English. You can hear it as a mantra in hospitals and doctors' offices throughout the United States, especially if you are a senior citizen or parent of a small child. "Did you get your flu shot this year?" Some of us simply shrug our shoulders and decide to rely on Theraflu and other over-the-counter remedies should we fall ill. After all, why all the fuss over such a simple virus that annually comes and goes like clockwork? We need to be convinced that waiting in the queues at the local medical center is worth our time.

Maybe we think this way because we have never heard of the 1918 outbreak of Spanish influenza, which caused between 20 and 40 percent of the global population to fall ill and killed 50 million people, mostly between the ages of 20 and 50.[49] Or maybe it is because we think that the avian influenza, which is 100 percent lethal in chickens, doesn't affect human beings. Having seemingly forgotten that we came through three flu pandemics in the last century alone, the world may be due for another one.

Scientists and other health care professionals have been looking to avian flu as the next potential threat for a number of reasons. Statistically and historically speaking, there is a relatively high likelihood of the flu being transmitted from migratory birds to poultry and then on to humans. As different countries, particularly those in Asia, become wealthier, the consumption of chicken has been noticeably increasing.[50] As the flu virus mutates each year when it's transmitted from one bird to another, the question arises, what if the mutation of the virus turns it into a strain that affects humans? Unfortunately, most scientists think this question should be phrased in terms of "when" instead of "if." To date, avian flu has killed less than 100 people, so the virus is starting to make the leap from birds to human beings.

The stakes are large: extrapolating the effects of an influenza outbreak like the one of 1918 on today's population, about 1.7 million people might be expected to die from the virus in the United States alone. Pushing out to the rest of the world, the total number of fatalities would probably reach an unfathomable 360 million, 20 percent greater than the entire U.S. population. HIV/AIDS has caused between 25 and 28 million deaths since its discovery until today.[51] It is not, however, only avian flu that has people scared. Some label it as one out of five potential global pandemics, the others being Super-TB, Super-Staph, Super-Malaria, and HIV.[52]

We have failed to realize that, in our world, bad health—whether a result of pandemics or poor lifestyle choices—greatly hinders economic development and prosperity. The WHO, serving as an international oversight body, could be responsible for insuring that governments accurately handle and report contagious disease threats to prevent the spread across borders.

Counterfeit Drugs

While the miracle of modern science has created pharmaceuticals to combat virtually all known diseases, there is currently a lack of leadership in providing access to pharmaceutical drugs to those persons needing them most. One of the biggest obstacles that must be addressed is how to handle intellectual property rights (IPR), because there is a conflict in the international regulation of IPR between the incentives to develop health technologies.[53]

In late October 2007, the U.S.-Central America Free Trade Agreement, CAFTA-DR was passed. One of the most controversial aspects of the vote centered around pharmaceutical drugs coming into Costa Rica from the United States and associated IPR regulations. More specifically, Costa Ricans would be prohibited from using or developing generic versions of the drug until U.S. patents expired. Hence, the free trade agreement would exclude many Costa Ricans from access to needed medicines, and potentially jeopardize the stability of the state-provided health care system. This is one example of how health issues in general, and pharmaceuticals in particular, have come to be integrated into international arenas such as trade. An even greater danger, however, exists. The problem of fake pharmaceuticals penetrating global markets puts the lives of people at risk every day.

Imagine being hospitalized in China and needing an intravenous drip in order to survive. What would you do if you knew that there was nearly a 20 percent chance of being given a drip that contained absolutely no active ingredient?[54] Or what if you were one of the approximately 400 million people living in Asia or Africa who became infected with malaria this year? When you go to purchase an over-the-counter, antimalarial antibiotic, the odds are good that you'll get a counterfeit version. More than 50 percent of these bogus drugs contain either no active ingredient, an older, ineffective version of the antibiotic, or simply a fever reducer that will temporarily help you to feel better.[55]

The black market industry of phony pharmaceutical drugs is expanding and unregulated. While individual country governments, such as China, have made efforts to curb the industry, the counterfeit drugs have an estimated value of $32 billion in annual sales.[56] In fact, it is thought that 50 percent of all pharmaceutical drugs sold in Asia are counterfeit, with the two largest producer countries being China and India. Producers have become increasingly sophisticated in their techniques, making it very difficult to tell the difference between the real drugs and the fake ones. The potential damage that can be caused by these fake drugs is frightening.

One of the problems with the fake drugs is their contribution to super-strains of diseases that are resistant to antibiotic treatment. When a phony drug contains a small amount of a needed medication, it allows the disease to develop a resistance to the real drug. Such strains of superbugs that exist today include cholera, salmonella, tuberculosis, and malaria, just to name a few.

Another aspect of the fake drug industry is criminality and associated deaths. Returning to the example of malaria, approximately 1.5 million people (90 percent of them being children) died from the disease in 2005.[57] While we may never know how many of these people received fake drugs, it goes without question that at least some of them did. Similarly, at least four infants in China died in 2008 and tens of thousands of others were sickened because the baby formula given to them was laced with the industrial chemical melamime. (http://www.time.com/time/world/article/0,8599,1844750,00.html) The producers of the phony, antimalarials and baby formula should be held accountable for contributing to the deaths.

Individual countries have been unable to control the growth of trade in false pharmaceuticals, and the penalties for being caught producing them have been kept minimal. Not only do the ramifications for participating in this industry need to be made more severe, but the international community also needs to come together to protect people from this threat to public safety and global health.

Health and Its Interlinkages

In the Macro Quantum world, health is linked to virtually every other policy area, including trade, security, immigration, and environment. With more trade comes the likelihood of greater health risks related to goods that cross borders. In March of 2007, more than 100 brands of pet food were recalled when they were found to contain wheat gluten imported from China that contained a chemical known as melamine. In the summer of 2007, toothpaste containing diethylene glycol, a toxic chemical used in engine coolants, was found in exports from China to Panama, the Dominican Republic, Canada, and Australia.[58] The scares have continued as toys containing hazardous levels of lead were also recalled in developed countries. Fortunately, in countries such as the United States, which enjoy organizations such as the Food and Drug Administration (FDA), a large number of these products have been found, recalled, and sent back to China. Nonetheless, the fact that these products have even made it to the shelves of importing countries points to a blatant gap in international trade. Despite international regulations it appears that there is nobody doing the regulating.

China is not the only country at fault. A growing pattern has been emerging. According to the WHO, "there are a number of trade-offs inherent in the globalization process that need to be resolved, taking full account of their health dimensions."[59] This includes, for example, the trade-off between food and safety regulations in developed countries and the export prospects of low-income countries. Consider China, where, in order to compete globally, regulations regarding the production of exported items are much more stringent than those for products destined for its domestic market. In light of the number of tainted products that have emerged even within the past year from China, this is cause for concern for both export markets and for the health of the Chinese population itself. Similarly, the developed world has been accused of pushing more dangerous industries into the laps of developing nations. Rich nations seem comfortable outsourcing hazardous industries to lower income countries, notably to export processing zones (EPZs).[60] While supranational organizations may give the appearance of playing a supervisory role in protecting the rights of workers in these countries, laissez-faire policies have a tendency to rule the day, putting the health and even the lives of many workers at risk.

Health has turned into a security issue deeply embedded in the foreign policies of many countries to address varied threats including everything from SARS and avian influenza to bioterrorism. As a result, health has become a foreign policy and security issue.[61] The subsequent dedication of large portions of foreign policy budgets to health-related fields has also had an impact in expanding the public's view on health. But what exactly are the threats that foreign policies are seeking to address?

As an example, look at SARS to see how a nationalized health problem can go global in a small amount of time. SARS, like the avian flu, is a disease that jumped across species to affect human beings. Initially, the disease was localized in civet cats, found throughout China. As the animals are also a Chinese delicacy, they were being consumed by patrons of restaurants throughout the country. There was a delay in recognizing what the source of the virus was. Hence, the civet cats continued to be served until the Chinese government intervened. By this time, however, an infected doctor who had been treating SARS patients had flown to Hong Kong, not realizing his condition. Hence, while the government was able to stabilize the situation on one end, the ability of a single individual to board a plane and land in another country unchecked allowed the virus to begin its global spread.[62] As the doctor checked into a hotel, other guests who would later return to their home countries (including Singapore, Malaysia, Canada, the Philippines, Vietnam, and Thailand) were also infected. At this point, the WHO stepped in and identified the disease (which Chinese authorities had previously described as a strange strain of pneumonia), but was unable to do much besides administer a warning to travelers. While it is true that the disease has been eradicated from the affected countries after an extensive quarantine, SARS illustrated the vulnerability of the world's population to natural and man-made biological diseases.

In thinking about man-made diseases, we must also consider the role of bioterrorism in today's world. According to prominent global health experts John Wyn Owen and Olivia Roberts, "since the events of [September 11] the health and development agenda has also been widely linked with the foreign policy priorities of improving global security and preventing state failure. Bioterrorism has formed a prominent part of the health and security agenda."[63] Modeling technology that can simulate what would happen to human beings if they were subject to such an attack is readily available. While access to such technology is allegedly restricted by the United States, the likelihood of it being secured is minimal. If the software were to fall into the wrong hands, then new forms of bioterrorism could be developed virtually undetected.

Biological weapons could cause equal amounts of damage with a much lower cost than nuclear weapons. Additionally, pathogens (disease-based organisms) can go virtually undetected, which means that preparing for such an attack is quite difficult. If a terrorist were to use certain strains of diseases, it would be nearly impossible to provide the necessary health care to infected individuals, unless stockpiles of vaccines or antibiotics existed. Many types of pathogens labeled by the CDC as potentially dangerous for bioterrorism are resistant strains of diseases that can't be cured. Additionally, highly communicable diseases put any population at risk, even if there are vaccines (such as in the case of smallpox). Additionally, bioterrorism can cause widespread panic and fear when it might not be necessary. The anthrax scare is undoubtedly within the memory of many readers of this book. While some of the fear was surely justified, the degree of panic that resulted was disproportionate to the degree of the actual number of infected letters.

Ultimately, how big is the threat? While the answer to this question might only ever be known fully to those working in the intelligence community, it is important that the world not be caught off guard should an act of bioterrorism occur. This means having plans in place to help at-risk populations, including stockpiling of vaccines for the pathogens most likely to be used in such an attack. The importance of information sharing and global coordination also needs to be highlighted.

The impoverished of today's world are disproportionately affected by diseases, many of which have already been eradicated in the developed world. HIV/AIDS, tuberculosis, malaria, and communicable diseases, which account for a total around six million deaths per year, are directly linked to poverty, gender inequality, government-driven development policy, and mismanaged health care reforms throughout the world.[64] An estimated 10 million children under the age of five die each year from these causes, almost exclusively in low-income countries or in poor sectors of middle-income countries.

Part of the problem is resource allocation. For example, about $125 billion are spent each year on health research, yet only 10 percent of the funding is dedicated to eradicating health problems in the developing world, which has about 90 percent of the world's population.[65] One reason for this is the current structure of the global health system.

Socialized medicine is not an ubiquitous reality. As a result, the ability to pay often overshadows those who need medical attention the most. Indeed, there is a pressing "need to prioritize research in line with health needs rather than ability to pay, and the affordability of medical technologies to low-income populations and developing countries."[66]

As we've seen, the limited economic opportunities in countries afflicted by poverty and poor health also cause immigration. A freer flow of people means greater exposure to, and faster transmission of, diseases, but also a greater possibility for developed countries with medical expertise to help countries in need more quickly than ever before.

For example, consider the case of Zimbabwe and the HIV/AIDS epidemic. Food shortages, impoverishment, forced removals, and drought have compelled many hundreds of thousands of Zimbabweans to migrate in search of livelihood opportunities.[67] Despite the fact that Zimbabwe is virtually the only country in sub-Saharan Africa to stabilize and decrease its HIV/AIDS rate, it is still one of the highest in the world, at about 20 percent of its population. As migrants leave for other countries, the likelihood of the disease spreading across borders increases.

And in countries where livelihoods can be had, the process of development itself is creating health challenges. Modern industrial processes continue to cause pollution, which has a high correlation with increased incidences of asthma, lung cancer, and other respiratory and cardiovascular diseases.[68] A large portion of today's health problems are the result of human activities. Urban development with poor regulations can result in a combination of poor infrastructure and sanitation locally but also affect the global community. Big polluters, such as China and the United States, are having such a large effect on the environment that their pollution can pose a health hazard to citizens of neighboring countries, as well.

The Prescriptions: More than a Band-Aid

If our world is going to be able to address health in the future, it becomes necessary to rework our health care system, as well as define new global leadership roles for the WHO, the World Bank, NGOs, MNCs, and national governments. We recognize fixing the health care system is not a simple process. Consider the 1,000-plus page act proffered the 1993 Task Force on National Health Care Reform, headed by then-First Lady Hillary Rodham Clinton. The report was mocked for being protracted even by congressional standards, but frankly it would have been difficult to navigate the United States' current system of HMOs, Medicare, private insurance, and health savings accounts in fewer pages. But even a quick overview can shed some light as to the general direction policy needs to move.

As a PricewaterhouseCoopers report notes, "globally, health care is threatened by a confluence of powerful trends—increasing demand, rising costs, uneven quality, misaligned incentives. If ignored, they will overwhelm health systems, creating massive financial burdens for individual countries and devastating health problems for the individuals who live in them."[69] In terms of health care reform, patients, insurers, hospitals, and physicians must collaborate to provide better preventative care and education. One critical reform is in the area of medical education and licensing. More grants to increase the supply of doctors and nurses, as well as the creation of more flexible roles so that nurse practitioners and physician's assistants can take on some of the roles currently reserved for doctors, can help to relieve the supply constraint.

While the United States' system may be the most expensive, other countries have problems as well. Countries such as Brazil, China, Russia, and India currently lose more than 20 million productive life-years annually to chronic disease, much of which is avoidable.[70] In 2002, the cumulative health spending of 24 OECD countries was $2.7 trillion; PricewaterhouseCoopers estimates that health spending for OECD countries will more than triple to $10 trillion by 2020. And completely socializing medicine (or making it tax-funded) is probably not the best solution. More than 75 percent of hospital administrators and other medical sector executives in 27 different countries surveyed believe that financial responsibility should be shared between taxpayers and patients. Even in systems where health care is largely socialized, such as in Europe and Canada, only 20 percent of respondents favored socialized care, while the vast majority preferred a system of taxpayer funding and cost sharing by patients.[71]

In the realm of cross-border disease management, the WHO could step up as the premier multilateral body. Today, the WHO's budget is only $1.66 billion annually (versus the United States' CDC and affiliates 2009 budget request of $8.8 billion[72]); this figure could be easily doubled, with the added financial burden divided between member countries. But not only does the WHO need increased funding it also requires internal reform in order to be useful. It might be time for the WHO to redirect its financial resources to actions such as distributing money for medications to more effective groups. Instead of trying to compete with private foundations on this front, a new role might be better. The rising instances of fake pharmaceuticals and inconsistent regulations on exported products show that there is a clear need for a global regulatory agency and watchdog. This is one way in which the WHO could stay relevant in tomorrow's world. During the SARS crisis, one of the WHO's strong suits was getting information out to the global community about the outbreak, even when China was hesitant to name the disease. WHO as a global communicator and regulator would help to fill an ever-widening gap in the arena of global health. For example, by acting as a global Food and Drug Adminstration, the WHO could administer standards for exported goods to avoid tainted products. It could also sponsor legislation that addresses the needs of internally displaced persons that often prevents the administration of pharmaceutical drugs to those in need.

Other organizations such as the World Bank, NGOs, and private foundations, could help fill a funding and service gap. The World Bank, along with many private foundations, has been successful in raising funds earmarked specifically for combating global health matters. Turning to them as the potential health financiers of the future allows them to focus their energies where they are most effective. A large part of the success of these organizations (and a large part of the failure of the WHO) has been their ability to function as individual organizations with specific projects. A consolidation would risk exchanging efficiency for bureaucracy. In identifying new projects, the different organizations could also look to an expanded G20, as the G7 has been successful in recent years at setting course for new global health objectives.

Health care systems worldwide face many of the same challenges. If we shift our thinking to see health as an essential competitive resource, the focus on preventative care and chronic illness at the national level will naturally follow, relieving the burden U.S. companies and individuals must bear compared to countries with socialized medicine systems. On the multilateral front, greater information sharing and management of cross-border disease and tainted or counterfeit goods is needed. By proposing a revitalized WHO as well as domestic initiatives that shift the burden of health care away from companies and increases the supply of medical professionals, the United States could recapture its role as a leader in global health. Without such changes, however, one can see how the United States' failure to promote tomorrow's health will hurt the nation's chances in the increasingly competitive global economy.

Where Are All the Doctors?

In her book *Overtreated*, Susan Brownlee notes the number of doctors per capita is lower in the United States than the median number in the rest of the developed world, but our doctors have much higher incomes. The root of high prices is a simple question of supply and demand. As the population ages and fewer people seek out preventative care before conditions become dire, demand for medical services has skyrocketed.

Now the supplies of qualified nurses and doctors are coming up short. This started when several national advisory groups, including the Institute of Medicine and the Council on Graduate Medical Education, issued reports forecasting a surplus of physicians.* To prevent creating a glut of doctors, medical schools voluntarily held enrollment relatively constant at about 16,000 new students a year. From 1980 to 2005, enrollment was flat. At the same time, the U.S. population grew by more than 70 million, according to the Association of American Medical Colleges (AAMC). Although schools have

---

*Robert Davis, "Shortage of surgeons pinches U.S. hospitals," *USA Today*, February 26, 2008, www.usatoday.com/news/health/2008-02-26-doctor-shortage_N.htm.

(*Continued*)

(*Continued*)

since lifted the cap, it takes three to seven years to train doctors. Not to mention the fact that new generations of doctors are shying away from less lucrative but critical practice areas such as general surgery and family practice medicine, instead choosing specialty areas that pay better. Rural areas are especially hard hit by the lack of doctors.

Can you really blame doctors? Students attending Harvard Medical School will be expected to foot a bill of $60,800 for the first year alone.* Multiplied by four, a physician will graduate with more than $240,000 of debt just from graduate school (never mind what kind of debt they may have lingering from their undergraduate days). No wonder they are demanding such high salaries. While medical schools do receive hefty government subsidies, tuition and fees remain much higher in the United States as opposed to other developed countries where educational fees are often covered in their entirety by the state.

It seems that the simple solution would be to open new medical schools or expand existing ones with federal money. But opening a new school eligible for government funding in the United States requires accreditation by the Liaison Committee on Medical Education (LCME), a group sponsored by the Association of American Medical Colleges and the American Medical Association. Twelve out of the 17 LCME members come from one of these two organizations. The comparable organization in the United Kingdom, the General Medical Council, has only two of its 35 members that come from similar interest groups, while 14 of its members come from the National Health Service—presumably representing public interest. The AAMC and AMA represent doctors and medical educators who are not necessarily motivated by what is best for the American public. In any event, the resulting.

---

*Harvard Medical School, "Costs," http://hms.harvard.edu/admissions/default.asp?page=costs.

medical industry monopoly over determining the supply of doctors clearly has impacted the marketplace for medicine

Moreover, consider the plethora of special U.S. licensing laws that have limited the supply of health care providers, thereby limiting competition and raising doctors' incomes. One study estimates the cost of health care regulation such as licensing ranges from $256 billion to $339.2 billion per year.[*] Almost 80 percent of adult primary care and 90 percent of child care services could be safely provided by nurse practitioners.[†]

Problematically, the United States is also in dire short supply of registered nurses (RNs). As the demand for RNs is expected to grow by 2 percent to 3 percent each year, the unmet demand for RNs could reach as high as 500,000 by 2025, according to a March 2008 report. Though a report from the American Association of Colleges of Nursing (AACN) showed a 5.4 percent enrollment increase in entry-level baccalaureate programs in nursing in 2007 over the previous year, this increase is not sufficient to meet the projected demand for nurses. According to the Health Resources and Services Administration (HRSA), "to meet the projected growth in demand for RN services, the U.S. must graduate approximately 90 percent more nurses from U.S. nursing programs." But there is also a shortage of faculty. The AACN states that U.S. nursing schools turned away 40,285 qualified applicants from baccalaureate and graduate nursing programs in 2007 due to an insufficient number of faculty, clinical sites, classroom space, clinical preceptors, and budget constraints. Also, more than 75 percent

---

[*]Christopher J. Conover, "Health Care Regulation: A $169 Billion Hidden Tax," Policy Analysis no. 527, October 4, 2004, www.cato.org/pub_display.php?pub_id=2466.
[†]Richard Leviton, The Medical Monopoly: Your Tax Dollars Limit the Competition, www.forhealthfreedom.org/Publications/Monopoly/TaxDollars.html.

(Continued)

(*Continued*)

of RNs believe the nursing shortage presents a major problem for the quality of their work life, the quality of patient care, and the amount of time nurses can spend with patients.* Survey results suggest this leads to greater nurse turnover—which is financially devastating to hospitals. Hospitals that perform poorly in nurse retention spend, on average, $3.6 million more than those with high retention rates.[†]

One PricewaterhouseCoopers' Health Research Institute report advanced several strategies for addressing the doctor and nurse shortages including developing more public-private partnerships, using technology as a training tool, and designing more flexible roles for advanced practice nurses given their increased use as primary care providers. Public-private partnerships would be a combination of hospitals, medical and nursing colleges, and government policy makers working together to find and increase the capacity of medical education institutes. Flexible roles means allowing physician's assistants and nurse-practitioners to play larger roles that are traditionally assumed by doctors, although this is currently prohibited by licensing practices. Greater funding for nursing schools will be key. Whereas less than 5 percent of medical school revenues come from tuition and fees thanks to government subsidies, the government is not nearly as generous with RNs.[‡] Moving away from the volume-based pay scale and turning instead to performance-based pay will help to lessen the burden by discouraging overtreatment and encouraging more effective treatment.

---

*"Nursing Shortage," American Association of Colleges of Nursing, April 2008, www.aacn.nche.edu/Media/FactSheets/.
[†]"What Works: Healing the Healthcare Staffing Shortage," PricewaterhouseCoopers, June 2007, www.pwc.com/extweb/pwcpublications.nsf/docid/674d1e79a678a0428525730d006b74a9.
[‡]Sue Blevins, "The Medical Monopoly: Protecting Consumers or Limiting Competition?" Cato Policy Analysis no. 246, Dec 15, 1995, www.cato.org/pubs/pas/pa-246.html.

Another means of cutting health care costs is tort reform. Patients can be awarded large settlements for personal injuries due to medical malpractice under current tort laws. The high costs of medical malpractice insurance and compensation awards are passed on to health care consumers. One suggestion is to cap the awards of damages.

The bottom line is that the supply-demand equation of medical care providers in the United States is simply off-kilter. However, with some modest public policy shifts, price pressure might subside, which will hopefully boost not only our nation's economic competitiveness, but our health as well.

Chapter 7

Environment

The Hidden Cost of Everything

Over the long haul of life on this planet, it is the ecologists, and not the bookkeepers of business, who are the ultimate accountants.

—STEWART UDALL

W hether or not you want to believe the inconvenient truth about global warming, environmental stewardship in the Macro Quantum world has become increasingly relevant to everyone —from the subsistence farmer in Malawi to the hybrid car driver in Seattle. By 2008, even erstwhile George W. Bush had changed his tune, announcing that his administration was working "toward a climate agreement that includes the meaningful participation of every major economy—and gives none a free ride."[1]

Unfortunately, the public discourse on the environment has focused almost exclusively on climate change to the detriment of other more pressing yet manageable environmental policy challenges, including water management and the establishment of balanced energy, agricultural, forestry, and fishing guidelines. This is not to say that we should forget global warming, but more to say that there are many other pressing, immediate ecological questions raised by the rapid industrialization and globalization of the past decades that deserve serious attention.

The past 50 years have brought profound changes in human global production and consumption profiles. Increased economic activity and population growth, coupled with greater prosperity and heightened demands for commodities and energy, are degrading ecosystems and creating shortages of potable water, clean air, healthy food, and fertile soil. And, unlike the effects of global warming, the negative effects of shortages are happening in the present and require our full attention today.

When the UN's Brundtland Commission first coined the term "sustainable development" in 1983, it identified poverty as one of the most important causes of environmental degradation. It argued that greater economic growth, fueled in part by increased international trade, could generate the necessary resources to combat what had become known as the "pollution of poverty": poor water quality, inadequate housing and sanitation, malnutrition, and disease.[2] While deprivation remains a problem in many pockets of our planet, burgeoning prosperity and growing consumption provide their own set of environmental trials. The average rates at which people consume oil and metals and produce waste like plastics and greenhouse gases, are 32 times higher in North America, Western Europe, Japan, and Australia than they are in the developing world.[3] Developing countries and the rich world alike are eating more (see Table 7.1) and using more energy (Table 7.2) than ever before.

And that's not all we are using more of: According to the Millennium Ecosystem Assessment, water withdrawals from rivers and lakes have doubled since 1960.[4] Increased agricultural use of chemical fertilizers has caused nitrogen emissions also to double since 1960, while phosphorous emissions tripled in the same period. Countless acres of forest have been cleared to feed growing appetites, while fuelwood used for energy has become scarce in many parts of the world. In turn, the ecosystems on which we have come to depend have sustained irreparable damage: 20 percent of the earth's coral reefs have been lost, and an additional 20 percent have sustained damage.[5] Approximately 35 percent of mangroves (the plants that form the basis of many subtropical intertidal ecosystems) have disappeared in the last two decades.[6]

Table 7.1 Per Capita Consumption of Calories, Cereals, and Meat in 1961 and 2003

	Category	Unit	1961	2003
Developed Countries	Cereals	kg/capita/year	148.26	131.19
	Meats	kg/capita/year	52.43	80.29
	Fish	kg/capita/year	10.77	23.95
	Calories	cal/capita/day	2949.6	3331.11
Developing Countries	Cereals	kg/capita/year	129.1	156.4
	Meats	kg/capita/year	9.19	28.91
	Fish	kg/capita/year	5.3	13.94
	Calories	cal/capita/day	1927.31	2668.76

SOURCE: FAOSTAT.

Table 7.2 Energy (million kwH) Consumption by Households in the G7 and E7, 1990 and 2005

Countries	1990	Households 2005
U.K.*	99,482	116,811
U.S.	99,482	1,359,227
Canada	130,084	150,986
Japan	184,845	334,061
France*	109,593	149,810
Germany	122,803	141,800
Italy*	104,990	66,960
G7 total	851,279	2,319,655
India	31,983	103,368
Indonesia	8,877	41,184
China	48,080	282,481
Brazil	51,865	83,193
South Korea	17,735	50,874
Mexico	20,389	42,628
Russia*	95,245	108,915
E7 total	274,174	712,643

*U.K., Italy, Russia, France data from 1992.
SOURCE: UN Statistics division.

Contrary to alarmist rhetoric, the disappearing coral reefs and doubling nitrogen levels are not putting humankind on the brink of extinction (any time soon, at least). But these phenomena do significantly detract from quality of life, and in certain prone areas are threatening livelihoods. Environmental degradation is responsible when a fisherman from Louisiana must travel further and work longer hours to get a decent catch; it is responsible when a Bangladeshi farmer must sit out a storm, hoping his roof will stand up to the increasingly intense floods that each year brings; and it is responsible when a jogger in Tokyo opts for the indoor track to avoid the dirty air outside.

Prosperity: The Problem or the Solution?

Some first-worlders take solace in the fact that degradation associated with increased wealth tapers off after a *nouveau riche* phase, but this is actually a false comfort. A much-lauded 1995 study by Princeton economists Gene M. Grossman and Alan B. Krueger, found an "inverted U"[7] relationship between income levels and air and water quality. As poor economies begin to grow, they initially experience deteriorating environmental quality, but after a certain point, as wealth increases, environmental quality improves as well.[8] (See Figure 7.1.)

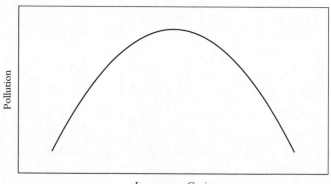

Figure 7.1   Pollution vs. GDP Inverted U

Throughout this book, we've discussed how vast swaths of East Asia, Central Europe and the Middle East are increasing industrial output, amassing wealth, and mimicking Western consumption patterns. This group, which represents a third or more of humanity, is on the upward slope of the curve, where the demand for a better life via economic growth outpaces the demand for clean air. Growing industry after all requires greater resources, and these emerging countries tend to be less efficient users of inputs. According to the Economist Intelligence Unit, China's generators use almost 20 percent more coal to produce one unit of electricity than do generators in developed countries and lose 50 percent more electricity during transmission. Chinese manufacturing companies use 3 to 10 times more water, depending on the product, than those in industrialized nations.[9]

Over the hump and on the other side of the curve, rich nations have acquired the resources and know-how to develop clean technologies, lessening the trade-off between growth and environment. But pollution reduction has less to do with technology and more to do with what the rich world is producing—and what it isn't. In 2007, 78.5 percent of U.S. GDP was tied to the service sector; compare this to a global average of 64 percent, and a mere 40 percent in China. Services are far less polluting than industry and far less resource-intensive than agriculture. The developed world isn't living on services alone; it still needs manufactured goods, but now it imports them (as discussed in Chapter 2) and lets the polluting production processes happen elsewhere.

So while the inverse-U relationship holds true for many pollutants—G7 industry is cleaner than its E7 counterpart—it is not necessarily what the G7 *produces* that pollutes, but more what it *consumes*. Today's economy spreads the impact of consumer choices across national boundaries by stretching the distance between the different phases of the production life cycle—from raw material extraction to processing, use, and disposal. A typical supply chain crosses several borders. To produce a simple consumer product, for example, wood from an Indonesian forest and Malaysian rubber may be exported to the Pearl River Delta, the industrial hub of Hong Kong and its environs, where local air and water pollution is created by the power generation

and factory effluents used to process our goods. These factories, powered by coal extracted from Shaanxi province in northern China, support the global business strategies of major international firms. The
goods they produce are destined for markets in Western Europe and
North America. At the end of the product life cycle, waste may be
exported to India in order to be disposed of.

As the end recipient of these manufactured goods, Americans and
other G7 citizens should shoulder some responsibility for the pollution. Not only is it good karma, but it makes sense. In our Macro
Quantum world, the most immediate impact of environmental degradation on human well-being may occur in poor countries, where
loosely regulated industry is allowed to extract resources and pollute
air and water, but eventually the products of poor stewardship are
shared by neighboring countries, and ultimately by the entire international community. Many countries rely on rivers that cross neighbor's
borders for most of their fresh water, including Botswana, Bulgaria,
Cambodia, the Congo, Gambia, the Sudan and many nations in the
Middle East. From Azerbaijan to Zimbabwe, we all rely on the rain
forests of South America to sequester carbon and provide us with
breathable air. Pollution does not respect man-made boundaries. Even
the best of unilateral efforts cannot make a difference without cross-
border as well as private-public sector coordination. And at the heart
of the debate is a lifestyle change: Americans (and all of the world's
burgeoning middle class) need to consider the hidden cost of what
they consume.

According to the World Values Survey, rich world attitudes shift
over time to favor a pristine environment over growth.[10] Unfortunately,
this attitude change is not always translated into enlightened policy
or lifestyle changes—indeed, the industrialized world's environmental
progress is hampered by retrogressive pricing policies and outmoded
American dreams of suburbs, steaks, and SUVs. Prices signal value to
consumers; and it is important for prices to reflect the increasing scarcity of resources as well as the difficulty in abating pollution. The value
we put on various inputs today does not reflect true costs associated
with the goods. Much of what is produced and consumed creates
what economists would call "negative externalities"— unintended bad
effects on others. When you buy an SUV that produces high emissions,

everyone suffers from reduced air quality. And when U.S. farmers are charged a pittance for water, they have no incentive to skimp on irrigation. As a result, water-intensive crops are planted in hot, dry places; consumers may temporarily benefit through cheaper produce but eventually lose out as fresh water becomes more and more scarce, threatening our health and way of life, and even causing conflict in certain prone areas.

By providing nearly free water to farmers, as well as direct financial support for agriculture, the U.S. government has subsidized cheap food for domestic consumers, creating negative externalities throughout the Macro Quantum world. In terms of health, two-thirds of Americans today are obese or overweight, putting them at elevated risk for coronary disease, type II diabetes, and even certain types of cancer. And as the foodstuffs gobbled up by newly prosperous countries continue to climb (but the United States and the G7 refuse to tighten their belts) this pricing scheme is hardly sustainable. In the first half of 2008, food and agricultural input prices in some parts of the world doubled. The United States has been apt to blame growing middle classes in China and India for rising costs, but Americans continue to eat one and a half times the calories that the average person in India eats.[11] Paying more for rice or corn would be a trifling cost for Americans, but it could mean the difference between 1,000 and 2,000 calories for the 40 percent of the world that lives on less than two dollars a day.

In addition to raising food prices, the United States' and the G7's natural resources binge can impact economic growth in several ways. Oil and other commodities witness similar price pressures; climate change, a product of our fossil fuel dependence, modifies weather patterns and thereby increases costs of damage from extreme weather (storms, hurricanes, typhoons, floods, droughts, and heat waves); soil and water degradation makes agriculture less productive, requiring more chemical fertilizer; air and water pollution raises human health costs. According to the landmark 2007 Stern Review on climate change, overall costs and risks of climate change alone will be equivalent to losing at least 5 percent of global GDP each year; under certain models the estimates of damage could rise to 20 percent of GDP or more.[12] In sum, environmental stress is a key detractor from prosperity, and thus the capitalist peace.

Simply stated, it's in everyone's long-term interest to preserve the environment. Poor management of natural resources disrupts business and threatens tranquility by displacing people in addition to fostering insecurity, poverty, and economic underperformance. By failing to cope with the diffuse global network of consumers and producers and by failing to include the replenishment cost of air, water, land, trees, fish, and other natural resources in the price of what we consume, the Micro Domestic approach to the environment fosters unsustainable development and makes producers and consumers both worse off. To counter the resource depletion and degradation that is occurring around the globe, international environmental cooperation must include the entire worldwide community of consumers and producers, no matter where a business is domiciled.

The fundamental challenge for human institutions in our Macro Quantum world is to create and maintain a sustainable combination of economic, social, and natural environmental conditions in an increasingly commercial and interconnected civilization.[13] The United States has fallen woefully short on this challenge. Americans' attitudes toward the environment are progressive relative to poorer countries, as our inverted-U curve might predict. The most recent World Values Survey showed 59.2 percent of Americans (up from 48.7 in the previous survey) favor environmental protection over economic growth, sandwiching the United States below Canada and most of Europe, but well ahead of low and middle income countries like Mexico, China, and India.[14] Yet the United States' current policy paradigm is stuck in the Micro Domestic phase, emphasizing its own economic interest at the expense of the world's holistic (environmental, physical, and social) well-being in a way that will ultimately make people poorer. The United States' body of environmental policies remains a disorganized incentive structure that favors a cheap, dirty, instant gratification style of production abroad and consumption and an unfortunate "not in my backyard" ethos.

However, our backyard is much bigger than ever before, now encompassing the entire globe. As the world's biggest consumers, Americans should lead the way in overhauling our lifestyle to avoid the real human and economic costs of environmental degradation, and the sooner the better. Such changes, perhaps even government mandated, combined with international cooperation aimed at promoting commerce while managing land and water use, developing green technologies and promoting sustainable agriculture and fishing practices can substantially alleviate the stresses on the global resource pantry and raise the standard of living for millions of people worldwide. Considering recent trends happening to our land, sea (and rivers, lakes, and streams), and air—the need for cooperation becomes all the more apparent.

Land

Land covers less than a third of the Earth's surface, but until we get better at swimming, it is where virtually all of our daily lives unfold. In terms of environmental challenges, forestry and agriculture issues top the land list. Rainforests once covered 14 percent of the earth's land surface; this is down to less than 6 percent today.[15] Rainforest loss is important primarily for two reasons. First, rainforests continuously recycle carbon dioxide into oxygen—more than 20 percent of the world's oxygen is produced in the Amazon rainforest—and without it, we are in trouble.[16] Second, as forests are cut down, we also lose biodiversity. Experts estimate that we lose 137 plant, animal, and insect species every single day due to rainforest deforestation.[17] Since many of our pharmaceuticals today come from plant-based substances, each species lost is a lost medical opportunity.

Agriculture is one of the most fundamental human activities. Today, 13.3 percent of the Earth's land surface is arable and currently 4.7 percent is dedicated to permanent crops. The World Watch Institute estimates more than 80 percent of arable land has been lost because of soil degradation.[18] Although some degradation is inevitable, better agricultural practices can prevent much of this shrinkage. Today, approximately 40 percent of the world's population is involved in agriculture,[19] and with expanding demand for bioenergy, more farmland (and former forest) is being dedicated to fuel plants such as corn, sugar cane, and switch grass. Even in our age of abundance, the reduction in cropland dedicated to food production has led to worries that there is simply not enough food to go around. We must reassess our land use—especially forestry, biofuel, and agriculture practices—to ensure we are getting the most out of this precious resource.

Forests: Growing Money on Trees

The value of world trade in wood forest products alone exceeded $200 billion in 2007.[20] An estimated 60 million people live in the rainforests of Latin America, Southeast Asia, and Africa. An additional 350 million people are directly dependent on forest resources for subsistence or income, and 1.2 billion people in developing countries use trees on farms to generate food and cash.[21] Yet the Earth's overall forest cover continues to steadily decline. Forests are essential for global carbon sequestration and soil retention. They are also a major pillar of local ecosystems, providing shade, shelter, and nourishment for animals, plants, and people. With the loss of forests, scientists fear not only the loss of peoples' livelihoods and biodiversity but also the exacerbation of global warming. While forest losses have stabilized in the G7 over the past 50 years, 50,000 square miles of tropical forest are being cleared every 12 months. That is a size equivalent to Mississippi or more than half of Britain.[22] The burning and clearing of forests contributes more than one-fifth of total global greenhouse gas emissions—more than the emissions of all of the world's cars, trucks, trains, and planes combined.[23] "We are living in a borderless world and what happens to forests and forestry in one country is very much dependent on what happens in other countries, whether it is increasing demand for wood and wood products, logging bans, taxes on exports, changes in exchange rates, invasive species, or a host of other trans-boundary issues," explains Jan Heino of the UN Food and Agriculture Organization (FAO).[24]

Biodiversity has suffered tremendously from the declining forests. More species are under threat than ever before, according to the World Conservation Union. Its "Red List," published in September 2007, warns that 16,306 of 41,415 species are under threat of extinction, nearly 200 more than in 2005 and a steady increase from the first report in 1996.[25] Many of these species provide critical goods and services in their habitats. Of the threatened figure, almost 1,200 species are birds.[26] That means roughly 12 percent of the world's 9,800 bird species may face extinction within the next century.[27] Birds disperse seeds, control insect and rodent populations, and pollinate plants—providing essential services in the food chain.

In addition to deforestation's long-term costs, ecosystem degradation comes with very real immediate human and financial costs. The burning of 10 million hectares of Indonesia's forests in 1997 resulted in additional health care costs of $9.3 billion and affected some 20 million people.[28]

Considering the costs to replant old growth forests as well as the human costs associated with deforestation, you probably paid less for the teak table in your living room than you should have. Legislation imposing the cost of replanting trees on logging companies would eventually pass the true higher price along to the consumer and curb incentives to overconsume.

Biofuels: Are They the Answer?

An increasingly substantial amount of forest is cleared to grow crops such as corn, soy, and sugarcane that can be converted to biofuels (thus reducing our fossil fuel reliance). Agribusiness companies are rapidly expanding fuel crop plantations into the Amazon rainforest and other tropical ecosystems throughout South America, Southeast Asia, the Pacific, and Africa. The expansion of palm oil (a source of biodiesel) farming is the primary cause of deforestation in Indonesia, where forests are disappearing at a rate of more than 2.8 million hectares a year—an area half the size of Belgium.[29] In other parts of the world, logging companies convert forests into sugarcane, corn, and other ethanol imputs.[30] While bioenergy is seen as part of the solution to climate change, sustainable use of bioenergy requires balancing many factors, including competition between food security and energy security, allocation of scarce water resources, effects on poverty and rural development, as well as the impacts on the biodiversity.

A study commissioned by the Swiss government examined 26 biofuels and identified striking differences in the environmental costs of different crops.[31] According to the study, fuels made from U.S. corn, Brazilian soy, and Malaysian palm oil actually may be *worse than fossil fuels* in terms of greenhouse gas emissions per unit of energy created (see Table 7.3). Biofuels from residual products, such as recycled

Table 7.3 How Green Are Biofuels? Use of Resources During Growing, Harvesting, and Refining of Fuel

Crop	Used to Produce	Greenhouse Gas Emissions*	Use of Resources During Growing, Harvesting and Refining of Fuel				% of U.S. Cropland Needed to Meet Half of U.S. Demand	Pros	Cons
			Water	Fertilizer	Pesticide	Energy			
Corn	Ethanol	81–85	High	High	High	High	157%–262%	Technology ready and relatively cheap	Reduces food supply
Sugar cane	Ethanol	4 to 12	High	High	Medium	Medium	46–57	Technology ready	Limited as to where will grow
Switch grass	Ethanol	−24	Medium–Low	Low	Low	Low	60–108	Won't compete with food crops	Technology not ready
Wood residue	Ethanol, biodiesel	N/A	Medium	Low	Low	Low	150–250	Uses timber waste and other debris	Technology not fully ready
Soybeans	Biodiesel	49	High	Medium–Low	Medium	Medium–Low	180–240	Technology ready	Reduced food supply

*Kg of CO_2 created per megajoule of energy produced.
Source: Conservation Biology.

cooking oil and ethanol from grass or wood, fared better. As part of a sustainable agriculture and energy policy, the total environmental impact of these fuels must be considered.

So, the answer to the question—are biofuels good for the environment?—is maybe; it depends on what the fuel comes from and where it is grown. A hectare of cane in Brazil can produce around four tons of ethanol, equivalent to around 5,000 liters of fossil fuel. After taking into account the fossil carbon needed to make the ethanol, approximately 13 tons less of carbon dioxide (CO_2) are released from fossil carbon for every hectare of land converted to sugar cane.[32] Corn, however, is not nearly as efficient.

In addition to biofuels' questionable impact on CO_2 emissions, the UN believes ethanol has contributed 10 to 15 percent of food price inflation, while the International Food Policy Research Institute suggests corn prices have risen 25 to 33 percent because of biofuels.[33] According to the Rainforest Action Network, the corn required to make enough ethanol to fill a 25-gallon SUV tank once could feed one person for a year.[34] Amid rising food prices, isn't there a better use for this land?

Agriculture: No Such Thing as a Free Lunch

In addition to changing our economy, the substantial mass of land dedicated to agriculture has literally changed the face of the planet. Significant land, water, and labor are dedicated to agriculture and food production. Agriculture is responsible for approximately 70 percent of water use worldwide.[35] In some circumstances, diverting land for agricultural use has resulted in substantial habitat loss and habitat fragmentation (dividing a habitat into pieces that are too small to maintain populations of some species), negatively impacting biodiversity.[36] The use of artificial fertilizers and pesticides is altering the chemistry of lakes, rivers, and streams. These pollutants lessen the safety of drinking water, harm fish and wildlife, and lead to the spread of oxygen-depleted "dead zones." Use of nitrogen fertilizer, considered a major cause of these zones, has increased eightfold since 1960.[37]

The use of pesticides also creates human health challenges. For example, in Central America, bananas are grown in huge, monoculture plantations where pesticides are applied directly by workers or through aerial spraying. The chemicals pollute the water supply and have been linked with increased cancer rates in local communities. A U.S. jury awarded $3.3 million to six workers who claimed they were left sterile by a pesticide used at a banana plantation in Nicaragua operated by Dole Fresh Fruit Co., a U.S. multinational corporation.[38]

Beyond questions of land use and pesticides, the age-old (and increasingly relevant today) question that agricultural policy must answer remains: How best to get food to hungry mouths? In his famous 1798 essay, Thomas Malthus predicted that the human population would grow without end, while a finite amount of arable land would prevent the global food supply from growing in stride. Malthus prophesied widespread famine, disease, and war would result. Fortunately, Malthus failed to predict the immense demographic and agricultural changes that were to follow the Industrial Revolution, and his bleak projections were largely avoided thanks to slowing population growth and technological innovation on the farm.

Although Malthus failed to get it right the first time around, his followers resurface whenever food supplies are looking low. In the early 1970s, a sharp jump in global population growth (averaging 2 percent per year) caused food prices to rise dramatically; however, the "green revolution"[39] eventually mitigated this famine scare. Once again, as grain prices skyrocketed in early 2008, neo-Malthusians seemed justified in singing a refrain of "I told you so." According to World Bank data, between January 2000 and March 2008, grain prices had tripled and fertilizer prices had quintupled.[40] In the first four months of 2008 alone, the cost of rice rose 141 percent. The World Bank announced that 33 countries are confronting food crises. In Haiti, protesters chanting "we're hungry" forced the prime minister to resign; 24 people were killed in riots in Cameroon. Food riots have also erupted in Mexico, Morocco, Egypt, Cote d'Ivoire, Guinea, Mauritania, Senegal, Uzbekistan and Yemen, while Vietnam, Cambodia, India, and Egypt have restricted rice exports to drive down domestic prices. Rising food prices have in turn generated high inflation rates, noticeably in Asia. In Vietnam, the year-on-year rate of consumer price inflation reached 19.4 percent in March 2008. Inflation in Pakistan hit 11.3 percent in February; in China, 8.7 percent in February; and in Indonesia, 8.2 percent.[41]

Since the last food scare, population growth slowed to 1.2 percent,[42] which would ostensibly suggest the world's food system should be able to cope with the challenge. But a new twist on the neo-Malthusian argument suggests that changing lifestyles—not an increase in head count but an increase in food consumption per head (shown in Table 7.4)—could lead to the food system's downfall. In all regions outside of Sub-Saharan Africa, food production per capita has increased over the last two decades. Yet, despite overall global increases in the amount of food available per capita, overconsumption and imbalances in the global agricultural and food distribution systems mean that even in this age of abundance, when one billion people are overweight, more than 800 million people remain undernourished.[43]

According to the UN Food and Agricultural Organization, Americans eat an average of 3,770 calories per capita a day compared with an average of 2,440 calories consumed per capita in India.[44] Moreover, the United States is the largest consumer of beef—an extremely inefficient source of calories. (Cutting out the middleman in the grain-cow-man food chain makes the process *54 times* more efficient in terms of calories.[45]) Traditionally, demand for food was thought to behave differently than that for other commodities. Engel's Law states that as income rises, the amount devoted for basic food typically declines. But the West's ever-expanding appetites, and waistlines, seem to be proving Engel wrong. If newly affluent Asian consumers begin to resemble their Western counterparts, indeed, greater trouble could be brewing. (See Table 7.5.)

The causes of the most recent food crisis—higher meat consumption, the dedication of more land for corn and other biofuel crops, and higher prices for agricultural inputs and global speculation—were exacerbated by paltry policy cure-alls in the form of inefficient subsidies and export caps. For example, the United States continues to subsidize domestic ethanol production, a wrongheaded attempt to grow more fuel, which used up a third of 2008's corn crop.[46] Food export bans have proliferated, tightening global food markets. Forty-eight of the 58 countries whose reactions are tracked by the World Bank have imposed price controls, consumer subsidies, export restrictions, or lower tariffs.[47] President of the World Bank Robert Zoellick believes that food inflation could push at least 100 million people into poverty.[48] While the

Table 7.4 Percent of Food Production and Consumption by Country, G7 and E7

Countries	% of World Food Production					% of World Food Consumption				
	1979–1981	1989–1991	1999–2001	2002	2003	1979–1981	1989–1991	1999–2001	2002	2003
G7										
Canada	1.37	1.41	1.62	1.50	1.45	0.64	0.59	0.65	0.65	0.64
France	3.49	3.45	3.73	3.38	2.80	1.62	1.41	1.27	1.26	1.23
Germany	3.38	2.85	2.55	2.45	2.54	2.30	1.89	1.67	1.67	1.62
Italy	1.94	1.41	1.20	1.19	1.08	1.78	1.43	1.25	1.21	1.19
Japan	4.04	3.63	1.92	1.74	1.50	2.80	2.45	2.09	2.03	2.00
United States	10.50	11.10	11.28	9.82	9.74	6.51	6.22	6.35	6.29	6.24
United Kingdom	3.86	2.65	1.85	1.53	1.72	1.56	1.30	1.19	1.17	1.16
E7										
Brazil	3.73	2.96	3.76	3.83	3.87	2.88	2.91	3.04	3.07	3.17
China	7.07	7.60	11.74	12.19	11.99	20.67	21.86	22.40	21.83	21.79
India	3.24	2.67	2.72	2.33	2.64	12.69	14.07	14.51	14.82	14.89
Indonesia	1.08	1.89	2.05	2.23	2.79	2.94	3.38	3.60	3.60	3.59
Korea, Republic of	0.72	0.80	0.82	0.83	0.76	1.01	0.91	0.84	0.83	0.82
Mexico	3.76	2.42	3.31	5.08	4.86	1.86	1.80	1.84	1.87	1.85
Russian Federation	n/a	n/a	1.21	1.27	1.28	n/a	n/a	2.54	2.56	2.52

SOURCE: FAO Statistical Yearbook, 2005–2006.

Table 7.5   2006 Consumption of Selected Goods (kg/person) by Country

	U.S.	Europe	India	China
Wheat	101	252	64	76
Rice	13	5.4	76.5	95.8
Corn	753	122.8	13	107.5
Vegetable oils	38.7	41.8	10.4	17.5
Milk	89	68.4	35	10.4
Beef	41.8	17.5	1.3	5.4
Chicken	44.5	15.3	1.8	7.6

SOURCE: U.S. Department of Agriculture.

rise of short-term commodity prices (including oil and food) has slowed, it already proved to be a devastating blow for the world's poorest, who often spend more than half of their income on food.

In the short run, emergency relief is the only Band-Aid for a food crisis. Despite the spiraling prices, farmers cannot increase output because they are unable to increase production. Short-term aid is not a substitute for long-term solutions, however. In the longer term, greater investment in rural infrastructure, appropriate technology, and easier access to credit for farmers are among the options on the table. Currently, market distortions that keep farmers from benefiting from higher food prices are the fiercest stumbling block in the fight against world hunger. The International Monetary Fund and the World Bank must play leading roles in discussions to improve both industrial and developing country policies, as well as in lending to the agricultural sector in poorer and middle-income countries to encourage and support good policies. And, as Chapter 2 addressed, the Doha rounds of WTO need to hammer out rich-world farm subsidies.

On the consumer front, eating less food—especially less red meat—makes the food chain more efficient. The resources required to produce meat outstrip that for grain or vegetables. One kilogram of bread requires about 1,000 liters of water to produce, while one kilogram of beef requires about 15,000 liters. Livestock production is estimated to be responsible for more climate change gases than all the motor vehicles in the world, accounting for 18 percent of human induced greenhouse gas emissions.[50] But small moves, short of converting to vegetarianism, could help make the food chain more efficient. Beef cattle raised organically on grass emit 40 percent fewer greenhouse gases and use 85 percent less energy to produce beef than cattle fed on grain.[51] In Latin America, 70 percent of former forests in the Amazon have been turned over to grazing. The seven billion livestock animals in the United States alone consume five times as much grain as is consumed directly by the entire U.S. population.[52]

Techno-Foods: A Solution to World Hunger?

In the last half-century, technology has transformed farming, one of the most fundamental human activities. While it took nearly 1,000 years for wheat yields to increase from 0.5 to 2 metric tons per hectare, in only 40 years, wheat jumped from two to six metric tons per hectare. During the "Green Revolution" of the 1960s, improved seeds, new farm technology, and better irrigation and chemical fertilizers spread throughout the developing world.

The modern seed varieties flourish with controlled irrigation and petrochemical fertilizers, dramatically improving harvests and creating more food. FAO data indicate that for all developing countries, wheat yields rose by 208 percent from 1960 to 2000; rice jumped 109 percent; corn was up 157 percent; potatoes 78 percent; and cassava yields increased more than 36 percent.★

Before the 1960s, conventional wisdom held that agricultural technology does not travel well. It is either too climate specific, as in the case of biological technology, or too sensitive to input prices, as with mechanical technology.† Well-funded government and NGO efforts helped to research these new technologies as well as develop infrastructure. Overall, it was estimated that 40 percent of all farmers in the Third World were using Green

★"Green Revolution: Curse or Blessing?" International Food Policy Research Institute.
†Prabhu Pingali and Terri Raney, "From the Green Revolution to the Gene Revolution: How Will the Poor Fare?" ESA Working Paper No. 05-09, November 2005.

Revolution seeds by the 1990s, and an even higher percentage had adopted its watering and fertilizer techniques.★

The next wave of innovation came in the early 1990s, when genetically modified (GM) crops became widespread. GM plants can be engineered to be tolerant to the herbicides and insecticides or for other desirable traits. In 2007, 12 million farmers from 23 countries planted GM crops (1.7 million farmers more than in 2006). Ninety percent of these farmers were small and resource-poor farmers from developing countries.† While most GM crops are grown in industrial countries, the proportion now grown in the developing world has increased consistently every year, especially in countries like India, the Philippines, Brazil, Paraguay, Uruguay, and South Africa. GM crops not only lead to higher yields but also to a reduction of pesticide use, which reduces their agricultural footprints. (See Figure 7.2.)

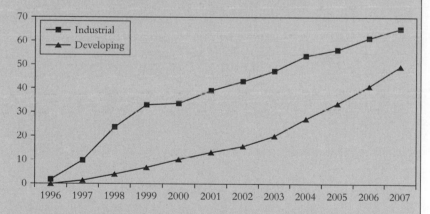

Figure 7.2   Global Area of GM Crops, 1996 to 2007, Industrial and Developing Countries
Source: Clive James, 2007.

★Peter Rosset, "Lessons from the Green Revolution," Food First, April 8, 2000, www.foodfirst.org/media/opeds/2000/4-greenrev.html
†C. James, "Global Status of Commercialized Biotech/GM Crops: 2007," ISAAA Briefs No. 37, ISAAA: Ithaca, NY.

(*Continued*)

(*Continued*)

Since GM plants are grown on open fields, there have been worries of cross-pollination creating "super-weeds" or other unintended side effects. Much of the controversy surrounding GM crops, however, is ethical—while modifying a plant seems mundane, applying genetic engineering to animals or people is a scary proposition for some. Yet what is undeniable is that GM crops are helping to feed more people and use less land, water, and pesticides to do it. Although the dual "green and gene" wave has revolutionized global agriculture, small farmers who cannot afford rising fertilizer prices or new seed varieties seek new options. Consider the system of rice intensification (SRI), a relatively low-tech but novel practice with great potential.

Rice, a staple food for more than half of the world's population, is a unique grain, amazingly tolerant to flooding. The conventional irrigated rice cultivation method capitalizes on this property, flooding rice paddies to reduce the amount of labor needed to weed the fields. Under this method, however, rice requires up to five times the irrigation withdrawals needed by the world's two other main cereal staples (corn and wheat) combined.

SRI involves using compost or manure (not synthetic fertilizers) in un-flooded nurseries. Under SRI, seedlings are transplanted one by one with wide spacing between each. Weeding, watering, and the timing of transplantations are increasingly important. The World Wide Fund for Nature (WWF) found that SRI has helped increase yields by more than 30 percent, to four to five tons per hectare from the current average of three tons per hectare, while using 40 percent less water than conventional methods.

From techno-food to low-tech, modern agricultural science has come a long way in keeping us fed. Balancing the food needs with sustainable agriculture will become even more important as the world grows wealthier each year, and more than 2.5 billion people are expected to inhabit the planet by 2050.

Water

Even among the most eco-conscious, "blue issues"—those concerning the health of our seas, rivers, and lakes—are often overshadowed by "green" land concerns. Evidence of our terrestrial bias abounds: Less than 1 percent of the ocean is protected by marine parks, compared with 12 percent of land.[53] However, the health of the sea is essential to the global economy as well as to human nourishment. We fish there; we transport goods there; and we already produce eco-friendly energy there via wave farms. Yet we are rapidly depleting fish stocks and, through pollution, changing the temperature and composition of our oceans.

Freshwater (water with less than 0.5 parts per thousand of dissolved salt) is also suffering from changing composition and depletion. The fresh water found in aquifers, ponds, lakes, and rivers is essential to health, disease control, agriculture, transportation and industry. Hydroelectric dams harness its energy. Yet less than 3 percent of the Earth's water is fresh (and only a fraction of that is readily accessible), making the availability of this precious resource one of the primary determinants of where and how people can live. In the past, people have not only moved for it but also fought for it. Indeed, water bears important linkages to immigration and security, as well as health, trade, and poverty.

Freshwater

The fresh water issues faced around the globe can be grouped into two general categories: those of quantity and quality. The two sets of issues are often interrelated and both have significant ramifications for the standard of living. According to the OECD, by 2025, global water use will rise by up to 30 percent in developing countries and more than 10 percent in the developed world.[54] The population living in water-stressed areas is set to double during the period between 1995 and 2025, and by 2030 some two-thirds of the world's inhabitants may experience moderate to high water stress.[55] More than 80 countries now have water shortages that threaten health and economies, while 40 percent of the world—more than two billion people—have limited access to clean water or sanitation.

The International Institute of Tropical Agriculture estimates that about a third of the population of sub-Saharan Africa, that is 300 million people, will suffer from malnutrition because of intensifying drought by 2010.[56] When combined with the current spike in commodities prices, drought has proved devastating. For example, drought in parts of Somalia and poor rainfall in others meant domestic food production was well below normal. Somalia already imports more than half its grain needs, and soaring commodity prices and a weakening currency have made those staples 375 percent more expensive than a year ago, according to the UN's Food and Agriculture Organization.[57] Nor is the United States exempt from the problems of drought: In May of 2008, Northern California's East Bay Municipal Utility District had to pass its first water-rationing resolution in 16 years.[58] And many may face a dry future: California and the other arid states of the western United States are expected to suffer from severe drought.[59] Computer models by the Hadley Center for Climate Prediction and Research predict a 3 percent to 18 percent increase in the amount of the Earth's surface that will be exposed to "extreme" drought by 2100; 40 percent of the world will suffer from "severe" drought, up from the current 18 percent and half the world will suffer from "moderate" drought.[60]

While some areas are naturally water-poor, drought can often result from poor policy choices. Agricultural policy is perhaps the key water offender. According to the WWF, Australian policies encouraging the growth of cotton in the 1960s, for example, and the advent of large-scale irrigation led to a dramatic over-allocation of water resources, resulting in a "range of dramatic natural resource impacts . . . including irrigation-induced salinity, growing evidence of decline in native fish populations, loss of vegetation, degradation of soils, and water quality decline resulting in algal blooms."[61]

In the United States, nearly a quarter of California's irrigation water is dedicated to alfalfa, which is harvested mostly for hay to feed dairy livestock and is a low-value crop that accounts for only 4 percent of state farming revenues.[62] That means California devotes 20 percent of its water supply to a crop that generates less than one-tenth of one percent of the state's economy.[63] And what's worse, many California farmers still pay the government between $2 and $20 per acre-foot for irrigation water, which is as little as 10 percent of the water's full cost.[64] Taxpayers foot the rest of the bill.

Or consider rising economic power China's water situation. Northern China is home to two-thirds of the country's cropland but only one-fifth of its water. As competing demands for water are made by cities, industry, and agriculture, the land is drying up. Between 1991 and 1996, the water table beneath the north China plain fell by an average of 1.5 meters a year, yet Chinese officials insist on subsidizing wheat production in the north to maintain grain self-sufficiency. Likewise, in the United States, farmers pay significantly lower prices per acre-foot of water than households, leading to the growth of water-intensive crops in desert areas.

Although not quite as exaggerated, poorly designed consumer water pricing schemes also lead to inefficient water use. Water pricing varies from country to country, depending largely on whether the water company is privatized or state-owned. Municipal water use is metered in most countries, but in some, such as most parts of Egypt and Lebanon and even certain parts of the United States, a flat-rate tariff is used. A century ago, the average American used only about 10 gallons of water a day, but today, Americans use 100 gallons a day per person, causing stresses on our sources of drinking water.[65] Applying metered and full cost pricing (meaning factoring all costs— past and future, operations, maintenance, and capital costs— into prices) would certainly help.

Inefficient infrastructure is also a leading water waster. Often, publicly held water infrastructure is woefully outdated and water management systems are plagued by waste and inefficiency. It is common for cities to lose 20 to 50 percent of their water to leaks and other problems in the distribution system.[66] Taiwan, for example, loses nearly two million cubic meters of water a day to leakage.[67] The good news is that fixing the problem will be a sound investment. The OECD estimates that halving the proportion of people without access to improved water sources by 2015 would produce benefits nine times the costs incurred.[68]

As for issues of quality, while clean water availability has increased in many regions of the world, half of the urban population in Africa, Asia, Latin America, and the Caribbean suffers from contaminated water. In the United States, 100 percent of the population has access to water, and 83 percent has proper sanitation. Compare this with 4 and 1 percent, respectively, in Afghanistan.[69] Even in middle income countries, substantial segments of the population lack adequate access to water and sanitation: 79 percent of the population has access to water and 45 percent has proper sanitation in Brazil, while those numbers fall to 69 percent and 22 percent, respectively, in China.

The international aspect of these policy and infrastructure investment choices cannot be ignored. There are more than 250 trans-boundary basins, accounting for 60 percent of the earth's freshwater volume.[70] Tensions between countries that share a river basin may hinder sustainable development, indirectly driving poverty, migration, and social instability.[71] Water conflicts also have the potential to exacerbate other nonwater-related stresses, like increased migration, poverty, and border tensions. Such is the case in India and Bangladesh, where the two neighboring states have long bickered over the Ganges River.[72] Despite a recent treaty signed in 1996, the failure of the two sides to cooperate has left the Sundarban wetlands and mangrove forests seriously threatened. High levels of arsenic threaten the population that draws drinking water from the Ganges. Environmental stress has in part provoked more than two million Bangladeshis to emigrate to neighboring regions of India, where in turn, this large influx has led to numerous ethnic conflicts. In the Indian border state of Assam, more than 4,000 people were killed in a series of violent incidents in the early 1980s, and tensions continue today.[73]

Without proper freshwater management, riparian conflict is likely to become a greater challenge in the future. In some cases, technological fixes—including desalinization plants, which are currently too pricey for all but a few wealthier regions—may be able to help lessen water woes. But for arid regions across the globe, reforming water-intensive agricultural policy will be key.

Fisheries

Today we are just beginning to dip our toes into the almost boundless potential of our seas. From desalinization plants, to fisheries and wave farms, which create energy boasting a cost-per-kWh equal to that of nuclear power by using freestanding turbine technologies,[74] our oceans could play an essential role in alleviating many of our resource deficits, but only if they're better cared for.

Of these commercial uses of the sea, fishing has been by far the most economically significant. Consider fisheries the farms of the sea. They are not just a source of food, but also an important source of foreign exchange and jobs. During the past three decades, employment in fishing and fish farming has grown faster than the world's population and faster than employment in agriculture.[75] In 2004, an estimated 41 million people worked as fishers and fish farmers, most of these in developing countries. World value of fish exports nearly tripled between 1976 and 2004, valued at over $71.5 billion in 2004.[76] According to the FAO, human consumption of fish increased from 93.6 million tons in 1998 to 100.7 in 2002, providing 2.6 billion people with at least 20 percent of their average per capita animal protein intake.[77]

Despite their importance to the economy and to human nutrition, the health of world's fisheries has deteriorated, with 76 percent of the world's fish stocks fished at or beyond their sustainable limits.[78] Numerous studies underscore an alarming decline in fish stocks, although the percentage of stocks exploited at or beyond their maximum sustainable levels varies greatly by region. In major fishing areas including the Western Central Atlantic, the Eastern Central Atlantic, the Northwest Atlantic, the Western Indian Ocean, and the Northwest Pacific, between 69 and 77 percent of stocks are depleted.[79] Moreover, there are growing hypoxic bodies like the Gulf of Mexico, water literally without oxygen, in which many bottom-dwellers such as snails, worms, starfish, and crabs die because they are unable to escape, while more mobile creatures like fish and shrimp are forced to flee the area.[80] (See Figure 7.3.)

Additionally, there is growing concern about destructive fishing practices such as trawling and blast fishing. Trawling cuts the living material from the sea bottom, reduces the future productivity of the ocean and stirs up huge sediment plumes. According to one author, "out-of-control demand for once premium foods has translated into grotesque and unsustainable forms of production. A taste for 'popcorn shrimp' in the strip malls of America translates into the cutting down of tropical mangrove forests in Ecuador and the destruction of wild

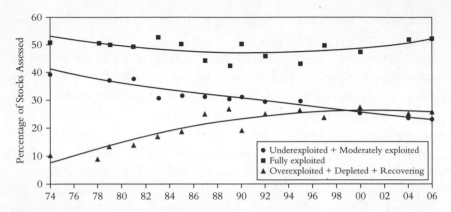

Figure 7.3   Global Trends in Marine Stocks since 1974
SOURCE: FAO.

shrimp stocks in Southeast Asia."[81] The Macro Quantum interlinkage of prosperity and increased consumption with environmental degradation couldn't be clearer.

"Stock depletion has implications for food security and economic development, reduces social welfare in countries around the world, and undermines the well-being of underwater ecosystems," says Ichiro Nomura of the FAO.[82] To ensure fishing occurs sustainably, fishing practices need to be monitored, and destructive techniques should be banned. Fish, like any other resource, are not free goods; the price paid for sushi should reflect just how scarce many piscine species are becoming.

Moreover, much of fishing occurs on the high seas (that is, the area outside the exclusive economic zone of any given country). The truly international status of these waters makes fish catches an issue particularly suited to multilateral management. Allocation of fishing rights is a slippery issue, however. According to the FAO, there has been a shift away from the classical management approach of simply limiting catches of fish to rights-based approaches that align commercial incentives and preservation objectives.[83] However, "negative perceptions about rights-based approaches persist, in part because they require resolving the fundamental fisheries management dilemma of who gets which fish."[84] International oversight and agreement on an allocation method must be set to prevent the global fishing industry from collapsing.

Air

The last of our environmental trinity—land, sea (and rivers, lakes, and streams), and air—has received the most attention recently. Air pollution, in the form of greenhouse gas emissions (such as carbon dioxide, nitrogen oxide, methane, and chloroflorocarbons), causes global warming, the ramifications of which scientists speculate will touch every aspect of our lives eventually. From coastal flooding to changing weather patterns, a warmer future could threaten our lifestyles dramatically. But air pollution—the gases, aerosols (solids or liquids suspended in gas), and particulates that are largely a product of our cars, fossil fuels, and factories—already impacts us through higher rates of respiratory diseases and birth defects, lower economic productivity, soil leeching, and lower fish catches.

Worldwide air pollution is responsible for large numbers of deaths and cases of respiratory disease. The WHO states that 2.4 million people die each year from causes directly attributable to air pollution, and research suggests women exposed to high levels of ozone and carbon monoxide may be up to three times as likely to give birth to a baby with heart defects.[85]

Air pollution also detracts from economic efficiency. Acid rain, a product of certain sulfur or nitrogen compounds reacting in the atmosphere with water vapor, has been shown to have adverse impacts on forests, freshwater and soil, killing off insects and fish, as well as causing damage to buildings. Smog—ground-level ozone—is a combination of sunlight and greenhouse gas emissions (hydrocarbons and nitrogen oxide).[86] Smog can reduce visibility and add to driving hazards and delays in ground and air traffic. Logistics costs per unit of GDP are more than three times higher in China (which is significantly smoggier) than in the United States.[87]

Now more than ever, a global solution for air pollution needs to be implemented. The dirtiest cities in terms of particulate matter (shown in Table 7.6) aside from Cairo, Egypt, are all Asian, but that does not mean their pollution stays close to home. Consider that in April 2007, a dense cloud of pollutants over northern China sailed to nearby Seoul. The dark cloud continued its trajectory over the Korean peninsula and across the Pacific. The cloud was visible to a U.S. satellite as it crossed the U.S.

Table 7.6 The World's Most Polluted Cities by Particulate Matter

G/M³Particulate Matter	City
169	Cairo, Egypt
150	Delhi, India
128	Kolkata, India (Calcutta)
125	Tianjin, China
123	Chongqing, China
109	Kanpur, India
109	Lucknow, India
104	Jakarta, Indonesia
101	Shenyang, China

SOURCE: World Bank.

West Coast. Unfortunately, this was not a one-time incident. Along with toys, clothes, and electronics, air pollution has become a major Asian export to the United States. "Occasional, large-scale Asian dust storms had led us to believe that this pollution traveled east in infrequent, discrete events," said University of California at Davis atmospheric scientist Steve Cliff. "As it turns out, Asian pollution, particularly in the Sierra-Cascade range and elsewhere in the American West, is the rule, not the exception."[88]

This kind of visible pollution—ambient particulate matter—in addition to greenhouse gases, plays an important role in climate, exerting both warming and cooling effects, and affecting precipitation and cloud cover. Scarce data from emerging countries make tracking emission sources, concentrations, transport patterns, and impacts difficult,[89] but it is estimated that the increase in global-warming gases from China's coal use will probably exceed that for all industrialized countries combined over the next 25 years, surpassing by five times the reduction in such emissions that the Kyoto Protocol seeks. India is right behind China in stepping up its construction of coal-fired power plants.[90]

Studies to date show that the growing amounts of microscopic pollutant particles coming from factories, vehicles, and power plants in China and India have changed U.S. Pacific coast weather patterns.[91]

Table 7.7 Total Carbon Dioxide Emissions
(million tons of CO_2 per year)

United States	2,790
China	2,680
Russia	661
India	583
Japan	400
Germany	356
Australia	226
South Africa	222
United Kingdom	212
South Korea	185

SOURCE: Center for Global Development.

High-altitude storm clouds over the northern Pacific have increased up to 50 percent over the past 20 years. Potential consequences of this change in weather patterns could be warmer air and more soot farther north into the Canadian Arctic, leading to accelerated melting of polar ice packs.[92] But also, as Table 7.7 shows, the United States and other G7 countries remain significant polluters.

This suggests we need a truly international policy to deal with air pollution. The much-touted Kyoto Protocol was meant to curb national CO_2 emissions relative to each nation's level in 1990. But the Kyoto Protocol has been highly ineffective as far as treaties go.[93] Kyoto's first problem is that the United States, the world's largest polluter, refuses to join. Secondly, developing countries, which are contributing a growing proportion of global emissions, have been left without firm commitments to do anything.

After coming under considerable scrutiny for not ratifying Kyoto, President Bush posited his first specific goal on the nation's emissions in April 2008, calling for the United States to halt the growth in greenhouse gases by 2025. Big business has been surprisingly responsive. There has been a push from industry to create user-friendly simplified federal regulation to avoid a complicated local web of conflicting measures. "We're in the worst of all worlds right now; we've got a dozen states that are forming their own regulations," says Jeffrey Immelt, CEO of General Electric.[94] This same logic should be carried to the international level, unifying emissions policies between countries. To discuss appropriate multilateral solutions that doesn't repeat Kyoto's mistakes and simplify regulations to facilitate clean business activity, let's first examine two primary air pollution sources: power generation and transportation.

Coal: Fueling the Fire

Coal is perhaps the dirtiest means of generating power. From the mining and transporting to the burning of coal, each step spews carbon dioxide, as well as mercury, sulfur dioxide, nitrogen oxides, soot, and particulate matter pollution as we described earlier. There are two methods of coal mining: underground and surface, both of which come with environmental price tags. The method used simply depends on where coal deposits are buried. Underground mining can have significant health impacts on its employees, particularly in developing countries, where health and safety policies are often subpar. In 2004, for example, China reported more than 6,000 coal mining related deaths and 10,000 new cases of black lung.[95] Surface coal mining, on the other hand, requires large tracts of land to be disturbed, raising a number of environmental challenges, including soil erosion, dust, noise, and water pollution, and impacts on local biodiversity. Once extracted, coal is generally transported by truck, train, or barge. These methods of coal transportation are not only expensive—in some cases accounting for 70 percent of the delivered cost of coal—they also burn fossil fuels in the process.[96] Alternatively, coal can be mixed with water, and this slurry can be transported via pipeline, cutting down on some of these transportation impacts, but not all.

When coal eventually reaches a power plant, even with new "clean coal" technologies such as coal capture and sequester (CCS) programs and a process called integrated gasification combined cycle (IGCC), its environmental footprint cannot be fully negated. CCS recovers and buries CO_2 emissions, but the process itself is actually extremely energy intensive, which could potentially double the operating cost of power plants. For a typical new CCS power plant to become financially viable, coal will need to be priced at $30 per ton (as opposed to the current price of $9 per ton).[97] IGCC, on the other hand, turns coal into gas, cutting down on sulfur dioxide and nitrogen oxide emissions, but it is also currently prohibitively expensive. Trying to clean up coal's act is proving to be a difficult and expensive task. Shifting focus to developing other less environmentally degrading forms of power might make more sense.

In Chapter 3, we saw how building alternative energy technology clusters could help the U.S. economy break out of its slump and maintain its innovative edge. As described in our solar grand plan, existing photovoltaic plants have demonstrated that concentrated solar power is practical, but costs must decrease to make it a viable energy source. By improving technology and capturing economies of scale, solar power could become viable within a decade or so, replacing increasingly damaging and expensive fossil fuels. Hydroelectric, geothermal, and wind power also should be supported as alternatives for fossil fuels.

Pollution on the Move

Pollution sources that move, such as trucks, cars, bulldozers, and trains, are known as "mobile sources"; [98] they rely on combustion engines that produce carbon monoxide and dioxide, as well as nitrogen oxide, hydrocarbons, and particulate matter. Because these mobile sources are such an essential part of commerce—including the trucks and trains that ship goods—as well as everyday life, an eco-friendly transportation policy must address consumer lifestyles, vehicle and engine design, and the fuels used by vehicles.

Stricter regulations for vehicle manufacturers and subsidizing alternatives to combustion engines are two avenues that could be explored. From the electric Tesla electric roadster to the zero-emissions hydrogen powered Honda FCX Clarity, a number of high profile substitutes have emerged recently, proving that a cleaner car is possible. These vehicles are currently out of reach for some consumers, but with continued advancements, prices will likely fall. For all vehicles, be they traditional, hybrid, or electric, providing improved information on fuel economy will also help consumers make better choices and shy away from gas-guzzlers.

In terms of gasoline, the price should be dramatically higher in the United States (as it is in most of Europe) to reflect gas' environmental damage. However, it is difficult to accurately price the potential costs of global warming, because projections are highly varied and spread over long time periods.[99] Yet, a carbon tax could at least partially offset the costs of technological research and environmental remediation. A taxation scheme similar to that applied to cigarettes will help drivers to understand the full cost of their transportation choice. Of course, this option is likely to be politically unpopular, given the U.S. public's recent concern over rising fuel prices. In a June 2008 Pew survey, 82 percent of Americans said they were watching gas and oil price news closely (up from 69 percent in August 2007).[100] On the other hand, a carbon tax on top of $3+ per gallon gas may not be as crazy as it sounds. Europeans have coped with $2 to $4 per gallon gas taxes for decades.

In terms of lifestyle, providing people better public transportation options is key. Appropriate solutions depend largely on local circumstances (what is appropriate in New York may not work in Nebraska). For dense urban areas, bus, light rail, and subway systems could be revamped. Better city planning can prevent the inefficient suburban sprawl that is happening today (see box at the of this chapter). While motor vehicles are likely to continue to play a substantial role in the U.S. economy as well as a growing role in China and India, making cars more environmentally friendly and providing alternatives to combat air pollution should remain an important goal.

Cultivating Environmental Consciousness

The lack of formal international structures is a significant impediment to better management of water, land, and resources. Several supranational organizations, from the World Health Organization to the World Trade Organization, play a part in environmental oversight and regulation, but there is no overarching coordination. Without a managing body, international environmental policy has been shaped haphazardly by treaties and ad hoc groups. While some treaties are useful, they are static documents unable to foresee changes in consumption and production patterns. This has not been aided by the plight of the well-known Kyoto Protocol. While it would be an unfair generaliza-tion to say all treaties encounter as many stumbling blocks as Kyoto, it is safe to say they cannot monitor pollution levels nor can they enforce themselves. This is why an international monitoring body is needed.

Of course, credit should be given to NGOs for attempting to fill some gaps. Where states have failed to venture (or have tried unsuccess-fully), pioneering nonstate actors have stepped in to lead preservation efforts. Private nonprofit organizations have done a fair job monitor-ing, raising awareness, and funding localized efforts. NGOs like the World Wide Fund for Nature, Greenpeace, and the Sierra Club are well known for their activism. But NGOs are inherently limited in their audience and authority. Expanding upon NGO efforts will require greater state support to enforce environment-friendly regulations and incentivize private sector participation. Not to mention, in many coun-tries government is the largest single purchaser of goods and services and can set procurement policies that support sustainability.

For these reasons, a multifaceted platform, reflecting the fact that environmental challenges are the product of many different sectors, should be designed to tackle these issues. Given the expanding role of nonstate actors, the G20 could form a working group to recommend a range of policies to better manage not only greenhouse gas emissions but also promote better conservation policies regarding water and land use, mining, fishing, and livestock rearing, among others. These may be easier to fix first.

Any platform that claims to address environmental challenges must incorporate the private sector. From commercial farms and fisheries to factories, environmental degradation is typically linked to private players. The government must shift subsidies away from heavily pol-luting industries toward private research for cleaner forms of energy. Private sector finance can also support capacity building and introduce international best practices. World Watch Institute's *State of the World 2008* report estimates that responses to climate change and other envi-ronmental problems are affecting more than $100 billion in annual cap-ital flows.[101] Twenty-seven major corporations are actively urging the U.S. Congress to pass legislation regulating greenhouse gas emissions, and 575 environmental and energy hedge funds are now in existence.[102] What's more, in 2007, Goldman Sachs released a study showing that companies with strong environmental, social, and governance policies outperformed the stock market in general by 25 percent.[103] Business is starting to respond to the changing environment—but this trend must expand exponentially to truly curb our environmental challenges.

More important, consumers must be brought into the fold. This can be accomplished by pricing goods to reflect their true costs—including the costs of disposal and negative externalities a product may cause. This applies equally to water, carbon emissions, forest products, and meat and fish, among other goods. The environmental oversight body we propose would work like an international Environmental Protection Agency (EPA), using market-based institutions to promote greater energy and resource efficiency, minimize waste generation, encourage environmentally sound purchasing decisions, and shift toward pricing systems that incorporate hidden environmental costs. The ultimate aim is to shift the calculus behind production and consumption. Some tools it would use include information sharing, penalizing countries that subsidize heavily polluting industries, liberalizing water and energy markets, and pollution tax schemes.

Information Sharing

One seminal role for our proposed environmental working body would be to manage information. While the OECD and World Bank compile basic information on fresh water use, there is currently no true marine monitoring system that actually looks at what is going on under the ocean. Monitoring fish stocks and catches, recording algae plumes in detail, and observing use of nitrogen-rich fertilizers is the first step to a more integrated ocean policy.

In the arena of river management, localized efforts will also be required to coordinate efforts in managing individual water basins. Between states, the development of shared data, water management institutions, and legal frameworks has helped to reduce the risk of water-related conflict. Since 1948, approximately 295 international water agreements have been negotiated and signed.[104] According to the OECD, relations among riparian states are typically more cooperative than in basins without treaties or water management mechanisms. The Mekong River Commission, for example, has been largely successful promoting equitable and sustainable water use and fostering good relations between Thailand, Vietnam, Laos, Cambodia, and China. Similar shared information could be gathered on fish catches and even carbon dioxide emissions.

A second part of monitoring is measuring, that is, providing a yardstick by which to judge our progress. When factories spew noxious and potentially carcinogenic fumes, it becomes clear that promoting human well-being is sometimes not the same as prompting GDP growth. According to World Watch's *State of the Earth 2008* report, green accounting programs are in place in at least 50 countries and at least 20 other countries are planning to initiate such programs soon.

Realigning Prices to Reflect Actual Costs

Subsidizing heavily polluting industries is simply unfair; but every day, consumers and industries receive hidden subsidies when they don't pay the full cost of the externalities their choices create. The WTO could actually work as an environmental policy manager to get rid of these secret subsidies. The World Trade Organization has set a precedent in the past of lessening inequitable burdens of pollution. In 2003, the United States prohibited the importation of Thai shrimp that had been caught in nets that caused unnecessary deaths of large numbers of endangered turtles. In this case, the WTO sustained the principle that global environmental concerns trump narrow commercial interests. The WTO's logic held that supporting low-cost unsound environmental practices can be viewed as a sort of subsidy; others must pay for the environmental damage caused by these poor practices. The principle can be extended to justify restricting importation of goods produced by technologies that unnecessarily pollute our atmosphere and river systems. Countries could use the WTO framework to prohibit or tax the importation of goods produced using energy intensive technologies.

This would include rationalizing agriculture policy to reflect the true costs of what we eat. The G7's $300 billion dollars of yearly subsidies have stalled the Doha trade talks and only caused harm to human well-being. By artificially depressing global prices, farmers in developing countries are hurt. By not accurately reflecting the true costs of production, including land and water degradation, environmental damage mounts, and future costs increase. Rationalizing agricultural subsidies and injecting competition and dynamism into the markets, while maintaining sustainable food security, would be a key goal of this global EPA.

Water and Energy Markets

The introduction of water markets is part of a shift away from command-and-control to more decentralized and market driven policies. This process has been promoted by the UN, the World Bank, and the OECD.

In most states, public authorities assume the double role of owners of the utilities (providing water supply and sanitation services) and regulators of both public and private providers. A clear distinction between these functions can help to improve water management. Market-based instruments, such as better pricing structures and tradable permits, could be introduced alongside government regulations, as well as cooperative efforts among water providers and users, spearheaded by local groups and NGOs. Forgoing flat rate water charges for fee structures that increase with usage could help align incentives correctly. Providing better information on how much water they are actually using, broken down by appliance, would help consumers to monitor their usage.

Increased competition in energy utilities would have a similar effect on energy sector. While coal remains the cheap staple of Chinese energy, increased market liberalization has brought some gains in efficiency. Until 2002, the State Power Corporation (SPC) accounted for 50 percent of power-generation assets and 90 percent of electricity supplied in China. In 2002, the SPC was broken into 11 firms and private investment was allowed into the market. While electricity prices remain regulated by the government and fuel costs are still artificially low, there has been a movement toward sector liberalization to improve efficiency and also create new opportunities for business.

Pollution Taxes

A tax on coal-based electricity, a gas-guzzler tax on SUVs, or a replenishment surcharge on forestry products and fish, are all examples of using taxes to discourage overconsumption. Progressive taxation is an essential part of the forward-looking Macro Quantum paradigm. After

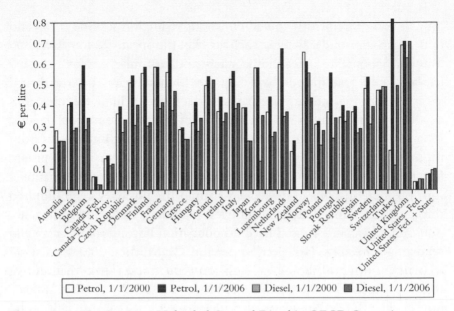

Figure 7.4 Tax Rates on Unleaded Gas and Diesel in OECD Countries
SOURCE: OECD, The Political Economy of Environmentally Related Taxes.

all, the costs of abating pollution are much higher than the expense of simply preventing pollution in the first place. (See Figure 7.4.)

Take the carbon tax, for example, what the *New York Times* calls the "most glamorous—and certainly the most unlikely—use of the tax code since Al Capone got hooked for tax evasion."[105] The rationale behind it is simple: The levels of carbon dioxide being added daily to the atmosphere create environmental damage. Climate change threatens to disrupt weather patterns, inundate coastal areas, accelerate the spread of diseases, and significantly change agricultural production patterns.

By levying tax on fuels according to carbon content, the incentive to save energy will be present at every level, from individuals' consumption choices to businesses' capital investment. While Denmark, Finland, Norway, and Sweden have had carbon taxes in place since the 1990s, only Denmark has experienced a significant reduction in emissions.[106] Experts speculate Denmark's success lies in the fact that carbon tax revenue proceeds are given back to industry, earmarked for environmental innovation.

The other frequently touted emissions reduction scheme is cap and trade. Cap-and-trade systems such as the European Union Emission Trading Scheme for greenhouse gases and a similar system to combat acid rain and nitrous oxide in the United States have achieved great localized successes. Under such a scheme, a limit for emissions of a certain pollutant is set and companies are given emissions credits. Companies that need to increase their emissions must buy credits from those who pollute less. The Kyoto Protocol's Clean Development Mechanism (CDM) is a cap-and-trade system that imposes national caps on the emissions of developed (Annex I) countries. One hundred thirty-seven of the ratifying countries, including India and China, are non-Annex I countries and have no obligation beyond monitoring and reporting emissions. However, under the CDM, these countries stand to benefit from greenhouse gas emission reduction projects that receive Certified Emissions Reduction Credits, which can be sold to Annex I buyers. The CDM stipulates that developed nations can help fund environmentally friendly projects in developing countries in return for additional credits. China accounts for approximately 60 percent of CDM carbon credits trading. But these projects alone cannot bring developing countries' energy practices up to international par. Kyoto has taught us that the political contentiousness and scale of a carbon trading system, combined with the lack of affordable carbon capture technology, makes cap-and-trade systems a poor solution for carbon reduction.[107]

Rather than an opaque and difficult to understand cap-and-trade system, carbon taxes and other polluter taxes, are transparent and easily understandable, making them more likely to elicit public support and quick implementation, according to the Carbon Tax Center. As Nobel Laureate Joseph Stiglitz points out, "polluting industries like the cap-and-trade system. While it provides them an incentive not to pollute, emission allowances offset much of what they would have to pay under a tax system."[108]

The capitalist peace is complicated by the need to forge an environmental consensus among a great diversity of interests from around the world. However, the terms of the debate are shifting as a growing number of people support the development of a global community based on greater respect for people and nature. While the debate over greenhouse emissions has obfuscated the profound changes in global production and consumption patterns, more people are realizing environmental regulation can complement economic growth and perhaps even make us healthier and safer. Environmental problems harm the basis for production, while in the global quest to meet growing energy and resource needs, a wide spectrum of business and investment opportunities for green investment has created a new environmental interest group.

As we embark upon our second century of globalization, we are much better equipped to make eco-friendly choices than we were 100 or even 10 years ago. The world now understands globalization's ecological impact well enough to craft more environmentally efficient policies and sustainable business plans from trunk to tail. Citizens everywhere have the tools to make informed choices about the way we feed, clothe, transport, and entertain ourselves. Instead of fretting over our dirty past, we need to focus on a cleaner future. By strategically managing our scarce natural resources, we stand to prevent environmental catastrophes from threatening to derail the capitalist peace.

Urbanization: Can It Help Save the Planet?

For most of history, humans were rural creatures, tied to forests and farms. But during the twentieth century, people flocked to the city; the ranks of urbanites swelled from 220 million people to roughly 2.8 billion.* By 2008, Homo sapiens hit a new milestone: More than half the species lived in cities.† The United Nations' *State of World Population 2007* report predicts that by 2030 some five billion people will be city dwellers, up

---

*Lisa Schlein, Joe De Capua, and Sven Krüger, "For Humanity's Sake, Developing World Must Prepare for Soaring Urbanization," *UN Population Fund*, June 28, 2007, www.citymayors.com/society/urban-population.html.
†"Urban" is generally defined as 1,000 people per square mile or 400 per square kilometer.

(Continued)

(*Continued*)

from 3.3 billion in 2008, as mankind continues to leave farms for factory and office work.

Today, as city centers, suburbs, and satellite towns merge into large metropolitan areas, we're witnessing the rise of megacities—immense urban areas with more than 10 million people. By 2020, the Earth will have 27 megacities, up from 21 today, and by then, cities of 5-plus million will have grown from 50 to 73.★ Despite the nightmarish images from old movies like *Blade Runner* and *Soylent Green* of a bleak urban future, there are plenty of reasons to cheer up about urbanization.

Cities don't have to be eco-unfriendly; on the contrary, they actually are less damaging to the environment than we might think. Recent studies show that a typical New York City resident, for example, is responsible for 7.1 metric tons of CO_2 per annum, a fraction of the 24.5 metric ton U.S. average. Urban settings require less energy to heat, light, cool, and fuel. Buildings are not only more densely packed, but city apartments are smaller than most suburban stand-alone houses. In addition, good public transit systems mean fewer people driving. Recent efforts by NYC Mayor Michael Bloomberg helped reduce emissions in the city by roughly 446,000 metric tons a year by using cleaner fuels, buying more energy-efficient equipment, planting street trees, and increasing the use of alternative fuel and hybrid vehicles.[†]

But to capture these benefits requires planning. If city growth is not strategically guided, urban sprawl can result in increased traffic (which emits CO_2 and particulates), as well as water pollution and land misuse. If growing megacities fail to properly plan for new water and sewer lines, power plants, schools, and increased police and fire protection, the results are not pretty. Smart cities enact growth boundaries and design

---

★Seewww.citymayors.com/statistics/urban_2020_1.html;www.citymayors.com/statistics/urban_2006_1.html.

[†]See *Inventory of New York Greenhouse Gas Emissions*, April 2007. www.nyc.gov/html/om/pdf/ccp_report041007.pdf

(*Continued*)

parks and open spaces, promote public transportation, revitalize and reposition already developed areas through rezoning, and prevent new development in floodplains and other disaster-prone areas—particularly given the unpredictability of weather patterns in the Macro Quantum world.

Thanks to their population density, cities also make for ideal laboratories for new eco-friendly trends in food, energy, water, transportation, and even entertainment. One interesting area is "vertical farming" (VF), a high-tech variation on hot-houses and hydroponics. The practice of growing food miles or even continents away from where consumers live uses an immense amount of energy and chemicals to preserve food. Growing food closer to where we live offers the world benefits including: (1) year-round crop production whereby one indoor acre can grow four to six times more than an outdoor acre (and even 30 times more for strawberries!); (2) higher predictable yields without weather-related crop failures due to droughts, floods, or pests; (3) organic food with no herbicides, pesticides, or fertilizers (also eliminating toxic runoff); (4) better land use by repurposing abandoned urban sites and returning farmland to nature (thereby restoring the global ecosystem); and (5) reduced fossil fuel use (no tractors, plows, or shipping).★

In energy, a variety of alternative technologies including solar paneling, wind power generated atop skyscrapers, tidal and wave turbines and hydrogen pipelines, coupled with mandatory eco-efficient building requirements (for example, insulation and appliance efficiency standards) could also dramatically reduce urban power needs. As services grow in importance to the global economy, policies to power office buildings—today's brain factories—could shape energy use around the world. Small efficiency gains would really add up.

★See www.verticalfarm.com or check out www.organitech.com, an interesting company that has commercialized several VF technologies.

(Continued)

(*Continued*)

There are many new developments designed to combat increasing water scarcity, from filter systems that capture rainwater, to robots that detect water pipelines leaks, to more efficient sewage treatment plans. Public metering, too, could encourage more efficient water usage. For cities near oceans, scalable desalination plants are becoming more economical.★

In transportation, futuristic "power sidewalks" that gather kinetic energy from footsteps, zero-emission buses and cars including taxis and delivery trucks, and high-speed intercity railways, are among dozens of possibilities to help stave off carbon emissions and pollution. In older cities, like Mexico City, one of the world's largest and most congested, even mundane retrofitting of municipal diesel buses with particulate filters is helping reduce soot from the city's more than four million cars. Congestion pricing, car-free zones, and a variety of public transportation subsidies can also greatly reduce vehicular usage and its ill effects.

On the entertainment front, imagine a dance club powered in part by a wind turbine and solar panels, as well as a dance floor that generates power from the motion of people dancing. It's in London and it's called Club Surya. The décor is strictly recycled and the food and drinks are organic and locally grown.

So while the images of ugly, unhealthy urban existence may pessimistically cloud our perspective on cities, through a combination of better planning, thoughtful employment of technology, and bold public policies, city living could be a remedy for growing global consumption and environmental degradation.

★A team of scientists at UCLA recently developed a nanotechnology process that dramatically reduces the cost of desalination. See "Engineers Develop Revolutionary Nanotech Water Desalination Membrane," *University of California, Los Angeles,* November 6, 2006, www.physorg.com/news82047372.html.

Chapter 8

Poverty

Remembering the Bottom of the Pyramid

> *Poverty is the parent of revolution and crime.*
>
> —ARISTOTLE

O ur nineteenth- and twentieth-century experience should make it clear that the capitalist peace and poverty eradication are linked by a virtuous cycle: Rising incomes and widespread prosperity create peace and allow trade to flourish; and in turn, a peaceful commitment to trade creates further prosperity. Nearly everyone in the world was poor at the start of the nineteenth century, but with the advent of trade, that rate is down to only 20 percent now. Moreover, today as we formulate poverty policy, we have the advantage of having seen poverty reduction in action. Much of the heavy lifting on this front has occurred in the last generation—according to the World Bank, the world poverty rate fell from 33 percent in 1981 (about 1.5 billion people) to 18 percent by the new millennium (about 1.1 billion people)[1]—providing us specific clues on what to do to accelerate poverty's end.

One thing we have learned in the last couple of decades is that charity is not a strategy. Multilateral efforts to combat poverty through stale foreign aid plans have encountered a desensitized audience. We've all seen advertisements to help end starvation and children's suffering on late-night TV or in magazines. Pictures of malnourished, raggedy, barefoot kids, stunned and smeared with dirt, almost always accompany these petitions that entreat you to act before it is (very ominously) "too late." Usually they feature celebrities asking you to "adopt" a child, and, for a modest donation, make a huge difference in their life. While the moral poignancy of these images is difficult to counter, the more compelling rationale behind tackling poverty is fostering collective global prosperity. It's in our economic self-interest to eliminate poverty.

In the past two decades the world economy has thrived as it expanded to include more and more workers and consumers, but there are still another two billion impoverished people who have yet to experience the benefits of globalization. Moreover, given how deeply interlinked it is with so many other areas—trade, security, immigration, and health, to name a few—pervasive poverty is perhaps the single greatest threat to our capitalist peace. Not only does poverty condemn two billion people to hunger, disease, and shortened life spans, but it also hurts the Macro Quantum world by breeding instability, environmental degradation, and civil conflict. But decades of stagnation in many aid recipient states have created donor fatigue in many G7 nations. Ending poverty in our lifetimes is more realistic than we might think, but we need a new attitude and policy mix that mobilizes both governments and nonstate actors synergistically and considers poverty as an economic, not moral, threat.

Poverty Trends: Some Bright Spots

What is poverty and who is a poor person? Clearly, poverty means different things in different places; living below the poverty line in the United States is very different from doing so in Bangladesh. For example, the U.S. Department of Health and Human Services classifies a single person in the United States earning $10,400 or less annually (roughly $30 a day) as living in poverty,[2] while the World Bank considers poverty as living on less than one-fifteenth of that amount or about $2 per day and extreme poverty at less than $1 per day).[3] But when we slice through quantitative definitions, poverty translates essentially into not fulfilling basic biological needs. The world's poor tend to have low daily caloric intake; they do not eat enough to have the energy to work eight hours in a field or factory. They cannot afford basic sanitation let alone medical care, and so they suffer from high rates of infectious disease, infant mortality, and illnesses linked to malnutrition. The poor also suffer from low literacy rates and a dearth of education, which impedes labor productivity and perpetuates substandard sanitary and environmental practices. As a result, even if the number of people in a poor country is quite large, the labor force is often small because potential workers are sidelined by hunger, disease, and a lack of education. What's worse, for many of the world's poor who are unable to integrate into the labor market, the benefits of globalization cannot be realized and poverty becomes a vicious trap. To reduce poverty, standards of nutrition, sanitation, and education must improve, but these very same things cannot improve unless poverty is reduced. But as we'll see, there are ways out of this cycle of deprivation.

The good news is that poverty has been steadily decreasing. Look at the trends: The proportion of the world's population in extreme poverty (living on less than $1 a day) has declined from about three-quarters in 1820 to less than one-fifth today,[4] and progress has only accelerated with this latest wave of globalization. (See Figure 8.1.)

These global summary statements, however, conceal some unsettling poverty trends across regions. As Figure 8.2 shows, East and South Asia have witnessed significant decreases in poverty, while Latin American and African reductions have been modest at best. The tremendous decreases in Asia are largely a product of shifts toward capitalism in two countries—China and India—where historically poverty was the worst in absolute numbers (remember, these two countries have a combined population of more than 2.2 billion, or one-third of the world). Of course, other economies have also successfully shared in the benefits of liberalization, such as Vietnam, where World Bank surveys of the country's poorest households show 98 percent of people became better off in the 1990s; and Uganda, where poverty fell 40 percent during the

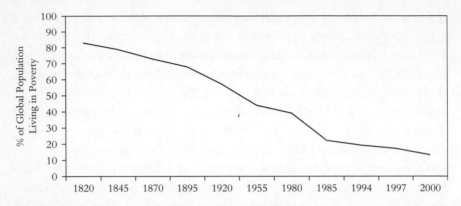

Figure 8.1   Poverty Head Count Ratio, 1800–2000
NOTE: Head count ratio demonstrated as a percentage. Poverty defined as US$1.50 a day 1993 PPP
prices.

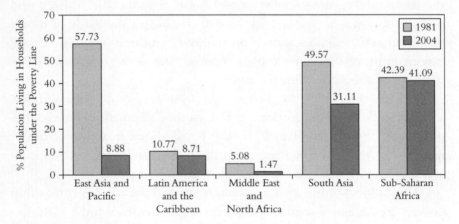

Figure 8.2   Global Poverty Trends by Region, 1981–2004
SOURCE: Povcal.

1990s and school enrollments doubled.[5] But according to Jose Antonio
Ocampo and Juan Martin, as well as other scholars who study inequality and poverty, the world outside of Beijing and New Delhi is in fact
becoming less equal, and poverty reduction has been less profound than
we would expect.[6] Indeed, the Chinese and Indian miracles distort the
picture of poverty reduction upon closer inspection.

Our track record from the last 20 years may not be perfect, but
it has provided us hints as to what kind of policies work in the battle

against poverty—and what kind don't. As Joseph Stiglitz notes, by the mid-1990s, the benefits of free trade gained wide acceptance by policy makers and intellectuals.[7] China, the current poster child for globalization, has sustained meteoric GDP growth around 10 percent year-on-year for 20 years, while India has almost hit 7 percent year-on-year for the last decade.[8] Likewise, poverty rates have plummeted in these two megacountries: The percentage of the population living in households with consumption or income per person below the poverty line has fallen from 1981 to 2003 by 62.54 percent in rural China and by 14.18 percent in rural India.

On the other hand, sub-Saharan Africa remains the region with the highest poverty rates. Unsurprisingly, it has also witnessed the least successful implementation of comprehensive liberalizing economic reforms. Many countries in this region actually have seen a decline in their economic growth, accompanied by hyperinflation and a decrease in per capita income and life expectancy.[9] According to David Dollar of the World Bank, Southeast Asian countries that were initially similar to these African countries were successful because they liberalized trade when agricultural products were their principal exports then moved quickly into labor-intensive manufacturing.[10] African economies, however, have investment climate issues that prevented this shift. In Africa, then, just reducing import tariffs did not have enough effect to overcome the nontariff barriers to capitalism. Dollar says, "tariffs were a barrier, certainly, but experience suggests that other barriers were more important. How easy is it to start a firm, hire labor, get reliable electricity? Even with formal tariffs lowered, can a firm get the necessary inputs through customs? The developing countries that have done well with globalization are those that fostered reasonably sound investment climates so that their firms can take advantage of opportunities on the world market."[11] Who would willingly invest in a country where most of the capital will be skimmed off to support the lavish lifestyles of the ruling elite?

The nations that have successfully liberalized and created sound investment climates have witnessed amazing economic performance and poverty reduction. Liberalization has also created political and economic challenges by increasing inequality between and within societies. It seems as if China and India have actually become several countries in one: super rich, middle class, lower middle class, and the super poor. The 14 percent that remains poor in China still numbers about 150 million people—roughly the population of Nigeria. India and China must therefore contend with economic equality issues between their newly minted millionaires (and billionaires) and their millions who go to bed barely fed. Underscoring this is the deep divide between urban and rural society in China and India. The rural populations in these massive countries are significantly worse off, and remain largely untouched by the positive effects of globalization that have lifted their urban compatriots out of poverty.

What China and India's relative success teaches us is that economic openness, free trade, export orientation, and foreign direct investment help poor countries to outgrow poverty. Indeed, in poor countries, a dollar of foreign investment is much more productive in terms of economic growth than a dollar of domestic investment.[12] Researchers speculate this is because investment from foreign firms generates "spill-over effects," or positive externalities, including new technologies and processes introduced by foreign companies, as well as providing competition to state monopolies. That being said, inequality within the fastest growing economies is increasing, and as Friedrich von Hayek argued, some inequality is inevitable if not desirable in order to grease the wheels of innovation. Still, a high degree of inequality between or within countries is undesirable, potentially destabilizing, and merits our attention.[13]

Even with the amazing reduction in poverty, there's more work to be done. Today, when more than two billion people live on less than $2 a day, poverty has hardly been eradicated. Allowing nearly two billion people to live on such scant resources not only leaves a vast market consumers and workers untapped, but also threatens all of our security, environment, and health. Today these people remain outside the reach of globalization, caught in a vicious cycle that perpetuates economic and political instability, shortened life spans, environmental degradation, and civil conflict. The incredible progress of a handful of countries, like India, China, Vietnam, and Uganda, toward reducing their number of poor shows us how useful globalization and trade liberalization can be in the battle against poverty. As corporations seek out new markets and investment in lesser-developed countries, more of the business community's attention should turn to the two billion–plus poor. Despite their limited incomes, the poor offer numerous business opportunities for large MNCs and small entrepreneurs alike that could help to give this huge segment of humanity a stake in the Macro Quantum world.

Unfortunately, to date, the United States and the G7 have viewed global poverty aid programs as a financial burden rather than part of a broader capitalist peace strategy. What little attention rich nations have paid to the poor, they have done through government aid, and they have rarely considered how their other policies impact the impoverished. The recent food crisis is an example of how the shortsighted agricultural and trade policies of the United States and G7 have exacerbated poverty around the world. Imbalances in energy policy and farm subsidies in the United States helped to spark spiraling food prices, disproportionately burdening the world's poorest. Through more carefully crafted policy and engagement of nonstate actors in the poverty arena, we could substantially reduce the number of poor. But first we need to shift our mind-set by realizing how intertwined poverty is with virtually every cross-border challenge we face today.

Poverty's Interlinkages

Throughout our discussion, we've noted how poverty is linked to other areas in our Macro Quantum world. In trade and investment, poverty impedes the creation of a more interdependent marketplace of workers and consumers. Globalization requires a large, constant supply of skilled workers, yet by reducing educational opportunities, poverty stunts this supply. For example, despite the fact that India has one of the youngest and largest workforces in the world, the head of leading tech company Infosys recently pointed out there was an "acute shortage of skilled manpower" in the country, while a study by Hewitt Associates projects that 2007 salaries for skilled Indian workers will rise 14.5 percent, a sign that demand for skilled labor is outstripping supply.[14] This is because India, while not short on workers, is short on skill. Indeed, the Indian literacy rate is only 61 percent (versus 82 percent in China).[15]

On the flip side, mismanaged trade can also aggravate poverty. Although typically a tool of poverty alleviation, when poorly coordinated, trade can create imbalances that exacerbate deprivation. Consider the food crisis that began in 2007. In Chapter 7, we saw the spiraling commodity and food prices resulted in part from the failure to reform agricultural subsidies. Most Americans take food for granted—even the poorest fifth of households in the United States spends only 16 percent of its budget on food. But in many developing countries, food is a much larger portion of spending: Nigerian families spend 73 percent, Vietnamese 65 percent, and Indonesians half of their budgets on food.[16] In turn, this makes poor households particularly susceptible to fluctuations in the price of staple crops. In 2007, when the food import bill of developing countries rose by 25 percent, it was the poor who suffered most. According to an April 2008 World Bank report, the "recent large increases in food prices appear likely to raise overall poverty in low income countries substantially."[17]

The food crisis has clear links to failure at Doha. Agricultural subsidies must be addressed if there is any hope for long-term poverty eradication. According to *The Economist,* "a successful Doha round could raise the global income by more than $500 billion a year by 2015. Over 60 percent of that gain would go to poor countries, helping to pull 144 million people out of poverty . . . the reduction of rich country farm subsidies and more open markets in the [global] north would also help."[18] The failure of the Doha round is a roadblock to international cooperation on poverty alleviation and shows the influence of the United States' and G7's Micro Domestic views. It is essential that developed countries adopt a more fair-minded and pragmatic approach to agricultural and trade policies in order for there to be any lasting gains against poverty.

Poverty is also the single largest enabler of disease in the world; it forces people to live in environments that make them sick, without decent shelter, clean water, or adequate sanitation. More than 800,000 African children per year still die of malaria—more than from any other disease—when there are medicines that cure for 55 cents a dose, mosquito nets that shield a child for $1 a year, and indoor insecticide spraying that costs about $10 annually for a household.[19] Unfortunately, even these relatively low costs are beyond the budgets of the world's impoverished.

Around 28 percent of all children in developing countries are estimated to be underweight or stunted. The two regions that account for the bulk of the deficit are South Asia and sub-Saharan Africa. It is no coincidence that there are 350–500 million cases of malaria annually with one million fatalities, and Africa accounts for 90 percent of malarial deaths and African children account for more than 80 percent of malaria victims worldwide.[20]

These diseases, oftentimes completely curable or treatable, are contributing to the ongoing instability in the region. Yet crucial medical treatment is too expensive for the poverty-stricken. The WHO's Commission on Macroeconomics and Health recently estimated that Ghana and other countries in the malarial zone need to spend only about $35 or $40 per person per year to keep people healthy enough to work. However, Ghana can afford only about $10 a person, which means there is a gap of roughly half a billion dollars ($25 for 20 million people).[21] These small costs continue the spread of malaria, a disease that is actually relatively cheap and easy to cure, and leave these nations sick and economically unproductive. Such health crises threaten the stability of governments as well as local economies, allowing poverty to disturb the capitalist peace.

Or consider that the International Agency for Research on Cancer (IARC) reports that the cancer rate is increasing in developing countries as a result of poverty. The IARC predicts that the number of new cases will double to 27 million by 2050. In fact, of the 7.6 million people who died of cancer in 2008, nearly two-thirds of them are in emerging markets. In most of these countries, there are few basic diagnostic oncology facilities, and when chemotherapy drugs are available, they are prohibitively expensive for most cancer patients.[22]

Poverty is also intertwined with environmental degradation. Developing nations and their impoverished citizens often fall victim to industrialized countries' pollution and environmental abuse. Globally, the richest quintile of the world accounts for 86 percent of total private consumption expenditures—the poorest quintile accounts for only 1.3 percent.[23] If the poor world were to consume in the same manner as the West to achieve the same living standards, "we would need two additional planet Earths to produce resources and absorb wastes."[24] Yet, according to the International Development Bank (IDB), poor people within developing countries are disproportionately at risk from the increased impacts of environmental degradation. Products of climate change, such as increased volatility in weather patterns (for instance, floods and droughts), will hit countries like Bangladesh the hardest, and yet it is the poor who are the least able to adapt to these changing circumstances.[25]

Poverty often leads to resource stripping just for local populations to survive or pay off debts. But sadly, unsustainable practices tend to also harm the poor the most, because the poor tend to depend on natural resources for their livelihoods. Nearly three-quarters of the extremely poor live in rural areas where they rely directly on forests for food, fuel, fiber, and building materials.[26] For instance, Indonesia's forests—once among the biologically richest and most expansive in the world—now rank among the most threatened. Impoverished locals, looking to make a profit, cleared more than 40 percent of the country's forests in the last 50 years. However, this has done little for Indonesia; incomes are down over the last decade.[27]

Poorer societies are much more likely than high-income societies to fall into conflict over water and arable land and other scarce natural resources such as oil, diamonds, and timber.[28] Such countries are also more likely to have weak governments, making it easier for would-be rebels to grab land and vital resources. Resource scarcity can also provoke migration and major population displacement that result in conflicts between social groups, such as in Darfur, Sudan, where conflict broke out as a partial result of diminishing rainfall.

Poverty drives migration; if you cannot make a living in one place, you will move to a more friendly economic locale. Indeed, immigration everywhere is a product of the economic circumstances of countries: The Irish emigrated in the wake of a potato famine, and the Mexicans immigrating to the United States are just the latest in a historical wave of people seeking greater stability. Take a look at South Africa. As the most developed country on the African continent, it has attracted a wave of economic and political refugees since the fall of apartheid in 1994. Most of them (as many as three million) hail from neighboring Zimbabwe where President Mugabe's repressive rule has pushed thousands of Zimbabweans across South Africa's northern border on a weekly basis.[29] However, in May 2008 violence and rioting erupted against these immigrant Zimbabweans carried out by impoverished and unemployed South Africans who viewed them as threats to their employment prospects. As a result, many of these persecuted Zimbabweans have fled South Africa, bringing their potential economic contributions with them and marring the record of South Africa's post-apartheid regime.

Poor countries are not just where pollution's effects are felt most, but also where it is made. Unless managed carefully, the path to wealth pursued by such states can bring about fundamental, irreversible, and unwise environmental change. But environmental protection is key to sustaining economic growth—vital for the G7 countries and the developing world alike.[30] As heavily polluting industries continue to migrate to lesser developed countries, tackling the pollution-poverty connection has an added dimension: By broadening the concept of economic growth in ways that includes environmental and human values, we can move to mitigate the problems of unsustainable, dirty growth.

Increased energy use has long been associated with higher development levels and lower poverty rates. It is no coincidence that the world's largest economy with the highest standard of living—the United States—also uses the highest amount of energy per capita (about one-fifth of global energy). As Figure 8.3 shows, the higher a nation's electricity usage, the higher its Human Development Index (HDI). One reason for this correlation is simple: Without access to power, industry and job creation is stifled.

Modern farming is extremely energy-intensive: The energy costs of producing fertilizer, running tractors, and, not least, transporting farm products to consumers are high. With oil prices oscillating wildly, doubling and even tripling at times, energy costs were a major factor driving up agricultural prices and exacerbating conflict in impoverished nations during the world food crisis of 2007–2008. These inflated agricultural prices, in turn, are passed on to consumers in developing countries, often with severe effects. The World Bank has estimated that 100 million individuals could be pushed below the poverty line by the recent food crisis, which equates to the loss of seven years of gains against poverty.[31] The world's poor are extremely sensitive to changes in industrialized countries' policies.

Fast growing countries such as China are competing with the developing world for increasingly scarce resources, including oil and farmland, driving up prices for raw materials of all sorts, food staples

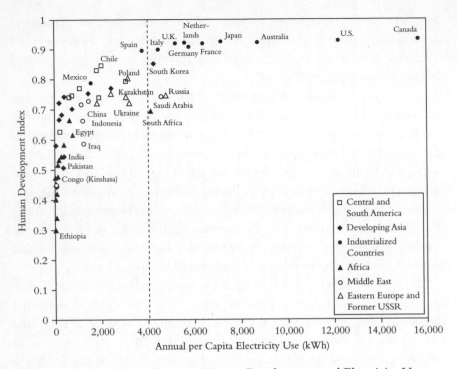

Figure 8.3   Correlation between Human Development and Electricity Usage
SOURCE: *Physics Today.*

included.[32] But the rich world is exacerbating these effects by supporting the production of biofuels. The International Monetary Fund estimates that corn ethanol production in the United States accounted for
at least half the rise in world corn demand in each of the past three
years. This elevated corn prices, as well as the prices of other crops—
especially soybeans—as farmers switched their fields to corn, according
to the U.S. Department of Agriculture. Furthermore, Washington provides a subsidy of 51 cents a gallon to ethanol blenders and slaps a tariff
of 54 cents a gallon on imports. In the European Union, most countries
exempt biofuels from some gas taxes and slap an average tariff equal to
more than 70 cents a gallon on imported ethanol.[33] These industrialized countries' practices, such as biofuel subsidies, are only inflating the
cost of food, thereby increasing the number of people mired in poverty.

The destabilizing influence of poverty on international and domestic security cannot be overstated. Since the Cold War's end, from Sierra

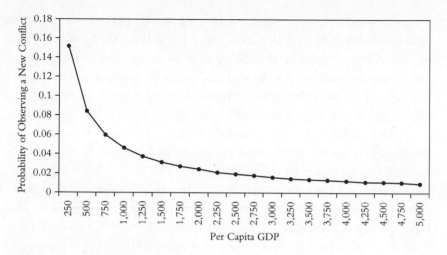

Figure 8.4   Risk of Civil War and GDP per Capita, 1960–1999
SOURCE: The Brookings Institution.

Leone to Indonesia, civil wars and insurgencies have erupted in places suffering from persistent poverty or sharp economic decline. According to a study done by Hoeffler and Rohner, the average GDP per capita for countries that had experienced war within five years is $1,100, while the average GDP per capita for countries that had not experienced war within five years is $5,764.[34] Figure 8.4 shows how the probability of civil war drops precipitously once a country achieves a GDP of approximately $1,000 per capita. Armed conflict can draw in neighboring countries, exacerbating regional instability and requiring costly military intervention by outside powers. These conflicts sap already depleted national resources and further cripple the fragile economies of some of the world's poorest countries while claiming millions of innocent lives. These countries are also incubators of transnational security threats like terrorism, weapons proliferation, and criminal activity.

Poverty breeds suicide bombers and terrorist camps. Consider what is happening in parts of the central Asian steppe and Middle East. There is a growing socioeconomic divide between the privileged few and the impoverished many. Poverty-stricken youth, with little hope for the future and even less attachment to their government, in search of glory and God, provide terrorist organizations with a seemingly endless supply of suicide bombers. It is estimated that up to 40 percent of the Arab population lives in extreme poverty—that is, on less than $1 a day.[35] The millions of impoverished young Muslims who struggle to subsist have no stake whatsoever in the existing socioeconomic or political order.

Without constructive alternatives, and facing a grim future, impoverished youth may have a sense of hopelessness, despair, and rage, which can lead to violence for material gain.[36] Participating in terrorism and joining militia groups becomes increasingly attractive, thereby posing a serious threat to global peace and security.

Poverty also contributes to drug trafficking, a significant impediment to both international security and international development. The United Nations Office on Drugs and Crime (UNODC)'s *World Drug Report* states that poverty leaves farmers "vulnerable to the temptations of illicit incomes" derived from drug crops.[37] Furthermore, the "recurrent conflicts and poverty in Afghanistan have provided an opportunity for illicit production to become widespread. Poverty and conflicts in Central Asia have also hindered the development of defenses against trafficking."[38] According to the UNODC, "a long-term reduction of the world's supply of coca depends not only on effective law enforcement, but also on eradicating the poverty that makes farmers vulnerable to the temptation of growing lucrative illicit crops."[39]

Consider the quantum connection between the world's heroin supply, poverty, and the U.S. campaign against terrorism. Afghanistan produces 93 percent of the world's opium poppies. After the U.S. invasion, Afghanistan fell into chaos and impoverished farmers, desperate to feed their families, made bargains with drug traders. For a small initial investment in seeds, farmers could grow poppy. Though few, if any, ever see direct profits from the crop, poverty-stricken rural Afghans strike these deals just to survive. This is hugely destabilizing to the Afghan state as well as the region as a whole: Poppy is illegal, and illegal profits cannot be taxed. Of more immediate danger to the Afghan state, however, is the debilitating relationship between drug barons who supply the Taliban with money and weapons and the militants who protect the growing regions and help get the drugs to market. Drugs enrich a few at the expense of many and cost the government a lot in eradication efforts, without contributing to either the domestic or the global economy. At the nexus of the loss of trade and investment, lack of economic development, and security concerns, stands poverty.

Foreign Aid and the Millennium Development Goals

Considering its role in promoting conflict, environmental degradation, and the spread of disease, it is clear global poverty is the primary stumbling block in maintaining the capitalist peace. This is why it is so essential we make poverty eradication a key feature of our economic policy. Yet in the past, the way we have thought about poverty—not in terms of economics but as a regrettable humanitarian problem—has severely limited our collective response.

Former president of Ireland Mary Robinson argues that poverty is the worst human rights problem in the world today.[40] She advocates making "globalization a more values-led and ethical process which benefits all people."[41] Robinson is likely correct in asserting that poverty remains a huge threat to human rights; however, her morality argument has failed to move countries to action, as a possible sign of frustration with charity-focused poverty eradication plans.

According to the 2005 Human Development Report, "with today's technology, financial resources and accumulated knowledge, the world has the capacity to overcome extreme deprivation."[42] We have seen that spreading capitalism is the best way to ensure impoverished countries' long-term participation in the global economy; it is also in the best interest of Western businesses and corporations, which stand to gain from the opening up of previously untapped markets and consumers. However, a gap remains between the rhetoric of the G7 countries and the steps they actually take to eradicate poverty. Poverty elimination strategies tend to be given low priority and tend to focus on aid—an incomplete (and inefficient) treatment for such a complex problem.

In *The End of Poverty* Jeffrey Sachs suggests that certain places on the planet, owing to geographical isolation, burden of disease, inhospitable climate, and poor soil, are mired in extreme poverty and unable to reap the benefits of globalization. Sachs' argument has some merit: A country's natural endowments directly contribute to the state of its economy. Without a pinch of geographic luck, for example, many of the Gulf states would likely be poor stretches of desert. Sachs argues that there is a market failure at the lowest level of development that requires aid to construct the "preconditions of basic infrastructure (roads, power, and ports) and human capital (health and education)."

But Sachs' suggestion that the way out of the poverty trap is through massive injections of foreign aid[43]—$135 billion per annum, rising to $195 billion by 2015,[44] like Robinson's argument, again seems to miss the point. Aid is a strictly voluntary effort, motivated perhaps by guilt or pity, but without any structural rationale and incentive to ensure it is carried out.

Time and time again, moral suasion has proved insufficient to generate solid commitments to humanitarian efforts, and international aid today remains modest. The average OECD country gives less than half a percent of its GNP as development assistance.[45] Despite much lip service toward ending poverty, it seems only in cases when poverty alleviation coincides with other strategic interests have we seen significant aid packages. Even then, the lack of a distribution network for aid, the red tape of donating governments' bureaucracies, and the influence of corrupt or failed domestic regimes significantly impede the efficacy of aid. This is not to say government aid is completely without a place in the Macro Quantum world. Increasing the role of nonprofit organizations and creating many competing channels of potential distribution could streamline the aid distribution process. The government and NGOs could also tackle areas that are difficult for businesses to venture, such as infrastructural projects. But in general, applying inefficient and haphazard charity instead of a cogent policy to deal with poverty sends the message that poverty is unfortunate but unimportant. And in the deeply interconnected Macro Quantum world, the poor are actually very important.

Consider the UN's Millennium Development Goals (MDGs). With much hullabaloo, the MDGs were launched in 2000, setting holistic objectives for 2015 aimed at reducing poverty. The eight broad Millennium Development Goals include: (1) eradicating extreme poverty and hunger; (2) achieving universal primary education; (3) promoting gender equality and empowering women; (4) reducing child mortality; (5) improving maternal health; (6) combating HIV/AIDS, malaria, and other diseases; (7) ensuring environmental sustainability; and (8) fostering global partnerships for development to include good governance and free civil societies. The MDGs as a whole are difficult to disagree with—but they are merely targets, not the means for achieving them.[46]

In order to achieve the goals, "poor countries have pledged to govern better and invest in their people through health care and education.

Rich countries have pledged to support them through aid, debt relief, and fairer trade," states the UN Development Program.[47] Industrialized countries have been enlisted to donate Official Development Assistance (ODA) of 0.7 percent of gross national income (GNI) annually. In spite of these commitments, ODA declined between 2005 and 2006 and is expected to continue to fall slightly in 2007 as debt relief declines.[48] The United States in particular, has lagged behind its fellow G7 members in government aid levels. This is reflective of a larger phenomenon mentioned earlier: Countries simply aren't motivated to give aid. A recent UN report states that the United States and Japan (the world's largest and third largest economies, respectively) have been named as the "least generous donors."[49] But shaming aside, the G7 is not so much uncharitable as much as it is disillusioned: The ardor of the United States and other G7 countries has been diminished by the failure of past poverty eradication efforts and the corrupt regimes that embezzled foreign aid rather than used it to help ease crippling poverty.

If we expand our focus beyond traditional government aid, Americans and other G7 citizens privately donate quite a bit. Despite the relatively low levels of official aid, privately the United States gives more than any country. In fact, as seen in Table 8.1 U.S. private giving is 3.5 times as high as U.S. official development assistance according to the 2007 *Index for Global Philanthropy*. U.S. private giving is estimated to be $95.2 billion, while U.S. Official Development Assistance is only estimated to be at $27.6 billion. Interestingly, NGOs that rely on directed giving have proven better outlets for charity than public donations.

One reason official donations are low is because such funds to developing countries—some $2.5 trillion has been provided over the past 50 years—has gone not to needy private citizens but largely to crooked leaders.[50] In fact, foreign aid may have worsened the plight of the impoverished by sustaining corrupt and inefficient governments that contribute to their misery and by leaving nations with mountainous debt. In such mismanaged countries, as many as 70 around the world, new ways forward must be found to change the basic system.[51] William Easterly makes the apt comment: "It should be obvious not to give aid to corrupt governments."[52] And as Figure 8.5 notes, African countries have been the most prone to corruption. For example, Nigeria received $3.5 billion in aid from 1980 to 2000, which

Table 8.1 Total U.S. Economic Engagement with Developing Countries, 2005

Category	Billions of US$	(%)
U.S. Official Development Assistance (ODA)	$27.6	14
U.S. private assistance	$95.2	50
Foundations	$2.2	2
Corporations	$5.1	5
Private and voluntary organizations	$16.2	17
Universities and colleges	$4.6	5
Religious organizations	$5.4	6
Individual remittances	$61.7	65
U.S. private capital flows	$69.2	36
U.S. total economic engagement	$192.0	100

SOURCES: Organization for Economic Development and Co-operation (OECD), Development Co-operation Report 2006, Vol. 8 No. 1, 2007, Hudson Institute 2007.

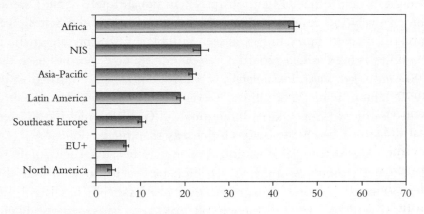

Figure 8.5 Demands for Bribery, per Region
SOURCE: Transparency International.
Note: Percentage of Respondents Asked to Pay a Bribe to Obtain Service During Past 12 Months.

is actually a few hundred million less than Sani Abacha, who ruled the country from 1993 to 1998, has been accused of stealing from public coffers.[53] While there have been several success stories of anticorruption efforts in Ghana and Tanzania, for instance, a study by the World Bank found that between 1996 and 2004, the quality of governance deteriorated in as many African countries as it improved.[54]

Toward a Poverty Strategy

In short, viewing the poor as charity cases that require handouts hasn't worked, especially because many handouts have often lined dictators' pockets instead of feeding hungry mouths. Poverty alleviation strategies should attempt to minimize the possibility of corruption, which in many situations means avoiding direct lending or aid to corrupt governments. Although liberalizing trade should be the primary strategy (as it has been in China and India), one must recognize that many tactics are necessary. Governments alone cannot eradicate poverty. The solution is not just writing a check—direct antipoverty efforts such as microfinance lending and other NGO initiatives are becoming far more important. Echoing some of the themes and ideas mentioned earlier, to successfully combat poverty will require cultivating capitalism at a grassroots level, engaging both private and public sector players, and reforming some multilateral institutions all of which, in combination, should work holistically toward promoting the capitalist peace.

Bottom of the Pyramid

P.C. Prahalad's seminal Bottom of the Pyramid (BOP) concept argues that there is room for business development at the BOP—that is, among the poorest of the poor. This theory flies in the face of conventional wisdom, which is characterized by the "dominant assumption that the poor have no purchasing power and therefore do not represent a viable market."[55] The private sector, specifically multinational corporations and lending institutions, have an enormous opportunity to play a huge role in alleviating poverty while at the same time making a profit, expanding brand recognition, and opening new market opportunities. And best yet, BOP strategies cut out the government middleman, avoiding needless bureaucracy and room for potential corruption.

Simply as a result of the enormous numbers of impoverished, the poor represent "a significant latent purchasing power that must be unlocked."[56] If even half of the current poor were incorporated in the global market, they could buy enormous quantities of goods and services in aggregate even if individual purchases are small. Moreover, because poverty is relatively concentrated, it is not difficult to reach vast swaths of poor at once. Consider that by 2015 there will be more than 225 cities in Africa, 903 in Asia, and 225 in Latin America. More than 368 cities in the developing world will have more than one million people in each, and at least 23 of these will have more than 10 million residents. Collectively, these cities will account for about 1.5 to 2 billion people. About 35 to 40 percent of these urban concentrations will comprise BOP consumers. The density of these settlements—approximately 15,000 people per hectare—will allow for relatively easy market penetration.[57]

BOP businesses have the potential to shift attitudes of many poor, showing them the "capitalist light" at the end of the tunnel. Dejected and disenfranchised, the poor don't have a reason to believe in globalization and commerce until they can physically touch it and see it. When someone in the neighborhood has a car, cell phone, and maybe even a laptop, the results seem more tangible. But until then, despair is pervasive for people stuck in the poverty trap.

The BOP strategy that has perhaps received the most attention lately is microcredit. Microcredit is an umbrella term for all programs extending small loans (microfinance lending—often as little as $25) and other financial services such as savings accounts, to very poor people for self-employment projects that generate income and a source of support for their families.[58] Virtually unheard of before the 1970s, microlending has become a global phenomenon as businesses and people realize its efficacy in fighting poverty and inequality. Microfinance develops a culture of trust and teaches basic concepts of having to pay back and understanding asset and liability matches or mismatches. The Microcredit Summit's latest report notes that small loans to the poor rose to 133 million people—up from 13 million people in 1998.[59] As of 2007, 3,316 microcredit institutions reported reaching 133,030,913 clients, 92,922,574 of whom were among the poorest when they took their first loan. Of these poorest clients, 85.1 percent are women.[60] Increasingly, banks and philanthropies are realizing that microlending provides an excellent way to both alleviate poverty and instill a sense of economic power including savings and ambition for the future.

In the past, banks in the developing world rarely lent to the poor, instead the poor had to go to moneylenders who often charged exorbitant interest rates. This trapped farmers and other low-income earners in a cycle of poverty and deprived developing country economies of small businesses. Grameen Bank of Bangladesh and its founder Muhammad Yunus, Nobel Peace Prize winners for their work using microcredit loans to lift millions of women out of poverty, have shown how poor borrowers can be as reliable as the rich, and that trust can motivate repayment as well as collateral. Yunus pioneered "social collateral," where he would give loans to a group of women who were then responsible for each other's repayment. This kind of peer pressure turned out to be remarkably effective. Think of this in contrast to securitization and credit ratings discussed in Chapter 2. Indeed, in Bangladesh today, Grameen's loan recovery rate is an astonishing 98.5 percent, as compared to 40 to 50 percent at conventional banks that offer loans to affluent families in Bangladesh.[61] Grameen's success lends support to a growing recognition that capitalism can be harnessed to curb poverty just as, if not more effectively than aid programs. (See Table 8.2.)

Other organizations besides Grameen Bank are increasingly recognizing the value of microfinance lending, both for their own economic well-being as well as that of their clients. Similar programs have popped up all over the globe, from Mexico to Indonesia. Making loans and expecting investment returns encourages a greater degree of accountability than simply making a grant. For the recipients, meanwhile, there are benefits apart from the capital received, including the opportunity to demonstrate their creditworthiness and fiscal responsibility. A loan from a foundation can serve as a credit history, key to obtaining more

Table 8.2 Microfinance Institution Activity (as of December 31, 2006)

Number of MFIs Reporting (1997–2006)	3,316
Number of MFIs Reporting in 2007 Only	873
Percent Poorest Clients Represented by 873 MFIs Reporting in 2007	92.4
Total Number of Clients (as of 12/31/06)	133,030,913
Total Number of Poorest Clients (as of 12/31/06)	92,922,574
Total Number of Poorest Women (as of 12/31/06)	79,130,581
Number of Poorest Family Members Affected (as of 12/31/06)	464,612,870

SOURCE: 2007 Microcredit Summit Report, 2.

traditional forms of capital, such as bank loans, and attracting for-profit investors. The recipients of microfinance loans are generally perceived as more credit-worthy by these institutions.[62] One of the more innovative NGOs in this space is Kiva (www.kiva.org, see box), an Internet-based platform that connects small lenders—who often lend just $25—to needy businesspeople in countries from Kazakhstan to Cambodia.

Given its aims and historical position, the World Bank should take the lead and the initiative on microfinance lending to ensure it becomes an engrained multilateral Macro Quantum strategy. Currently, World Bank projects focus on the goals of its 1999 Comprehensive Development Framework, which encourages countries to own their development agendas and be active stakeholders.[63] By working almost exclusively with governments, the World Bank is in danger of both making itself obsolete as well as abetting corrupt regimes. Microfinance lending, on the other hand, has the power to reach impoverished citizens, bypassing crooked governments, and cultivating commercial culture. The World Bank could give out leveraged loans to microlending institutions in order for them to expand. In the spirit of microlending itself, by making loans to microlending organizations deemed "too risky" by traditional commercial banks and investors, the World Bank could provide an important stimulus for local growth.

But BOP development means more than just microlending and has greater impact by broadly engaging the lowest strata of developing countries. Oftentimes, poor people cannot afford to buy greater volumes of goods that they would like; a reasonably priced small packet would have great appeal. For example, figure 8.6 shows the growing number of single-serve packages of shampoo that are sold in the Indian market. Measured in tons, the Indian shampoo market is as large as that of the United States. Large MNCs, such as Unilever and Procter & Gamble (P&G), as well as local firms have penetrated the BOP through scaled down products. Today, the penetration of shampoo in India is about 90 percent.[64]

There are numerous examples of BOP success. "Emerging markets are our key growth areas," says François Perraud of Nestlé. "Our best sellers in Africa are 3-for-1 products, where granulated coffee, cream, and sugar are all sold in one powder sachet." As Gunender Kapur, of Unilever Nigeria, says, "Our well-recognized brands are sold in small, low-priced packs. This ensures that consumers towards the bottom of

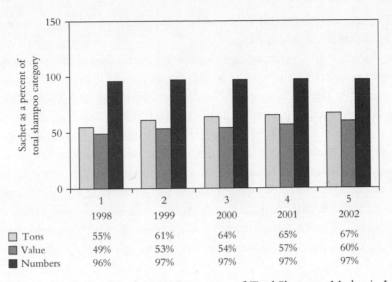

Figure 8.6   Single-Serve Sachet as a Percentage of Total Shampoo Market in India
Source: www.whartonsp.com/articles/article.asp?p=389714&seqNum=4.

the economic pyramid, earning daily wages, can buy our brands with a relatively modest cash outlay.[65] Or consider that India's Tata Motors just developed what it calls the world's cheapest car, the Nano. Unveiled in January 2008 with a retail price of about $2,500, the cars have no radios, no airbags, no passenger-side mirror and there is only one windshield wiper.[66] However, Tata Motors is hoping that the introduction of the Nano not only empowers the poor but also opens up a previously unexplored market niche for the company. This should be a wake-up call to other automobile manufacturers, particularly in industrialized countries. As GM and Ford continue to struggle with huge financial losses in the face of growing competition from more efficient overseas firms, perhaps they should look to expanding their market share in developing markets with no-frills, inexpensive automobiles.

The U.S. government could do a lot to promote these BOP opportunities through increased funding for government agencies that support U.S. business abroad, such as the Export-Import Bank and the Overseas Private Investment Corporation (OPIC). Moreover, governments can subsidize or give tax breaks to corporations that invest in the developing world. With government support between NGOs, multilateral assistance, and corporate efforts, poverty can be eradicated while at the same time promoting the capitalist peace.

These BOP opportunities cannot be easily leveraged without the cooperation of all these players. At the core of all poverty arguments is essentially the promotion of wealth, stability, and more solid citizenship. G7 countries, particularly the United States, have failed to realize these can be achieved by accessing BOP populations—some two billion people worldwide. BOP should be a win-win: The more Fortune 500 companies that venture out to emerging markets, the more seeds of capitalism are spread while simultaneously opening up new markets and building brand recognition. As long as developing countries' poor are excluded from target markets, G7 countries will continue to miss out on incomparable business opportunities.

NGOs and Social Entrepreneurs

All around the world, nongovernmental organizations (NGOs) have become the frontline warriors in the fight against global poverty, often working with multilaterals and MNCs to turbo boost the effort. There are thousands of such philanthropies around the world, with more than 3,000 of them having UN consultative status today.[67] These nonstate ninjas have been essential in filling the gap between what the state and the international community are willing and able to provide and what the people need. In many cases, the largest NGOs provide more in direct funding than parts of the United Nations.

For example, the Gates Foundation, the world's largest private charity founded by U.S. billionaire and Microsoft founder Bill Gates and his wife Melinda, runs a global development program that works with "motivated partners to create opportunities for people to lift themselves out of poverty and hunger."[68] The operating budget for the Gates Foundation in 2006 ($33 billion) was actually 10 times greater than the operating budget for the World Health Organization in the same time period. Similarly, Oxfam International—one of the oldest and best known NGOs—is a confederation of 13 entities working together with more than 3,000 partners in more than 100 countries to combat and eradicate poverty.[69] Oxfam has a presence in virtually every corner of the world, sponsoring development programs and responding to crises such as the Darfur tragedy. Oxfam also maintains campaigns for policy and practice change on fair trade, conflict and humanitarian response, climate change, and issues such as debt relief, the global arms trade, poverty reduction, and universal basic education.[70] In the fiscal year 2005–2006, Oxfam disbursed $638.25 million through its global programs.[71] All told, the sophisticated and experienced staff and large budgets of these NGOs help them provide vital services to the world's poor.

One of the more exciting NGO trends is the emergence of "social entrepreneurs," the venture capitalists of the nonprofit sector.[72] These small players recognize a social problem and use entrepreneurial principles to organize, create, and manage specific ventures to make social change. Whereas traditional venture capitalists measure performance in investment returns and profit, a social entrepreneur focuses on broader societal impact. These groups tend to be smaller than most NGOs (often just one or two people and often very young). They sometimes partner with NGOs, multilaterals, or other citizen groups (in both the public and private sectors). By using private sector savvy and taking advantage of market forces, social entrepreneurs are playing an important role in alleviating poverty throughout the world. The Schwab Foundation even sponsors the attendance of social entrepreneurs at the Davos World Economic Forum.

One headline grabbing organization founded to support these activities is Ashoka, started in 1980 by former McKinsey consultant Bill Drayton, often called "the godfather" of social entrepreneurship."[73] Drayton likes to say that social entrepreneurs neither hand out fish nor teach people to fish—their aim is to revolutionize the fishing industry. Responding to the demand, many universities are now offering classes in social entrepreneurship, and there are a growing number of role models.[74] The emergence of more social entrepreneurs and their improved access to growth capital as they get better connected to philanthropists, is creating enormous productivity opportunities for the citizen sector.[75] The first Ashoka fellow was named in India in 1981. There are now about 1,800 fellows in 60 countries and Ashoka has a $30-million annual budget funded by donations. Fellows often come from Ashoka's private sector partners like consultants McKinsey & Co. and public relations firm Hill & Knowlton.[76]

Ending Agricultural Subsidies

As we've pointed out several times now, failing to bring the Doha trade negotiations to a successful and equitable conclusion has wreaked havoc on the global economy. A well-greased trade system is an integral part of the international development agenda: All development partners should collaborate in devising a shared global strategy to address this global problem. G7 farm subsidies should be eliminated; the returns on this concession would be far greater than the sacrifice. In addition to making impoverished farmers' crops more competitive in the international market, ending subsidies would give G7 countries remarkable leverage with developing country governments in the manufacturing sectors. Over the long term, agricultural productivity must increase in the developing world in order to both avert food crises as well as to combat poverty. In order for this to happen, however, the Doha round must be settled in a way that allows developing countries' agricultural products to compete fairly in the global marketplace.

Even the World Bank Group President Robert Zoellick has suggested rich countries could help finance a "green revolution" to increase farm productivity and raise crop yields in Africa. One measure the U.S. Congress failed to pass in 2008 aimed to create a pilot program to buy $25 million in food grown locally in poor countries. Currently, the United States buys food from U.S. suppliers and pays high shipping fees to send it to needy countries.[77] By implementing this legislation, the United States could have saved money as well as encourage local production by buying directly from local farmers.

World Bank Reform

Aside from the Doha round, the World Bank itself has become part of the poverty problem. It focuses on governments, ignoring grassroots groups. The IMF and the World Bank have sometimes extended funds to governments that either have no interest in reform or are unable to pull it off, thereby providing some additional financial breathing space to malfeasant rulers. Despite good intentions, World Bank funds may actually be subverting the spread of pro-market policies.[78] By seeking cooperation primarily with governments, the World Bank is, quite literally, banking on the local government infusing cash into the economy rather than hedging its bets by engaging the impoverished themselves.

Furthermore, while the World Bank has taken positive steps toward poverty eradication, the organization's resources could be used more efficiently to do more. As discussed in Chapter 2, creating a permanent fund based on gold reserves could help foster many areas that may fall outside traditional World Bank lending programs today. For example, funding venture capital for microlending, alternative energy projects, sustainable agriculture, and other BOP sectors could dramatically accelerate progress on the World Bank's mission to end poverty. Ending poverty cannot be achieved by the public sector alone, and initiatives like this are the best way to ensure long-term sustainability and growth.[79] The broadening of the World Bank's shareholder base, as discussed earlier, would also help this effort by making more capital available.

Capitalist Peace Corps

The United States could do much to promote capitalism, provide aid, and alleviate poverty in the long-term through the formation of a "Capitalist Peace Corps," a group modeled on the current Peace Corps, with an expanded budget and a renewed focus on commerce, finance, and trade. One of the Peace Corps' stated missions is to "help promote a better understanding of Americans on the part of the peoples served." What better way to do that than to use it to promote capitalism, a core American value. Initiatives like this provide a crucial basis for inspiring good will toward the United States and other developed countries as well as providing a useful platform from which to combat poverty.

The U.S. Peace Corps was officially established in March of 1961 and has had 190,000 volunteers and trainees to date in 139 different countries. According to the Peace Corps website, there are 8,079 current volunteers. Currently, however, only 15 percent of the Peace Corps budget is being put toward business development. The rest is dedicated to other important areas as education (36 percent), health and HIV/ AIDS (21 percent), environment (14 percent), youth development (6 percent) and agriculture (5 percent),[80] with the aim of helping: (1) the people of interested countries in meeting their need for trained men and women; (2) to promote a better understanding of Americans on the part of the peoples served; and (3) to promote a better understanding of other peoples on the part of Americans. While these are admirable goals, "dollars and sense" deserves its own focused organization. This more specialized Capitalist Peace Corps would aim to identify business/entrepreneurship opportunities in developing countries, mobilize needed resources in social entrepreneurial fashion, and tie in American industry where feasible. In addition to creating greater potential for business, such a group would also indirectly promote the U.S. image abroad. The Peace Corps fiscal year 2008 budget was $330.8 million, which could easily be increased by at least $1 billion to accommodate the creation of the new Capitalist Peace Corps.

Alleviating Poverty as a Macro Quantum Strategy

While poverty has been decreasing, there is still work to be done. As trade, foreign investment, and technology have spread, the gap between the economic haves and have-nots has widened, not only in wealthy countries like the United States but also in poorer nations like Mexico, Argentina, India, and China. There are pockets of ultra-wealthy people now living in these countries alongside some of the world's poorest. This widening not only exacerbates antiglobalization sentiment (which is not in the interest of either the G7 or impoverished people), but also makes the battle lines less clear in the fight against poverty. It is necessary for the G7 as well as rising powers to step up and address poverty before our collective economic interests are threatened.

Imagine the potential if these last two billion impoverished were brought into the Macro Quantum economy. The capitalist peace thrives on differentiated labor, on competition, on economies of scale and on innovation—all things that poverty severely inhibits. There are still hundreds of millions of people barely eating enough calories each day to survive, let alone to dream about participating in the global economy—these are the people we need to incorporate and raise out of the vicious cycle of poverty. Therefore it is in everyone's collective interest to cultivate new markets and labor sources throughout the world.

With momentum in the Millennium Development Goals stalled, and 2015 MDG targets not likely to be met, global poverty reduction requires a renewed focus not only from the G7 countries led by the United States but also from new rising powers. Moreover, the foreign-aid strategies of the past need broader support from NSAs geared toward engaging populations not simply governments. Beyond greater trade engagement, the better use of NGOs and social entrepreneurs, MNCs and microlenders, as well as more effective multilateral platforms, are necessary to alleviate poverty and ensure that we continue striving to achieve the capitalist peace.

Social Entrepreneurs

Social entrepreneurs prove that a worldwide impact can be made by relatively few individuals. Some of these efforts are modest. For example, Soraya Salti, a 37-year-old Jordanian woman is trying to transform the Arab world by teaching entrepreneurship in schools. Her organization, Injaz, is now training 100,000 Arab students each year to find a market niche, construct a business plan, and then launch and nurture a business. The program has spread to 12 Arab countries and is aiming to teach one million students a year. Girls, in particular, have flourished in the program, which has had excellent reviews and is getting support from the U.S. Agency for International Development.

Or consider Cinepop, the brainchild of Ariel Zylbersztejn, a 27-year-old Mexican. Ninety percent of Mexicans can't afford to go to movies, so he started his own Cinepop, which shows movies on inflatable screens in public parks for free. He sells sponsorships to companies to advertise to the thousands of viewers who come to watch the free entertainment. Cinepop is only three years old, but already 250,000 people a year watch movies on his screens—and his goal is to take the model to Brazil, India, China, and other countries.

But perhaps the most far-reaching and global of the social entrepreneurial projects is Kiva.org. In 2005, more than 20 years after Grameen Bank pioneered the idea of microlending, Matt

(Continued)

(*Continued*)

and Jessica Flannery brought a touch of Silicon Valley innovation to the practice. Kiva is "the world's first person-to-person micro-lending web site, empowering individuals to lend directly to unique entrepreneurs in the developing world." Its model is simple: Kiva partners with existing microlending organizations that choose qualified entrepreneurs. The organizations use kiva.org to post profiles of these entrepreneurs and their projects. The stories of the people found on Kiva are often very detailed. A random perusal of the site brings up Grace from Uganda, whose $500 loan allowed her to buy refrigeration equipment for her peanut butter business; and Angel, a Roma gypsy from Bulgaria, who used $850 to start his own bicycle repair shop.

On the giving side, potential lenders are able to browse potential recipients, then lend using a credit card or Pay Pal account. Over time, the entrepreneur repays the loan (without interest). Repayment and other updates are posted on Kiva and e-mailed to lenders if they chose. When lenders get their money back, they can re-lend to someone else in need, donate their funds to Kiva for operational expenses, or withdraw their funds. In only a couple of short years, Kiva has become an extremely popular tool. The web site gives statistics on the loans made and repaid in the last week. A typical week looks like this: $680,600 was lent; 1,574 entrepreneurs funded; 9,103 lenders made a loan; and 644 loans were completely repaid. Not only has Kiva brought a new degree of transparency to microlending, it has fostered a personal rapport between lenders and recipients, reinforcing the sentiment that, through technology, it really has become a small world, after all.

The increasing prominence of social entrepreneurs has the potential to generate huge benefits by spreading capitalist culture abroad and identifying unfulfilled societal needs. America Forward (www.americanforward.org), a consortium of social

entrepreneurs, proposes an expanded concept of national service and federal matching of private social investment funds that
invest in community-run programs to increase the number of
social entrepreneurs in the future.

---

* Nicholas D. Kristof, "The Age of Ambition," the *New York Times*,
January 27, 2008, www.nytimes.com/2008/01/27/opinion/27kristof.
html?scp=4&sq=social+entrepreneurship&st=nyt.

Chapter 9

Driving with a New Dashboard in the Macro Quantum World

There are three kinds of lies: lies, damned lies, and statistics.
—Benjamin Disraeli

It would be an understatement to say that the world today is a very different place than it was just 20 years ago. Throughout our discussion, we've described, from trunk to tail, the tremendous opportunities and challenges presented by the new elephant in our living room: globalization. Its ripple effects have touched virtually every facet of our daily lives—from how we feed ourselves to what we do for a living, and from how we teach our children to what we aspire to be, have, and do.

Down but Not Out

In the Macro Quantum world, greater cross-border exchange and the rise of emerging powers and NSAs have reshaped the face of the global economy. To continue to survive and thrive in this ecosystem, we've discussed how the United States must adapt from a unipolar to a multipolar (or what Richard Hass calls a "nonpolar") system where dozens of players—states and NSAs alike—exercise power and influence.[1] One popular adage on Wall Street is, "the trend is your friend," meaning you profit by trading with the market not against it. While the United States once was *the* market, the market now has many players that America cannot control. And before we let other countries control, or even corner, the market, it is in our collective interest to solidify the rules and sanction the referees of the globalization game. This will require not only acknowledging but actually welcoming new players through more inclusive multilateral architecture and policy stances. Cultivating a multilateral "strength in numbers" attitude will be key to avoiding the calamities of unchecked globalization that befell the world in the early twentieth century.

The recommended adjustments in trade, energy, security, immigration, health, environment, and poverty policies aim to strengthen and modernize our current institutional infrastructure—including NATO, the WHO, the WTO, the World Bank, and the UN, among others. Lately, many of these organizations have been left to languish, but with a little attention and extra funding, a revived multilateral system could shepherd the capitalist peace forward based on the rule of law not the law of the jungle. In addition to reforming such multilaterals, the United States needs to turn a critical eye to policies, attitudes, lifestyle trends, and institutions at home. Small adjustments at the domestic level could have quantum reverberations beyond our borders. But this will not be easy.

While the United States has lost economic ground to new players and tarnished its reputation abroad through its own knee-jerk unilateral reactions, it is still capable of evolving and thriving in the Macro Quantum world. Although American government has been slow to adopt the new thinking and policies necessitated by globalization, our private sector has been at the forefront of these megatrends for decades. The United States has topped the World Competitiveness Yearbook rankings for 15 straight years through 2008, a study that surveys 55 economies according to 331 criteria measuring how nations create and maintain conditions favorable to businesses.[2] And despite the financial body blows it has taken recently, the United States still has arguably the world's most sophisticated economy and financial system. Moreover, the United States is the global vanguard of venture capital and technology as well as the leader in measures of individual productivity across many key industries. While the global credit crisis, bank failures, and mounting government deficits seem ominous, they are hardly intractable. The United States has a uniquely entrepreneurial and pragmatic culture, finding the means to reinvent itself even at the darkest hour. U.S. business has always been adept at Joseph Schumpeter's "creative destruction"—the Darwinian process whereby visionary, radical innovation continuously propels the economy forward; this must become an integral feature of our government as well.

For much of the last decade, the United States' intoxicating post-Cold War confidence as the world's sole superpower deluded our government into believing that we could control globalization by sheer will. This has proven to be a myopic and unfortunate miscalculation. Now, the United States must begin to dismantle entrenched Micro Domestic attitudes. Even if these strategies brought success 50 years ago, we must part with them in search of something more fitting for today's very different world. More important, these changes could serve as a model for the world to emulate. The United States is still in many ways the world's leader, but clearly the recent administration has misconstrued the source of this power. The esteem the United States has been afforded by the international community comes not from brute economic and military strength, as recent officials have believed, but the enduring admiration, trust, and respect its pioneering form has garnered during the twentieth century. The United States has long been viewed as both experiment and inspiration. Even as early as 1630, famous Puritan preacher John Winthrop told the members of the Pilgrim settlement in Massachusetts that they would serve as a "city upon a hill," a standard for the rest of the world. As the United States settles into maturity after 230-plus years as an independent entity, it must fight off the inertia of old habits and remember its role as a great innovator and leader. While global markets deal with the credit crisis triggered by America's subprime woes, United States leadership on the financial front may be truly appreciated by the world.

One factor preventing the United States from abandoning the Micro Domestic paradigm is simply how charmed and effortless our lives have been under this old perspective. Few alive today remember firsthand the Great Depression or World Wars I or II. Postwar babies have grown up bathed in prosperity, free to pursue individual happiness, but this has sometimes translated into unsustainable instant material gratification, mountains of debt, and displays of angry, armed aggression. Today, the circumstances have changed. What if such attitudes were to spread globally? How would we deal with a world where 6.7 billion people "pursue happiness" through thoughtless consumption, and countries flex their military muscles to enforce their national agendas? Happiness is surely more than endless consumption with no regard for the true quantum costs to others. So what policies do we craft to achieve a more thoughtful, responsible happiness? To answer these questions requires new modes of thinking, and new ways of measuring where the United States stands, where it is going and how far it is from where it wants to be. Many critics have noted the structural flaws inherent in our economic metrics for measuring progress and failure. Our Macro Quantum world requires different ways to analyze root causes to problems, identify possible solutions, and monitor and evaluate policies and their outcomes. To move forward, we will need to view the world through radically different lenses and monitor ourselves on a new, multigauged dashboard. Driving with only a speedometer might tell us how fast we're going, but it doesn't tell us if we're going in the right direction or if we have enough fuel to get there.

Living by Numbers

A man enters the lobby of an apartment building and greets his neighbor on her way out. "What's the temperature like outside?" she asks. "Feels like thirty-five or so," replies the man. Without further context, this single number doesn't tell us much. Perhaps this exchange happens in New York, and the woman will turn back to grab a heavier coat. Or maybe it occurs in London, where she'll brace herself for the sweltering 35 degrees Centigrade (95 degrees Fahrenheit). Or it may be the case that (regardless of locale) the man's running a fever and his response may not accurately correspond with the actual air temperature.

While this particular ambiguity is readily dispelled, the scenario draws attention to perhaps the greatest Macro Quantum challenge—devising, gathering, and interpreting appropriate measurements and statistics. Specifically, what measures should we be using to judge well-being, success, wealth, progress, and happiness? Temperature is fairly objective and easy to quantify, but measuring complex phenomena like economic advancement is messier and more subject to distortion than one might imagine. How do we best collect and aggregate data? How can we account for observational error and intentional statistical manipulation? Can we compare figures across borders? And is just measuring GDP alone enough to give us the best barometer for advancement?

While Adam Smith is often considered the father of modern economics, English economist and philosopher William Petty actually tried to get a scientific handle on the country's economic health almost a century before Smith and made some of the first estimates of national accounts (an accounting measure of the entire country's income and output) in 1665. Petty, Oliver Cromwell's chief economist and assistant to philosopher Thomas Hobbes, was one of the first thinkers to note that a country's wealth was larger than its sum of gold and silver. In trying to estimate the size of Britain's economy, he discovered that England's stock market was worth more than all its hard assets—land, metals, and livestock—and the difference must be the "value of people"—human capital.[3] Petty was one of the first to recognize money in circulation and the velocity of it changing hands had much to do with economic value. It was here that the basic notion of analyzing and quantifying a country's economic activity was born.

The next major breakthrough in national accounting didn't come until the early twentieth century, as Ted Halstead and his colleagues describe:

> In 1931 a group of government and private experts were summoned to a congressional hearing to answer basic questions about the economy. It turned out they couldn't; the most recent data were for 1929, and they were rudimentary at that. In 1932, the last year of the Hoover administration, the Senate asked the Commerce Department to prepare comprehensive

estimates of the national income. Soon after, the department set a young economist by the name of Simon Kuznets to the task of developing a uniform set of national accounts. These became the prototype for what we now call the GDP.[4]

Since the implementation of a formal system of national income and production accounting in the depression era, economic activity, whether tallied as gross national product (GNP) or as gross domestic product, has been the premiere measure of economic well-being. GDP, defined as the total market value of all final goods and services produced in a country in a given year, has become the most accepted standard and has changed forever how we look at public policy. Before the advent of national accounting, economists rarely had been consulted on public policy. Equipped with powerful new statistical tools, they became *the* policy authorities of the postwar era.

Yet even the forefather of national accounting realized the limitations of GDP. Already in 1934, Kuznets warned that, "the welfare of a nation can scarcely be inferred from measurement of national income." He wrote again in 1962: "Distinctions must be kept in mind between quantity and quality of growth, between its costs and return, and between the short and the long run. Goals for more growth should specify more growth of what and for what."[5] In other words, GDP and its components give us a measure of how much we produce and consume—but it doesn't reflect any of the qualitative aspects of the economy. It cannot answer essential questions: Are we consuming too much? Is some of today's registered consumption simply a waste? Will an increase in GDP today have a negative effect on GDP in the future? And, perhaps most important, are we producing goods and services that benefit society as a whole? Kuznets' critique has since been echoed by many prominent economists including Nobel laureates Joseph Stiglitz, Amartya Sen, and Muhammad Yunus.

GDP is a powerful indicator, but it is by no means a complete measure of socioeconomic activity. On the one hand, as economist and Nobel Laureate John Kenneth Galbraith reported, prosperity spread rapidly in the era after WWII in part thanks to "little observed but spectacular improvements in the statistical measures of the current output of the U.S. plant."[6] But GDP is not a wholly accurate or objective measure. It excludes a number of factors that contribute to economic well-being, like the value of nonmarket goods and services (especially natural resources) and informal and unpaid activities. The contributions of stay-at-home mothers (or fathers) are ignored as well as in-kind trade. Yet anytime a dollar changes hands GDP is boosted, even if well-being or value is not created. If a housekeeper and lawn care company are hired to perform some domestic duties previously performed by a family member without pay, GDP is boosted.

Since GDP includes all activities where money changes hands, it necessarily views cash-generating activities related to natural disasters and crime in terms of economic *gains*. For example, earthquakes and hurricanes register immense damage and disrupt thousands of lives, yet they also typically generate economic and labor expansion through rebuilding efforts. While disasters may raise GDP by causing money to change hands, they do not create well-being. French classical liberal theorist Frédéric Bastiat pointed out this faulty rationale nearly 160 years ago in his parable of the broken window.[7] Bastiat describes a shopkeeper whose window is broken by a boy. Because repairing the busted window makes work for the glazier, who will then buy bread, benefiting the baker, who will then buy shoes, benefiting the cobbler and so on, the townspeople hail the mischievous boy as an economic benefactor, ignoring the opportunities the shopkeeper may have had if he had not been forced to spend his money on a new window. Perhaps he would have spent the money to hire a new worker for his store, or saved for his daughter's education. Likewise, GDP is unable to capture the fact that victims of floods, hurricanes, wildfires, and earthquakes are merely replacing destroyed property (if even possible), not adding to their wealth or happiness. By this equation, the most productive citizens for a national economy are "terminally ill cancer patients going through a costly divorce," because they generate a lot of economic activity.[8] Figure 9.1 illustrates some of the concepts—such as leisure, health, and satisfaction—that GDP cannot measure, as well as some concepts that are included in GDP but do not contribute to well-being, such as depreciation and "regrettables" such as spending on crime and disaster remediation.

If, for a moment, we set aside the philosophical issue of what we want to measure and consider GDP not as a proxy for well-being

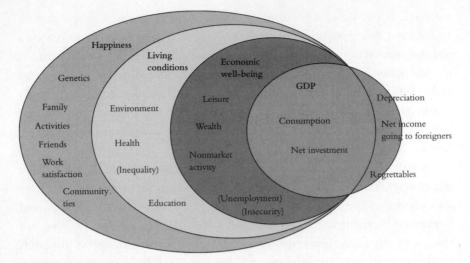

Figure 9.1   What GDP Does (and Does Not) Measure
SOURCE: Deutche Bank.

but simply as a measure of economic activity, there are still significant statistical challenges surrounding how GDP is actually measured.
In his 1950 book *On the Accuracy of Economic Observations*, Princeton
Economics Professor Oskar Morgenstern reminded us that national
income may only be measured within a 10 percent margin of error,
although economic policy advisers often propose policies based on
adjustments in national income of 1 percent or less—a shift that is
statistically insignificant.[9] Although data collection has become more
sophisticated since Morgenstern's book was published, accuracy remains
as elusive as ever. Many countries lack adequately trained professionals
capable of observing economic data and rely instead on GDP estimates
made by the Word Bank. Some developing countries are experiencing
fundamental economic and social changes that bring more stakeholders
into the market, changing the way people invest, get employed, earn
money, and consume; statisticians may have a difficult time keeping up.
Nor can aggregate statistics at a national level capture regional disparities within these states. Even in OECD countries, only within the last
70 years have government agencies and private economic researchers
systematically collected economic data, and this data is still prone to
manipulation and error.

Moreover, there may be strong incentive for governments to adjust, or even falsify, statistics. Improving economic performance can increase the responsible party's chances of staying in power. Consider China, where regional officials' performance is measured by provincial GDP growth.[10] Rampant massaging of local growth figures has resulted. Statistical manipulation can also help to gain entry into international organizations, like when Greek government officials distorted budget deficit numbers in order to gain entrance into the European Monetary Union (EMU).[11] Up until 1995, Greece maintained high government deficits, often more than 10 percent of GDP. The number dwindled incredibly rapidly, and by 2000, Greece's deficit was below 3 percent making the country eligible for EMU membership. After Greece was accepted to the EMU, the Statistical Office of the European Communities refused to validate figures prepared by the National Statistical Service of Greece (NSSG). In reaction, the NSSG was forced to revise its debt estimate several times until the surplus became a deficit.

Even the United States is not immune to such tampering. U.S. political commentator Kevin Philips notes:

> The use of deceptive statistics has played its own vital role in convincing many Americans that the U.S. economy is stronger, fairer, more productive, more dominant, and richer with opportunity than it actually is.... The corruption has tainted the very measures that most shape public perception of the economy— the monthly consumer price index (CPI), which serves as the chief bellwether of inflation; the quarterly gross domestic product, which tracks the U.S. economy's overall growth; and the monthly unemployment figure, which for the general public is perhaps the most vivid indicator of economic health or infirmity. Not only do governments, businesses, and individuals use these yardsticks in their decision-making but minor revisions in the data can mean major changes in household circumstances—inflation measurements help determine interest rates, federal interest payments on the national debt, and cost-of-living increases for wages, pensions, and Social Security benefits. And, of course, our statistics have political consequences, too. An administration is helped when it can mouth banalities

about price levels being "anchored" as food and energy costs begin to soar. [12]

Philips believes most American presidents from John F. Kennedy through George W. Bush have made a variety of tweaks to the methodologies of inflation and unemployment that give Americans a distorted view of the economy. As a result, the U.S. economy can seem up even when average Americans are feeling pretty down.

A second statistical concern surrounding GDP is its standardization across the globe. Even without manipulation, national income statistics are poor bases for international comparison due to different classifications, definitions, price systems, population growth rates, and exchange rates, as well as different measurements of inflation between countries. Consider how just one small piece of the puzzle can throw off the whole picture, such as the varying accounting treatments of depreciation across countries. Since estimates of depreciation are made by corporations themselves and are guided by tax considerations and local regulations, the results can provide misleading ideas about the value of enterprises. For example, the same equipment may be worth more on the books under U.S. accounting rules as opposed to those of, say, Thailand. A useful indicator of national economic activity should be internationally comparable given that other countries are the benchmarks by which we measure our own progress. For example, in Chapter 6 we saw that Americans spend $2.3 trillion annually on health care. Without knowing that this is more than double on a per capita basis what most industrialized countries spend, that information would not tell us much. How can we adjust for statistical manipulation and cross-border differences? While the best we can do to combat manipulation is to enforce unified statistical standards and better monitoring, there are several methodologies currently employed to account for differences, including purchasing power parity comparisons and per capita adjustments.

Purchasing Power Parity

The effect of exchange rates and varying living standards can also skew cross-border economic comparisons leaving us with a distorted worldview. In theory, market exchange rates should adjust perfectly so that the same good and service have the same price in different countries. But in practice, imperfect capital mobility (currency controls in the extreme case) and practical concerns such as transportation costs prevent exchange markets from working perfectly. Each year the World Bank gathers data from countries in their local currency and adjusts that to a base value relative to U.S. dollars. If a country's currency weakens, like Argentina's did in 2001, for example, the economy looks dramatically different from just a year earlier. Argentina's economy theoretically shrank by two-thirds in dollar terms from 2000 to the end of 2001. Does that mean that Argentina produced only one-third in 2001 of what it produced in 2000? No. It is likely the amount of food consumed and things bought were about the same. But in U.S. dollar terms, the ultimate "value" was much less. Conversely, a country whose currency is gaining against the dollar will see its economy grow dramatically.

To avoid this, several organizations, including the World Bank, have opted to look at economies on a purchasing power parity (PPP) basis—a measurement that equalizes the purchasing power of currencies in their home countries for a given basket of goods. Of course, this causes concerns over what we include in this basket but still is probably more accurate than a GDP measurement at market exchange rates.[13] By defining a set of comparable goods across countries and asking how many units of the local currency are needed to buy this in relation to a base currency (usually U.S. dollars), PPP helps to avoid the flaws of exchange markets. When GDP is adjusted by this recalculated exchange rate, the figure is effectively adjusted to mirror the real purchasing power.[14]

To see PPP in action, consider that the 2006 GDP per capita of Germany in USD market prices is 17 times that of China ($35,000 versus $2,000). However, taking proper account of the fact that the products and services people need to sustain their standard of living are substantially cheaper in China than they are in Germany and adjusting the GDP figures by this we find that the PPP adjusted per capita GDP in Germany is only four times that of China ($31,000 vs. $7,600).[21] Indeed, the result of a PPP adjustment will most commonly be a reduction of the spread between rich and poor countries in terms of GDP levels.

Population Growth and Per Capita GDP

Another simple but overlooked issue with GDP relates to population growth: The more a population grows, the more GDP grows. Remember our earlier equation: GDP = Population $\times$ Per Capita Output. When a government reports its country's GDP has expanded 3 percent this year, if the population has also increased by 3 percent, per capita GDP is actually flat. In this respect, it is amazing that everyone on Wall Street frets and quibbles about whether real GDP growth will be fractionally positive or negative every 90 days. Given that the U.S. population is growing by roughly 1.0 to 1.5 percent a year, a GDP growth rate below that means the real per capita income is actually contracting. Isn't this a more insightful way of looking at GDP?

If you look at a recent five-year snapshot of a country's economic performance, you get a very different picture using per capita versus using aggregate data. Comparing Japan and the United States from 2003 through 2007 reveals interesting results. The popular perception is that the United States' dynamic economy was outperforming Japan's. While America's annualized GDP growth of 2.9 percent beat Japan's 2.1 percent, the per capita calculation adjusts GDP surprisingly. The U.S. population increased about 1 percent per annum during this period while Japan's was fairly flat (and even began to shrink). Considering U.S. population growth, Japan's economy actually grew slightly faster.

Moreover, using growth in GDP per capita rather than simple aggregate GDP growth reveals a strikingly different picture of other countries' economic health. For example, for the recent 2003–2007 period, Australia looked like it had one of the fastest growth rates among the major industrialized nations, expanding by 3.3 percent annually on average. But Australia also had one of the biggest increases in population during these five years. When GDP is adjusted to a per capita figure, Australia and Japan actually grew at roughly the same pace. Likewise, Spain has been perceived as one of the fastest growing economies in the Eurozone, but from 2005–2008 output per person grew more slowly than in Germany, which like Japan, was depopulating.

With similar population adjustments, even some lauded emerging economies in recent years look less attractive. For example, Brazil's per capita expansion was only 2.3 percent per annum from 2003–2007 because of population growth, not that much different from the G7's, while Russia sped by with a remarkable 7.4 percent per capita growth because its population shrank by nearly 0.5 percent per annum. In the case of India and China, India's growing population cuts its per capita growth rate to 6.8 percent versus 10.2 percent for China, whose population growth has been slowing.

Focusing on GDP per person also affects comparisons of global economic health over time. From 2002–2007, world GDP grew by an average of 4.5 percent a year, its fastest for more than three decades though not as fast as during the golden age of the 1960s when annual growth exceeded 5 percent. Because the world's population is now growing at half the pace it grew in the 1960s, per capita world income has actually increased by more over the past five years than during any other period on record (see Figure 9.2). *The Economist* notes that "the world has never had it so good."[15]

Today we define recession as two consecutive quarters of aggregate GDP stagnation or contraction, but if we think about it relative to population, we may have had more recessions than official government data has suggested. The whole notion of recession—and the corresponding policies to combat recession—may be very different. For example, stagnant GDP in depopulating countries like Italy, Russia, Germany, or Japan actually isn't so bad. But in countries with growing

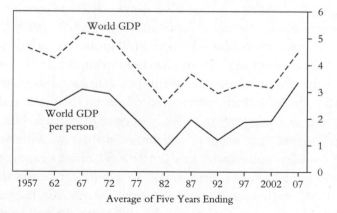

Figure 9.2   Per Capita vs. Gross GDP
SOURCES: IMF; Angus Maddison; EIU estimates.

populations like the United States (and most developing countries), the average citizen may be worse off. But one can see the political issues—and distortions—such statistical debates create. For example, if a country likes to boast about its total size—like some have accused the United States of doing[16]—then it would be unpopular to switch away from absolute GDP growth (although this, too, can be impacted by the value of the U.S. dollar, as discussed above).

GDP can be adjusted to a PPP or per capita basis to gain some accuracy, but it is difficult to check the challenges of intentional manipulation and poor data collection. We've also seen that GDP fails to measure noncash economic activity; nor can it distinguish between productive uses of cash and so-called regrettables, spending on crime and disaster remediation. While GDP has a wide margin for error and distortion, it is doubtful other indicators will be entirely immune from these problems. But a more important question is whether we can rely on this economic indicator to guide us on policy debates and decisions. After all, what is progress? Economic indicators for the last century have become the main gauge for most national and global policies, but there are enough limitations and deficiencies with such numbers that the indicators we use warrant reconsideration in the Macro Quantum world.

Debt-Funded "Growth"

As we've seen, GDP expansion is not necessarily per capita growth. But this becomes even more blurred when GDP growth is fueled by soaring debt levels. Consider the plight of Thailand during the 1997–1998 Asian financial crisis. Before the Thai government abandoned its currency peg to the U.S. dollar, it had experienced phenomenal GDP growth for decades; indeed, from 1965 to 1990, its economy expanded by an average of 7.1 percent per annum.[17] As the dollar rose in value and made the Thai baht less competitive in the 1990s, Thailand's export machine slowed and domestic investment took over as a bigger part of the country's GDP, although strong growth continued, averaging 8.2 percent in 1991–1996.[18] The growth of the early 1990s was a result of domestic investment in factories, real estate, and other assets—predicated on the availability of cheap credit. The Thai economy looked quite buoyant, but it was being propped up by borrowed money. While some would argue this is a perfectly fine economic strategy, wasteful investment leads to overcapacity and asset bubbles, and possibly lessens the efficiency of the entire economy. So while the country looked like it was still humming, debt needing to be repaid loomed on the horizon. Allowing the baht to float in 1997 helped revive the export sector in Thailand, but the precrisis economy—fueled by easy money, exorbitant debt, and asset bubbles—probably wasn't nearly as strong as GDP indicated.

This happens in wealthier countries, too. For the past two decades, the United States has had relatively low interest rates that have kept Americans borrowing money to buy everything from houses to flat screen TVs. As the property boom continued, people borrowed against inflated real estate values through home equity loans. Using these borrowed funds for consumption in turn pumped up GDP even more. The high GDP growth rates experienced in the early part of the millennium may simply reflect elevated debt. U.S. consumer credit card debt during the 2000–2007 period jumped from \$574 billion to \$915 billion.[19] And as witnessed in other boom-bust cycles, some of this debt may not be paid, while future economic activity may slow because of such overhang, actually reducing U.S. GDP somewhere down the road as the current credit crisis seems to suggest.

According to Freddie Mac (before nationalization!), the number of risky mortgages has also increased. In 2000 approximately 1 percent of adjustable rate mortgages (ARMs) were interest only, but this grew to more than 20 percent by 2005: Negative amortization loans, grew from roughly 3 percent of all adjustable rate mortgages to more than 30 percent in 2005.[20] Undoubtedly this will impact GDP down the road.

Or consider government spending. If the U.S. government borrows \$500 billion to \$1 trillion dollars annually from investors abroad to cover deficit spending, current GDP may appear inflated as that money circulates in the economy, but eventually servicing this debt will reduce GDP in one way or another. Borrowing money pumps up the economy in the short run but may deflate it over the longer run and could hurt the country's currency, too.

Some borrowing can be good. Companies generally borrow money to invest in productive assets that generate long-term value that is greater than the debt service (although as Thailand showed, it can also lead to overcapacity). That's generally not what consumer and government borrowing does. For example, an extra few hundred billion for defense spending, generally goes toward short-term versus productive investments. So, if government borrows $500 billion, or 3.5 percent of GDP to finance foreign invasions, is it 100 percent true, sustainable GDP expansion? Will this produce future GDP? Perhaps if we devised and monitored a GDP credit deflator statistic, we might have been less sanguine over American growth over the last decade.

While economists may debate the value of debt, there clearly comes a time when the use of debt is bad for an economy; at a minimum, there is a point at which it distorts our state of economic health. If you borrow today and inflate today's GDP, but this in turn sets us up for a slowdown later, is headline GDP that meaningful? GDP alone is not enough to paint a true economic picture; it must be supplemented by other economic and financial data to allow for better fine tuning.

Defining Progress in the Macro Quantum World

As Halstead and others noted in 1995, economic indicators "define the economic problems that the political arena seeks to address. If the nation's indicators of economic progress are obsolete, then they consign us to continually resorting to policies that cannot succeed because they aren't addressing the right problems."[21] Due to its ease of use, GDP is often used as a proxy indicator of more difficult-to-measure concepts, such as progress and well-being—a purpose for which it is woefully ill-suited. While there is a logical relationship between economic prosperity and well-being, GDP is too limited in scope to paint a sufficient picture of societal welfare, and therefore too limited to be the only standard by which we make policy. *It's like driving with only a speedometer.*

One popular modification of GDP is "green GDP," which is also reflected in the World Bank's genuine savings model. Although there are numerous versions of green GDP, they essentially correct GDP to counter natural resource depletion. As John Hicks noted in his *Value and Capital* in 1947, "Can a nation's entire GDP be consumed without undermining its ability to produce and consume the same GDP in the future?"[22] In 1989, Barber Conable, then the president of the World Bank, reiterated Hicks' concern that "Current calculations ignore the degradation of the natural resource base and view the sales of non-renewable resources entirely as income."[23] GDP focuses on short-term economic activities, leading to underinvestment in natural, economic, and social capital, essential to long-term sustainable development. The myopic focus of GDP is especially obvious in natural resource intensive and heavily polluting industries. Flying against the logic of most standard accounting principles, resource depletion makes no dent on GDP. Imagine if a copper mining company did not have to account for its exhausted mines—the mining company only has finite resources but it would appear as if its current actions had no effect on its future supplies.

Adjusting GDP to promote sustainable practices may lead to long-term economic gain but may curb current profits or require a more forward-looking policy that spreads resource depletion over a longer time period, causing GDP to decline in the short term. This makes switching measures politically difficult. For example, China's President Hu Jintao unrolled an ambitious attempt to change the GDP growth-obsessed culture in early in 2007. Hu promoted a green GDP that would reflect the cost of pollution to be used for evaluating the performance of provincial officials. When adjusted GDP results from several provinces were reported, double-digit GDP growth was reduced to near zero. Leaders were alarmed by the sobering results of Hu's experiment. Instead of deploying more resources for environmental cleanup, the project was shelved. The long-term hazards of high pollution, like greater health care costs due to nonpotable water and higher respiratory disease, were swept under the rug for political expediency. Instead of adjusting GDP itself, the UN has proposed supplementing it with a set of environmental accounts. What is useful about this approach is that disaggregating the two indicators allows us to focus specifically on environmental concerns—more gauges for our dashboard.

Similar measures could be developed to look at a range of issues—not just environmental impact. For example, under GDP, more production and more consumption, no matter what their side effects, register as positive. Not only does this ignore the value of the environment,

but it also encourages unsustainable levels of consumption and too little savings. At the same time Kuznets was leading the effort to imple-
ment national income accounting, the Keynesian revolution was taking
hold in the United States, shifting economists' focus to the demand
side. Policy makers no longer saw people solely as workers, farmers, and businesspeople, but primarily as consumers. Keynesians view
more consumption as a way to lead to a higher GDP and thus greater
economic well-being. In the United States where we borrow to support our consumption habits, this is arguably not the case. Landfills full
of plastic soda bottles, chronic obesity, and mounting debt tell us that
more consumption is not always better.

Changing our dashboard, that is, amending or supplementing GDP
as our predominant measure of well-being, would not be without precedent. In 1991 the United States switched from using gross national
product to gross domestic product in order to conform with international standards. Statistical indicators perform an essential function by
setting the tone for policy makers. They serve as red flags for the public
attention. But if political leaders "are trying to maximize GDP and GDP
is not a good measure, you are maximizing the wrong thing sometimes
at the expense of others and it can be counterproductive," says Nobel
Laureate Economist Joseph Stiglitz, who was tapped in early 2008 to
head a new French study on the measurement of well-being.[24]

Stiglitz's study is expected to propose a more holistic measure of
well-being. Several alternative measures like the Genuine Progress
Indicator, the Human Development Index, Environmental Performance
Index, Genuine Savings, and Ecological Footprint already exist. These
measures attempt to correct GDP through different methods, adjusting
for climate change, economically unproductive activities (such as costs
associated with crime), inequality, and pressure on resources. While the
economic community has long recognized the inherent imperfections
of GDP, these alternatives have been criticized for lacking the clarity
and conciseness of GDP.

Take the Genuine Progress Indicator (GPI), an ambitious yardstick created by the thinktank Redefining Progress, for example: GPI
attempts to distinguish between good and bad GDP growth. Under
GDP for example, resource depletion contributes to GDP, but GPI
deflates GDP by amortizing such depletion as a cost. GPI starts with

the same consumption data as GDP, but then adjusts for income distribution, and adds factors such as the value of household and volunteer work and higher education, while subtracting factors such as the costs of crime, pollution, and defense expenditures. The GPI is adjusted for nonmonetary factors such as income inequality, dependence on foreign assets, leisure time, the lifespan of consumer durables, and capital investments. While GDP itself is subject to interpretation and estimation, GPI requires a staggering number of calculations. Consider that the costs associated with crime alone include aggregating and deleting legal fees, medical expenses, and property damage. [25]

While GPI and other indicators have their own set of methodological challenges, they could complement traditional GDP to create a more accurate picture of progress. While GDP's simplicity may be attractive, it fails to mirror an increasingly complex world. The GPI's approach of amalgamating several indicators creates a single benchmark in monetized terms, which is useful for at-a-glance comparisons, but does not avoid the problems of exchange rates mentioned earlier. Nor does it serve as a single indicator specific enough to help with policy making. But disaggregating GPI and looking at its components individually does provide useful snapshots on quality of life trends. Therefore, using several indicators in combination could create a more holistic barometer of well-being without sacrificing accuracy. There are plenty of alternative GDP measures (as Table 9.1 shows), but in order for them to be taken seriously they must try to maintain high standards of accuracy and international comparability as well as guard against manipulation and accurately reflect economic activity as well as health, inequality, well-being, and environmental impact.

Rethinking Consumption, Debt, and Savings

A new expanded, reconfigured dashboard with many instruments—including debt ratios, biosocial indicators, environmental quality standards, and measures of regrettables—could help to curb the rampant overconsumption and overspending occurring in the United States (and to a lesser extent the rest of the G7); it may even spare us some fatal financial meltdowns. More consumption makes for a higher GDP

Table 9.1 Alternative Indicators

Indicator	Rationale	Creator
Genuine Progress Indicator	Tries to correct GDP by monetizing environmental and social factors.	Redefining Progress
Green GDP	Tries to correct GDP by monetizing environmental factors.	Chinese government
Genuine Savings	Provides estimates for savings by considering natural, environmental, and human capital aspects (i.e. education expenditures add to savings; degradation detracts).	World Bank
Human Development Index	Combines GDP with social indicators; emphasis on life expectancy, adult literacy, school enrolment and GDP.	UN
Ecological Footprint	Measures the ecological impact of human consumption relative to Earth's carrying capacity.	WWF and Global Footprint Network
Happy Planet Index	Life satisfaction data combined with environmental footprint data.	New Economics Foundation
Environmental Sustainability Index	Tracks a society's capacity to improve environmental performance.	Yale
Regional Quality of Development Index	Combines social, environmental and economic data.	Sbilanciamoci!
System of Economic Environmental Accounts	Combines environmental and economic data; environmental accounts are "satellite accounts" that accompany the System of National Accounts to track the interaction between the environment and the economy in detail.	UN, OECD, Eurostat, national governments

in the short run, but it may actually do more harm in the long run. Overconsumption depletes both our bodily and environmental health at unsustainable rates. What's worse, by financing this destruction through debt, we are also chipping away at our economic health.

As we mentioned before, GDP cannot distinguish between different types of consumption. Purchasing schoolbooks and purchasing beer both ratchet GDP up a notch. Some types of consumption are necessary and beneficial, but even then, there is a tipping point where you can have too much of a good thing. Every time you dip into your savings or use your credit card to buy a bigger flat-screen television, for example, you may damage your ability to later purchase a home, finance a higher education, start a business, or ensure a comfortable retirement. In the United States, personal savings has declined dramatically over the last three decades, from 18.5 percent in 1982 to negative 1 percent in 2006, only to turn moderately positive in 2007/2008.[26]

This sentiment also applies to government spending. Just as we can distinguish between useful and wasteful personal consumption, there is a difference between using government funds to build infrastructure projects that may eventually be productive assets and using government funds to give consumers a small tax rebate to finance a shopping spree at the mall.

The problem of too little savings will only get worse as working-age populations in most major industrialized countries shrink and the developed world continues to age. Aging populations are a problem because, as Franco Modigliani and Richard Brumberg's widely accepted "life cycle theory of savings" suggests, saving rates rise throughout a worker's active career and then decline in retirement. As baby boomers start to retire, pension systems the world over are straining. But instead of readjusting fiscal prerogatives in preparation for these changes, the United States and many of its G7 peers are running large deficits—creating debt-funded illusory GDP growth.

The United States was not always like this. "The whole idea of a consumption-driven economy is only about a hundred years old," according to University of Michigan's Thomas Princen: "For much of U.S. history, until roughly the end of the nineteenth century, underproduction was the big problem. Then we suddenly had plenty of production capacity. To become an industrial power, the problem then became, how do we stimulate purchase of all the output? If people were thrifty and frugal, as they had been for generations, there wouldn't be enough demand to drive the production that would make the country great."[27]"

This new emphasis was reinforced by the 1930s advent of national accounting, which defined progress in terms of consumption. As mentioned earlier, the focus on GDP and consumption came about during the Great Depression, when stimulating demand was America's primary economic challenge. This policy emphasis has dominated the American government and our cultural mindset for two to three generations now. As growth slows, politicians have urged us to spend with patriotic zeal. Tax codes have given Americans mortgage interest deductions to encourage home ownership, and all the spending that goes with it. Globalization has further fed into this phenomenon, bringing down the price of virtually all consumer goods, thereby democratizing consumption across most income groups. Cheap, plentiful finance supplied by Wall Street has added more fuel to the fire. As David Brooks has observed, this cultural shift, plus rising house princes in the last generation, have given people the impression they could take on more risk, distorting expectations of what constitutes a "middle-class" lifestyle, encouraging us to borrow and buy more.[28] No doubt this cultural shift has contributed to the credit crisis.

Perhaps U.S. hyperconsumption has been exacerbated by the country's sense of exceptionalism. America's unique view of its role in the world can be amazingly positive, or, if left unchecked, can be extremely destructive. Consider that upon arriving in the new world, American settlers pushed to the Pacific, helping themselves to endless acres in the name of Manifest Destiny. Indigenous populations were wiped out or displaced. Great forests that took centuries to mature were logged and cleared away for farms, then railroads, then highways and subdivisions. Mighty rivers were dammed, bays were bridged, seacoasts were fished, and minerals and oil were extracted and depleted. For many around the world, it looks like when we exhausted our country, we went global. For decades now, America has been draining the rest of the planet, consuming roughly 25 percent of the world's resources while accounting for only 5 percent of the population.

Clearly it's time for a change, and curbing American consumption-driven lifestyle will require some attitude adjustments, pain, and sacrifice; perhaps this will be the silver lining to our credit crisis and the slowdown in consumer lending. It will mean not overextending ourselves in energy-intensive 3500 square-foot McMansions we cannot afford, when 2500 square feet will do just fine. It will mean shifting from gas-guzzling SUVs to smaller hybrid cars, and not trading them in for something new every three years. It will mean eating with a focus on quality and not quantity, with less beef and chicken, and more fish, grains, and vegetables. On a societal level, it will mean producing fewer weapons and being less militaristic abroad. It will mean dedicating more time and resources to eradicating poverty at home and around the world.

The United States has a choice: It can transform itself through thoughtful Macro Quantum policy or wait for external forces (the depletion of fossil fuel, CO_2 emissions, greater instability in poorer countries, imbalances in the financial system, foreigners refusing to finance deficits, and terrorist attacks, among others) to mandate such evolutions. But isn't it far better and safer to guide managed change now rather than having it forced on us later? Can America channel its historic sense of exceptionalism away from destructive over-consumption into setting new global standards for sustainable life in the new millennium, thereby rebuilding its leadership role? To do this, Americans must abandon old "not in my backyard" thinking. Today, our backyard has become everyone's backyard. We share the same planet, the same finite resources, and increasingly the same wants and needs.[29] By acting collectively, we can abandon our Micro Domestic territoriality and start making cooperative decisions about what is most effective and logical in the Quantum Macro world.

One can see how alternative socio-economic indicators like GPI should be encouraged, to help shift the economy away from reliance on foreign debt, resource depletion, and regrettables. This can start with government. Clearly we need to distinguish between wasteful and productive spending. Government projects likely to create broader societal value in the future, like modern infrastructure, innovative education, effective health care, or a renewable energy industry, should be encouraged. On the other hand, excessive defense expenditures, or subsidies to limited-value sectors (like farming) need to be seriously reconsidered.

Part of the solution will be a greater future time bias and a shift toward saving and investing for tomorrow, versus spending today. The United States—both citizens and government—need to cultivate a savings culture. For over three decades, most Americans have saved little of their income compared with others overseas. Today, according to studies by the New America Foundation, half of Americans have few or no net assets.[30] Our troublesome currency, our imbalanced housing market, and our faltering banks are, in part, symptoms of this problem.

Programs spreading financial literacy, sweeping reform of current popular savings products such as IRAs, and perhaps even establishing and funding lifelong assets accounts for all citizens could help to instill a culture of thrift. One suggestion is to create a "saver's bonus," in which the government would match savings accounts dollar-for-dollar up to a limit (say $500) to encourage this behavior in low-income individuals, similar to a program started in the United Kingdom. This could be easily realized by linking tax refunds to savings products. Each year, the IRS issues refunds averaging more than $2,000 to 130 million tax filers.[31] By simply ticking a box on your tax return, these rebates could easily be put toward savings. Small changes to our lifestyles today could greatly enhance security and prosperity tomorrow.

Cooperation in a Multipolar World

Our new rubric for progress should also provide guidance in measuring the quality of GDP globally. If we want a cleaner planet, why do the negative effects of pollution go unrecorded in our measure of economic activity? And if we want a world with fewer weapons of mass destruction, why, then, does the upkeep of our arsenal of WMDs count as an economic good? Some have eschewed the inclusion of these factors because they are not "value neutral," that is, some people may value a clean environment more than others. Yet by completely omitting these criteria, we are not creating a value-neutral measure, we are actually making an extreme judgment call by saying the value of these things is zero, or maybe worse—value subtracted versus value added.

Our set of global metrics must reinforce basic universal commitments to sustainability and cooperation. Because the challenges that define the Macro Quantum world are truly worldwide, the only way to make progress is for people and governments the world over to have an agreed upon standard that a dollar spent on funding the UN is worth more than a dollar spent on buying a pack of cigarettes. Multilateral cooperation and greater private–public sector coordination after all are the cornerstones of capitalist peace.

Much of the economic progress and rise in living standards of the past 20 years has been a product of the deepened global dedication to trade liberalization, crafted under the guidance of multilateral institutions. As Harvard professor Dani Rodrik argues, markets are only as strong as their institutional context: "The paradox of markets is that they thrive not under *laissez-faire* but under the watchful eye of the state."[32] Public policy and multilateral organizations have an important role to play in the Macro Quantum world. First, free markets and free trade are predicated on information being readily available. Reviving and strengthening the UN, NATO, the World Bank, WHO, WTO and new institutions will create a network of specialized oversight bodies that can track flows of capital, weapons, immigrants, and diseases that can thwart our capital peace. A multilateral, multidimensional solution to our current financial crisis may just be the tonic for this new era.

Moreover, working through these institutions will strengthen the Macro Quantum cooperative spirit. In an era where many new actors—from MNCs to formerly "third world" countries—can influence the global system. These institutions provide an invaluable transparent channel of communication, as well as opportunities for divergent peers to work side-by-side. Multilateral institutions are also the ideal stage for the United States to exercise its softer brand of persuasive leadership, as opposed to brute force. Globalization need not be the daunting, dangerous elephant in the room. While it is large and complex, with a new dashboard and a renewed commitment to global cooperation, along with revised policies to face Macro Quantum realities, the United States has the tools and resources to tame the beast.

Whether we focus on refining how we measure economic activity, or even take a more holistic set of quality of life indicators as our guideposts, the Macro Quantum world needs not one but many new gauges to reinforce our integrated approach with a forward time bias, less reliance on debt, and the inclusion of a wide range of players. There's an old saying that people don't change when they see the light but when they feel the heat. From all the indicators we've been discussing, it's getting hot.

If the world's foremost power and consumer voluntarily shifts its lifestyle patterns and philosophy, think of the global implications for America's reputation. The United States has been presented with a tremendous opportunity to lead the world into the an unprecedented capitalist peace era; but to seize this opportunity we need to steer our thinking and lifestyle in a new direction. With a broader focus beyond economics and with a Macro Quantum philosophy to guide us, now we simply need to make the commitment not just to see but to lead our elephant.

Notes

Introduction

1. It would be impossible to name all the important writers on every aspect of globalization, but in addition to Friedman and Gore, a few others stand out. Jagdish Bhagwati, Amartya Sen, Joseph Stiglitz, and Martin Wolf are among my favorites on economics and business. For international diplomacy and security issues, works by Philip Bobbitt, Francis Fukuyama, Robert Kagan, Sam Huntington, and Michael Mandlebaum have been particularly enlightening. On ethnic conflicts and immigration, writings by Amy Chua and Michele Wucker are very useful. Bjorn Lomborg, Bill McKibben, Bill McDonough, Michael Braungart, and Fred Singer have produced encouragingly sober books on the environment, and on poverty and economic inequality Jeffrey Sachs and Paul Collier have covered key issues extremely well. One writer who deserves special mention is Fareed Zakaria, whose recently published *The Post-American World* tries to tackle many of the issues I'll be covering.
2. For those familiar with quantum physics, this may sound like the theory of particle duality.

3. I find Levitt's seminal research into how lower crime rates in the United States were linked to legalized abortion and a reduction in unwanted births inspirational. While several critics have subsequently attacked his analysis, I nonetheless applaud the attempt to understand quantum relationships in our unbelievably complex world.

4. This trend has been captured in the canon of "dumb-down" literature beginning with Richard Hofstadter's 1966 classic, *Anti-Intellectualism in American Life*, and continuing with Harold Bloom's *The Closing of the America Mind* (1988), or more recently the Postmans' *Amusing Ourselves to Death* (2005), Al Gore's *The Assault on Reason* (2007), and Susan Jacoby's *The Age of American Unreason* (2008).

Chapter 1: Seeing the Elephant in the Twenty-First Century

1. Henry Thompson, *International Economics: Global Markets and Competition*, 2nd ed. (Hackensack, NJ: World Scientific, 2006), 86.

2. Heita Kawakatsu and A. J. H. Latham, *Asia Pacific Dynamism 1550–2000* (London: Routledge, 2000), 26.

3. For a compilation of sources, see "Source List and Detailed Death Tolls for the Twentieth Century Hemoclysm," available at http://users.erols.com/mwhite28/warstat1.htm#Second.

4. This is unadjusted for inflation, putting total costs at perhaps $40 trillion to $60 trillion in today's terms. See "Costs of War," http://abob.libs.uga.edu/bobk/coopc20.html.

5. See Worldbank.org for historical data on GDP growth rates; UNDP.org for life expectancy and health indicators.

6. There are numerous books on the subject, including my two previous books, *Money Changes Everything* and *From Third World to First Class*, as well as Brink Lindsey's *Against the Dead Hand*.

7. The Human Development Index (HDI) is a comparative measure of life expectancy, literacy, education, and standard of living for countries worldwide promoted by the United Nations. It is a standard means of measuring well-being, especially child welfare. It is often used to determine and indicate whether a country is a developed, developing, or underdeveloped country and also

to measure the impact of economic policies on quality of life. This index takes a variety of indicators—including daily caloric intake, literacy, and life expectancy, among others.

8. Here, we use the World Bank definition of an emerging market. An emerging market is a transitional economy (moving from a closed to an open system) with low-to-middle per capita income. Most former Soviet and Eastern bloc countries would qualify; although the term is sometimes applied to the Gulf states, it is questionable whether these countries meet either criteria.

9. Angus Madison, *The World Economy: Historical Statistics* (Paris: Organization for Economic Cooperation and Development, 2004).

10. Ibid.

11. Indeed, Indonesian President Yudhoyono's offer to help with Iran's nuclear negotiations offers a glimpse into a potentially strong new ally.

12. "Mexico," *CIA World Factbook*, https://www.cia.gov/library/publications/the-world-factbook/print/mx.html.

13. My firm, HSBC, has 20,000 offices in 83 countries, employs 300,000 people, and has more than 150 million customers.

14. John L. Graham, "Trade Brings Peace," in *War and Reconciliation*, Joseph Runzo and Nancy M. Martin, eds. (Cambridge: Cambridge University Press, 2006).

15. Consider the exception to the rule, Venezuela's Hugo Chávez. According to the *International Herald Tribune*, Chávez's decisions to nationalize oil, steel, cement, and coal scared off many investors. In 1998, the Venezuelan central bank reported foreign investment of approximately $5 billion. By 2007, this figure had fallen to only $646 million. Meanwhile, Chávez's approval rating fell to 51.8 percent in February 2008 from 75.4 percent in June 2006. Matthew Walter, "Chávez's Mixed Blessing for Venezuelan Economy," *International Herald Tribune*, May 26, 2008, http://www.iht.com/articles/2008/05/26/business/control.php.

16. For 1950 numbers, see Angus Madison's *The World Economy: Historical Statistics* (Paris: OECD, 2004), and see www.worldbank.org for 2005 statistics.

17. Ibid.

18. For an excellent primer on economic freedom, see the Heritage Foundation and the *Wall Street Journal*'s "Economic Freedom Index" methodology, http://www.heritage.org/research/features/index/chapters/pdf/Index2008_Chap4.pdf.

19. See Mueller's excellent book *Capitalism, Democracy, and Ralph's Pretty Good Grocery* (Princeton, NJ: Princeton University Press, 2001).

20. Milton Friedman, *Capitalism and Freedom* (Chicago: University of Chicago Press, 1962), 8.

21. "The Changing Face of Global Violence" in *The Human Security Report 2005*, published by the Human Security Centre (www.hsrgroup.org).

22. Ibid.

23. Erik Gartzke, "The Capitalist Peace," *American Journal of Political Science* 51, no. 1 (2007): 166–191.

24. Dennis K. Berman, "Russians Are Coming, Wallets in Hand," *Wall Street Journal*, July 22, 2008, C1.

25. "Sarkozy in Drive to Give EU Global Role," *Economist*, August 28, 2007.

26. The Chinese renminbi is theoretically pegged to a basket of currencies heavily weighted towards the U.S. dollar. It floats in a narrow band controlled by the government.

27. IMF International Financial Statistics Database, www.imfstatistics.org (last accessed May 29, 2008).

28. Ibid.

29. "Sovereign-Wealth Funds: Keep Your T-Bonds, We'll Take the Bank," *Economist*, July 26, 2007.

30. Mangal Goswami, Ceyla Pazarbaşıoğlu, and Jack Ree, "The Changing Face of Investors," *Finance and Development*, March 2007, 6.

31. Ibid.

32. "Financial Integration among Developing Countries," 2006 Global Development Finance Report, World Bank (2006).

33. Ruchita Beri, "China's Rising Profile in Africa," *China Report* 43, no. 3 (2007): 297–308.

34. For more, see http://www.equator-principles.com.

35. Joseph Khan, "China Courts Africa," *New York Times*, November 3, 2006.

36. Somini Sengupta, "Take Aid from China and Take a Pass on Human Rights," *New York Times*, March 9, 2008.

37. Ibid.
38. "China Denies Report of Arms Sales to Sudan," Xinhua Newswire, March 14, 2008, http://news.xinhuanet.com/english/2008-03/14/content_7792198.htm.
39. Gerhardt Schroeder, speech given at Columbia University, December 11, 2007.
40. Chris Giles, "Globalisation Backlash in Rich Nations," *Financial Times*, July 22, 2007.
41. Nancy M. Wingfield, "Book Review: The Problem with 'Backwardness': Ivan T. Berend's Central and Eastern Europe in the Nineteenth and Twentieth Centuries," *European History Quarterly* 34, no. 4 (2004): 535–551.
42. Glyn Ford, "In the Wake of Xenophobia: The New Racism in Europe," *UN Chronicle* 44 (2007).
43. "EU 'Blue Card' to Target Skilled," *BBC News*, October 2007.
44. Joanna McKenna, "Protectionism on the Rise, Warn Global Executives—Annual Global Growth Rates Could Drop by One Percentage Point," *Economist Intelligence Unit*, press release, November 2006.
45. Lee Hudson Teslik, "Fast-Track Trade Promotion Authority and Its Impact on US Trade Policy," Council on Foreign Relations, June 2007.
46. "Top 7 Political Risks for 2007," Eurasia Group, February 2007, 3.
47. Ibid., 4.
48. "Financial Integration Among Developing Countries," 2006 Global Development Finance Report, World Bank, 21.
49. Robert McMahon and Lee Hudson Teslik, "New Push for Doha Talks," Council on Foreign Relations, February 2007.
50. Jayant Memon, "Bilateral Trade Agreements and the World Trading System," Asian Development Bank Institute, November 2006.
51. Applying quantum physics concepts in social science is a nascent, fascinating field. Many of my ideas have been in spired by writings from Dina Zohar and Joseph Fris, among others.

Chapter 2: Trade and Finance: Money, Money Everywhere

1. The N-11 countries are Indonesia, Nigeria, South Korea, Mexico, Turkey, Vietnam, Iran, Philippines, Egypt, Pakistan, and Bangladesh.

2. UBS, August 23, 2007. Keep in mind that much of this trade is linked to intermediate processing, which may seem a little like double counting. Nonetheless, it underscores how much more emerging markets countries are connected than in the past.

3. This is an overly simplistic example. There are other costs, such as insurance, tax, and transportation, that would figure into the decision to use overseas production.

4. David Ricardo's nineteenth-century corollary to free trade holds that countries (that is, those that do not have the absolute advantage) can gain from trade if they exploit cost differentials.

5. There are many overlapping phases in trade. One would rarely find such a neat example when industries simply start and stop, and labor shifts overnight. These phases can last years or even decades.

6. "The Coming Demographic Deficit: How Aging Populations Will Reduce Global Savings," McKinsey Global Institute, December 2004.

7. Ibid.

8. Bureau of Economic Analysis, s.v., "U.S. International Transactions, 1960–Present," *International Economic Accounts*, http://www.bea.gov/national/index.htm#gdp.

9. U.S. Census Bureau, s.v., "Persons Below Poverty Level and Below 125 Percent of Poverty Level by Race and Hispanic Origin: 1959 to 2005," *2008 Statistical Abstract*, http://www.census.gov/compendia/statab/cats/income_expenditures_poverty_wealth.html

10. U.S. Census Bureau, s.v., "Money Income of Households—Percent Distribution by Income Level, Race, and Hispanic Origin in Constant (2005) Dollars: 1980 to 2005," *2008 Statistical Abstract*, http://www.census.gov/compendia/statab/cats/income_expenditures_poverty_wealth.html

11. Jim O'Neil et al., "Getting Globalization Right: Meeting the Challenge of the Century," *Goldman Sachs Global Economics Paper* 95 (2003).

12. "Emerging-Market Multinationals: The Challengers," *Economist*, January 10, 2008.

13. Mansoor Dailami, "Globalization of the Corporate Sector in Emerging Markets," lecture presented at the World Bank Conference, Zurich, Switzerland, May 2008.

14. For example, in May 2008 the Indian telecom operator Bharti made an $18 billion-plus offer to take control of South Africa's MTN, valuing the South African entity at more than $35 billion, one of the largest cross-border emerging market deals. Agence France-Presse, "Bharti, MTN Merger Talks Could Wind Up This Weekend," *Yahoo! News*, May 17, 2008, http://news.yahoo.com/ s/afp/20080517/bs_afp/indiasafricasingaporetelecommergercom-panybhartimtn.

15. "That Empty Nest Feeling," *Economist*, September 6, 2008.

16. The Brady Plan was designed to address the least developed coun-try (LDC) debt crisis of the 1980s. LDCs had more than $700 billion in debt; the high debt loads made them very unstable eco-nomically. Under the plan, bank creditors would grant debt relief in exchange for greater assurance of collectability in the form of principal and interest collateral; debt relief needed to be linked to some assurance of economic reform, and the resulting debt should be more highly tradable, to allow creditors to diversify risk more widely throughout the financial and investment community.

17. "Economic & Trade Information on Hong Kong," HKTDC, http://www.tdctrade.com/main/economic.htm.

18. John Tagliabue, "Nestle's Aim: New-Market Growth," *New York Times*, October 15, 1994.

19. Mangal Goswami, Ceyla Pazarbaşıoğlu, and Jack Ree, "The Changing Face of Investors," *Finance and Development*, March 2007, 3.

20. "PEI Fifty," Private Equity International, May 2007, http:// www.peimedia.com/resources/Conference/downloads/PEI50_ Brochure_final.pdf.

21. To go long refers to holding stock; to short refers to selling stock before owning it (a technique that bets the price of a given stock will fall). Market risk is hedged because the hedge fund portfolio does not necessarily move with the market.

22. Some use excessive leverage, depending on strategies pursued— the infamous Long Term Capital Management in the late 1990s reportedly used leverage of nearly 50:1.

23. Associated Press, "Former PM Mahathir to Meet Financier George Soros in Malaysia," *International Herald Tribune*, December 12, 2006.

24. Simon Johnson, *Finance and Development IMF Magazine*, September 2007, http://www.imf.org/external/pubs/ft/fandd/2007/09/straight.htm.

25. The first sovereign wealth fund was formed in 1956. British administrators in the Gilbert Islands (now known as Kiribati) attempted to minimize the impact of international price fluctuations on the South Pacific atoll's export-dependent economy. They created the Kiribati Equalization Reserve Fund by levying a tariff on the export of phosphates contained in bird manure—one of their primary exports alongside fish and coconuts. The small country's supply of phosphates was rapidly depleted, but the tariff proceeds have grown into a $520 million portfolio—nearly seven times the nation's annual GDP.

26. "The Invasion of the Sovereign-Wealth Funds," *Economist*, January 17, 2008.

27. One of the only potentially shady SWF political maneuvers to date concerns Singapore's Temasek Holdings, which purchased a stake in the company owned by the prime minister of Thailand, Thaksin Shinawatra. This deal contributed to corruption charges against Thaksin and his eventual ouster.

28. See www.hsh.com for the latest and historical data on U.S. mortgage rates.

29. Joe Millman, "Latin America Feels Pain of U.S. Housing Slump," *Wall Street Journal*, April 23, 2007, A2.

30. The Basel group includes 13 countries: Belgium, Canada, France, Germany, Italy, Japan, Luxemburg, Netherlands, Spain, Sweden, Switzerland, United Kingdom, and United States.

31. Walter Molano, "Blame It on Basel," *Emerging Markets Adviser* (BCP Securities, Greenwich, CT), February 7, 2008.

32. Many of these securities were aggressively purchased by collateralized debt obligation (CDO) special purpose companies, another ratings-arbitrage variation of the SIV idea that often had more slices of risk than SIVs. The ultimate bastardizations of these Wall Street creations were SIVs and CDOs that bought tranches of other SIVs and CDOs, creating a phenomenally intricate web of risk and entanglement.

33. Ibid.

34. See the International Fund for Agricultural Development's web site, www.ifad.org.

35. Mira Kamdar, "The Threat of Global Food Shortages—Part III," *YaleGlobal*, May 7, 2008, http://yaleglobal.yale.edu/display .article?id=10766.

36. As a child in the 1960s I vividly remember hearing discussions and jokes about things "Made in Japan." At that time Japanese goods were considered cheap with little quality. How things have changed!

37. Defined as percentage of a country's GDP divided by its World Bank purchase power parity adjusted GDP.

38. Ambrose Evans-Pritchard, "China Threatens 'Nuclear Option of Dollar Sales," *Telegraph*, October 8, 2007, http://www.telegraph. co.uk/money/main.jhtml?xml=/money/2007/08/07/bcnchina 107a.xml.

39. Ibid.

40. Barry Eichengreen, "Global Imbalances and the Lessons of Bretton Woods," *National Bureau of Economic Research Working Paper* 10947, May 2004.

41. "Somewhere Over the Rainbow," *Economist*, Jan 24, 2008.

42. Friedrich von Hayek, "The Use of Knowledge in Society," *American Economic Review* 35, no. 4: 519–530.

43. Joseph Stiglitz, "The Roaring Nineties," *Atlantic*, October 2002, http://www.theatlantic.com/doc/prem/200210/stiglitz.

44. Consider two high-profile cases where the United States was hostile toward foreign investment, both of which were read globally as discriminatory and sending the world the wrong message. In June 2005, an unsolicited, all-cash $18.5 billion bid by a state-owned subsidiary of China National Offshore Oil Corporation (CNOOC) for Unocal was shot down for security reasons, which was more damning to the American reputation abroad than beneficial to U.S. security. Again, in February 2006, the sale of port management contracts in six major U.S. seaports to Dubai Ports World (an United Arab Emirates state-owned company) triggered a national security debate. The contracts had already been foreign-owned, by a British company!

45. Pioneered in the aftermath of World War II, Bretton Woods was shaped largely by the United States, which in 1944 produced half

the world's coal, two-thirds of the oil, and more than half of the electricity, and held three-quarters of world gold reserves.

46. Deborah Solomon and Bob Davis, "G-7 Cites New Yuan Concern and Weighs Rules for Funds," *New York Times*, October 20, 2007, A5.

47. Jim O'Neill and Robert Hormats, "The G8: Time for a Change," *Goldman Sachs Global Economics Paper* 112, June 2004.

48. It is estimated that passage of the bill will cost the average U.S. family $5,650. PRNewswire-USNewswire, "WashingtonWatch .com Federal Legislative Update," news release, May 27, 2008, http://www.foxbusiness.com/story/costing-farm-upcoming-war-spending-debate/.

49. Sallie James and Daniel Griswold, "Freeing the Farm: A Farm Bill for All Americans," *Cato Institute Trade Policy Analysis* 34, April 14, 2007.

50. Carol A. Jones, Hisham El-Osta, and Robert Green, "Economic Well-Being of Farm Households," *Economic Brief* 7, U.S. Department of Agriculture, Economic Research Service, March 2006, www.ers .usda.gov/publications/EB7/EB7.pdf.

51. Jonathan Lynn, "WTO Says Cannot Solve Food Price Crisis," Reuters, May 7, 2008, http://www.reuters.com/article/topNews/ idUSMAN14118020080507.

52. Yilmaz Akyuz, "Multilateral Financial Institutions: Overhauling Development Finance," *Social Watch Report 2006*, 14–17.

53. "That Empty Nest Feeling," *Economist*, September 6, 2007.

54. Edmund Conway, "Invest in Equities, Expert Tells IMF," *Telegraph*, February 18, 2008, http://www.telegraph.co.uk/money/main.jhtml? view=DETAILS&grid=&xml=/money/2008/02/18/cnimf118.xml.

55. Stephen Jen, "A US$100 Billion Supra-Sovereign Wealth Fund?" Morgan Stanley, February 8, 2008, http://www.morganstanley .com/views/gef/archive/2008/20080208-Fri.html#anchor6024.

Chapter 3: The Twilight of the Hydrocarbons

1. Daniel Yergin, *The Prize: The Epic Quest for Oil, Money & Power* (New York: Free Press, 1991), 17.

2. According to the U.S. Energy Information Administration (EIA), world energy consumption was about 447 quadrillion Btu (4.7 × 10^{16} Btu, EIA 2004). The energy expended by an individual doing a hard day's work is about 4,000 Btu, or 1,460,000 Btu a year (R. Loftness, *Energy Handbook*, 1984: 2, 756). Energy consumption in the United States is 105.63 quadrillion Btu (EIA, 2007). U.S. population is 304 million (*CIA World Factbook*, 2008).

3. Bureau of Economic Analysis, s.v., "National Income and Product Accounts Table: Table 7.1, Selected Per Capita Product and Income Series in Current and Chained Dollars," *National Economic Accounts*, http://www.bea.gov/national/nipaweb/TableView.asp?SelectedTable =253&ViewSeries=NO&Java=no&Request3Place=N&3Place=N& FromView=YES&Freq=Qtr&FirstYear=1929&LastYear=2008&3Pla ce=N&Update=Update&JavaBox=no#Mid.

4. "International Energy Outlook 2007," Energy Information Administration, May 2007, http://www.eia.doe.gov/oiaf/ieo/ index.html.

5. Ibid.

6. Ibid.

7. "Energy for China," *Economist Intelligence Unit Briefing*, July 12, 2007.

8. "How Many Drivers in China?" *China Car Times*, April 7, 2007, http://www.chinacartimes.com/2008/04/08/how-many-drivers-in-china/; for U.S. figures see http://www.unece.org/stats/trends 2005/transport.htm.

9. Katie Merx, "Competition for China's Growing Auto Market Is Heating Up," *Detroit Free Press*, April 20, 2008, http://www.freep.com/ apps/pbcs.dll/article?AID=/20080420/BUSINESS01/804200588.

10. Some suggest the world has entered a peak-oil period, referring to Shell geophysicist M. King Hubbert's 1956 theory that oil production mimics a bell curve, rising to a peak when half an oil field had been extracted, and then going into decline. Hubbert focused on continental U.S. production, and in 1956 he forecasted that U.S. oil production (excluding Alaska, which was not a state until 1959) would peak in 1970. He was correct for the 48 states, and the top of the bell curve in oil production became widely known as a "Hubbert peak."

11. A 74 percent increase in total coal consumption. "International Energy Outlook 2007," Energy Information Administration.

12. Keith Bradsher and David Barboza, "Pollution from Chinese Coal Casts a Global Shadow," *New York Times*, June 11, 2006, http://www.nytimes.com/2006/06/11/business/worldbusiness/11chinacoal.html?_r=1&oref=slogin.

13. "Asthma and Air Pollution," National Resources Defense Council, http://www.nrdc.org/health/effects/fasthma.asp (last accessed June 6, 2008).

14. Ibid.

15. Ibid.

16. María Antonieta Uribe and Héctor Tobar, "Leftist Guerrilla Group Claims It Bombed Mexican Pipelines," *Los Angeles Times*, September 12, 2007, http://articles.latimes.com/2007/sep/12/world/fg-guerrillas12.

17. Rüdiger Falksohn, "A Nuclear Power Renaissance," *Der Spiegel*, January 16, 2007, http://www.spiegel.de/international/spiegel/0,1518,460011,00.html.

18. Jack Spencer and Nick Loris, "Dispelling Myths about Nuclear Energy," *Heritage Foundation Backgrounder*, December 3, 2007, http://www.heritage.org/Research/EnergyandEnvironment/bg2087.cfm.

19. "The Nuclear Fuel Cycle," Uranium SA, http://www.uraniumsa.org/fuel_cycle/waste.htm.

20. Frank Barnaby and James Kemp, "Too Hot to Handle," *Oxford Research Group Briefing Paper*, July 2007, http://www.oxfordresearchgroup.org.uk/publications/briefing_papers/pdf/toohottohandle.pdf.

21. Sam Roe, "An Atomic Threat Made in America," *Chicago Tribune*, January 28, 2007, http://www.truthout.org/docs_2006/013007E.shtml.

22. Cyrus Safdari, "Iran Needs Nuclear Energy, Not Weapons," *Le Monde Diplomatique*, November 2005, http://mondediplo.com/2005/11/02iran.

23. See the 2007 National Intelligence Estimate (NIE), which stated that Iran has not frozen its nuclear program.

24. As we discuss in the security chapter, uranium enrichment is a huge issue among the nonproliferation community.

25. "International Petroleum Consumption," Energy Information Administration, http://www.eia.doe.gov/emeu/international/oil consumption.html (last accessed June 6, 2008).

26. Ibid.

27. International Energy Agency, *World Energy Outlook 2006*, "Summary and Conclusions," 4f.

28. Michael Klare, "Oil Wars: Transforming the American Military into a Global Oil-Protection Service," *TomDispatch.com*, October 8, 2004, www.commondreams.org/views04/1008-23.htm.

29. See Joseph Stiglitz and Linda Bilmes, *The Three Trillion Dollar War* (New York: W. W. Norton, 2008).

30. Jay Inslee and Bracken Hendricks, *Apollo's Fire: Igniting America's Clean Energy Economy* (Washington, DC: Island Press, 2007), 14.

31. Zhao Xingjun and Wu Yanrui, "Determinants of China's Energy Imports: An Empirical Analysis," *Energy Policy* 35 (2007): 4235–4246.

32. "Oil/Black Gold/Texas T," *Global Security.org*, www.globalsecurity .org/military/intro/oil.htm (last accessed June 6, 2008).

33. "The Role of Oil Wealth in the World Economy," McKinsey Global Institute, *McKinsey on Finance* 26 (Winter 2008): 14.

34. See note #10.

35. Charles Levinson, "Saudis Announce Slight Oil Output Increase," *USA Today*, May 17, 2008, http://www.usatoday .com/news/world/2008-05-15-saudi_N.htm.

36. Roger Stern, "Iran Actually Is Short of Oil," *International Herald Tribune*, January 8, 2007, http://www.iht.com/arti-cles/2007/01/08/opinion/edstern.php.

37. Steven Mufson, "High Oil Prices Push Giant Shifts in Wealth, Power," *Washington Post*, November 10, 2007; Bloomberg for recent reserve figures.

38. "Country Briefing: Russia," Energy Information Administration, www.eia.doe.gov/emeu/cabs/Russia/Background.html.

39. Judy Dempsey, "Russia Takes Heat over Energy Supply," *International Herald Tribune*, February 12, 2006.

40. "European Customers Hit by Gas Cuts," *CNN*, January 2, 2006, http://www.cnn.com/2006/WORLD/europe/01/02/russia .ukraine.impact/index.html.

41. "Ukraine Stealing Europe's Gas," *BBC News*, January 2, 2006.

42. In this deal, prices of gas sold to the Ukraine range from around $50 per 1,000 cubic meters of natural gas to $230, with a certain amount of cheaper oil coming from Central Asian supplies. "Russia, Ukraine Agree on New Gas Prices," *Kommersant*, January 4, 2006.

43. See note 10.

44. Steven Mufson, "Nigeria's Oil Morass," *Washington Post*, February 1, 2008, http://www.washingtonpost.com/wp-dyn/content/article/2008/01/31/AR2008013103634.html.

45. Ibid.

46. Ibid.

47. Peter Brokes and Ji Hye Shin, "China's Influence in Africa: Implications for the United States," Heritage Foundation, February 22, 2006, http://www.heritage.org/Research/AsiaandthePacific/bg1916.cfm.

48. Esther Pan, "China, Africa, and Oil," Council on Foreign Relations, January 26, 2007, http://www.cfr.org/publication/9557/.

49. Associated Press, "Brazil Oil Find May Be World's 3rd Largest," *CBS News*, April 14, 2008, http://www.cbsnews.com/stories/2008/04/14/world/main4013564.shtml.

50. Magali Devic, "South America's Great Gas Pipeline," *Washington Report in the Hemisphere* 27, no. 4 (April 2007).

51. "Chavez vs. ExxonMobil War Escalates," *Energy Bulletin*, February 11, 2008, http://www.energybulletin.net/40184.html.

52. See Roubini's web site at http://www.rgemonitor.com for a variety of interesting articles on Latin American politics related to oil.

53. "Ecuador Moves to Take Over Occidental Oil Operations," *International Herald Tribune*, May 16, 2006, http://www.iht.com/articles/2006/05/16/business/ecuador.php.

54. "Ecuador President Wants New Oil Contracts," *MSNBC*, November 28, 2006, http://www.msnbc.msn.com/id/15936476/.

55. Jad Mouawad, "Rising Demand for Oil Provokes New Energy Crisis," *New York Times*, November 9, 2007.

56. "Fighting Poverty: Findings and Lessons from China's Success," World Bank (2002).

57. "Energy and Poverty: The World Needs Far More Electricity to Power Development." *IAEA Bulletin*, February 2002.

58. Ibid.

59. "The Dark Continent," *Economist*, August 16, 2007.

60. "South Africa Gold Mines Shut by Power Cut," *BBC*, http://news .bbc.co.uk/go/pr/fr/-1/hi/world/Africa/7208542.stm.

61. "The Dark Continent," *Economist*, August 16, 2007.

62. Intergovernmental Panel on Climate Change (IPCC), *Climate Change 2007: The Physical Science Basis*, "Summary for Policy Makers," http://www.ipcc.ch/SPM2feb07.pdf.

63. "International Energy Outlook 2007," Energy Information Administration, May 2007, http://www.eia.doe.gov/oiaf/ieo/ index.html.

64. Inslee and Hendricks, *Apollo's Fire*, 220.

65. Associated Press, "Study Calls for 'Energy Revolution,'" *New York Times*, June 6, 2008, http://www.nytimes.com/aponline/business/ AP-Japan-IEA-ClimateChan.html?ex=1213416000&en=6b1cf64 bf9f14336&ei=5070&emc=eta1.

66. Nicholas Stern, *The Stern Review on the Economics of Climate Change*, HM Treasury, October 30, 2006, http://www.hm-treasury.gov.uk/ media/3/2/Summary_of_Conclusions.pdf.

67. See critiques of the Stern report by Yale's William D. Nordhaus and Cambridge's Partha Dasgupta, available at http://nordhaus.econ .yale.edu/SternReviewD2.pdf and http://www.econ.cam.ac.uk/ faculty/dasgupta/Stern.pdf.

68. Inslee and Hendricks, *Apollo's Fire*, 20.

69. Ibid., 19–20.

70. "Fuel for Friendship," *Economist,* March 7, 2007, 14.

71. "Beyond Three Gorges in China," *International Water Power*, January 10, 2007, http://www.waterpowermagazine.com/story .asp?storyCode=2041318.

72. "The Coming Wave," *Economist,* June 5, 2008, http://www.economist .com/search/displaystory.cfm?story_id=11482565.

73. Mathias Akselsson, "The World's Leader in Wind Power," *Scandinavia.com,* November 20, 2007, http://www.scandinavica .com/culture/nature/wind.htm.

74. Tyghe Trimble, "Turbine Turbulence: How to Fix U.S. Wind Power," *Popular Mechanics*, May 17, 2007, http://www.popularmechanics .com/science/earth/4216776.html?page=1&series=15.

75. Office of Harry Reid, U.S. Senator for Nevada, "Democrats' Energy Independence Legislation Will Protect Consumers, National Security, Environment," news release, May 14, 2007.

76. Office of the Defense Undersecretary, Defense Budget Materials (2007), www.defenselink.mil/comptroller/defbudget/fy2007/.

77. Office of the Defense Undersecretary, Defense Budget Materials (2006), www.defenselink.mil/comptroller/defbudget/fy2006/.

78. Inslee and Hendricks, 19.

79. "Curbing Global Energy Demand Growth: The Energy Productivity Opportunity," McKinsey Global Institute, May 2007, 12.

80. Neil King Jr., "A Difficult Road Awaits for Energy Conservation," *Wall Street Journal*, July 22, 2008, A14.

81. "Curbing Global Energy Demand Growth: The Energy Productivity Opportunity," McKinsey Global Institute, May 2007.

82. There are literally countless small power changes like these that can save enormous amounts of energy in the United States. See McKinsey study, "Curbing Global Energy Demand Growth: The Energy Productivity Opportunity."

83. Union of Concerned Scientists, "House Reaches Historic Breakthrough on Fuel Economy," news release, December 3, 2007, http://www.ucsusa.org/news/press_release/house-reaches.html.

84. Janet Swane et al., "American Energy: The Renewable Path to Energy Security," Worldwatch Institute and Center for American Progress, September 2006, 21, http://images1.americanprogress.org/i180web20037/americanenergynow/AmericanEnergy.pdf.

85. "Curbing Global Energy Demand Growth: The Energy Productivity Opportunity," McKinsey Global Institute, May 2007, 15.

86. National Renewable Energy Laboratory, *Fuel from the Sky: Solar Power's Potential for Western Energy Supply*, July 2002, SR-550-32160, 47–52 passim.

87. Ken Zweibel, James Mason, and Vasilis Fthenakis, "A Solar Grand Plan," *Scientific American*, December 2007, http://www.sciam.com/article.cfm?id=a-solar-grand-plan.

88. Ibid.

89. The NREL's web site at www.nrel.gov has some of the latest data on renewable energy development.

90. "New Solar Photovoltaic Cell Efficiency Record: 42.8%," *FuturePundit*, July 23, 2007. See http://www.futurepundit.com/archives/004418.html.

91. Martin Feldstein, "Reducing America's Dependence on Foreign Oil Supplies," presented at the American Economic Association meetings, January 2003, 5.

92. "Transportation Energy Facts," Energy Information Administration, http://www.eia.doe.gov/kids/energyfacts/uses/transportation.html.

93. See Zweibel, Mason, and Fthenakis, "Solar Grand Plan."

94. Ibid.

Chapter 4: Defense and Security: Preventing the Next War, Not Fighting the Last

1. Norman Angell, *The Great Illusion* (New York: Knickerbocker Press, 1913), ix–xiii passim, 381–382.

2. Thomas L. Friedman, *The World Is Flat* (New York: Farrar, Straus and Giroux, 2005), 421. This was an offshoot of Friedman's Golden Arches Theory, which argued that countries that both have McDonald's restaurants do not fight wars against each other. Some note that the Dell Theory evolved as the result of the Israeli-Palestinian fighting that undermined Friedman's original Golden Arches Theory.

3. Trade protectionism and nationalism were fed by escalating militarization, which, in turn, exacerbated tensions and stoked further anxieties. The Russo-Japanese war of 1904–1906, in which upstart Japan used its new British-designed fleet to soundly beat old Russian boats, and the 1906 introduction of the big-gunned *Dreadnought* class by Britain sparked a naval arms race with Germany. Even the United States, isolated as it was from Continental affairs at this time, responded with its own shipbuilding program.

4. Services include schools (e.g., madrassas) and insurance (e.g., payments for suicide bomber families).

5. Graham Allison, "How to Stop Nuclear Terror," *Foreign Affairs*, January–February 2004, 2.

6. University of Colorado at Boulder, "Regional Nuclear War Would Trigger Mass Death, Devastating Climate Change," news release, December 11, 2006.

7. Ibid.

8. Ibid.

9. Allison, "How to Stop Nuclear Terror," 2.

10. Bertil Lentner, "North Korea's Missile Trade Helps Fund Its Nuclear Program," *YaleGlobal Online*, May 5, 2003, http://yaleglobal.yale.edu/display.article?id=1546.

11. Ibid.

12. Abraham Wagner, lecture, Columbia University, New York, September 26, 2007.

13. "The Terror Next Time?" *Economist*, October 4, 2001.

14. Joseph Cirincione and Andrew Wade, "Get Smart on Ballistic Missiles," *Center for American Progress*, May 8, 2007, http://www.americanprogress.org/issues/2007/05/missiles.html.

15. "Iran's Ballistic Missile Capabilities," *CRS Report for Congress*, August 23, 2004, 4.

16. Cirincione and Wade, "Get Smart on Ballistic Missiles."

17. "China's Ballistic Missile Update 2004," *Risk Report, Wisconsin Project on Nuclear Arms Control* 11, no. 1 (November–December 2004), http://www.wisconsinproject.org/countries/china/ChinaBMupdate.html.

18. Ibid.

19. Ibid.

20. "China-U.S. Relations: Current Issues and Implications for U.S. Policy," *CRS Report for Congress*, 2007, 6.

21. Ibid.

22. Richard Grimmett, "Conventional Arms Transfers to Developing Nations 1998–2005," *CRS Report for Congress*, RL33696, October 23, 2006.

23. "Hard to Make Friends," *Economist*, January 17, 2008, http://www.economist.com/world/africa/displaystory.cfm?story_id=10534464.

24. Ann Calvaresi Barr, "Export Controls: State and Commerce Have Not Taken Basic Steps to Better Ensure U.S. Interests Are

Protected," Government Accountability Office, Testimony Before the Subcommittee on Oversight of Government Management, the Federal Workforce, and the District of Columbia, Committee on Homeland Security and Governmental Affairs, U.S. Senate, April 24, 2008. This testimony cited that the number of arms licensing officers was at the same level in fiscal years 2003 and 2006, despite an almost 20 percent increase in cases over that period.

25. Mitsuro Donowaki, "The Challenge of Terrorism for International Security and Disarmament: Global and Regional Impact," lecture, Fifth UN Conference on Disarmament, Kyoto, Japan, August 7, 2002.

26. "Somali Militia Group 'Surrounded,'" *BBC News*, January 4, 2007, http://news.bbc.co.uk/1/hi/world/africa/6230809.stm.

27. John Diamond, "Small Weapons Prove the Real Threat in Iraq," *USA Today*, September 29, 2003, http://www.usatoday.com/news/world/iraq/2003-09-29-cover-small-arms_x.htm.

28. Owen Bowcott and Richard Norton-Taylor, "War on Terror Fuels Small Arms Trade," *Guardian*, October 10, 2003, http://www.guardian.co.uk/world/2003/oct/10/armstrade.richardnortontaylor.

29. Lanka Business Online, October 10, 2003, http://www.lankabusinessonline.com.

30. Bowcott and Norton-Taylor, "War on Terror Fuels Small Arms Trade."

31. Karen Ballentine and Jake Sherman, *The Political Economy of Armed Conflict: Beyond Greed and Grievance* (Boulder, CO: Lynne Rienner Publishers, 2003), 2.

32. "Frequently Asked Questions," Small Arms Survey, http://www.smallarmssurvey.org/files/sas/home/FAQ.html#FAQ2 (last accessed June 3, 2008).

33. Katherine Heine, "Small Arms Threaten Sri Lanka's Stability," Reuters, September 30, 2003.

34. Ballentine and Sherman, *Political Economy of Armed Conflict*, 82.

35. Kofi Annan, "Small Arms, Big Problems," lecture, United Nations Conference on the Illicit Trade in Small Arms and Light Weapons in All Its Aspects, New York, July 9, 2001.

36. For the latest news on such programs, see the web site at http://www.gunpolicy.org, which includes a daily news feed on gun control efforts.

37. Emira Woods, "Somalia," *Foreign Policy in Focus* 2, no. 19 (1997), Interhemisphere Resource Center and Institute for Policy Studies, http://www.fpif.org/pdf/vol2/19ifsoma.pdf.

38. Frances Steward, "Root Causes of Violent Conflict in Developing Countries," *British Medical Journal* (February 9, 2002), http://www.pubmedcentral.nih.gov/articlerender.fcgi?artid=1122271.

39. Ibid.

40. Ibid.

41. Philip Bobbitt, "Get Ready for the Next Long War," *Time*, September 9, 2002, http://www.time.com/time/magazine/article/0,9171,1003220-1,00.html/.

42. "Port Security Task Force Report," Port Authority of New York and New Jersey, December 2006, http://www.cfr.org/publication/12301/port_security_task_force_report.html.

43. Ibid.

44. Ibid.

45. "Opinion Leaders Turn Cautious, Public Looks Homeward," America's Place in the World Survey Results, Pew Research Center, November 17, 2005, http://people-press.org/report/263/opinion-leaders-turn-cautious-public-looks-homeward.

46. Anup Shah, "World Military Spending," *Global Issues*, http://www.globalissues.org/Geopolitics/ArmsTrade/Spending.asp#WorldMilitarySpending (last accessed June 3, 2008).

47. "China's Defense Budget," *Global Security*, http://www.globalsecurity.org/military/world/china/budget.htm (last accessed June 3, 2008).

48. Tim Johnson, "China Announces Largest Military Budget Ever," *McClatchy Newswire*, March 4, 2008, http://www.mcclatchydc.com/world/story/29351.html.

49. "India's Military Budget," *Global Security*, http://www.globalsecurity.org/military/world/india/budget.htm (last accessed June 3, 2008).

50. Christopher Hellmann, "The Runaway Military Budget: An Analysis," *Friends Committee on National Legislation Washington Newsletter*, no. 705, March 2006, 3.

51. Ibid., 2.

52. Chalmers Johnson, *Nemesis: The Last Days of the American Republic* (New York: Holt Paperback, 2008).

53. Ibid.

54. Special thanks to President Clinton for his candid remarks in response to my questions in March 2008. He said that rebuilding the U.S. military and intelligence from the ground up would be one of the key responsibilities for any new president in the 2008 election.

55. Will Dunham, "Strained U.S. National Guard Has Hurricane Relief Role," Reuters, August 30, 2005.

56. Steve Coll, "Military Conflict," *New Yorker,* April 14, 2008.

57. National Security Archive, http://www.gwu.edu/~nsarchiv/NSAEBB/NSAEBB214/index.htm (last accessed June 10, 2008).

58. Mark Thompson, "America's Medicated Army," *Time,* June 5, 2008.

59. "Fighting Fires," *Economist,* February 16, 2007, http://www.economist.com/world/na/displaystory.cfm?story_id=8696412.

60. Hellmann, "Runaway Military Budget," 2.

61. "FY2009 Intelligence Budget," *Global Security,* http://www.globalsecurity.org/intell/library/budget/index.html. Note that this is an estimate, because intelligence budgets are classified. The last disclosed budget, for 2007, was $43.5 billion.

62. *The 9/11 Commission Report,* "Executive Summary," September 2006, 2, http://www.gpoaccess.gov/911/pdf/execsummary.pdf.

63. Central Intelligence Agency (CIA), Bureau of Intelligence and Research (INR) of the Department of State, Defense Intelligence Agency (DIA), National Security Agency (NSA), National Reconnaissance Office (NRO), National Geospatial-Intelligence Agency (NGA), Federal Bureau of Investigation (FBI), Army Intelligence, Navy Intelligence, Air Force Intelligence, Marine Corps Intelligence, Department of Homeland Security (DHS), Coast Guard (CG), Treasury Department, Energy Department, Drug Enforcement Agency. See: "Intelligence Issues for Congress," *CRS Report for Congress,* RL33539, March 10, 2008, 2–3.

64. *The 9/11 Commission Report,* "Executive Summary," September 2006, 2, http://www.gpoaccess.gov/911/pdf/execsummary.pdf.

65. Ibid., 2–3.

66. "The National Security Strategy of the United States of America," National Security Council, September 2002, http://www.whitehouse.gov/nsc/nss.html.

67. "Intelligence Issues for Congress," *CRS Report for Congress*, RL33539, March 10, 2008, 13.

68. "Iraq Coalition Casualty Count," http://icasualties.org/oif/.

69. "Iran: Nuclear Intentions and Capabilities," National Intelligence Estimate (NIE), November 2007.

70. "Iran Weapons Project 'Continued,'" *BBC News*, February 26, 2008, http://news.bbc.co.uk/2/hi/middle_east/7264090.stm.

71. "Intelligence Issues for Congress," *CRS Report for Congress*, March 10, 2008, 2–11.

72. Interpol, "Interpol: An Overview," Fact Sheet COM/FS/2008-03/GI-01.

73. Eric Schmitt, "Experts See Gains Against Asian Terror Networks," *New York Times*, June 8, 2008, http://www.nytimes.com/2008/06/09/world/asia/09terror.html?pagewanted=print. In fact, Azhari Husin, one of the most feared bomb makers in Asia, was killed by Indonesia's elite antiterrorism unit in 2005.

74. Testimony of Secretary of State Condoleezza Rice, Senate Foreign Relations Committee, February 8, 2007, http://foreign.senate.gov/testimony/2007/RiceTestimony070208.pdf.

75. See www.nypdshield.org for more information on the NYPD Shield program.

76. Adam Gopnik, "The Human Bomb: The Sarkozy Regime Begins," *New Yorker*, August 27, 2007, http://www.newyorker.com/reporting/2007/08/27/070827fa_fact_gopnik?currentPage=all.

77. "U.S. Public Diplomacy: Background and the 9/11 Commission Recommendations," *CRS Report for Congress*, 32607, October 19, 2006, 1.

78. "The Budget in Brief: Fiscal Year 2009," U.S. Department of State, February 4, 2008, http://www.state.gov/s/d/rm/rls/bib/2009/pdf/.

79. "Straight Talk on Staffing and Resources," American Foreign Service Association, http://www.afsa.org/040908Staffing.cfm (last accessed June 9, 2008).

80. "Diplomacy for the 21st Century: Transformational Diplomacy," *CRS Report for Congress*, 34141, January 29, 2008, 11.

81. Fred Kaplan, "What It Will Take to Heal U.S. Diplomacy," *Slate*, March 30, 2008, http://www.slate.com/id/2187579/.

82. Sheryl Gay Stolberg and Jim Rutenberg, "Bush Assails 'Appeasement,' Touching Off Storm," May 16, 2008, http://www.nytimes.com/2008/05/16/us/politics/16obama.html?ref=world.

83. Anne Gearan, Associated Press, "Rice Less Optimistic about Quick Peace Deal," *Yahoo! News*, June 3, 2008, http://news.yahoo.com/s/ap/20080603/ap_on_go_ca_st_pe/us_israel.

84. Condoleezza Rice, "On-the-Record Briefing to Press in London," U.S. Department of State, London, United Kingdom, March 1, 2005.

85. "Russia's Defense Budget," *Global Security*, http://www.globalsecurity.org/military/world/russia/mo-budget.htm (last accessed June 3, 2008).

86. "India and China Launch War Game," *BBC News*, December 20, 2007, http://news.bbc.co.uk/2/hi/south_asia/7153179.stm.

87. Andrew Tully, "Central Asia: Is It Time to Withdraw U.S. Troops?" *Radio Free Europe*, July 7, 2005, http://www.rferl.org/featuresarticle/2005/07/D14A9FDA-0EF0-4E6E-B5AF-AF28C63A2C08.html/.

88. The UN headquarters, for example, is so antiquated that New York City Mayor Michael Bloomberg called it a "hazard to school-children," and has threatened to stop allowing field trips to the UN. Catherine Donaldson-Evans, "New York City Mayor Says United Nations Building Is a Hazard to Schoolchildren," *Fox News*, November 12, 2007, http://www.foxnews.com/story/0,2933,310816,00.html.

89. Chelsea Trull, "China Opposes Japan's Bid for Security Council," *Michigan Daily*, April 15, 2005, http://media.www.michigandaily.com/media/storage/paper851/news/2005/04/14/News/China.Opposes.Japans.Bid.For.Security.Council-1430322.shtml.

90. "U.S., Russia, China Rejecting G4 UN Reform Bill," *China Daily*, May 13, 2005, http://au.china-embassy.org/eng/xw/t203436.htm.

91. UN General Assembly, "Report of the Open-Ended Working Group on the Question of Representation on and Increase in the Membership of the Security Council," A/58/47, July 21, 2004.

92. For many years, it was thought that China would be an obsta-cle to India's inclusion. The two had come to blows during the

30-day Sino-Indian war in 1962, and historically China had been an ally of India's archrival, Pakistan. However, in Tang Jiaxuan, China's foreign minister from 1998 to 2003, India found an unlikely ally who advocated India's bid for a permanent seat, but without a veto. Similar support came from former UK Prime Minister Tony Blair.

93. My thanks to Bob Orr of the UN for clarifying this important point.

94. See Carlos Seignie's "Efficient Peacekeeping for a New World Order," *Peace Economics, Peace Science and Public Policy* 11, issue 2, article 2 (2005), available online at www.bepress.com/.

95. "Russia Condemns NATO Expansion," *BBC News*, April 1, 2004, http://news.bbc.co.uk/2/hi/europe/3587717.stm.

96. Melissa Eddy, Associated Press, "Russia Warns NATO Expansion Will Sour Relations," *Google News*, June 6, 2008, http://ap.google .com/article/ALeqM5hlC-mIlvKeJbGeOOpckmkNY2cnCAD 91442T00.

97. Judy Dempsey, "U.S. Rejects German Calls to Withdraw Nuclear Weapons," *New York Times*, May 3, 2005, http://www.nytimes. com/2005/05/03/international/europe/03cnd-nuke.html.

98. "NATO Nuclear Policies," Nuclear Age Peace Foundation, http://www.nuclearfiles.org/menu/key-issues/nuclear-weap-ons/issues/nato-nuclear-policies/index.htm (last accessed June 9, 2008).

99. "Final Communiqué," Ministerial Meeting of the Defense Planning Committee and the Nuclear Planning Group, Brussels, Belgium, June 9, 2005, http://www.nuclearfiles.org/menu/key-issues/nuclear-weapons/issues/nato-nuclear-policies/2005-06-09_defence-planning-committee.html.

100. George P. Shultz, William J. Perry, Henry Kissinger, and Sam Nunn, "World Free of Nuclear Weapons," *Wall Street Journal*, January 4, 2007.

101. For a full transcript of Des Browne's proposal, see http://www.mod .uk/DefenceInternet/DefenceNews/DefencePolicyAndBusiness/ BrowneCallsForDevelopmentOfNuclearDisarmamentTechnologies .htm.

102. Ian Traynor, "Pre-Emptive Nuclear Strike a Key Option, Nato Told," *Guardian*, January 22, 2008, http://www.guardian.co.uk/world/2008/jan/22/nato.nuclear.

103. Judy Dempsey, "Report Calls for a Radical Overhaul of NATO," *International Herald Tribune*, January 31, 2008, http://www.iht.com/articles/2008/01/31/europe/nato.php.

104. For an excellent guide, see David A. Ochmanek's *Nato's Future: Implications for U.S. Military Capabilities and Posture* (Santa Monica, CA: Rand Corporation, 2000).

Chapter 5: Immigration: People, People Anywhere

1. Tamar Jacoby, "Immigration Nation," *Foreign Affairs*, November–December 2006, http://www.foreignaffairs.org/20061101faessay 85606/tamar-jacoby/immigration-nation.html.

2. In addition to women being able to work and support themselves in industry and service sectors, the later introduction and prolif- eration of modern birth control helped to speed the transition to smaller family size.

3. Lloyd Miller, "The Economic Impact of an Aging Europe," *McKinsey Quarterly*, May 2005, 1.

4. Ibid.

5. OECD, *International Migration Outlook: SOPEMI 2007 Edition* (Organization for Economic Cooperation and Development, 2007: 7, no. 7), 32.

6. Lloyd Miller, "The Demographic Deficit: How Aging Will Reduce Global Wealth," *McKinsey Quarterly*, March 2005.

7. William Larsen, "Worker to Retiree Ratio," October 10, 2002, http://www.justsayno.50megs.com/wr_ratio.html.

8. According to pension consultant Watson Wyatt (see http://www.watsonwyatt.com/news/featured/wef/germany.pdf).

9. David C. John, "2007 Social Security Trustees Report Shows the Urgency of Reform," Heritage Foundation, April 24, 2007, http://www.heritage.org/research/SocialSecurity/wm1429.cfm

10. "The Coming Demographic Deficit: How Aging Populations Will Reduce Global Savings," McKinsey Global Institute, December 2004.

11. Ibid.

12. "One-child policy" is a misnomer: Actually, minorities and rural families whose first child is female or disabled are allowed multiple children.

13. Ibid.

14. Amy Yee, "Stars of India," *Financial Times*, June 30, 2007.

15. S. Mitra Kalita, "A Reversal of the Tide in India: Tech Workers Flow Home to More Success," *Washington Post*, February 28, 2006, A01.

16. Ibid.

17. John Boudreau, "Behind the Boom, Emigres Tackle Poverty," *Mercury News*, December 6, 2006.

18. Kalita, "Reversal of the Tide in India," A01.

19. Raghunath A. Mashelkar, "India's R&D: Reaching for the Top," *Science* 307, no. 5714 (March 4, 2005): 1415–1417.

20. "The Role of Outsourcing in Reversing the Brain Drain into Brain Gain," *Development Gateway Foundation*, January 14, 2005.

21. Kalita, "Reversal of the Tide in India," A01.

22. UN Department of Economic and Social Affairs, Population Division, *International Migration 2006* (New York: United Nations Publications, 2006), http://www.un.org/esa/population/publications/2006Migration_Chart/Migration2006.pdf.

23. "Migration and Migrant Integration in the Atlantic Region Conference Report," Atlantic Conference 2007, March 22–24, 2007, Seville, Spain.

24. UN Department of Economic and Social Affairs, Population Division.

25. OECD, *International Migration Outlook: SOPEMI 2007 Edition*, 3.

26. Ibid.

27. "The Effect of Outsourcing and Offshoring on Productivity Change," U.S. Bureau of Labor Statistics, March 26, 2004.

28. "Monthly Statistical Snapshot, April 2008," Social Security Administration, http://www.ssa.gov/policy/docs/quickfacts/stat_snapshot/#table2.

29. Dan Griswold, "When Employment Lines Cross Borders," *Star Telegram*, April 21, 2008, http://www.cato.org/pub_display.php?pub_id=9346.

30. Jacoby, "Immigration Nation."

31. William A. Wolf, "The Importance of Foreign-Born Scientists and Engineers to the Security of the United States," 109th Congress, Immigration, Border Security, and Claims Subcommittee, Committee on the Judiciary, U.S. House of Representatives, September 15, 2005, http://www7.nationalacademies.org/ocga/testimony/Importance_ of_Foreign_Scientists_and_Engineers_to_US.asp.

32. Ibid.

33. Jacoby, "Immigration Nation."

34. Ibid.

35. Oscar Avila and Antonio Olivo, "Western Union Boycott Divides," *Chicago Tribune*, October 21, 2007.

36. For example, Western Union recently organized a 3:1 fund-matching program between immigrants from Zacatecas living in Illinois and local government offices in Mexico. As a result of the program, Western Union has already given $1.2 million to the Mexican community, earmarked for a computerized irrigation system and job creation.

37. Ibid.

38. Polaris Project, http://www.polarisproject.org/index.php?option= com_frontpage&Itemid=1 (last accessed June 18, 2008).

39. Mark Chaplin, "Agents in the UEFA Spotlight," *UEFA Online,* September 29, 2006, http://www.uefa.com/uefa/keytopics/ kind=2048/newsid=462974.html.

40. UNGIFT, Asia, "Briefing Note 8: Statistics on Human Trafficking in South Asia," http://www.giftasia.in/index.php? option=com_content&task=view&id=207&Itemid=347.

41. "Mexico and NAFTA: Tariffs and Tortillas," *Economist,* January 26–February 1, 2008, 38.

42. Ibid.

43. Jacob Hill, "Free Trade and Immigration: Cause and Effect," *Council on Hemispheric Affairs,* July 18, 2007, http://www.coha.org/ 2007/07/18/free-trade-and-immigration-cause-and-effect/.

44. "2005 Outsourcing Bills," National Conference of State Legislatures, http://www.ncsl.org/programs/employ/outsourcing05.htm.

45. "The Emerging Global Labor Market: The Demand for Offshore Talent in Services," McKinsey Global Institute, June 2005.

46. Martin N. Bally and Diana Farrell, "Exploding the Myths about Offshoring," McKinsey Global Institute, April 2004, 4.

47. Ibid., 5.

48. "Who Wins in Offshoring?" McKinsey Global Institute, February 4, 2004.

49. Bally and Farrell, "Exploding the Myths about Offshoring," 6.

50. Jacob Hacker of the New America Foundation has suggested that using innovative insurance schemes could help manage occupational transitions. Using a small percent of the savings from offshoring, for instance, corporations could purchase insurance for their displaced workers to cover a percentage of lost wages until they gain new employment.

51. Nor could a Procter & Gamble or Wal-Mart simply expect Chinese managers to follow global corporate protocol: Newly opened China had a business culture that still bore many peculiar relics of the Mao era. Bribery was rampant; Communist Party officials routinely wielded more authority than business owners; and a culture of paternalism meant that firing a middle manager could lead to a factorywide insurrection. For more anecdotes about the business climate in the early 1990s in China, see Tim Clissold's *Mr. China*.

52. Katherine Rosman, "Expat Life Gets Less Cushy," *Wall Street Journal*, October 26, 2007, http://online.wsj.com/article/SB119335069837572103.html.

53. Ibid.

54. Quality of life is on the rise in emerging markets, and cushy ex-pat packages are no longer needed to attract talent to foreign posts; many employees voluntarily relocate. According to consultancy ORC Worldwide, today the average package given a family of four moving from the United States to Tokyo is worth 1.8 times the executive's base salary, as opposed to 3.6 times in 1994.

55. Workforce Mobility Facts Page, "Worldwide Employee Relocation Council," http://www.erc.org/who_is_ERC/facts.shtml.

56. Business education has vastly improved in many former ex-pat destinations; the 2007 Economist Intelligence Unit includes MBA programs from Hong Kong, Singapore, South Africa, China, and

India in its list of the top 100 programs. In fact, many Westerners are now clamoring to study business abroad—the University of Pennsylvania's Wharton School offers students programs in Beijing and Israel, while the University of Southern California's Marshall School of Business requires its entire incoming class to take a field trip to one of a selected set of Pacific Rim or Latin American countries. As human capital consultancy Hewitt Associates explains, "conventional wisdom has been that expatriates were chosen based on the fact that they not only had the know-how to get a job done, but also were the corporate ambassadors who could spread a company's culture to new and existing regional offices. But in our increasingly globalizing world, organizations have discovered that having a 'replica' corporate culture in every corner of the globe in which they operate is not always necessary or even advantageous."

57. Danielle Guichard-Ashbrook, "International Students at MIT Post 9-11," *MIT Faculty Newsletter*, March/April 2006, http://web.mit .edu/fnl/volume184/guichard_ashbrook.html.
58. Ibid.
59. Institute of International Education, "International Student Enrollment in U.S. Rebounds," *Open Doors 2007: International Students in the United States*, November 12, 2007, http://opendoors .iienetwork.org/?p=113743.
60. Gregory Chenin and John Bidwell, "How the Patriot Act Is Affecting MHC's International Students and What the College Is Doing about It," *Mount Holyoke Alumnae Quarterly*, Spring 2005, http://www.alumnae.mtholyoke.edu.
61. Alan M. Webber, "Reverse Brain Drain Threatens U.S. Economy," *USA Today*, February 23, 2004, http://www.usatoday .com/news/opinion/editorials/2004-02-23-economy-edit_x.htm.
62. "Immigration Statistics," Department of Homeland Security, http://www.dhs.gov/ximgtn/statistics/. The Diversity Lottery awards U.S. visas by lottery to foreigners who were born in countries with low rates of immigration to the United States.
63. Webber, "Reverse Brain Drain."
64. David Heenan, as quoted by Stephanie Clifford, "America's Reverse Brain Drain," *INC.com*, December 12, 2005, http://www .inc.com/articles/2005/12/qaheenan.html.

65. Ilya Shapiro, "Foolish Misuse," *National Review*, April 1, 2008, http://www.cato.org/pub_display.php?pub_id=9311.

66. Although we typically think of how these visa shortages for engineers and scientists affect the U.S. technological lead, actually the H-1B visa covers a wide category of workers in "specialized occupations," such as models. A New York congressman proposed reclassifying models in a separate immigration category—what some jokingly call a "beautiful people" visa. But the fashion industry generates tons of revenue for the United States each year, and fewer and fewer foreign models are granted visas each year.

67. Ibid.

68. Bill Gates, "Strengthening American Competitiveness for the 21st Century," Oral Testimony, U.S. Senate Committee Hearing on Strengthening American Competitiveness, United States Senate Committee on Health, Education, Labor, and Pensions, Washington, D.C., March 7, 2007.

69. Ibid.

70. Carl F. Horowitz, "An Examination of U.S. Immigration Policy and Serious Crime," Center for Immigration Studies, April 2001, http://www.cis.org/articles/2001/crime/toc.html#fear.

71. "Immigrants and Crime: Setting the Record Straight," Immigration Policy Center, March 2008.

72. Ibid.

73. Horowitz, "Examination of U.S. Immigration Policy."

74. Office of the Press Secretary, "President Bush Discusses Comprehensive Immigration Reform in Glynco, Georgia," speech, Federal Law Enforcement Training Center, Glynco, Georgia, May 29, 2007, http://www.whitehouse.gov/news/releases/2007/05/20070529-7.html.

75. Anup Shah, "Brain Drain of Workers from Poor to Rich Countries," *Sustainable Development*, April 14, 2006, http://www.globalissues.org/TradeRelated/Development/braindrain/.

76. "The World Health Report 2006: Working Together for Health," World Health Organization, http://www.who.int/why/2006/en/.

77. Moyiga Nduru, "Brain Drain Is Killing People," *Inter Press Service*, May 25, 2007, http://ipsnews.net/news.asp?idnews=37898.

78. World Health Organization, "World Health Report 2006."

79. Mil Arcega, "Rising Health Care Costs One of 'Biggest Challenges,'" *Voice of America*, June 17, 2008.

80. See *The MetLife Market Survey of Nursing Homes and Assisted Living Costs*, October 2007, available online at http://www.metlife.com/ FileAssets/MMI/MMIStudies2007NHAL.pdf.

81. Chris Hawley, "Seniors Head South to Mexican Nursing Homes," *USA Today*, August 15, 2007, http://www.usatoday.com/news/ nation/2007-08-15-mexnursinghome_N.htm?POE-click-refer.

82. Ibid.

83. Mario Gonzalez, "Lake Chapala: The Oasis of Mexico's Retirement Destinations," *Security Corner*, September 20, 2007, http:// www.securitycornermexico.com/index2.php?option=com_ content&do_pdf=1&id=290.

84. Ibid.

85. For example, Mexico has immigrant and nonimmigrant *rentista* visas for people of any age who do not work in the country and are economically self-sufficient (this includes income from pensions or investment). Panama has enacted a similar policy, with two visas—the *pensionado* and *rentista*—that specifically target retirees. In addition to making the visas easier to obtain for retirees, the Panamanian government is luring foreigners to relocate with several perks, including a special 20-year property tax exemption on newly constructed homes, as well as discounts for seniors on entertainment, restaurant meals, hotels, utilities, and medical care.

86. Ibid.

87. Ibid.

Chapter 6: Promoting Tomorrow's Health Instead of Paying for Yesterday's Ills

1. Lee Jong-wook, "Launch of the Chronic Disease Report," presentation at Mauritius Institute of Health, World Health Organization, March 7, 2006, http://www.who.int/dg/lee/speeches/2006/mauri-tius_chronic_disease/en/index.html.

2. "Chronic Disease Overview," Centers for Disease Control and Prevention, http://www.cdc.gov/nccdphp/overview.htm.

3. Jeanne Lambrew, "Consumer-Driven Health Plans Prevent Prevention," Center for American Progress, April 10, 2008, http://www.americanprogress.org/issues/2008/04/prevention .html/#article1.

4. Lee Jong-wook, "Launch of the Chronic Disease Report."

5. Angela Zimm, Bloomberg News, "Chronic Illnesses on Rise, Study Says," *Boston Globe*, June 27, 2007, http://www.boston.com/news/ nation/articles/2007/06/27/chronic_illnesses_on_rise_study_says/.

6. J. A. Poisal et al., "Health Spending Projections Through 2016: Modest Changes Obscure Part D's Impact," *Health Affairs*, February 21, 2007, W242–253.

7. For fiscal year 2009, Medicare (the U.S. government program that supports 44 million elderly and disabled) will receive $420 billion in federal funding, while Medicaid (which provides health coverage and long-term care assistance to over 44 million low-income individuals and 14 million elderly and disabled people) will receive $224 billion.

8. P. T. Huynh, C. Schoen, R. Osborn, and A. L. Holmgren, "The U.S. Health Care Divide: Disparities in Primary Care Experiences by Income," Commonwealth Fund, April 2006.

9. Michael D. Tanner, "The Grass Is Not Always Greener: A Look at National Health Care Systems Around the World," *Policy Analysis* 613, March 18, 2008, http://www.cato.org/pub_display .php?pub_id=9272.

10. "Justification of Estimates for Appropriation Committees," Centers for Disease Control and Prevention, Department of Health and Human Services Fiscal Year 2009, http://www.hhs.gov/budget/ docbudget.htm#brief.

11. Ibid.

12. "China Accused of Sars 'Cover-Up,'" *BBC News*, April 9, 2003, http://news.bbc.co.uk/2/hi/health/2932319.stm.

13. Brian Knowlton, "2 Flights Carried Man with Deadly TB," *New York Times*, May 29, 2007, http://www.nytimes.com/2007/05/29/ health/29cnd-tb.html?_r=1&ref=health&oref=slogin.

14. Jeanne M. Lambrew and John D. Podesta, "Promoting Prevention and Preempting Costs: A New Wellness Trust for the United States," Center for American Progress, October 5, 2006, 3.

15. Nanci Hellmich, "Childhood Obesity, a Lifetime of Danger," *USA Today*, January 13, 2008, http://www.usatoday.com/news/health/weightloss/2008-01-13-childhood-obesity_N.htm.

16. Ibid.

17. United Nations Department of Economic and Social Affairs, Population Division, *World Population Prospects: The 2006 Revision* (New York: United Nations, 2007), http://www.un.org/esa/population/publications/wpp2006/WPP2006_Highlights_rev.pdf. See Figure 2 for a full ranking of life expectancies.

18. "Tobacco Timeline," *2000 Surgeon General's Report—Reducing Tobacco Use*, http://www.cdc.gov/tobacco/data_statistics/sgr/sgr_2000/highlights/highlight_historical.htm.

19. Centers for Disease Control and Prevention, "Cigarette Smoking Among Adults—United States 2006," *MMWR Weekly* 56, no. 44 (November 6, 2007): 1157–1161, http://www.cdc.gov/mmwr/preview/mmwrhtml/mm5644a2.htm.

20. "Higher Cigarette Taxes Reduce Smoking, Save Lives, Save Money," Tobacco Free Kids, May 12, 2007, http://www.tobaccofreekids.org/reports/prices/.

21. "Smoking and Tobacco Use," Centers for Disease Control and Prevention, http://www.cdc.gov/tobacco/data_statistics/tables/economics/expdcom.htm.

22. "10 Facts on the Tobacco Epidemic and Global Tobacco Control," World Health Organization, http://www.who.int/features/factfiles/tobacco_epidemic/en/index.html.

23. Ibid.

24. U.S. Department of Agriculture Economic Research Service, "Food Consumption," *Briefing Rooms*, May 25, 2007, http://www.ers.usda.gov/Briefing/Consumption/.

25. "A Way Out of the Mess?" *Time*, July 23, 1973, http://www.time.com/time/magazine/article/0,9171,878617-1,00.html.

26. Christine Sismondo, "Children of the Corn," *Toronto Star*, May 14, 2006, http://www.michaelpollan.com/press.php?id=51.

27. "Soda Warning? High-Fructose Corn Syrup Linked to Diabetes, New Study Suggests," *Science Daily*, August 23, 2007, http://www.sciencedaily.com/releases/2007/08/070823094819.htm.

28. "Study: Vegan Diets Healthier for Planet, People than Meat Diets," University of Chicago Press Office, April 13, 2006, http://www-news.uchicago.edu/releases/06/060413.diet.shtml.
29. University of Chicago Press Office.
30. Lambrew and Podesta, "Promoting Prevention and Preempting Costs."
31. Jeanne M. Lambrew and John D. Podesta, "Health Prevention as a Priority: Creating a 'Wellness Trust,'" *Washington Post*, October 17, 2006, http://www.washingtonpost.com/wp-dyn/content/article/2006/10/16/AR2006101600880.html.
32. Shannon Brownlee, *Overtreated: Why Too Much Medicine Is Making Us Sicker and Poorer* (New York: Bloomsbury, 2007), 6.
33. Ibid., 6–7.
34. Ibid., 5.
35. Catharine W. Burt, Esther Hing, and David Woodwell, "Electronic Medical Record Use by Office-Based Physicians," National Center for Health Statistics, http://www.cdc.gov/nchs/products/pubs/pubd/hestats/electronic/electronic.htm.
36. Brownlee, *Overtreated*, 4.
37. Samuel Uretsky, "Healthcare in the United States," *Medhunters*, http://www.medhunters.com/articles/healthcareInTheUsa.html.
38. Lambrew, "Consumer-Driven Health Plans."
39. "Background Basics on Prevention," http://www.americanprogress.com.
40. Josef Woodman, *Patients Beyond Borders*, http://www.patientsbeyondborders.com/media-room/faq.php.
41. "Medical Tourism Growing Worldwide," *UDaily*, July 25, 2005. http://www.udel.edu/PR/Udaily/2005/mar/tourism072505.html.
42. "600,000 Medical Tourists Visit Thailand," *Globe Health Tours*, November 26, 2006. http://news.globehealthtours.com/category/medical-tourism-statistics/.
43. Woodman, *Patients Beyond Borders*.
44. "Why Harvard Is Coming to India: Brand Name Healthcare Boosts Medical Tourism," *Health and Medical Tourism*, http://www.ealthmedicaltourism.org/Blogs/The_Shabana_Medical_and_Dental_Tourism_Blog/Why_Harvard_Is_Coming_to_India/.

45. "CDC's Origins and Malaria," Department of Health and Human Services, Centers for Disease Control and Prevention, http://www .cdc.gov/malaria/history/history_cdc.htm.
46. "History of WHO," World Health Organization, http://www.who .int/about/history/en/index.html.
47. "Declaration of Alma-Ata," World Health Organization, 1978, http://www.who.int/hpr/NPH/docs/declaration_almaata.pdf.
48. According to the WHO web site at www.who.int, its six-point agenda includes the following: promoting development; fostering health security; strengthening health systems; harnessing research, information, and evidence; enhancing partnerships; and improving performance.
49. "Pandemics and Pandemic Threats Since 1900," available online at www.pandemicflu.gov.
50. "The Threat of Global Pandemics," transcript, Council on Foreign Affairs, June 16, 2005, http://www.cfr.org/publication/8198/ threat_of_global_pandemics.html.
51. Ibid.
52. Ibid.
53. D. Woodward et al., "Globalization and Health: A Framework for Analysis and Action," *Bulletin of the World Health Organization* 79 (2001): 875–881.
54. Reuters, "China Hospitals Using 'Fake Plasma' Drip," *Alertnet*, November 9, 2007, http://www.alertnet.org/thenews/newsdesk/ PEK134452.htm.
55. Georgia Institute of Technology, "Fake Pharmaceuticals: Increase in Counterfeit Anti-Malarial Drugs Prompts Call for Crackdown and Better Detection," *Science Daily* 20, June 2006, http://www .sciencedaily.com/releases/2006/06/060619005440.htm.
56. Peggy B. Hu and Berta Gomez, "Public Safety Jeopardized by Chinese Counterfeiters," U.S. Information Agency, U.S. Department of State, May 20, 2005, http://usinfo.state.gov/eap/ Archive/2005/May/20-45620.html.
57. Georgia Institute of Technology.
58. "China Probes 'Tainted' Toothpaste," *BBC News*, May 23, 2007, http://news.bbc.co.uk/2/hi/asia-pacific/6684563.stm.
59. Woodward et al., "Globalization and Health."

60. Ronald Labonte and Ted Schrecker, "Globalization and Social Determinants of Health: Introduction and Methodological Background," *Globalization and Health* 3 (2007): 5, http://globalizationandhealth.com/content/3/1/5.

61. John Wyn Owen and Olivia Roberts, "Globalization, Health and Foreign Policy: Emerging Linkages and Interests," *Globalization and Health* 1 (2005): 12.

62. Melissa Curley and Nicholas Thomas, "Human Security and Public Health in Southeast Asia: The SARS Outbreak," *Australian Journal of International Affairs* 58, no. 1 (2004): 17–32.

63. Owen and Roberts, "Globalization, Health and Foreign Policy."

64. Labonte and Schrecker, "Globalization and Social Determinants of Health."

65. Global Health Council, October 30, 2007.

66. Woodward et al., "Globalization and Health."

67. UNAID report, 17.

68. "Emerging Threats," Global Health Council, www.globalhealth.org/view_top.php3?id=229.

69. "HealthCast 2020: Creating a Sustainable Future," PricewaterhouseCoopers' Health Research Institute.

70. "Working Towards Wellness: The Business Rationale," World Economic Forum, 2008.

71. "HealthCast 2020."

72. See the CDC web site at http://www.cdc.gov/about/business/budget.htm.

Chapter 7: The Hidden Cost of Everything

1. Office of the Press Secretary, "President Bush Discusses Climate Change," news release, April 16, 2008.

2. UN General Assembly, 42nd Session, Official Records, "Report of the World Commission on Environment and Development: Our Common Future," A/42/427, 1983.

3. Jared Diamond, "What's Your Consumption Factor?" *New York Times*, January 2, 2008.

4. Daniel Prager and Valerie Thompson, "Findings of the Millennium Ecosystem Assessment: How Do the Poor Fare?" *World Resources*

2005: The Wealth of the Poor—Managing Ecosystems to Fight Poverty, World Resources Institute, September 2005, http://population.wri .org/worldresources2005-pub-4073.html.

5. Ibid.

6. Ibid.

7. The inverted-U curve showing the relationship between economic growth and environmental degradation is sometimes called the environmental Kuznets curve, since it resembles the curve by the same name that illustrates the relationship between economic growth and income inequality.

8. Matthew Brown and Jane S. Shaw, "Does Prosperity Protect the Environment?" *PERC Reports* 17, no. 1 (1999): 12. This holds true for particulate matter and certain other air pollutants.

9. Jim Yardley, "Choking on Growth," *New York Times*, September 28, 2007.

10. World Values Survey Online Data Analysis, http://www.world valuessurvey.org/ (accessed May 29, 2008). The World Values Survey is an ongoing study that has examined the basic values and beliefs of more than 80 societies around the globe approximately every five years since 1990.

11. Heather Timmons, "Indians Bristle at U.S. Criticism on Food Prices," *International Herald Tribune*, May 13, 2008, http://www.iht .com/articles/2008/05/13/business/food.php#.

12. *Stern Review on the Economics of Climate Change*, "Executive Summary," http://www.hm-treasury.gov.uk/independent_reviews/ stern_review_economics_climate_change/sternreview_summary. cfm.

13. Richard Andrews, "Sustainable Enterprise: Implications for International Finance and Investment," February 28, 2003, http://www.newamerica.net/publications/policy/sustainable_ enterprise.

14. World Values Survey Online Data Analysis, http://www.world valuessurvey.org/ (accessed May 29, 2008).

15. "Rain Forest Facts," Rain-Tree, http://www.rain-tree.com/facts .htm (last accessed June 4, 2008).

16. Ibid.

17. Ibid.

18. "Trends and Facts—Cultivating Food Security," *State of the World 2005*, Worldwatch Institute, http://www.worldwatch.org/node/73.

19. *CIA World Factbook*, s.v., "The World," https://www.cia.gov/library/publications/the-world-factbook/geos/xx.html (last accessed June 4, 2008).

20. "Trade in Forest Products and Services," Food and Agriculture Organization, http://www.fao.org/forestry/trade/en/ (last accessed June 4, 2008).

21. Ibid.

22. Edward Harris, "Rain Forests Shrink at 'Alarming' Rate," Associated Press, February 3, 2008, http://www.livescience.com/environment/080203-ap-forest-decline.html.

23. "Saving Forests," Conservation International, http://www.conservation.org/learn/forests/Pages/overview.aspx (last accessed June 2, 2008).

24. Food and Agriculture Organization, "Globalization Altering the Forest Landscape in Asia-Pacific," news release, Chiang Mai, Thailand, October 16, 2007, http://www.un.or.th/presscentre/documents/071016FAOGlobalizationAlteringtheForestLandscapeinAsiaPacific.pdf.

25. "Summary Statistics for Globally Threatened Species," International Union for the Conservation of Nature, http://www.iucnredlist.org/info/stats (last accessed June 8, 2008).

26. Howard Youth, "Winged Messengers: The Decline of Birds," *Worldwatch Paper* 165, March 2003.

27. Ibid.

28. Daniel Prager and Valerie Thompson, "Findings of the Millennium Ecosystem Assessment: How Do the Poor Fare?" *World Resources 2005*, September 2005, http://earthtrends.wri.org/features/view_feature.php?fid=61&theme=4.

29. "Rain Forest Agribusiness," Rain Forest Action Network, http://ran.org/campaigns/rainforest_agribusiness/spotlight/getting_real_about_biofuels/ (last accessed June 2, 2008).

30. Ibid.

31. J. P. W. and W. F. Laurance, "How Green Are Biofuels?" *Science* 319 (2008): 52–53.

32. "Greenhouse Gas Emissions and Avoided Emissions in the Production and Utilization of Sugar Cane, Sugar and Ethanol in Brazil: 1990–1994," Macedo, Copersucar Technological Centre, www.mct.gov.br/clima/ingles/comunic_old/coperal.htm.

33. Gerry Shih, Cox News Service, "Ohio Rides the Boom in Ethanol Production," Environmental Working Group, May 27, 2008, http://www.ewg.org/node/26611.

34. "Rain Forest Agribusiness," Rain Forest Action Network, http://ran.org/campaigns/rainforest_agribusiness/spotlight/getting_real_about_biofuels/ (last accessed June 2, 2008).

35. "Facts and Figures: Water Use," UNESCO, http://www.unesco.org/water/iyfw2/water_use.shtml (last accessed June 8, 2008).

36. Jessica Forrest, "Protecting Ecosystems in a Changing World," World Resource Institute, July 2003, http://earthtrends.wri.org/features/view_feature.php?theme=7&fid=47.

37. Worldwatch Institute, "From Drinking Water to Disasters, Investing in Freshwater Ecosystems Is Best Insurance Policy," news release, July 11, 2005, http://www.worldwatch.org/node/1819.

38. Alex Veiga, Associated Press, "LA Jurors Award $3.3 Million to Banana Workers in Pesticide Case," *Panama-Guide.com*, November 6, 2007, http://www.panama-guide.com/article.php/20071106150552588.

39. The Green Revolution refers to the spread of the use of pesticides, irrigation projects, synthetic nitrogen fertilizer, and high-yield variety seeds outside the industrialized world in the 1960s.

40. Indur Goklany, "Fuels v. Food," *New York Post*, April 17, 2008, http://www.nypost.com/seven/04172008/postopinion/oped columnists/fuels_vs__food_106836.htm.

41. "The Political Cost of Inflation," *Economist*, April 4, 2008, http://www.economist.com/displaystory.cfm?story_id=10987640.

42. "Malthus, the False Prophet," *Economist*, May 15, 2008, http://www.economist.com/finance/displaystory.cfm?story_id=11374623.

43. "Obesity and Overweight," World Health Organization, http://www.who.int/dietphysicalactivity/publications/facts/obesity/en/ (last accessed June 6, 2008).

44. Heather Timmons, "Indians Bristle at U.S. Criticism on Food Prices," *International Herald Tribune*, May 13, 2008, http://www.iht.com/articles/2008/05/13/business/food.php#.

45. Cornell University, "U.S. Could Feed 800 Million People with Grain That Livestock Eat," news release, August 7, 1997, http://www.news.cornell.edu/releases/aug97/livestock.hrs.html.

46. "Grain and Bear It," *Economist*, May 23, 2008, http://www.economist.com/agenda/displaystory.cfm?story_id=11435966.

47. "The New Face of Hunger," *Economist*, April 17, 2008, http://www.economist.com/opinion/displaystory.cfm?story_id=11049284.

48. Ibid.

49. "Food Crisis: Soaring Prices Are Causing Hunger Around the World," *Washington Post,* March 14, 2008, A16.

50. FAO Newsroom, "Livestock a Major Threat to Environment," news release, November 29, 2006, http://www.fao.org/newsroom/en/news/2006/1000448/index.html.

51. "Innovations," *State of the World 2008*, Worldwatch Institute, http://www.worldwatch.org/node/5567.

52. Cornell University, "U.S. Could Feed 800 Million People."

53. "Blue in Green," *Economist*, December 10, 2007, http://www.economist.com/research/articlesBySubject/displaystory.cfm?subjectid=7933604&story_id=10272759.

54. "Improving Water Management: Recent OECD Experience," *OECD Policy Brief*, February 2006.

55. Ibid., 2.

56. Brian Fagan, "Learning from Our Arid Past," *Los Angeles Times*, April 29, 2008, http://www.latimes.com/news/opinion/commentary/la-oe-fagan29apr29,0,4871853.story.

57. Reuters, "Drought, Food Prices Threaten Millions of Somalis," May 19, 2008, http://africa.reuters.com/top/news/usnBAN953741.html.

58. Ryan Flimn, "California Utility Imposes First Water Rationing in 16 Years," *Bloomberg*, May 14, 2008, http://www.bloomberg.com/apps/news?pid=20601103&sid=aXfOhojHq.X8&refer=us.

59. Fagan, "Learning from Our Arid Past."

60. Ibid.

61. Tom Le Quesne, Guy Pegram, and Constantin Von Der Heyden, "Allocating Scarce Water," *WWF*, April 2007.

62. "Alfalfa: The Thirstiest Crop," Natural Resources Defense Council, http://www.nrdc.org/water/conservation/fcawater.asp.

63. Ibid.

64. Ibid.

65. U.S. Geological Survey, "Estimated Use of Water in the United States in 1995," *U.S. Geological Survey Circular* 1200, Denver, Colorado, 1995.

66. Abid Aslam, "Protecting, Conserving Water Resources Could Save Communities Immense Sums—Report," *One World US*, July 20, 2005, http://www.commondreams.org/headlines05/0720-05. htm.

67. "Nature's Water 'Factories' Under Threat," *People and Planet*, August 5, 2005, http://www.peopleandplanet.net/doc. php?id=2513.

68. Barrie Stevens, "Assessing the Risks," *OECD Observer*, http:// www.oecdobserver.org/news/fullstory.php/aid/1808/Assessing_ the_risks.html.

69. World Health Organization 2007 figures.

70. "Improving Water Management."

71. "Water and Violent Conflict," *OECD Issues Brief.*

72. Robie I. Samanta Roy, "India-Bangladesh Water Dispute," November 1997, http://www.american.edu/ted/ice/indobang .htm.

73. Ibid.

74. "The Coming Wave," *Economist*, June 5, 2008, http://www .economist.com/search/displaystory.cfm?story_id=11482565.

75. "The State of World Fisheries and Aquaculture 2006," Food and Agriculture Organization, http://www.fao.org/docrep/007/ y5600e/y5600e05.htm.

76. Ibid.

77. Ibid.

78. Worldwatch Institute, "SOS for Fading Ocean Life," news release, 2008, http://www.worldwatch.org/node/5360.

79. "State of World Fisheries and Aquaculture 2006," FAO.

80. Originally occurring every two to three years, the Gulf of Mexico dead zone now appears every spring, linked to the increased use of chemical fertilizers. In the spring, fresh thaws increase the flow of the Mississippi and Atchafalaya Rivers into the Gulf. The watershed for the Mississippi River covers 41 percent of the continental

United States and approximately 52 percent of U.S. farms. Runoff from the Mississippi River basin carries a heavy load of phosphorus and nitrogen-rich waste from animal manure and chemical fertilizers. The nutrient-laden wastewater promotes excessive algae growth. When the algae eventually sinks to the bottom to decompose, the bacteria that feed off it consume all the available oxygen, making the water unviable for other animal life. The impact of the dead zone on commerce has not been fully measured, but studies suggest that the occurrence of this dead zone forces fishing vessels to change their normal fishing patterns, expending more time and fuel to harvest their catches and potentially forcing marginal operators out of business. The forced concentration of fishing outside of the dead zone has resulted localized overfishing. The lost catch resulting from death of shellfish in the zone and long-term damage to the food chain and ecosystem caused by hypoxia is unclear, but is potentially quite large. The Gulf dead zone is one of the largest human-caused hypoxic zones in the world, but it is not unique. In the United States, hypoxic zones develop annually in western Long Island Sound off New York and Connecticut, in the Chesapeake Bay, and in the Neuse River in North Carolina. Outside the United States, dead zones are found in the Adriatic, Baltic, Black, and North Seas.

81. Bee Wilson, "The Last Bite," *New Yorker*, May 19, 2008, http://www.newyorker.com/arts/critics/atlarge/2008/05/19/080519crat_atlarge_wilson?currentPage=all.

82. FAO Newsroom, "Depleted Fish Stocks Require Recovery Efforts," news release, March 7, 2005, http://www.fao.org/newsroom/en/news/2005/100095/index.html.

83. "State of the World's Fisheries and Aquaculture 2006," Food and Agriculture Organization, http://www.fao.org/docrep/009/a0699e/A0699E06.htm#6.3.1.

84. Ibid.

85. "Pollution Linked to Birth Defects," *BBC News*, December 30, 2001, http://news.bbc.co.uk/1/hi/health/1731902.stm.

86. Robert Malone, "America's Most Polluted Cities," *Forbes*, March 21, 2006, http://www.forbes.com/2006/03/21/americas-most-polluted-cities-cx_rm_0321pollute.html.

87. Ibid.

88. Wayne Freedman, "Pollution in China Could Impact Our Air," *KGO-TV*, November 7, 2007, http://abclocal.go.com/kgo/story?section=news/environment&id=5747398.

89. Michelle L. Bell et al., "Global Impacts of Particulate Matter Air Pollution," *Environmental Research Letters* (2007): 2, http://www.iop.org/EJ/abstract/1748-9326/2/4/045026.

90. Keith Bradsher and David Barboza, "Pollution from Chinese Coal Casts a Global Shadow," *New York Times*, June 11, 2006.

91. Ibid.

92. Ibid.

93. Scott Barrett, "Barrett Proposal: A Multitrack Climate Treaty System," Belfer Center for Science and International Affairs, September 5, 2007, http://belfercenter.ksg.harvard.edu/experts/1294/scott_barrett.html.

94. Steve Gelsi, "Bush Calls For Halt in Greenhouse Gas Growth by 2025," *MarketWatch*, April 16, 2008, http://www.market-watch.com/news/story/bush-calls-halt-greenhouse-gas-growth/story.aspx?guid=%7B4E95F81E-4F34-4AE9-80A7-723DB5FE9B80%7D&dist=msr_3.

95. "The Search for Clean Coal," *Globe-Net*, May 28, 2008, http://www.climatebiz.com/feature/2008/05/28/the-search-clean-coal?page=0%2C2.

96. "Coal Mining," in *The Coal Resource: A Comprehensive Overview of Coal* (London: World Coal Institute, 2005).

97. "Search for Clean Coal."

98. "Mobile Sources," Environmental Protection Agency, http://www.epa.gov/oms/invntory/overview/pollutants/index.htm.

99. For example, varied discount rates applied to the costs of global warming for 100 years can generate widely different cost scenarios.

100. "Gas Prices Dominate the Public's Economic News Agenda," News Interest Index, Pew Research Center for the People & the Press, June 19, 2008, http://people-press.org/report/431/gas-prices-public-agenda.

101. "State of the World 2008: Innovations for a Sustainable Economy," Worldwatch Institute, http://www.worldwatch.org/stateoftheworld.

102. Ibid.

103. Ibid.

104. Meredith A. Giordano and Aaron T. Wolf, "The World's International Freshwater Agreements: Historical Developments and Future Opportunities," *Atlas of International Freshwater Agreements*, http://www.transboundarywaters.orst.edu/publications/atlas/.

105. Monica Prasad, "On Carbon, Tax and Don't Spend," *New York Times*, March 25, 2008, http://www.nytimes.com/2008/03/25/opinion/25prasad.html.

106. "The Elusive Negawatt," *Economist*, May 8, 2008, http://www.economist.com/displaystory.cfm?story_id=11326549.

107. "Introduction," Carbon Tax Center, http://www.carbontax.org/introduction/#why (last accessed June 16, 2008).

108. "Joseph E. Stiglitz Stands Up for a Carbon Tax," *Courrier International*, December 12, 2007, http://europe.courrierinternational.com/eurotopics/article.asp?langue=uk&publication=12/12/2007&cat=REFLECTIONS&pi=1.

Chapter 8: Remembering the Bottom of the Pyramid

1. "Pessimistic on Poverty? Economics Focus," *Economist*, April 10, 2004.

2. "The 2008 HHS Poverty Guidelines: One Version of the [U.S.] Federal Poverty Measure," United States Department of Health and Human Services, http://aspe.hhs.gov/poverty/08poverty.shtml.

3. "Pessimistic on Poverty?"

4. www.treasury.gov.au/documents/110/PDF/Round2.pdf.

5. "Questions and Answers with David Dollar," World Bank, 2004, http://www1.worldbank.org/economicpolicy/globalization/dollarqa.htm.

6. Jose Antonio Ocampo and Juan Martin, *Globalization and Development: A Latin American and Caribbean Perspective* (Stanford University Press, World Bank, and ECLAC, 2003), 192.

7. Joseph Stiglitz et al., eds. *Stability with Growth: Macroeconomics, Liberalization and Development* (New York: Oxford University Press, 2006), 241.

8. Economist Intelligence Unit Country Data for 1980 to present. Taken from World Bank figures.

9. Amarnath Singh, "The Year of Africa's Economic Turnaround?" *eAfrica*, March 8, 2005, http://yaleglobal.yale.edu/display.article?id=5388. Keep in mind that the high incidence of AIDS in sub-Saharan Africa has burdened these economies in many ways, and has hurt biosocial statistics such as life expectancy.

10. "Questions and Answers with David Dollar."

11. Ibid.

12. Erich Weede, *Balance of Power, Globalization, and the Capitalist Peace* (Berlin: Liberal Verlag GmbH, 2005), 47, www.fnst-freiheit.org/uploads/1044/Druckfahne.pdf.

13. One of the most noticeable inequities—wage differences between countries—is a product of the *lack* of liberalization within labor markets. By limiting the movement of people, labor markets become unbalanced; some countries have shortages, pushing up labor prices, while other countries have abundances of workers, pushing down wages. If immigration were an easier process, people could move to where they were needed most, equalizing wages.

14. James Surowiecki, "India's Skills Famine," *New Yorker*, April 18, 2007, http://yaleglobal.yale.edu/display.article?id=9074.

15. "India," *CIA World Factbook*, 2008 ed., https://www.cia.gov/library/publications/the-world-factbook/geos/in.html#People.

16. "The World Food Crisis," *New York Times*, April 10, 2008, available at http://www.nytimes.com/2008/04/10/opinion/10thu1.html.

17. Maros Ivanic and Will Martin, "Implications of Higher Global Food Prices for Poverty in Low-Income Countries," World Bank Development Research Group: Trade Team, April 2008, http://econ.worldbank.org/external/default/main?pagePK=64165259&piPK=64165421&theSitePK=469372&menuPK=64166093&entityID=000158349_20080416103709.

18. Weede, *Balance of Power*, 72.

19. Celia W. Dugger, "Push for New Tactics as War on Malaria Falters," *New York Times*, June 30, 2006, http://yaleglobal.yale.edu/display.article?id=7709.

20. http://www.globalissues.org/TradeRelated/Facts.asp#src9.

21. Michael Weinstein, "Economic Paradox of Ghana's Poverty," *Financial Times*, November 9, 2003, http://yaleglobal.yale.edu/display.article?id=2918.

22. Maggie Fox, "Tobacco Increases Cancer in Developing World," Reuters Africa, December 20, 2007, http://africa.reuters.com/wire/news/usnN20213145.html.

23. Anup Shah, "Linking the Environment and Poverty," *Global Issues*, February 12, 2005, http://www.globalissues.org/TradeRelated/Development/PovertyEnv.asp.

24. Ibid.

25. World Bank, "U.N. Climate Change Conference, Bali, Indonesia, 3–14 December, 2007," *World Bank Group Media Guide*, December 3, 2007. http://siteresources.worldbank.org/EXTSDNETWORK/Resources/2007Bali_Media_Guide_final.pdf?resourceurlname=2007Bali_Media_Guide_final.pdf.

26. Don Melnick and Mary Pearl, "Not Out of the Woods Just Yet," *New York Times*, April 20, 2006, http://www.nytimes.com/2006/04/20/opinion/20melnick.html.

27. Nigel Purvis, "Greening U.S. Foreign Aid through the Millennium Challenge Account," Brookings Institution, June 5, 2003, http://yaleglobal.yale.edu/display.article?id=1781.

28. "Poverty Breeds Insecurity," *Millennium Project*, January 19, 2005, http://yaleglobal.yale.edu/display.article?id=5150.

29. James Kirchik, "South Africa's Immigrant Shame," *Wall Street Journal*, May 28, 2008, http://online.wsj.com/article/SB121193274723s724561.html.

30. Purvis, "Greening U.S. Foreign Aid."

31. C. Peter Timmer, "The Threat of Global Food Shortages—Part I," *YaleGlobal*, May 5, 2008, http://yaleglobal.yale.edu/display.article?id=10749.

32. Paul Krugman, "Grains Gone Wild," *New York Times*, April 7, 2008, http://www.nytimes.com/2008/04/07/opinion/07krugman.html.

33. "The World Food Crisis," *New York Times*, April 10, 2008, http://www.nytimes.com/2008/04/10/opinion/10thu1.html.

34. Susan E. Rice, Corinne Graff, and Janet Lewis, "Poverty and Civil War: What Policymakers Need to Know," *Brookings Institution, Global Economy and Development Working Paper*, December 2006, 8, www.brookings.edu/views/papers/rice/poverty_civilwar.pdf.

35. ShawBlog, "Affluence and Poverty in the Middle East," http://shawblog.wordpress.com/2007/03/29/affluence-and-poverty-in-the-middle-east/.

36. "Poverty Breeds Insecurity."

37. "2007 World Drug Report," United Nations Office on Drugs and Crime, 1, https://www.unodc.org/pdf/research/wdr07/WDR_2007.pdf.

38. Ibid., 182.

39. "Coca Cultivation in the Andean Region: A Survey of Bolivia, Colombia, Ecuador and Peru," United Nations Office on Drugs and Crime, June 2007, http://www.unodc.org/pdf/andean/Andean_report_2007.pdf

40. Open Democracy, "Making 'Global' and 'Ethical' Rhyme: An Interview with Mary Robinson," Open Democracy, http://www.opendemocracy.net/globalization-open_politics/article_1627.jsp.

41. Robinson, Mary, "Globalization, Migration and Children: The Need for a Human Rights Approach," Columbia University Institute for Child and Family Policy, lecture series on "The Future of Children in a Global Society," October 18, 2004, www.childpolicyintl.org/publications/Mary%20Robinson_Speech.pdf.

42. "International Cooperation at a Crossroads: Aid, Trade and Security in an Unequal World," *Human Development Report 2005*, United Nations Development Programme, 1, http://yaleglobal.yale.edu/pdfs/hdr05.pdf.

43. Martin Wolf, "How to Help Africa Escape Poverty Trap," *Financial Times*, January 12, 2005, http://yaleglobal.yale.edu/display.article?id=5128.

44. John Cassidy, "Always with Us?: Jeffrey Sachs's Plan to Eradicate World Poverty," review of *The End of Poverty: Economic Possibilities for Our Time*, by Jeffrey Sachs, *New Yorker*, April 11, 2005, http://www.newyorker.com/archive/2005/04/11/050411crbo_books?currentPage=all.

45. Anup Shah, "US and Foreign Aid Assistance," *Global Issues*, April 27, 2008, http://www.globalissues.org/article/35/us-and-foreign-aid-assistance.

46. United Nations, "Millennium Development Goals Report: 2007" (New York: United Nations, 2007), 4–5, www.un.org/millenni umgoals/pdf/mdg2007.pdf.

47. United Nations, "Millennium Development Goals," http://www .undp.org/mdg/.

48. United Nations, "Millennium Development Goals Report: 2007," 4–5.

49. Celia W. Dugger, "U.N. Report Cites U.S. and Japan as the 'Least Generous Donors,'" *New York Times*, September 8, 2005, http://query.nytimes.com/gst/fullpage.html?res=9F06E0DC1231F93 BA3575AC0A9639C8B63.

50. George C. Lodge and Craig Wilson, "Multinational Corporations: A Key to Global Poverty Reduction—Part I," *YaleGlobal Online*, January 2, 2006. http://yaleglobal.yale.edu/ display.article?id=6657.

51. Ibid.

52. Pablo Pardo, *El Mundo*, May 26, 2007, 8–9, http://www.nyu.edu/ fas/institute/dri/Easterly/File/ElMundoArticle_052607.pdf.

53. Sharon LaFraniere, "Africa Takes Graft with Billions in Aid in Play," *New York Times*, September 6, 2005, http://www.nytimes. com/2005/07/06/international/africa/06lagos.html?_r=1& pagewanted=2&oref=slogin.

54. Ibid.

55. C. K. Prahalad, *The Fortune at the Bottom of the Pyramid: Eradicating Poverty Through Profits* (Upper Saddle River, NJ: Wharton School Publishing, 2004), 10.

56. Ibid., 11.

57. Ibid.

58. Microcredit Summit Campaign, "About Microcredit: A Small Introduction to a Huge Movement," http://www.microcreditsummit .org/Aboutmicrocredit.htm.

59. Sam Daley Harris, "State of the Microcredit Summit Campaign Report 2007," 2, http://www.microcreditsummit.org/pubs/ reports/socr/2007.html.

60. http://www.microcreditsummit.org/pubs/reports/socr/2007.html.

61. Amelia Gentleman, Anand Giridharas, and Keith Bradsher, "Micro-Credit Pioneer Gets Nobel for Peace," *International Herald*

Tribune, October 13, 2006, http://yaleglobal.yale.edu/display. article?id=8289.

62. Rachel Emma Silverman, "Giving … and Receiving," *Wall Street Journal*, December 10, 2007, R10, http://online.wsj.com/article/ SB119680029080513464.html.

63. World Bank Projects and Operations, "Strategies," http:// web.worldbank.org/WBSITE/EXTERNAL/PROJECTS/ 0,,contentMDK:20120702~menuPK:41386~pagePK:41367~piPK: 51533~theSitePK:40941,00.html.

64. http://www.whartonsp.com/articles/article.asp?p=389714& seqNum=4.

65. Lincoln Mali, "Africa's Newest Pyramid," *Africa-Investor.com,* January 1, 2005, http://www.africa-investor.com/article.asp?id=564.

66. "Tata Unveils Nano, Its $2,500 Car," *MSN Money*, January 10, 2008, http://articles.moneycentral.msn.com/Investing/Extra/Worlds CheapestCarArrivesTomorrow.aspx.

67. "Consultative Status with ECOSOC," United Nations Department of Economic and Social Affairs, http://www .un.org/esa/coordination/ngo/.

68. Bill & Melinda Gates Foundation, "Agricultural Development," http://www.gatesfoundation.org/GlobalDevelopment/Agriculture/.

69. "About Us," Oxfam International, http://www.oxfam.org/en/ about/.

70. "Programs and Campaigns," Oxfam International, http://www .oxfam.org/en/programs/.

71. "Oxfam International: Annual Report 2006," Oxfam International, http://www.oxfam.org/en/about/.

72. Katsuhiro Harada, "Social Entrepreneurs Gain Cred," *Nikkei Weekly* (Japan), August 20, 2007.

73. David Brooks, "Thoroughly Modern Do-Gooders," *New York Times*, March 21, 2008.

74. Nicholas D. Kristof, "The Age of Ambition," *New York Times*, January 27, 2008, http://www.nytimes.com/2008/01/27/opinion/ 27kristof.html?scp=4&sq=social+entrepreneurship&st=nyt.

75. "The Rise of the Social Entrepreneur," *Economist*, February 25, 2006.

76. Sarah Dougherty, "Entrepreneurs with Ethical Fibre," *Gazette* (Montreal), April 26, 2008.

77. David M. Herszenhorn, "Farm Income Up, but Subsidies Stay," *New York Times*, April 24, 2008, http://www.nytimes.com/2008/04/24/washington/24farm.html.

78. Weede, *Balance of Power*, 71.

79. Andrew Mitchell, "The Emerging Emerging Market," *Wall Street Journal*, October 23, 2007, http://online.wsj.com/article/SB119308908958267577.html.

80. Peace Corps, "Peace Corps Fact Sheet 2008," http://www.peacecorps.gov/index.cfm?shell=learn.

Chapter 9: A Different Lens, a Better Dashboard

1. Richard N. Haass, "The Age of Nonpolarity: What Will Follow U.S. Dominance," *Foreign Affairs*, May/June 2008, http://www.foreignaffairs.org/20080501faessay87304/richard-n-haass/the-age-of-nonpolarity.html.

2. International Institute for Management Development (IMD), "*World Competitiveness Yearbook 2008* (and Looking Back at 1989)," news release, May 15, 2008, http://www.imd.ch/research/publications/wcy/upload/PressRelease.pdf.

3. Tony Aspromourgos, "The Life of William Petty in Relation to His Economics," *History of Political Economy* 20 (1988): 337–356.

4. Clifford Cobb, Ted Halstead, and Jonathan Rowe, "If the GDP Is Up, Why Is America Down?" *Atlantic*, October 1995, http://www.theatlantic.com/politics/ecbig/gdp.htm.

5. Ibid.

6. Ibid.

7. Frédéric Bastiat, *Selected Essays on Political Economy*, trans. Seymour Cain, ed. George B. de Huszar (Irvington-on-Hudson, NY: Foundation for Economic Education, 1995).

8. Zubin Jelveh, "Beyond GDP," *Condé Nast Portfolio.com*, January 9, 2008.

9. Oskar von Morgenstern, *On the Accuracy of Economic Observations*, 2nd ed. (Princeton, NJ: Princeton University Press, 1963).

10. Li Deshui, "China's Official Statistics: Challenges, Measures and Future Development," Permanent Mission of the People's Republic of China to the United Nations, March 3, 2005.

11. "Finmin Says Fiscal Data Saga Has Ended in Wake of EU Report," Athens News Agency, December 8, 2004, http://www.hri.org/news/greek/ana/2004/04-12-08.ana.html#09.

12. Kevin Phillips, "Numbers Racket: Why the Economy Is Worse Than We Know," *Harper's*, May 13, 2008.

13. "Grossly Distorted Picture," *Economist,* March 13, 2008, http://www.economist.com/finance/displaystory.cfm?story_id=10852462.

14. Ibid.

15. Ibid.

16. Ibid.

17. See http://www.tdri.or.th/library/quarterly/notes/gsp_n.htm#txt-9.

18. Economist Intelligence Unit Country Data.

19. This doesn't even begin to include other consumer-linked debt, such as home equity loans. Peter Gumbel, "The $915 Billion Bomb in Consumers' Wallets," *Fortune*, October 30, 2007, http://money.cnn.com/2007/10/29/magazines/fortune/consumer_debt.fortune/index.htm. For 2001 figure, see http://www.truthaboutcredit.org/truth.asp?id2=6153&id3=credittruth&.

20. See Amy Crews Cutts, "Facts and Figures on New Mortgage Products," *Federal Trade Commission Workshop*, May 24, 2006, http://www.ftc.gov/bcp/workshops/mortgage/presentations/cutts.pdf.

21. Cobb, Halstead, and Rowe, "If the GDP Is Up."

22. "Genuine Progress Indicator," *Redefining Progress*, http://www.rprogress.org/sustainability_indicators/genuine_progress_indicator.htm.

23. Cobb, Halstead, and Rowe, "If the GDP Is Up."

24. Agence France-Presse, "Stiglitz Says GDP May Be Poor Indicator of Economy," *Google News*, January 8, 2008, http://afp.google.com/article/ALeqM5i8WXcpn59kDray5lHqtu5PSvzl-A.

25. For a complete explanation of GPI, see www/redefiningprogress.org.

26. Federal Reserve Bank and Deutsche Bank Economics Research, November 2008.

27. "U-M Professor Confronts America's Over-Consumption," University of Michigan Science Blog, December 2002, http://

www.scienceblog.com/community/older/2002/B/20026323.
html.

28. David Brooks, "The Culture of Debt," *New York Times*, July 22,
    2008, http://www.nytimes.com/2008/07/22/opinion/22brooks
    .html?sq=david%20brooks&st=cse&scp=2&pagewanted=print.

29. This was a key subject of my last book, *Money Changes Everything:
    How Global Prosperity Is Changing Our Needs, Values, and Lifestyles*
    (Upper Saddle River, NJ: Financial Times Prentice Hall, 2003).

30. "Asset Building Program,"http://www.newamerica.net/programs/
    asset_building/about_this_program.

31. Reid Cramer, "Don't Spend Your Tax Rebate!" *American Prospect
    Online*, April 15, 2008.

32. Dani Rodrik, "Feasible Globalizations," *NBER Working Paper*
    9129, August 2002, http://www.nber.org/papers/w9129.

Index

AACN. See American Association of
   Colleges of Nursing
AAMC. *See* Association of American
   Medical Colleges
Abramovich, Roan, 54–55
Abromovich, Ivan, 40
Abu Dhabi, 64, 69, 113–115
Abu Dhabi Investment Authority
   (ADIA), 69
Acid rain, 275
ADIA. *See* Abu Dhabi Investment
   Authority
Afghanistan, 147
Africa
   development, xix
   global financial system and, 116–117
Age
   demand for services and, 192–193
   immigration and, 183–188
Agriculture, 150, 261–266
   consumption of goods by country, 265
   global area of GM crops, 267
   spiking and collapsing markets, 94

   subsidies, 87–88, 132, 316–317
   vertical farming, 289
AIDS, 2, 36, 156, 196, 233, 234, 240,
   307, 318. *See also* Developing
   countries
AIG, 65, 74
Air, 275–280
Aircraft Carrier Replacement Program, 158
Algeria
   energy surplus and, 112
   as leading natural gas producer, 106
Ambani brothers, 55
American Association of Colleges of
   Nursing (AACN), 245
American Express, 56
American Foreign Service Association, 162
American Geophysical Union, 142
American Intl. Group, 60
American Medical Association, 244
Angell, Norman, 15, 137
Angola, 23, 110–111
Annan, Kofi, 145
Anti-Ballistic Missile Treaty, 162

Anti-Semitism, 26
Apartheid, 7
Apple, 38, 138
Arcelor-Mittal, 59
Argentina, emerging market companies
    in, 56
Arms race, 178–180
ASEAN, 86
Ashy, Joseph W., 178
Association of American Medical Colleges
    (AAMC), 243, 244
AT&T Inc., 60
Australia, 20, 62, 167
    energy surplus and, 112
    as leading coal producer, 104
    number of migrants, 205
Austria, 26
    as exporter of small arms, 146
Automobiles, 133–136
    electric-only, 135
    health care and, 221

Bank of America, 60
Bank of England, 68
Bank of Japan, 77
Banks, 67
    remittance flows, 194
    transfer services, 193–194
Basel Accord, 73
Basel II Accords, 73, 74
Bastiat, Frédéric, 329
BCG. See Boston Consulting Group
Bear Stearns, 65, 74
Belgium, 90
    as exporter of small arms, 146
    immigration, 184
Benin, energy deficits and, 109
Berkshire Hathaway, 60
Bernanke, Ben, 208
Bernard, Andrew, 41
BHP Billiton PLC, 60
Bilateral Trade Agreements (BTAs), 28
Bilmes, Laura, 154–155, 156
Biofuels, 259–261
Bio-social markers, 3
Bioterrorism, 237–238, 239. See also
    Terrorism

Blackhawk Corporation, 14
Blackstone, 67
"Black Wednesday," 68
Blogs, 14
Bloomberg, Michael (Mayor), 288
BLS. See Bureau of Labor Statistics
BMW, 49, 131
Bobbitt, Philip, 148
Bolivia, 19
Bonds, 63
    U.S. Treasury, 20
BOP. See Bottom of the pyramid
Boston Consulting Group (BCG), 56
Bottom of the pyramid (BOP), 60–61,
    310–314
Boxing, 40
BP PLC, 59
Brady Plan, 7
Brazil, 27, 167
    development, xix
    as "Emerging 7," 9
    emerging market companies in, 56–57
    energy consumption, 97
    as exporter of small arms, 146
    percent of food production and
        consumption, 264
    population and economy, 10
    productivity due to cardiovascular
        disease, 222
    as rising power, 11
    sustainable energy and, 124
Bretton Woods Agreement, 5, 77, 80, 84
Bribery, 309
BRIC (Brazil, Russia, India, China)
    countries, 45, 60–61, 90, 91
Brown, Gordon (Prime Minister), 175
Browne, Des (Defense Secretary), 175
Brownlee, Susan, 243
Brumberg, Richard, 343
Brundtland Commission, 250
Brunei, 70
BTAs. See Bilateral Trade Agreements
Bureau of Labor Statistics (BLS), 191
Buse, Meghan R., 41
Bush, George W. (President), xvii, 30, 72, 81,
    87, 124, 156, 159–160, 162, 179,
    206, 212–213, 249–250, 332

CAFE. *See* Corporate average fuel
    economy
CAFTA-DR. *See* U.S.-Central America
    Free Trade Agreement
Calderon, Felipe (President), 212
California Public Interest Research Group,
    123–124
Cambodia, energy deficits and, 109
Cameroon, 75–76
Canada, 20, 167
    energy consumption, 97
    energy intensity, 129
    as exporter of small arms, 146
    Group of Seven participation, xviii
    as leading natural gas producer, 106
    as leading nuclear producer, 107
    life expectancy, 217
    number of migrants, 205
    percent of food production and
        consumption, 264
    population and economy, 10
Capitalism, xxi
    capital access, 61–64
    capital flows, 61
    capitalist peace, 15–17
    credit crisis, 63, 64
    Group of Seven and, 82–83
    peace corps for, 317–318
Carbon dioxide emissions, 277
Carbon Tax Center, 286
Carlyle Group, 67
Caterpillar, 56
CCS. *See* Coal capture and sequester
CDC. *See* U.S. Centers for Disease Control
    and Prevention
CDM. *See* Clean Development Mechanism
Cemex, 59
Center for American Progress, 220–221
Central Bank of Turkey, 85
Central Hujin Investment Corp., 70
Chad, 116
Chagaev, Ruslan, 40
Chávez, Hugo (President), 18, 117–118
Chemical Weapons Ban, 162
Chernobyl, 121
Chevron Corp., 60
Chile, emerging market companies in, 57

China, 4, 54, 69, 70, 86, 167
    communism, 6, 173
    consumption of goods, 265
    currency and, 78, 79
    defense budget, 151–152
    development, xix
    economic growth, 52–53
    economy of, 44–45
    as "Emerging 7," 9
    emerging market, 44–45
    emerging market companies in, 57
    energy consumption, 97, 99–100
    energy intensity, 129
    as exporter of small arms, 146
    free trade, 7
    as leading coal producer, 104
    as leading oil producer, 102
    life expectancy, 217
    market crises, 20
    migration, 190
    percent of food production and
        consumption, 264
    population and economy, 10
    power shifts, 5
    productivity due to cardiovascular
        disease, 222
    relations with the United States,
        20–21
    as rising power, 11
    Sudan and, 24
    water situation, 271
China Const. BA-H, 60
China Institute of International
    Studies, 23
China Investment Company Ltd., 69, 70
Chirac, Jacques (President), 87–88
Chrysler, 58, 223
Cinepop, 320
Citigroup Inc., 59
Civil wars, 146–147
    risks, 303–304, 303
Clean Development Mechanism
    (CDM), 286
Clinton, Bill (President), 17, 157, 158
Clinton, Hillary Rodham (Senator), 241
Club Surya, 290
CNN, 14

Coal, 103–105, 278–279
  leading producers, 104
  as source of global energy, 101
Coal capture and sequester (CCS), 279
Coast Guard, 149
Cobden, Richard, 15
COBRA, 200
Coca-Cola Co., 59
Cody, Richard A., 157
Colbert, Steve, xvii
Cold War, xv, 16–17, 31, 41, 140, 178, 303
Colgate-Palmolive, 56
Commercial Bank ZI, 59
Commission on Macroeconomics and
      Health, 299
Commodities, 19
  prices, 94
Communications
  foreign languages, 160
  technology, 51–52
Communism
  in China, 6, 173
  war against, 30
Comprehensive Test Ban Treaty, 175
Conable, Barber, 339
Consumer price index (CPI), 331–332
Corporate average fuel economy
      (CAFE), 127
Côte d'Ivoire, 23
  number of migrants, 205
Council on Graduate Medical
      Education, 243
CPI. See Consumer price index
Credit
  crisis, 63, 64
  IMF's gold holdings and credit
      outstanding, 92
  macro quantum crisis, 71–76
Crime, immigrants and, 206
Cromwell, Oliver, 327
CSN, 59
Cultural Revolution, 200–201
Currency. See also Exchange rate; United
      States, dollar value
  exchange rates, 76–77
  foreign debt and, 77–78
Cyprus, 54

Czech Republic, 173
  as exporter of small arms, 146

Darfur, 24, 147, 315
DARPA. See Defense Advanced Research
      Projects Agency
Da Silva, Lula (President), 124
Davos World Economic Forum, 316
Debt, 343–346
  currency and, 77–78
  -funded growth, 337–338
Defense, 33, 150. See also Terrorism; United
      Nations
  civil wars, 146–147
  framework, 163–164
  future and, 177–180
  history of, 140–141
  number of state-based armed conflicts by
      type, 139
  strategies, 150–151
  U.S. intelligence and diplomacy, 158–163
  U.S. military reform, 151–158
  weapons, 141–146
Defense Advanced Research Projects
      Agency (DARPA), 130
"Dell Theory of Conflict Prevention"
      (Friedman), 138
Deng Xiaoping, 7
Denmark, 124
  immigration, 184
Department of Homeland Security, 202
Developing countries, 29. See also AIDS;
      HIV; Poverty; individual
      countries
  emerging versus, 52–53, 53
  energy demand, 98
  natural resource development, 117
  population growth, 185
  remittances to, 195
  U.S. economic engagement, 308
Diplomacy, 158–163
Dobbs, Lou, xvii
Doha Round, 28–29, 85, 87, 88, 298, 317
Doha trade talks, xxi
Dole Fresh Fruit Co., 262
Dollar, David, 295
Dot-com bubble, 93–94

Drayton, Bill, 316
Drugs, 36, 304–305
  counterfeit, 235–236
  over-the-counter, 233
Dubai, 64, 113, 114, 201

E7. See "Emerging 7"
Economic development, 150
Economics
  laissez-faire, 87
  power, 138–139
  pre-World War I, 25
  rising affluence, 16
The Economist, 64–65, 298, 335
Ecuador, 19, 118
Education, 150
  in Great Britain, 3
  literacy, 8
  medical, 243–246
  non-U.S. citizens' share of degrees
    awarded, 203
  in South Korea, 6, 7
Egypt
  development, xix
  emerging market companies in, 57
  migration, 190
  weapons of mass destruction, 142
EIA. See U.S. Energy Information
    Administration
Eisenhower, Dwight D. (President),
    122–123, 131
Electricity. See also Energy
  correlation between human development
    and usage, 301, 302
Electromagnetic warfare, 178–180
Electronic medical records (EMRs), 229
Eli Lilly & Co., 60
EM. See Emerging market
"Emerging 7" (E7), 9
  energy consumption by households, 251
  global imports and exports, 46
  versus Group of Seven, 10
  other rising powers and, 10–13
  percent of food production and
    consumption by country, 264
Emerging market (EM), 45
  assets, 65, 66

capital flows, 61
companies by country, 56–58
growth and, 49, 50
most valuable companies, 59–60
"Next 11," 45
stock and bond markets, 63
structural changes, 48, 49
Employee Relocation Council
    (ERC), 201
Employment, 150, 191. See also Labor
  outsourcing, 191
EMRs. See Electronic medical
    records
EMU. See European Monetary Union
The End of Poverty (Sachs), 306
Energy, 33, 35, 150
  balances, 108–110
  consumption, 97, 98, 99
    by fuel, 104
  consumption by households, 251
  deficits, 109–110, 109
  demand, 96–100
  in developing countries, 98
  efficiency, 125–128
  global financial system and, 111–118
  hydropower, 124
  instability, 118–121
  intensity by region, 129
  legislation, 126
  renewable, 121–125, 122
  shortages and imbalances, 132–133
  solar, 129–132
  sources, 101
  supply, 110–111
  surpluses, 112
  sustainable, 124–125
  types, 101–108
    coal, 103–105
      leading producers, 104
    natural gas, 105–106
      leading producers, 106
    nuclear, 106–108
      leading producers, 107
    petroleum, 101–103
      leading producers, 102
    solar, 129–132
    wind, 131

Environment, 34, 36–37, 150
  air, 275–280
  carbon dioxide emissions, 277
  environmental consciousness, 280–287
    information sharing, 282–283
    prices and costs, 283–284
  genetically modified crops, 267–268
  land, 257–266
  per capita consumption of calories, cere-
    als, and meat, 251
  pesticides, 261–262
  pollution versus GDP inverted U, 253
  prosperity, 252–257
  water, 269–280, 284
Environmental Protection Agency
    (EPA), 282
Environmental Sustainability Index, 342
EPA. See Environmental Protection Agency
EPZs. See Export processing zones
Equator Principles, 23
ERC. See Employee Relocation Council
Escape, 134–135
Ethanol, 124
EU. See European Union
European Commission, 26
European Monetary Union (EMU), 331
European Union (EU), 8, 26, 86, 88
Exchange rate, 85. See also Currency
Export-Import Bank, 314
Export processing zones (EPZs), 237
Exxon Mobil Corp., 59, 118

Fannie Mae, 65, 74
FAO. See United Nations Food and
    Agriculture Organization
Farm Bill (2007), 88
FDA. See U.S. Food and Drug
    Administration
FDI. See Foreign direct investment
Federal Aid Highway Act, 122–123, 131
Federov, Sergei, 39
Ferguson, Niall, 24–25, 139
Finance, 32–35, 33, 43–94
  capital access, 61–64
  crisis, 65
  financial hubs, 64–65
  key players, 67

  market crises, 19–24
  microfinance institution activity, 312
  rise of nonstate actors, 13–14
Finland, as exporter of small arms, 146
Fisheries, 273–275
  global trends in marine stocks, 274
Flannery, Jessica, 320
Flannery, Matt, 320
Food, 227–228
  per capita consumption of calories,
    cereals, and meat, 251
  percent of food production and
    consumption by country, 264
  riots, 262–263
  shortages, 75–76
  spiking and collapsing markets, 93–94
  techno-foods, 266–269
Forbes, 54, 55
Ford, Henry, 49, 130
Ford Motor Company, 58, 59, 131,
    134–135, 223, 314
Foreign aid, 305–309
Foreign direct investment (FDI),
    22–23, 61
Foreign languages, 160
Forests, 258–259
Fortune 50056
Fossil fuel, 133, 259–260
Fox News, 14
France, 26, 167
  energy consumption, 97
  as exporter of small arms, 146
  Group of Seven participation, xviii
  as leading nuclear producer, 107
  life expectancy, 217
  number of migrants, 205
  percent of food production and
    consumption, 264
  population and economy, 10
  power shifts, 5
"Freakonomic" world, xvii
Freddie Mac, 65, 74, 338
Free trade, 45–47
  in China, 7
  in India, 4, 7
Freshwater, 269–272
Friedman, Milton, 16

Friedman, Tom, xiii, 15, 138
Fund of the Russian Federation
(SFRF), 70

G6. *See* Group of 6
G7. *See* Group of Seven
G20, 86
Galbraith, John Kenneth, 329
GAO. *See* Government Accountability
Office
Gartzke, Erik, 16
Gasoline, 127–128
pricing, 280
use in the United States, 128
Gates, Bill, 55, 130, 205, 315. *See also*
Microsoft Corp.
Gates, Melinda, 315
Gates Foundation, 14, 233, 315
GATT/WHO. *See* General Agreement on
Tariffs and Trade/World Trade
Organization
Gazprom, 59, 115–116
GDP. *See* Gross domestic product
GE. *See* General Electric
General Agreement on Tariffs and Trade/
World Trade Organization
(GATT/WTO), 5, 87. *See also*
World Trade Organization
General Electric (GE), 56, 59, 62, 278
General Motors (GM), 58, 131, 223, 314
Genetically modified (GM) crops, 267268
Genocide, 2, 172
Genuine Progress Indicator (GPI),
341, 342
Germany, 26, 167
energy consumption, 97
as exporter of small arms, 146
Group of Seven participation, xviii
immigration, 184
as leading nuclear producer, 107
life expectancy, 217
number of migrants, 205
percent of food production and
consumption, 264
population and economy, 10
Ghana, 299
weapons of mass destruction, 142

GIC. *See* Government of Singapore
Investment Corporation
Gilder's Law, 51–52
Ginobili, Manu, 39
Gleneagles G8, 233
Globalization. *See also* Energy
backlash, 24–29
challenges, 37–42
emerging markets, 21, 29
energy and, 111–118
global convergence, 8
health care, 215–247
overview, 2–3
sports and, 38–42
GM. *See* General Motors; Genetically
modified crops
GMAC Global Relocation Services, 201
GNI. *See* Gross national income
GNP. *See* Gross national product
Gold, 119–120
IMF's holdings and credit
outstanding, 92
Goldman Sachs, 45, 282
Golf, 40
Gore, Al, xiii, 2
Government, 150
Government Accountability Office
(GAO), 144
Government of Singapore Investment
Corporation (GIC), 69
Government Pension Fund Global
(GPFG), 69
GPFG. *See* Government Pension Fund
Global
GPI. *See* Genuine Progress Indicator
Grain. *See also* Agriculture
per capita consumption of calories,
cereals, and meat, 251
prices, 75–76
Grameen Bank of Bangladesh, 14, 311
The Grand Illusion (Angell), 138
Great Britain
currency and, 79
education system, 3
as exporter of small arms, 146
industrialization, 3–4
Greece, 331

Greenpeace, 14, 281

Gross domestic product (GDP), 6, 8, 16, 41–42. *See also* Macro Quantum theory

  emerging versus developed, 52–53, 53

  increase in spending, 152

  measurements, 330, 330

  versus per capita income, 336

  population growth and, 334–336

  projected in 2050, 22

  risk of civil war and, 303–304, 303

Grossman, Gene M., 252

Gross national income (GNI), 307

Gross national product (GNP), 328

Group of 6 (G6), 6

Group of Seven (G7), xviii, 6–7, 9

  capitalism and, 82–83

  challenges, 37–42

  currency and, 80

  derailment, 17–19

  economic growth, 52–55, 52

  as economic model, 86

  versus "Emerging 7," 10

  energy consumption by households, 251

  evolution, 84–86

  imports and exports, 46

  percent of food production and consumption by country, 264

Guerilla movements, 14, 106

Gulf Cooperation Council, 86

Gulf Wars, 121, 155

Hadley Center for Climate Prediction and Research, 270

Haiti, 75–76

Halstead, Ted, 328

Hass, Richard, 324

Hayek, F., 82

HDHPs. *See* High-deductible health plans

HDI. *See* Human Development Index; United Nations Human Development Index

Headquarters Allied Command Europe Rapid Reaction Corps, 173

Health care, 34, 36, 150, 187. *See also* Macro Quantum theory

  counterfeit drugs, 235–236

  doctors and nurses, 243–246

  immigrants and, 206–209

  increase in labor supply with decrease in global chronic illness, 218

  interlinkages and, 236–240

  international health infrastructure, 232–234

  life expectancy by country, 217, 219

  lost productive years due to cardiovascular disease, 222

  medical tourism, 207–208, 230–232

  per capita spending, 219

  providers and insurance, 228–230

  solutions, 240–243

  unhealthy lifestyles, 224–228

  U.S. smokers by gender, 226

"Health for All by the Year 2000" program, 232–233

Health Resources and Services Administration (HRSA), 245

Health savings accounts (HSAs), 229–230

Hedge funds, 67–68, 70–71

Heritage Foundation, 107

Hicks, John, 339

High-deductible health plans (HDHPs), 229–230

High-occupancy vehicle (HOV), 134

High-powered microwaves (HPMs), 179–180

Hill & Knowlton, 316

Hindu religion, 11

HIV, 36, 196, 234, 240, 307, 318. *See also* Developing countries

Hobbes, Thomas, 327

Home Depot, 71

Honda, 58

Hong Kong, 69

  as economic and political power bloc, 6

  as emerging economic economy, 21

  life expectancy, 217

  stock market, 64

Hong Kong Monetary Authority Investment Portfolio, 69

House Armed Services Committee, 213

Housing assistance, 150

Houston Rockets, 38

HOV. *See* High-occupancy vehicle

HPMs. *See* High-powered microwaves
HRSA. *See* Health Resources and Services
    Administration
HSAs. *See* Health savings accounts
HSBC, 56, 60
HSH Associates, 71
Hu Jintao (President), 339–340
Human Development Index (HDI), 301,
    302, 342
Human Development Report, 305–306
Human rights, 16–17, 166. *See also* United
    Nations
Human Security Report, 16
Human trafficking, 196–197
Hungary, 26
    emerging market companies in, 57
Hunter, Duncan, 213
Hydrocarbons, 95–96. *See also* Energy
Hydroelectric dams, 269
Hydro energy, 101
Hydropower, 124
Hyundai, 58

IAEA. *See* International Atomic Energy
    Agency
IARC. *See* International Agency for
    Research on Cancer
IBM, 60, 62
IBRD. *See* International Bank for
    Reconstruction and
    Development
Iceland
    immigration, 184
    life expectancy in, 217
IDB. *See* International Development Bank
IEA. *See* International Energy Agency
IGCC. *See* Integrated gasification
    combined cycle
Illness. *See* Health care; Pandemics;
    individual illnesses
IMF. *See* International Monetary Fund
Immelt, Jeffrey, 278
Immigration, 34, 36
    age and, 183–188
    by category, 182
    countries with largest international
        migrant stock, 205

crime rates, 206
destination countries, 188–190
efforts to block, 211–212
health care and, 206–209
illegal, 206
involuntary migration, 196–197
outsourcing, 191, 197–202
policies, 209–212
population growth, 185
poverty and, 195–196
returnee trend, 189
security and, 202–206
"south-to-south" migration, 189–190
trends and implications, 190–194
IMSS. *See* Mexican Social Security Institute
Index for Global Philanthropy, 307
India, 54, 313
    consumption of goods, 265
    development, xix
    as "Emerging 7," 9
    emerging market companies in, 56
    energy consumption, 97
    energy intensity, 129
    free trade, 4
    as leading coal producer, 104
    migration, 190
    number of migrants, 205
    as part of the UN Security Council,
        170–171
    percent of food production and con-
        sumption, 264
    population and economy, 10
    power shifts, 5
    productivity due to cardiovascular dis-
        ease, 222
    as rising power, 11
Indonesia
    development, xix
    as "Emerging 7," 9
    as leading coal producer, 104
    as leading natural gas producer, 106
    life expectancy in, 217
    migration, 190
    percent of food production and
        consumption, 264
    population and economy, 10
    as rising power, 12

Industrial and Comm. Bk., 59

Industrialization, in Great Britain, 3–4

Industrial Revolution, 3, 15, 52

Infant mortality, 8

Inge, Lord Peter, 176

Initial public offerings (IPOs), 65

Injaz, 319–320

Institute of Medicine, 243

Insurance companies, 67

Integrated gasification combined cycle
      (IGCC), 279

Intel Corp., 59

Intellectual property rights (IPR), 235

Intelligence, 158–163

International affairs, 150

International Agency for Research on
      Cancer (IARC), 299

International Atomic Energy Agency
      (IAEA), 159

International Bank for Reconstruction and
      Development (IBRD), 89–90

International Court of Justice, xxi, 5

International Criminal Police Organization
      (Interpol), 160

International Development Bank
      (IDB), 300

International Energy Agency (IEA),
      110, 120

International Finance Corporation, 62

International Food Policy Research
      Institute, 261

International Institute of Tropical
      Agriculture, 270

International Monetary Fund (IMF), 23, 69,
      265, 302
   emerging market economies, 21
   gold holdings and credit outstanding, 92

International Network on Small
      Arms, 144

International Organization for Migration
      (IOM), 210

Interpol. See International Criminal Police
      Organization

IOM. See International Organization for
      Migration

IPOs. See Initial public offerings

IPR. See Intellectual property rights

Iran
   energy surplus and, 112
   as leading natural gas producer, 106
   as leading oil producer, 102
   weapons of mass destruction, 142

Iraq
   cost of war, 154–157
   invasion, xvii, 19, 31, 121
   war in, 111

Ireland, 305

Israel
   energy deficits and, 109
   number of migrants, 205

Italy, 167
   as exporter of small arms, 146
   Group of Seven participation, xviii
   life expectancy in, 217
   percent of food production and
         consumption, 264
   population and economy, 10

Jagr, Jaromir, 39

Jaguar, 59

James, Harold, 24–25

Japan, 167
   energy consumption, 97
   as exporter of small arms, 146
   foreign trade, 4
   Group of Seven participation, xviii
   immigration, 184
   as leading nuclear producer, 107
   life expectancy in, 217
   number of migrants, 205
   percent of food production and
         consumption, 264
   population and economy, 10
   population transition, 186, 186
   yen, 76–77

Jazeera, Al-, 14

Jen, Stephen, 91

Johnson, Lyndon (President), 80

Johnson & Johnson, 60

Jordan
   energy deficits and, 109
   number of migrants, 205

J.P. Morgan, 21

Justice, 150

Kapur, Gunender, 313–314

Kazakhstan
as leading coal producer, 104
migration, 190
number of migrants, 205

Kennedy, John F. (President), 332

Khaldon Khalifa al Mubarak, 114

KIA. *See* Kuwait Investment Authority

Kissinger, Henry, 175

Kiva.org, 320–321

KKR. *See* Kohlberg Kravis Roberts & Co.

Klitschko, Vitali, 40

Klitschko, Wladimir, 40

Kohlberg Kravis Roberts & Co.
(KKR), 67

Komatsu, 56

Kovalev, Alexei, 39

KP Singh, 55

Krueger, Alan B., 252

Kuwait, 69, 70
energy surplus and, 112
as leading oil producer, 102

Kuwait Investment Authority (KIA), 69

Kuznets, Simon, 328

Kyoto Protocol, 36–37, 125, 131, 140,
161–162, 277, 278, 286

Labor, 47. *See also* Employment
increase if global chronic illness is
reduced, 218
skilled workers, 62

Laissez-faire economics, 87

Lambrew, Jeanne, 220–221

Lamy, Pascal, 88

Land, 257–266. *See also* Agriculture
biofuels and, 259–261, 260
forests, 258–259

Land Rover, 59

Lanxade, Jacques (Admiral), 176

Latin America, global financial system and,
117–118

LCME. *See* Liaison Committee on Medical
Education

League of Nations, 163

Legislation
energy, 126
Farm Bill (2007), 88
Federal Aid Highway Act, 122–123, 131
Marine Transportation Security Act,
149–150
National Security Presidential
Directive, 179
Sarbanes-Oxley Act of 2002, 65
U.S. Patriot Act, 202

Lehman Brothers, 2, 65, 74

Levi's, 47

Levit, Steven, xvii

Levitte, Jean-David, 161

Liaison Committee on Medical Education
(LCME), 244

Library Group, 6

Libya, weapons of mass destruction, 142

Life expectancy, 8, 216–217, 217

Lifestyles, 256–257
of children, 224
sedentary, 224
unhealthy, 224–228

Literacy, 8

Luxembourg, immigration, 184

Macau, 21

Macro Quantum theory, xvi, xix, 30–37,
323–348. *See also* Environment;
Gross domestic product; Health
care
to alleviate poverty, 318–321
consumption, debt, and savings, 343–346
crisis and, 71–76
debt-funded growth, 337–338
institutional reform, 84
labor and, 47
versus micro domestic, 32
policy areas, 33–34
population growth and per capita GDP,
334–336
poverty and, 297–305
progress and, 338–341, 342
purchasing power parity, 333–334
spiking and collapsing markets, 93–94

Macy's, 47

MAD. *See* Mutual assured destruction
policy

Maher, Bill, xvii

Major League Baseball (MLB), 39–40

Malaysia, emerging market companies
        in, 57
Malthus, Thomas, 262
Marine Transportation Security ACT
        (MTSA), 149–150
Matsui, Hideki, 39–40
Matsuzaka, Daisuke, 39–40
Mbenga, DJ, 39
McCain, John (Senator), xviii, xx, 131
McDonald's, 56, 227
McKinsey & Co., 65, 112, 186, 199, 316
MDGs. See United Nations Millennium
        Development Goals
Media, 14
Medicaid, 208
Medical outbreaks, 36, 148. See also AIDS;
        HIV
Medical tourism, 207–208, 230–232
Medicare, 150, 208
Medvedev, Dmitri (President), 18, 24, 174
Merck & Co., 59
Mercosur, 86
Metcalfe's Law, 51–52
MetLife, 208
Metric tons of oil equivalent (MTOE), 103
Mexican Social Security Institute
        (IMSS), 208
Mexico, 21–22, 167
    development, xix
    as "Emerging 7," 9
    emerging market companies in, 57
    energy intensity, 129
    immigration and, 212–213
    as leading oil producer, 102
    life expectancy in, 217
    migration, 190
    percent of food production and
            consumption, 264
    population and economy, 10
    as rising power, 12
    skilled workers, 62
MFN. See Most Favored Nation
Microcredit Summit, 311
Micro domestic, 325
    versus macro quantum, 32
    policy areas, 33–34
Microsoft Corp., 59. See also Gates, Bill

MICs. See Middle Income Countries
Middle East, global financial system and,
        112–115
Middle Income Countries (MICs), 90
Military (U.S.)
    reform, 151–158
    spending, 152
Millennium Ecosystem Assessment,
        250–251
Mini Cooper, 49
Missile warheads, 143, 179
Mittal, Lakshmi, 55
MLB. See Major League Baseball
MNCs. See Multinational corporations
Modigliani, Franco, 343
Mohamad, Mahathir, 68
Molano, Walter, 74
Montesquieu, Charles de, 15
Moore's Law, 51–52
Morgan Stanley, 91
Morgenstern, Oskar, 330–331
Morocco, energy deficits and, 109
Mortgages
    bubble crisis, 71–73
    ratings, 73
Most Favored Nation (MFN), 87
Mozambique, life expectancy in, 217
MTOE. See Metric tons of oil
        equivalent
MTSA. See Marine Transportation Security
        ACT
Mugabe, President, 301
Muhammad Yunus, 311, 329
Mukherjee, Pranab, 164
Multinational corporations (MNCs), xix
    emerging market companies, 56–58
    growth of, 55–61
    health care and, 221–223
    institutional reform, 84
    most valuable companies, 59–60
    poverty and, 297
    rise of, 13
Musk, Elon, 135
Muslims, 11, 171, 304
Mutombo, Dikembe, 39
Mutual assured destruction (MAD)
        policy, 151

Mutual funds, 67
MySpace, 14

NAFTA. *See* North American Free Trade
    Agreement
Nano, 314
NASA. *See* National Aeronautics and Space
    Administration
NASDAQ, 72
National Academy of Sciences, 192
National Aeronautics and Space
    Administration (NASA), 178
National Basketball Association (NBA),
    38–39
National Guard, 157
National Health Service (NHS), 230, 244
National Intelligence Estimate (NIE), 159
National Rifle Association, 213
National Security Presidential Directive, 179
National Statistical Service of Greece
    (NSSG), 331
NATO. *See* North Atlantic Treaty
    Organization
Natural disasters, 93–94, 120, 157, 173
Natural gas, 105–106
    leading producers, 106
    as source of global energy, 101
Natural resources, xv, 150
Naumann, Klaus (General), 176
NBA. *See* National Basketball Association
Nepal, 196
Nestlé, 65, 313
The Netherlands, 26, 167
    as leading natural gas producer, 106
New America Foundation, 345
New York Police Department (NYPD), 161
New York Stock Exchange, 65
New York Times, 285
New Zealand, 62
"Next 11" emerging markets, 45
NGOs. *See* Nongovernmental organizations
NHS. *See* National Health Service
Nicaragua, 262
NIE. *See* National Intelligence Estimate
Nigeria, 13, 23, 110–111, 117
    development, xix
    energy intensity, 129

energy surplus and, 112
    labor problems, 94
Nike, 38
9/11, xvii, 18, 72, 142, 147, 156, 162, 202,
    238. *See also* Terrorism
    policies following, 204
9/11 Commission, 158–159
"NINJA" (no income, no job, no assets)
    borrowers, 72, 73
Nippon Telegraph, 59
Nissan, 58
Nixon, Richard (President), 227
Nobel, 329
Nobel Prize, 193, 286, 311
Nokia, 56
Nomura, Ichiro, 274
Nongovernmental organizations (NGOs),
    xix, 14, 233
    social entrepreneurs and, 314–316
Nonstate actors (NSAs), xviii
    rise of, 13–15
North American Free Trade Agreement
    (NAFTA), xviii, 12, 197–198
North Atlantic Treaty Organization
    (NATO), xv, 5, 18, 20, 33, 163
    allies and, 31
    reform, 173–176
North Korea
    per capita income, xx
    weapons of mass destruction, 142
Norway, 69
    energy surplus and, 112
    as exporter of small arms, 146
    government pension fund, 69–70
    immigration, 184
    as leading natural gas producer, 106
Novartis AG-REG, 59
Nowak, Lisa Marie, 178
Nowitzki, Dirk, 39
NPT. *See* Nuclear Nonproliferation Treaty
NSAs. *See* Nonstate actors
NSSG. *See* National Statistical Service of
    Greece
Nuclear energy, 106–108
    accidents, 121
    leading producers, 107
    as source of global energy, 101

Nuclear Nonproliferation Treaty (NPT), 108, 174
Nuclear proliferation, 35–36
Nuclear war, 151
Nuclear weapons, 174–175
Nunn, Sam, 175
Nutrition, 227–228
NYPD. See New York Police Department

Obama, Barack (President), xviii, xx, 131
Obesity, 224–225
Occidental Petroleum, 118
ODA. See Official Development Assistance
OECD. See Organization for Economic Cooperation and Development
Office of Malaria Control in War Areas, 232
Official Development Assistance (ODA), 307
Oil, 101–103
    Angola and, 23
    in the Caspian Sea, 120–121
    currency and, 78
    leading producers, 102
    leading sovereign wealth funds, 69–70
    mortgage bubble crisis and, 72
    Nigeria and, 23
    Russia and, 17–18
    as source of global energy, 101
    spiking and collapsing markets, 93–94
Olympics, 40–41
Oman, 54
O'Neill, Jim, 45
On the Accuracy of Economic Observations (Morgenstern), 330–331
OPEB. See Other postemployment benefits
OPEC countries, 125
OPIC. See Overseas Private Investment Corporation
O'Reilly, Bill, xvii
Organization for Economic Cooperation and Development (OECD), 5, 207, 241, 270, 283, 306, 331
    tax rates on unleaded gas and diesel in OECD countries, 285
Ortiz, David, 39–40

Osama bin Laden, 147
Other postemployment benefits (OPEB), 223
Outsourcing, 191, 197–202
Ovechkin, Alex, 39
Overseas Private Investment Corporation (OPIC), 314
Overtreated (Brownlee), 243
Owen, John Wyn, 238
Oxfam International, 14, 315
Oxford Research Group, 108

P5, 168. See also China; France; Russia; United Kingdom; United States
    expansion, 171
    veto power, 169
Pacific Gas & Electric, 124
Pakistan, 19
    energy intensity, 129
    migration, 190
    number of migrants, 205
    weapons of mass destruction, 142
Pandemics, 233–234
Paramilitary groups, 14
Particulate matter (PM), 105
Pax Americana, 15
Peace Corps, capitalist, 317–318
Peacekeeping missions, 170, 177
    of the United Nations, 172–173
Pension funds, 67, 187
Pension reform, 223
People miles per gallon (PMPG), 134
Pepsi, 50
Per-capita income, 41–42
    versus gross domestic product, 336
Perraud, François, 313
Perry, William J., 175
Pesticides, 261–262
Petrobras Pref., 59
Petrochina CO-H, 59
Petrodollars, 113–115
Petroleum. See Oil
Petty, William, 327
Pew Research Center, 82, 151, 280
Pfizer Inc., 60
The Philippines, 75–76
    migration, 190

Philips, Kevin, 331–332
Platinum, 119–120
Plaza Accord, 77
PM. *See* Particulate matter
PMPG. *See* People miles per gallon
Poland, 13, 26
    emerging market companies in, 57
    as leading coal producer, 104
Politics, European, 27
Pollution, 279–280
    coal, 278–279
    versus GDP inverted U, 253
    most polluted cities by particulate
        matter, 276
    taxes, 285–287
Population, 135
    depopulation, 186
    growth, 185
    growth and per capita GDP, 334–336
    Japan's transition, 186, 186
Poverty, 2, 34, 37, 41, 85. *See also*
        Developing countries
    demands for bribery, 309
    disease and, 298–299
    eradication, 91–92
    immigration and, 195–196
    linkages to Macro Quantum world,
        297–305
    Macro Quantum strategy and,
        318–321
    strategizing, 309–318
    trends, 293–297
        global trends, 294
        head count ratio, 294
PPP. *See* Purchasing power parity
Prahalad, P.C., 310. *See also* Bottom of the
        pyramid
PricewaterhouseCoopers, 241, 245–246
Prius, 134
Private equity funds, 67
Privatization, 7
Procter & Gamble (P&G), 60, 313
Prosperity, 252–257
Protectionism, 26, 27
Pujols, Albert, 40
Purchasing power parity (PPP), 10–11, 16,
        333–334

Qaeda, Al-, 14, 140, 142
Qatar, 87

Railroads, 4
Rainforest Action Network, 261
Rand Corporation, 176
Reagan, Ronald (President), 30
Real estate, mortgage bubble crisis, 71–73
Red Cross, 14
Regional Quality of Development
        Index, 342
Registered nurses (RNs), 245, 246
Reliance group, 55
Renmindi (RMB) exchange rate, 85
Retirement, 221–222
REVA, 135
Rice, Condoleezza, 160, 161, 162–163, 170
RMB. *See* Renmindi exchange rate
RNs. *See* Registered nurses
Roberts, Olivia, 238
Robinson, Mary, 305
Roche Hldg-Genus, 60
Rodrik, Dani, 347
Romania, 13, 26, 54
Royal Dutch Shell, 59
Russia, 17, 54, 69, 70, 70, 86
    development, xix
    as "Emerging 7," 9
    emerging market companies in,
        57–58
    energy consumption, 97
    energy surplus and, 112
    as exporter of small arms, 146
    global financial system and, 115–116
    as leading coal producer, 104
    as leading natural gas producer, 106
    as leading nuclear producer, 107
    as leading oil producer, 102
    number of migrants, 205
    percent of food production and con-
        sumption, 264
    population and economy, 10
    power shifts, 5
    productivity due to cardiovascular
        disease, 222
    as rising power, 11–12
    wealth in, 54–55

Sachs, Jeffrey, 306

Salti, Soraya, 319–320

Sánchez de Lozad, Gonzalo "Goni," 118

Sarbanes–Oxley Act of 2002, 65

Sarkozy, Nicolas (President), 20, 161

SARS outbreaks, 36, 148, 220, 237, 238, 242

Saudi Arabia, 19, 69, 70, 111
  energy surplus and, 112
  as leading oil producer, 102
  number of migrants, 205

Savings, 343–346

Schröder, Gerhard, 24, 87–88, 174

Schultz, George P., 175

Schwab Foundation, 316

Science, 150

SCO. See Shanghai Cooperation Organization

Security, 33, 35–36. See also Terrorism; United Nations
  civil wars, 146–147
  collective, 163–164
  framework, 163–164
  future and, 177–180
  history of, 140–141
  immigration and, 202–206
  number of state-based armed conflicts by type, 139
  risks, 177–178
  strategies, 150–151
  U.S. intelligence and diplomacy, 158–163
  U.S. Military reform, 151–158
  weapons, 141–146

Sen, Amartya, 329

Serbia, 54

SEVIS. See Student Exchange Visitor Information System

SFRF. See Fund of the Russian Federation

Shalikashvili, John (General), 175–176

Shanghai Cooperation Organization (SCO), 164

Sibneft, 54–55

Siemens, 56

Sierra Club, 281

Sierra Leone
  energy deficits and, 109
  small arms weapons, 144

Silicon Valley, 72, 130, 189, 205

Singapore, 64, 69, 70
  as economic and political power bloc, 6
  number of migrants, 205

SIPRI. See Stockholm International Peace Research Institute

SIV. See Special Investment Vehicle

Slim, Carlos, 55

Smith, Adam, 3, 15, 327

Snapple, 50

Soccer, 40, 120, 196

Social entrepreneurs, 314–316, 319–321

Socialized medicine, 240

Social security, 150

Social services, 150

Solar energy, 129–132

Somalia, energy deficits and, 109

Sony, 138

Soros, George, 25, 68

South Africa
  development, xix
  as leading coal producer, 104
  productivity due to cardiovascular disease, 222

South Korea, 167
  development, xix
  as economic and political power bloc, 6
  education, 6, 7
  as "Emerging 7," 9
  as leading nuclear producer, 107
  per capita income, xx
  percent of food production and consumption, 264
  population and economy, 10
  as rising power, 12

Sovereign wealth funds (SWFs), 14, 22, 67, 68–71
  leading countries, 69–70

Soviet Union, 41. See also Russia
  collapse, 8–9

Space programs, 150

Spain, 167
  as exporter of small arms, 146
  number of migrants, 205

SPC. See State Power Corporation

Special Investment Vehicle (SIV), 73–74

Sports. *See also* individual sports
    globalization and, 38–42
SRI. *See* System of rice intensification
Sri Lanka, small arms weapons
            and, 144
State of the World 2008, 282, 283
State of World Population 2007, 287
State Power Corporation (SPC), 284
Stern, Sir Nicholas, 123
Stiglitz, Joseph, 25, 83, 154–155, 156, 286,
            329, 340
Stockholm International Peace Research
            Institute (SIPRI), 154
Stocks, 63
    Hong Kong, 64
Stojakovic, Peja, 39
Strauss-Kahn, Dominique, 90
Student Exchange Visitor Information
            System (SEVIS), 202–203
Sudan, 147
    China and, 24
    migration, 190
    small arms weapons, 144
Suez Canal, 4
Suez Crisis, 79
Suzuki, Ichiro, 39–40
Swaziland, life expectancy in, 217
Sweden
    energy intensity, 129
    immigration, 184
    as leading nuclear producer, 107
SWFs. *See* Sovereign wealth funds
Switzerland, 167
    as exporter of small arms, 146
    immigration, 184
Syria, 163
    weapons of mass destruction, 142
System of Economic Environmental
            Accounts, 342
System of rice intensification (SRI), 268

Taiwan, as economic and political power
            bloc, 6
Taliban government, 147
Task Force on National Health Care
            Reform, 241
Tata Motors, 59, 314
Taxes

pollution, 285–287
    rates on unleaded gas and diesel in
            OECD countries, 285
Techno-foods, 266–269
Technology
    advances after World War II, 9
    communications, 51–52
Temasek Holdings, 70
Tennis, 40
Terrorism, 2, 148–150. *See also*
            Bioterrorism; 9/11
    rise of incidents, 148–149, 149
    weapons of mass destruction, 141
Tesla Motors, 135
Texas pacific Group, 67
Thailand, 4
    emerging market companies in, 58
Theraflu, 233
Three Gorges Dam, 124
*The Three Trillion Dollar War: The True Cost
            of the Iraq Conlict* (Stiglitz and
            Bilmes), 154–155
Tobacco industry, 225–226, 226
Togo, energy deficits and, 109
Tourism, medical, 207–208, 230–232
Toyota Motor, 58, 60, 131, 134
TPA. *See* Trade Promotion Authority
Trade, 32–35. *See also* World Trade
            Organization
    with Japan, 4
    labor patterns and, 47
    during the nineteenth century, 5–6
    routes, 47
Trade Promotion Authority (TPA), 27
Training, 150
Transportation, 150
Tuberculosis, 233
Turkey, 13, 26
    emerging market companies in, 58
    as exporter of small arms, 146
Turkmenistan, as leading natural gas
            producer, 106

Uganda, small arms weapons and, 144
Ukraine, 13
    as leading nuclear producer, 107
    number of migrants, 205
    weapons of mass destruction, 142

UNHCR. *See* United Nations High Committee on Refugees
Unilever, 313–314
Union of Concerned Scientists, 127
United Arab Emirates, 69, 70
    energy surplus and, 112
    as leading oil producer, 102
    number of migrants, 205
United Auto Workers, 223
United Kingdom, 86, 167
    energy consumption, 97
    Group of Seven participation, xviii
    as leading natural gas producer, 106
    as leading nuclear producer, 107
    life expectancy in, 217
    number of migrants, 205
    percent of food production and consumption, 264
    population and economy, 10
    power shifts, 5
United Nations, xvii, xxii, 5, 20
    budget assessment and payments, 167
    budget reform, 166–168, 167
    peacekeeping, 172–173, 177
    Security Council reform, 168–171
    security system, 164–166
United Nations Children's Fund, 166
United Nations Development Program, 166
United Nations Food and Agriculture Organization (FAO), 258, 263, 270
United Nations General Assembly, 164
United Nations High Committee on Refugees (UNHCR), 210
United Nations Human Development Index (HDI), 9
United Nations Initiative to Fight Human Trafficking, 196–197
United Nations International Fund for Agricultural Development, 75
United Nations Millennium Development Goals (MDGs), 307, 319
United Nations Office on Drugs and Crime (UNODC), 304
United Nations Security Council, xxi, 12, 18–19, 159–160
    reform, 168–171

United States, 167
    capitalism and, xxi
    consumption of goods, 265
    dependency on foreign capital, 81–82
    dollar value, 19, 20, 25, 75, 76–82, 84
        (*See also* Currency)
    economy, xiv
    energy consumption, 97
    energy intensity, 129
    as exporter of small arms, 146
    federal defense budget request, 150
    gasoline use, 128
    Group of Seven participation, xviii
    immigration, 184
    intelligence and diplomacy, 158–163
    international relations, 19
    labor productivity, 48
    as leading coal producer, 104
    as leading natural gas producer, 106
    as leading nuclear producer, 107
    as leading oil producer, 102
    life expectancy in, 217
    lifestyle, 102
    micro domestic approach, 30
    military
        reform, 151–158
        spending, 152
    mortgage bubble crisis, 71–73
    non-U.S. citizens' share of degrees awarded, 203
    number of migrants, 205
    percent of food production and consumption, 264
    policies, xvi
    population and economy, 10
    post–Cold War, 16–17
    productivity due to cardiovascular disease, 222
    relations with China, 20–21
    role of renewable energy consumption, 122
    in the twenty-first century, 29–37
UNODC. *See* United Nations Office on Drugs and Crime
Urbanization, 287–290
U.S. Agency for International Development, 320

U.S. Census Bureau, 229
U.S. Centers for Disease Control and
    Prevention (CDC), 216, 232
U.S.-Central America Free Trade
    Agreement (CAFTA-DR), 235
U.S. Congress, 27, 88, 316–317
U.S. Customs and Border Protection, 149,
    203
U.S. Department of Agriculture, 226–227
U.S. Department of Defense, 110–111, 153
    spending, 154
U.S. Department of Energy, 103, 110
    National Renewable Energy Laboratory,
    130
U.S. Department of Health and Human
    Services, 293
U.S. Diversity Visa Lottery, 204
U.S. Embassy, 208
U.S. Energy Information Administration
    (EIA), 97
U.S. Federal Reserve Bank, 72
U.S. Food and Drug Administration (FDA),
    237
U.S. Information Agency (USIA), 161
U.S. Navy, 111, 180
U.S. Patriot Act, 202
U.S. Peace Corps, 318
U.S. Public Health Service, 232
U.S. Treasury, 74
    bonds, 20
USIA. See U.S. Information Agency

Value and Capital (Hicks), 339
Van den Breemen, Henk (General), 176
Venezuela, 19
    energy surplus and, 112
    as leading oil producer, 102
Vertical farming (VF), 289. See also
    Agriculture
Veterans Affairs, 208
Veterans benefits, 150
VF. See Vertical farming
Vietnam War, 80
Virgin Islands, energy deficits and, 109
Visa, 38
Volt, 134
Von Hayek, Friedrich, 296

Wake Island, energy deficits and, 109
Wall Street, 72
Wal-Mart Store, 60, 71
Wang Hongyi, 23
War on Terror, 19
Waste, 101
Water, 269–280, 284
    fisheries, 273–275
    freshwater, 269–272
    situation in China, 27
Wealth of Nations (Smith), 3
Weapons, 141–146. See also Nuclear
    weapons
    black market for, 145
    conventional, 142–144
    missile warheads, 143
    small arms, 144–145, 146
    exporters, 146
Weapons of mass destruction (WMDs),
    141–142
Wen Jiabao, 169
Western Union, 194
White House, 27
WHO. See World Health Organization
Wilson, Woodrow (President), 163
Wind energy, 131, 290
Winthrop, John, 326
WMDs. See Weapons of mass destruction
Women, sports and, 40
World Bank, xviii, xxii, 5, 14, 20, 23,
    61, 82, 85, 140, 193, 262, 295,
    316–317
    reform, 89–93, 317
    repositioning, 90
World Development Report, 82
World Drug Report, 304
World Food Program, 166
World Health Organization (WHO), 14,
    207, 226, 232, 237, 242, 281
World Trade Organization (WTO), xxii,
    85, 139–140, 281, 283. See also
    General Agreement on Tariffs and
    Trade/World Trade Organization;
    Trade
    accession talks, 88–89
    trade progress, 86–89
World Values Survey, 254

World War I, 4–5, 225, 326
World War II, 5, 326
    postwar economy, 5–8
    postwar technology advances, 9
World Watch Institute, 257, 282, 283
World Wide Fund for Nature (WWF),
        268, 281
Wrangler, 47
WTO. See World Trade Organization
WWF. See World Wide Fund
        for Nature

Xia Bin, 78

Yacimientos Petrolíferos Fiscales Bolivianos
        (YPFB), 118
Yao Ming, 38–39
Yashin, Alexei, 39
Yemen, weapons of mass destruction, 142
Yen, 76–77
Yergin, Daniel, 95
YouTube, 14
YPFB. See Yacimientos Petrolíferos Fiscales
        Bolivianos

Zoellick, Robert, 263, 265, 316–317
Zylbersztejn, Ariel, 320